THE MAKING OF MEDIEVAL DERRY

The Making of
MEDIEVAL
DERRY

CIARÁN J. DEVLIN

FOUR COURTS PRESS

Published by
FOUR COURTS PRESS LTD
7 Malpas Street, Dublin 8, Ireland
www.fourcourtspress.ie
and in North America for
FOUR COURTS PRESS
c/o IPG, 814 N Franklin St, Chicago, IL 60622

First published by Veritas in 2013.
Second edition (revised) 2018.

A catalogue record for this title is available
from the British Library.

ISBN 978–1–84682–755–6

Printed in England
by TJ International Ltd, Padstow, Cornwall.

DEDICATION
Don Easpag Seosamh Ó Dufaigh
ceannródaí

Foreword

IN THE FIVE YEARS SINCE I HAD THE HONOUR OF OFFICIATING at its launch, Ciarán J. Devlin's book on the history of the medieval diocese of Derry has established itself firmly in the affections of that select band who have close to their hearts the Gaelic past of that area of the north-west of Ireland now comprised in the modern diocese of Derry. It is probably true to say that that position was secured not only by the quality of research and scholarship which it displays but even more because of the empathy with which otherwise remote historical figures are presented, as well as the lightness of touch and the irony even with which the feats and follies of humanity, then as now, stand forth from the historian's page.

This may well be so because the author was, in the best sense of the word, an amateur. Born in Muintir Luinigh in north-west Tyrone in the heart of the diocese and educated in St Columb's College, Derry, and in Maynooth, he appears, as indeed he himself implies in one of the early pages of his book, to have felt the fascination of history from his adolescent years. His university education in Maynooth endowed him with a firm grasp of the French cultural tradition together with an excellent command of both spoken and written Irish.

In Maynooth too, he belonged to that generation of students who came under the inspiring influence of the then professor of modern Irish, Donnchadh Ó Floinn. It was an influence which stimulated many of Ó Floinn's alumni to such varied achievements for the rebuilding of our religious and cultural traditions as the restoration of Holy Cross Abbey and Ballintubber, the modern translation of the Bible into Irish, and not least to a renewed enthusiasm for the local history of the Christian Church in Ireland.

In the spirit of the time, the cultural life of the country was seen as, to use the title of one of Ó Floinn's essays, 'The Integral Irish Tradition'. It was viewed as the lifeblood of a living continuity and therefore writing its history could never be reduced to a recital of facts and figures or of dead documentation. However precise its information or prudent its judgment, the result would always be warmed by the human breath shared with our predecessors and the conviction of a common destiny.

After his primary degree and during his theological studies, Ciarán Devlin had his first opportunity of a training in historical method, where he came under the demanding direction of his professor of ecclesiastical history, Patrick J. Corish, and began to draw attention to himself by his early essays in historical research.

Once ordained, his life was to be that of a diocesan priest, first teaching in St Columb's, where he had studied, and then ministering initially as curate in the Co. Derry deanery of the diocese and finally as parish priest in his native parish in Tyrone. Active as he was in those years in the theological life and the pastoral work of his fellow clergy, not to mention the upkeep of the physical fabric of his parishes, he maintained and developed his initial impulse towards history, building up a fine personal library of medieval sources and reading widely and methodically in all that pertained to the diocesan past, being finally appointed official historian of his diocese.

For many years and because of the limits on his time and energies, the fruits of his industry were to be seen chiefly in the many historical essays which enriched various parish and church anniversaries and jubilees, but towards the end of his life he set about collecting these *disiecta membra* and working them into a sustained narrative and a single volume, *The Making of Medieval Derry*.

On its publication, the work met with an immediate welcome from all those whose interest in the history of Gaelic Ulster left them keenly aware that there had been practically no major work on this diocesan area based on Gaelic sources since the appearance more than sixty years before of Séamus Ó Ceallaigh's seminal *Gleanings from Ulster History* in 1951.

In contradistinction to that remarkable achievement, *The Making of Medieval Derry* presents a less daunting aspect, introducing the reader as it does to a whole gallery of remarkable personages, ranging from the early saints of the diocese like Colm Cille, Eoghan of Ardstraw and Mura of Fahan, through the unique figure of the female airchinneach, Bébhinn, to later heroes of even more turbulent times, like the colourful Vicar Apostolic at the Plantation of Ulster, Tarlach Ó Ceallaigh, or the wandering sheep dealer and clandestine friar, the Bráthair Bán. Native scholars who brought intellectual life back to Benedictine monasteries in the Rhineland or anarchic noblemen who exhausted the patience even of their own political allies and kinsmen, all stand forth from these pages in an unforgettable parade of human diversity.

Such a result could only have been achieved by the author's long-term tenacity in grappling with often discouraging source material, marrying annal entries with genealogical lines and saints' lives, clarifying frequently corrupt family names and reconciling the deformed place-names of Plantation records or papal documents with their Gaelic originals. To such dedication we may confidently attribute the authenticity and the freshness which are the distinguishing marks of the entire work.

The first edition of the book sold out and is no longer available. It is therefore a pleasure for me to welcome this second edition. Sadly, Ciarán Devlin died unexpectedly before being able to complete his book with the critical apparatus which is essential to making a serviceable research tool of a work of this kind. It is timely that in the new edition this deficiency has been ably made good by a scholar of the experience and standing of Dr. Nollaig Ó Muraíle through the addition of a series of indexes containing more than three thousand references (personal names, surnames, place-names and so forth). In this contribution of his he has manifested a precision and a thoroughness which can only add to the esteem in which the book has been held. The ease with which it can now be consulted must be a cause of great satisfaction to all those who have enjoyed and profited from the original.

Seosamh Ó Dufaigh,
Bishop emeritus of Clogher

Preface

THIS ALL BEGAN ABOUT SIXTY YEARS AGO IN AN ANCIENT history class in St Columb's College, Derry, with the Ionian Revolt against the Persians, as the late Vincent McGeown analysed the progress of the revolt and the ideas that lay behind it, introducing us to the reality of history and its meaning in the lives of the people whose story it told. The interest that had been awakened there went into abeyance in the sameness of the academic day until Mgr Patrick Corish, doyen of Irish Church historians in St Patrick's College, Maynooth, brought drama through his inimitable style of lecturing to the intricacies of theological debate and to the broad lines of Church history. Once again it was his introduction to the character of the participants that brought their choices to life.

This turned my attention to what might have been going on nearer home, which was encouraged by Mgr Corish's use of the Gilmartin Prize to develop historical research among his students. In addition to that, I had had the benefit of what one might call the 'holistic approach' to our past inspired by Fr Donnchadh Ó Floinn, professor of Irish, who saw language, history and religion as skeins in the cultural web to which we are heirs and which helps shape our identity. Of course that does not mean that our heritage is to be seen as nobler than that of others, just that it is ours, own or disown it.

What to do about it? The first glimmer of life came from the fresh approach to Gaelic history of the group of local historians in Ulster, many of them priests, who formed the first diocesan historical societies and who brought into focus what they discovered from the use of local tradition and placenames, taken in conjunction with genealogies, the various annals and poetry. With the promptings of the late Bishop Mulligan, Mgr John Quinn and Cardinal Ó Fiaich, work was produced by Eamon Devlin, Peadar Livingstone and Bishop Joseph Duffy that brought a new sense of purpose into the field.

The greatest influence for me at the time was the late Fr Paddy Gallagher because he was not far from me when he was a curate in Dromore, where I could go to experience his hospitality and watch him argue with his pipe – which seemed more a prop to conversation than any source of gratification – as he moved effortlessly through the machinations of *Sliocht Airt* (Ó Néill) of Omagh or followed Aodh Rua through his own *Magh Ene*. Too late I thought of the opportunities I had missed to press him further about west Tyrone and east Donegal as they now are, which he knew so well. Important to the effort too was the perceptiveness and the grasp of language and placenames of the late Fr Brendan McGinn.

Armagh, Clogher, Co. Donegal and Kilmore had already well-established historical societies. In emulation, and with the support of Mgr Ben Kielt,we set up the Derry Diocesan Historical Society with its publication *Derriana*, named in tribute to the book of historical essays published by Bishop John Keyes O'Doherty in 1902. We organised tours and lectures and produced five editions of *Derriana*, edited by Fr Kevin McKenna. Unfortunately the Troubles intervened, which meant that it became unwise to bring people together in any centre of population, and meetings of that kind are essential if such a society is to gather a membership that would make it self-perpetuating.

Although the society did not achieve as much as was hoped, it had the result that some of my colleagues began to seek historical background material for parish celebrations like the opening or rededication of a church after the liturgical changes following the Vatican Council. One striking thing to be noticed in reading many parish histories produced around that time was that they mostly followed a similar format: an introduction describing geography and geology, followed by a study in general terms of the early Church and of any local figure who fitted into the picture. Then the story usually leaped to the Plantation of Ulster, the Penal Era and then modern times. In between, there is a thousand years during which, it might seem, nothing much happened, except maybe for rampaging Vikings, Brian Boru and St Malachy of Armagh.

That is caricature, naturally, but the impression was that the Middle Ages in Ireland were of no particular interest. Those who compiled these histories so painstakingly bore little blame for this of course. Few academic historians then wished to specialise in medieval Gaelic Ireland and rarely did any one of them set out to probe even the broad political spectrum to say nothing of religious conditions in the blank space on the map that was the diocese of Derry. Only with the advent of Katharine Simms, Kenneth Nicholls and Brendan Bradshaw in academia did it begin to appear that something of medieval north-west Ulster might be resurrected.

At this point, there arises a further challenge for the Church historian – how to document and explain the recovery of the Church when the chances of survival seem minimal, while at other times an apparently flourishing Church gives in to seeming collapse. In Ireland, every 300 years or so such seeming collapse has led on to reformation and renewed life. To follow the movement of the tides of history became an enthusiasm that at first was largely a matter of frustration, because few sources had survived the devastation of wars, particularly in the long and grim seventeenth century, followed by the poverty and insecurity of penal times.

The fascination of local medieval history lies in the way that the search becomes a sort of detective story that you write yourself, often because it seems as if you have stumbled into a world into which few have found access for ages. At the same time, being a priest working in a parish is also fascinating because two consecutive days are rarely the same and because human living rarely succumbs to typecasting. One's timetable is frequently uncertain; there are days when everything seems to happen at once and where night and day seem to merge. Reconciling the two at times raises anxiety about the morality of making time to delve into the past, but then one discovered the delight with which many people greeted some aspect of the history of their parish or townland or ancestry, or of some local saint unknown to them up until then. One learnt that there is a hunger in many people to understand their roots and that there are many pathways leading to vital faith. There, to a large extent, lies the nub of the issue. In Northern Ireland many of us have, at best, a hazy idea of our history and particularly of what happened a few hundred years ago. Most of the information is not readily available so that we can find it hard to grasp how events are related to each other and why things happened as they did. Consequently, we can fall prey to analyses that are based on misconceptions of the past or on the whataboutery of partisan argument. This does not make for a society at peace with itself, as recent events have shown. Neither is it good for religion or for the Church, in that it brings into being a certain uneasiness in life and speech due to fear of offending 'the other side'.

As a result, we can read back into medieval history attitudes that people of that time would not recognise as theirs. Such is the case, it

3

seems to me, with the view that consideration of the Gaelic past can only be a 'Catholic thing', neglecting the obvious fact that many who are not Catholic are of Scots Gaelic stock whose ancestors were just as much part of the medieval Gaelic world. There is of course no such thing as neutral, impartial history. We all come to it from our own perspectives. The recent Troubles have taught us that what actually happened is less important than what people think happened. However, we get nowhere unless as much as is possible of all perspectives are put 'out there' for all to grasp.

In many ways, what makes a person feel that he or she belongs in any community is shared memory. Some realisation of what has happened in the past gives a sense of meaning and purpose to the present and the deeper the realisation the deeper the sense of belonging. Should the process become exclusivist, problems result. We inherit the past. We owe it to those who created it to try to understand the choices they faced, how they saw and coped with responsibility, and what clarification or correction in our perception might now be worthwhile.

In writing about the history of the diocese of Derry the author is writing obviously from a Catholic perspective, with definite purpose in mind. Hopefully anyone reading these pages who is not Catholic may find some insight into what has made the northern Catholic such a different species, since here is no such thing as 'a Catholic' *simpliciter*. There are French Catholics and Polish Catholics and Mexican Catholics and Nigerian Catholics – as well as lapsed Catholics – sharing attitudes, doctrine and practice, hopefully, but all somewhat different as a result of what faith has experienced in their lives and in their countries.

My aim in writing is to try to recall from neglect some of the people who influenced the course of events over the more than 1,400 years of the history of the Christian faith in Derry, and in the process point to a past that still has meaning for us. The aim is not to give information simply but to reawaken a sense of continuity and heritage as a source of pride and as a realisation of the hand of God at work with his people in the many leaps and lunges that life can take. Furthermore, since all our teaching and preaching is no more than preparing the ground for God's gift of faith, is it not part of the duty of a priest in communicating the faith to hand on the story of our religious past as well? Is an account of our history that is as open-minded and critical as possible not equally an account of what God has accomplished over centuries in the lives of our people? Should we not attempt to get in touch with their spirituality and forms of prayer when others have discovered and developed from them what they choose to call 'Celtic spirituality', which can be selective in what it particularises from the past?

Much, of course, is due to the loss of memory and self-esteem, resulting from the rejection in the nineteenth century of the language in which that spirituality was expressed, even though much of it can still be found in manuscript and in folklore collections. One problem for many is that in medieval times, Ireland seems to be a catalogue of wars and cruelties. Such a conclusion is understandable since the annals are like collections of newspaper headlines that prefer to report bad news. Some of the fighting was little more than an aggressive form of tax collection, whilst other lifestyles went on alongside as best they could. However, as one reads Shakespeare's historical plays or contemplates the Italy or France of that time, one discovers that European nobility were often in the same mould. Engaging other people to work and produce the food and wealth, noblemen could have the leisure to defend their honour and prove their virility.

Our concern is with one era in the long history of the Christian faith in the diocese of Derry, roughly the 1,000 odd years we call the Middle Ages: from the coming of Christianity to the country and the fall of the Roman Empire to the suppression of the Church in the seventeenth century. It is an age which extends from the days of the great missionaries like Patrick and Columba and Cainneach, of monks like Mura and Cairbre, religious like Cognat and Sáfann, bishops like Eoghan and Lurach. It extends through the great reform of the Church all over twelfth-century Europe, accomplished here in Ireland under the leadership of St Malachy and St Giolla Mac Liag (Gelasius). It was that reform which gave us dioceses as we now have them, as well as a system of lay involvement in Church life through the erenaghs (medieval Irish office responsible for receiving parish revenue from titles and rents), which prepared well for an unforeseen time of dispossession and persecution, a time culminating in that 120-year-long period when the diocese did not even have a bishop. All these events that our forefathers lived through, whether in achievement or in adversity, have left their mark on us, sometimes even without our conscious awareness of them.

In putting together these historical essays as an amateur and in the interstices of the pastoral ministry, one can be only too aware of the inadequacy, the gaps and possible errors in such an endeavour. In these days of academic specialisation, to try to aim at the sweep of 1,000 years is to give many hostages to fortune. My defence is simply that it needs to be done and that an inadequate account of our medieval past is surely better than no history at all. If nothing else it provides some sort of basis for others to build on. The effort to improve on it will bring our ancestors in faith something of the recognition they have long merited and consequently enrich the lives of generations to come.

A Note on Nomenclature

A difficulty arises in books of this kind in the treatment of proper names when writing on Irish medieval topics. The literary tradition in Irish is nearly 1,500 years long and in such a period change is only to be expected in the forms of the language and in the orthography in which these forms were rendered. A practical simplification will allow us to recognise three orthographical standards: that of Old Irish before the year 1,000, that of Classical Irish down to the twentieth century, and contemporary standard spelling, referred to as the *Caighdeán Nua*.

While academics put chronological accuracy first, using the spelling of the period they write about, this can become preciosity and a source of irritation in the case of words which are still perfectly familiar in contemporary speech and writing to anyone with a working knowledge of Irish. Why write *Cenél nEogain*, when *Cineál Eoghain* is the natural expression; or *Cenél nOengusso* for *Cineál Aonghasa*?

The older standard is acceptable when the word has not survived its own period, be it Old Irish or Classical Irish. But if the word or expression is natural in contemporary Irish, the medieval spelling looks ossified, seeming sometimes to have little connection with the modern forms of the names, and therefore becomes an obstacle to identification. To ask: 'What is that in English?' is of little help, because in actual fact the form of our names that we have accustomed ourselves to using is not English, either by root or meaning. To transmute medieval Gaelic names into the colonial forms imposed upon them is hardly an acceptable solution since we owe their bearers the courtesy we would claim for ourselves, that our names be spelt as we would wish them to be.

Accordingly, it was decided that if a name or word is natural in contemporary Irish, it should be written in contemporary spelling – the *Caighdeán Nua*. To do otherwise would smack of academic snobbery, if not an assumption that this language is long dead. This is particularly true of personal and family names. Why write Ó Gairmleadhaigh, Mac Rudhraighe, even Ó Domhnaill, when today we recognise Ó Gormlaigh, Mac Ruairí, Ó Dónaill? Thus names like Ua Cobhthaigh, Ua Donnghaile, Ua Tuathghaile, Ua Cearbhaill, Flaithbheartach and Laithbheartaigh have been simplified to read Ó Cofaigh, Ó Donnaile, Ó Tuathaile, Ó Cearúill, Flaitheartach and Laifeartaigh, being closer to modern pronunciation and easier for most readers to recognise. On occasion, giving the Gaelic form of names is essential to avoid confusion, as in the case, for example, of Ó Cairealláin and Ó Cearbhalláin, which have often both been made Carlin in 'English', and yet are obviously distinct names.

EDITORIAL NOTE
Sadly, Ciarán Devlin did not live to review the text of his book, or to provide the maps and genealogical charts which he had planned. *Grásta ó Dhia air.*

Contents

Illustrations

1
Derry Through the Ages

T HE DIOCESE OF DERRY INCLUDES THE MOST NORTHERLY point of the island of Ireland, extending from Lough Swilly to the River Bann and including most of the basin of the River Foyle. The ecclesiastical centre of the diocese nowadays is the city of Derry, founded originally by *Colm Cille* (St Columba) in AD 546 as a staging post between Ireland and what would become his more important foundation at Í in Scotland, now known as Iona.

The area making up the present diocese was, in those days, a grid of *tuatha* or small kingdoms established by closely related kin groupings, for whom were founded the churches – many of them as episcopal centres – of Ardstraw (by St *Eoghan* or Eugene), Carndonagh (associated with St *Mac Cairthinn* or Macartan), Coleraine (by St *Cairbre*, friend of St Eoghan), Fahan (founded by St *Mura*), Maghera (by St *Lurach*), and the churches of St *Fionnlugh* and St *Neachtán* in the valley of the Roe. Many of the churches of the diocese are so ancient that they were later claimed with some verisimilitude to have been founded by St Patrick himself.

With the passage of time, the stronger of these kingdoms began to absorb the weaker until eventually the whole area was ruled by one kin group, *Cineál Eoghain* (the descendants of Eoghan, son of High King Niall Naoighiallach – of the Nine Hostages –who died in AD 453). This process coincided with the movement to reform the Church, associated with St *Maolmhóg* or Malachy of Armagh in the twelfth century – both movements, the political and the ecclesiastical, being inspired due to travel abroad and by contemporary developments on the continent and in Scotland. One of the most crucial aspects of the ecclesiastical programme, modelled on the reform initiated in Rome by the monk Hildebrand, later Pope Gregory VII, was the establishment of bishops with spiritual authority over a clearly-defined territory. In the north west, as we will see, this bishop was to be based at Ardstraw in modern Tyrone, but because it suited the secular power of the time better, the new diocese of Derry was in fact centred at first on Ráth Luraigh, now Maghera.

By this time, in AD 1100, Derry had become the centre of the religious order of monks founded by St Columba and which had houses as far afield as Iona in Scotland and Kells and Durrow in central Ireland. The great enterprise of reform involved many compromises and settlements and part of it would seem to have been that the order conceded monastic primacy to Armagh. The Abbot of Derry, Giolla Mac Liag, or Gelasius as he was known in Latin, became Archbishop of Armagh in succession to St Malachy. His successor in turn, *St Conchúr Mac Con Choille*, had family associations with the abbey, which perhaps enabled him to persuade the monks there to accept the continental rule of the Canons Regular of Arrouaise in France. In any case, Derry lost its Columban order, and in the thirteenth century became the seat of the bishop of the diocese, an area co-extensive with the then *Mac Lochlainn* kingdom of northern *Cineál Eoghain*.

The story of the later medieval diocese has a fitful light cast on it by documents preserved in Rome which testify that, like the rest of western Europe, Derry had its quota of 'Rome-runners', ambitious clerics seeking preferment at the papal court in Rome, or during the papal exile up to AD 1376 at Avignon in France. As a result of the Norman invasion and the extension of English power to part of the island, candidates for the episcopacy also had to get permission from the medieval English king, although this ceased to be a problem when, during the Reformation in the sixteenth century, English power broke with Rome.

The Plantation of Ulster from 1609 onward dispossessed all native leadership, political or ecclesiastical, and with the wars of the seventeenth century and the Penal Laws of the eighteenth, the diocese entered its own 'dark ages'. Catholics were henceforth tenants on the lands owned by their ancestors and were no longer allowed any recognised place of worship. Being Catholic was not, technically speaking, illegal but the English government made religious confession a test of loyalty, which it chose to constrain or persecute whenever it felt its position in the country threatened.

Catholics, for example, had to live outside town precincts, which explain the 'Irishtowns' still commemorated in street names in places like Omagh. The atmosphere in the city of Derry was especially unsympathetic. Priests were discouraged, particularly those educated in continental seminaries, and bishops were forbidden. In fact, the diocese lacked a bishop for 119 years after the martyrdom of Réamann Ó Gallachair in 1601, a period when vicars apostolic ran affairs. It is not even clear where clergy at this time were educated – seminaries were forbidden in the country and the continental colleges beyond the reach of most.

The Church they served was one of great poverty, with discreet liturgies held in barns or often in the open air, as witness the many 'Mass-rocks' still venerated in the countryside. The Catholics of Ireland, the vast majority of the population, were without influence over their own destinies, except to the extent that the government needed to keep them quiescent and intimidated. When oppression began to wane at the end of the eighteenth century, these people were at once faced with the necessity of a huge programme of building since only the remotest parishes had any place of worship and there were no schools. That this building programme was accomplished with the pennies of the poor amid all the travail of nineteenth-century Ireland – in particular in the teeth and aftermath of one of the worst European disasters, the Great Famine of the 1840s – is a tale of heroic perseverance, leadership and faith. It was accomplished furthermore by a people ravaged by wholesale emigration, itself a strenuous test of morale. One of the results of the church and school building effort was a conviction of the importance of religious practice and a thirst for education. With the contemporary change in their spoken language, people began to replace the homely Gaelic piety of their ancestors – being reborn these days in an *ersatz* 'Celtic Spirituality' – with forms of prayer and devotion based on Franco-Italian patterns and devoid of native roots. In that same century, an irredentist political tradition inclined to violence developed throughout the country as a result of the obstinate refusal of government to react favourably to constitutional protest from Daniel O'Connell onwards. This led eventually in the twentieth century to the War of Independence and, after the foundation of Northern Ireland, to a diocese split between two jurisdictions, to endemic political instability and to tension within the Church.

The people who faced the War of Independence from 1916 to 1921, the two World Wars of the twentieth century and the economic collapse between those wars, were, because of their religious history, a people with a high level of sacramental practice (they had taken to the ideas of Pope St Pius X at the beginning of the century with enthusiasm). They were a prayerful people, both in private and in the family, and their vigorous faith showed itself in the abundance of vocations to the priesthood and the religious life. However, they were a people whose history had conditioned them to accept religious practice as normative and whose lack of self-assurance left them liable to view any sort of theological speculation as aberrant, in that it might upset the cohesion that had so long been necessary for self-protection.

Since the new state, in which two-thirds of the people of the diocese of Derry now lived, had accorded them scant recognition, many were deeply suspicious of the legal system, of government, government supporters and indeed of any arm of government, especially the police whose *modus operandi* and allegiance seemed alien. When government in Northern Ireland operated a policy of positive inhibition and proved itself incapable of evolving a democratic system of equality, hindsight suggests that it was a matter of time until the dam would break. No one, however, could have foreseen the distress and cruelty that would result, or the ways in which moral fibre and religious conviction would be tested.

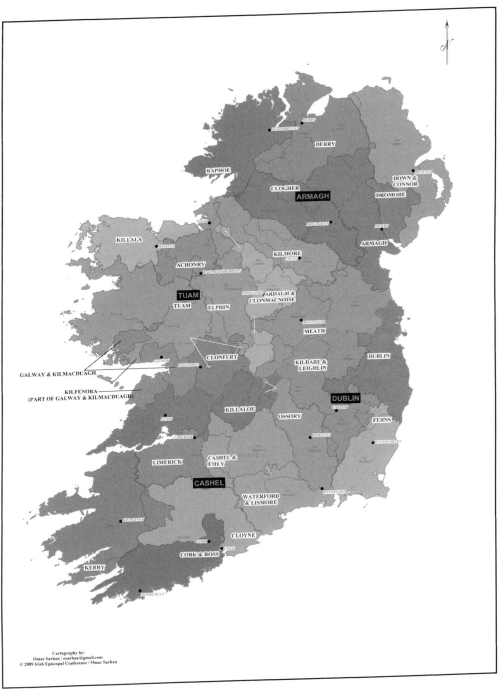

THE DIOCESES OF IRELAND

The following labels appear on the map:

LANGFIELD — Parish Name
(*Drumquin*) — Secondary Name

CLONCA
(*Malin*)

CLONMANY
CULDAFF
DONAGH
(*Carndonagh*)
MOVILLE

BUNCRANA

MAGILLIGAN
COLERAINE
(*Dunboe, Macosquin and Aghadowey*)

FAHAN
(*Burt Inch*)

STRATHFOYLE
LIMAVADY
AGHADOWEY

ERRIGAL

TEMPLEMORE
FAUGHANVALE
DUNGIVEN
KILREA

GLENDERMOTT
(*Waterside*)
ARDMORE

CAMUS
(*Strabane*)
LECK-
PATRICK
CLAUDY
BANAGHER
GRANAGHAN
(*Swatragh*)
GREEN-
LOUGH

DONAG-
HEADY
(*Dunamanagh*)

MOURNE
(*Melmouni*)
CLONLEIGH
(*Lifford*)
MAGHERA
LAVEY

URNEY AND
CASTLEFIN
(*Duneyloop*)

BADONEY UPPER
(*Plumbridge*)
BALLINA-
SCREEN
DESERT-
MARTIN
BALLYSCULLION
(*Bellaghy*)

DONAGHMORE
(*Killygordon*)

ARDSTRAW
WEST /
CASTLEDERG
BADONEY LOWER
(*Gortin*)
GREEN-
CASTLE

TERMONAMONGAN
(*Aghyaran*)
CAPPAGH
(*Killyclogher*)
ARDSTRAW EAST
(*Newtownstewart*)

LANGFIELD
(*Drumquin*)

DRUMRAGH
(*Omagh*)
SION MILLS

Lough Swilly
ISKAHEEN
Lough Foyle

0 Miles 12
0 Kms 20

Drawn by M. Murphy Geography Dept. UCC

THE CATHOLIC PARISHES OF DERRY TODAY

2
Medieval Personalities

IN SEARCH OF COLM CILLE

THERE ARE FEW PERSONALITIES IN THE EARLY CHRISTIAN centuries in the islands of the North Atlantic who have left a more profound impress both on the history of these lands and the popular imagination than Colm Cille, for he is at one and the same time a historical person and a figure of myth.

Let us be clear first of all about the value of myth. Myth is not the opposite of history. It often expresses something that is beyond cold facts and the words that record them and failure to grasp this can lead to profound misunderstanding. For example, a nationalist when pressed about the year 1689 might think of Derry, Aughrim and the Boyne, with the subsequent inception of the Penal Laws, whereas to an Orangeman it means the *Glorious Revolution*. The resulting difference of perception can be explosive. For a Frenchman, the term 'revolution' implies more than the activities of a Danton or a Robespierre, redolent as it is for him of the ideals of *Liberté*, *Égalité*, *Fraternité*, not to mention probably *laïcité*. Every country has its myths, which may strike the outsider as odd, but to penetrate their meaning it is important to weigh up the purpose, content and hope borne by the myth. To deal with it simply in intellectual terms will be likely to do damage to the foundations of people's world view, whether we are considering the stable at Bethlehem, or the 1916 Rising, or the American Constitution. Examining such matters merely in terms of logic and intellect results in that sterile cerebration that appears likely to be a doubtful legacy of the late twentieth-century mind, dismissing as it does any view of the human condition that is not 'scientific'.

Therefore, in our search for Colm Cille we must consider both the historic Columba and the figure that grew up in popular belief, reflecting both people's human needs and religious experience. Both realities are actual, if not necessarily factual.

Paternal

Colm was born at Gartán, near Kilmacrenan, according to folk-belief, the oldest of five children of his parents Féilimí and Eithne. Féilimí belonged to Cineál Chonaill, third in direct descent from Niall Naoighiallach (of the Nine Hostages) who died in AD 453 and whose name was to be borne by his descendants, the *Uí Néill*.[1] Niall was high king at Tara, allegedly of the *Connachta*, the descendants of the mythological kings Cormac, son of Art Aonfhear, son of Conn Céadchathach (Conn of the Hundred Battles – probable a euhemerised ancestor-god after whom the Connachta are named). The genealogy was probably invented to give respectability to a war band that had achieved influence and power by raiding and capturing slaves abroad, a band such as that which had captured St Patrick. Niall himself had been killed in just such a raid on the continent, it was said. Nonetheless, as the son of Conall, son of Niall, Féilimí's pedigree was royal. A cousin, nephew and grandnephew of Féilimí were high kings,[2] a fact which meant that Colm himself could have been king as well, since he belonged to the *deirbh-fhine* or 'true kin' (those descended from the same great-grandfather in the male line), who were eligible to succeed.

Maternal

In his latest superbly detailed and invaluable contribution to the study of the Irish saints, Pádraig Ó Riain posits the maternal descent of Colm Cille from the *Corbraighe* of *Fánaid*/Fanad, to whom his mother Eithne belonged according to some of the genealogies. The Corbraighe of Fánaid as a group are not found amongst the population group names in other genealogies. The only possible originators of such a group to occur in the genealogy of Cineál Chonaill are *Cairbre Liath* and *Cairbre Beag*, both sons of *Séatna*, brother of Féilimí, both sons of *Fearghus Ceannfhada*, which makes Féilimí their uncle and Colm their cousin. There is clearly a generational problem here.

---

1. This *clann* name must be distinguished from the family surname Ó Néill, descended much later from High King Niall Glúndubh, who died in 919.
2. Muircheartach Mac Earca (of *Cineál Eoghain*); Ainmhire and his son Aodh Mac Ainmhireach (of *Cineál Chonaill*).

One genealogy adds that Cairbre was the son of *File*, son of *Eichin* from Buais, which brings us eastwards to the River Bush in Co. Antrim, but the genealogies show no Corbraighe/Cineál Chairbre, etc., in the population groups in that area. *File* is surely an occupation rather than a first name. One epithet applied to Eithne in a genealogy –which casts further doubt on the substance of the said genealogy – is *béalfhada* (long-mouthed), scarcely a compliment one would think, particularly as DIL records just two uses of the epithet, one as used here of Eithne, and the other to describe the blade of a sword. 'Cairbre son of File' suggests that it is a confused version of that which makes Eithne descend from the *Uí Bairrche* of south Leinster: Eithne, daughter of Aengus or Dimma, son of Noe, son of Féichín, son of Cairbre file, son of Aileall Mór.

To confound things even more, O'Rahilly pointed to a relationship between the Uí Bairrche of Leinster and two groups of the *Manaigh*, one who gave their name to Fermanagh and the other, according to one version of the tale, given refuge by *Eochaidh Gunnat*, King of the Ulaidh, after they had killed the son of the King of Leinster. This might throw some light on the reference to the River Bush.

It is worth bearing in mind that at the time the Uí Néill were engaged in a long struggle to overcome the Laighin, which ended with the death of High King *Aodh mac Ainmhireach*, cousin of Colm Cille at the battle of Dún Bolg near Baltinglass in 598. Genealogy hints also at a connection between the Uí Bairrche and the area between Bann and Bush in modern Co. Antrim, and later with Bangor of St Comhghall. Such a connection might indicate how the marriage of Féilimí and Eithne (south east to north west) could have come about. The reference in genealogy to Eithne as *queen of the Cairbri of Fánaid* may well mean that a branch of the Uí Bairrche called the Cairbri (or Corpraigi) descended from Cairbre file ('the poet'), came north along with her and were settled in Fanad. The descendants of Cairbre/Corpre, son of Niall Naoighiallach and brother of Conall and therefore uncle of Fearghus Ceannfhada, were settled in Sligo. That it is not claimed in any genealogy that Eithne was related to this Cairbre, son of Niall, is surely significant in the issue.

Genealogical tradition asserts that Eithne was *deirbhfhionn dualfhada* – 'of the long truly fair tresses'. If the folk belief that Colm was red-haired is accurate, he did not take after his mother.

The genealogy that seems most coherent is that which gives Eithne's descent from the Uí Bairrche, a branch of the royal line of the *Laighin*,[3] which had given kings to the Laighin and had occupied the lands between the Barrow and Slaney Rivers in what is now Wexford – Carlow and, at some stage, as far as south Kildare. Before the year AD 500, they were defeated in battle by the *Uí Chinsealaigh*, who established themselves in the middle of the area. This divided Uí Bairrche territory into two distinct parts not long before Eithne married Féilimí.

It may well be asked why Féilimí should marry a woman from the other end of the country. At the time, the Uí Néill were trying to establish political control over the *Laighin* since they already controlled the province of Meath, their own province Connacht and much of west Ulster. Uí Bairrche saw themselves being shunted farther from the centre of power in Leinster and had hopes of regaining something of what the dynasty had lost. Since Cairbre is described as *file* he may have resorted when his political fortunes declined to *filíocht* or native learning, as it might be called, like many in his position over the centuries. It would suit both Uí Bairrche and Uí Néill to link up, and what better way than through a political dynastic marriage.

The location of the Uí Bairrche is particularly interesting when we see it in the context of how Christianity first came to Ireland. It is a fact of history that new ideas and new cultures follow the trade routes, the main channels of communication, at sea or on land, often skipping from one population centre to another. (This is said to explain how Indonesia became Islamic, or the odd way Christianity spread within the Roman Empire, or indeed how the Irish language declined in Ireland.) It follows that the continent-facing valleys of south-east Ireland must have seen the stirrings of Christianity because of their commercial links with Gaul (now France) and Britain.

Eithne's Religious Background
It is in the south and south east of Ireland that many of the pre-Patrician churches are found, those which are connected with Declan, Ibar, Iserninus and perhaps Palladius himself (who was sent by Pope Celestine in AD 431 to the 'Irish believing in Christ'). The Uí Bairrche had laid claim at a very early stage to the area around Naas in *Magh Life* (the Liffey valley) where is found the church of Killashee (*Cill*

---

3. Who gave their name to the province of Leinster. NB: The kingdom of Meath was not then part of the province of Leinster.

Ausaille) associated with Auxilius, one of Palladius' companions. The church of *Sléibhte* (Sletty) in Laois founded by Fiacc, the first bishop of the Laighin, according to very early tradition, was in Uí Bairrche territory. It is reasonable then to state that Eithne brought a tradition of Christianity with her when she went north, whereas it is not in any sense as clear that the family of Fearghus Ceannfhada, Colm's grandfather, was Christian. Her influence may have been decisive and radical since in Irish law even then 'the rearing of children is usually the responsibility of both parents.'[4]

Colm's Family

There were five children in their family. There were three girls, all of whom subsequently married and had children,[5] and two boys, *Eoghan* known as *Eoghan Beag*, the father of St *Earnán*, and the oldest who was named *Crimhthann* (pronounced 'criffan'). Crimhthann meant fox and carried with it the nuance of craftiness or deceit. It was then common for people to have names that indicated a reverence for a special animal.[6] Later folklore explained that the boy was called Crimhthann ('foxy') because he had red hair. The word *colm* means 'dove'.

Be that as it may, there is no clear explanation as to why he came to be called Colm Cille. One explanation refers the name 'dove of the church' to the other children commenting on the frequency of his visits to the church, but one wonders about the centrality of churches at the time. There is little anecdotal evidence of the presence of other children during his education. It is also suggested that the new name reflected his character. It is possible that he received the name in two stages, *Colm* first and then *Cille*.

Perhaps of relevance to the metaphor of 'dove' was the pyx containing the Blessed Sacrament that was suspended above the altar in the early European Church. It was shaped like a dove and was called a *columba* after the reference in Psalm 84:3 to a turtle dove by the altar in a translation of Scripture that was well known at the time (later

---

4. See Fergus Kelly, *Guide to Early Irish Law* (Dublin: Dublin Institute for Advanced Studies, 1988), p. 85.
5. *Mínchloth* was the mother of the sons of *Éanán* (cf. *Cill mhac nÉanáin* – Kilmacrenan); *Bran*, one of the four sons of another sister, was buried in Derry. *Síneach* was married to *Cian* and one of their sons, Aidan the monk, was buried at Cúl Uisce, which, according to Colgan, is Iskaheen, near Muff.
6. Many surnames in their anglicised forms hide the Irish *cú* – 'a hound', e.g. McNamee, Conway, McCullagh, Conroy, Ó Connor, McGonagle.

translations have the swallow, however). A chrismal was sometimes carried on the person for sick calls or for devotional reasons. *Columba* in this sense may or may not be relevant to our quest, but it would translate as *colm*, perhaps indicating devotion to the Blessed Eucharist. As a personal name it is symbolic and metaphorical, which makes it difficult to elucidate. Three spellings of his name are found in Irish: *Colm*, *Colum* and *Colam*, all with *Cille* usually added. As well as the word *colm* meaning 'dove' (cognate with Latin *columba*), there exists a homonym *colm* meaning 'scar'. The reputation of Colm Cille as a saint subsequently led to one of the most common names, both of saints and non-saints, *Colmán* 'little dove', Latinised as Columbanus.

Colm Cille was born on Thursday, 7 December AD 521 at *Ráth Cnó* near Gartán, according to late tradition and laid on 'the flagstone of nostalgia'/*Leac na Cumha*.[7] Thursday was seen as St Colm's special day in Donegal tradition, and even more so in the tradition of the Gàidhealtachd of Scotland, down to the present day. The year 521 can be deduced from St Adhamhnan's biography of the saint but is nowhere stated explicitly. The child was baptised at *Tulach Dubhghlaise* ('hill of the dark stream') now Templedouglas, near Kilmacrenan.

Youth and Early Education

For Colm's education, according to later sources, his parents chose a foster father, the priest *Cruithneachán*. Perhaps a word should be said first about *altram* or fosterage. This was not the result of parental vagary. *Altram* or *altramas* was an institution, a system of education, so common that the expression for 'in fosterage with', *in aice le*, has come to mean in modern Irish 'near' or 'beside'. Children were placed in the care of foster-parents between the ages of seven and seventeen. Since there was little social mobility, it was the responsibility of these foster parents to keep and instruct their *dalta* according to his class and rôle in life.[8] There was a distinction between *altram seirce* ('fosterage for love'), when no fee was payable, and *cáin iarraith*, a legal term indicating a fosterage fee (which, interestingly, was greater for a girl

---

7. A local flagstone, so called from the custom of prospective emigrants lying on it as a cure for homesickness.
8. The son of a king, for example, was to be provided with a horse and proper clothing and taught horsemanship, swimming, marksmanship and the board games *ficheall* and *brannamh*; a daughter was taught embroidery, sewing and dressmaking.

than for a boy).[9] This was a binding legal contract. Strong bonds of loyalty were created with foster parents and foster brothers and sisters, to the extent, indeed, that the intimate names children use for their parents were used in Old Irish for their foster parents: *aite* 'daddy', now in modern Irish *oide*, 'teacher' and *muimme*, now *buime* 'nurse'.

Cruithneachán (Cronaghan)

Why then did Féilimí and Eithne choose to send their oldest child to be fostered by this Cruithneachán (Cronaghan)? Cruithneachán is always described as *cruimhthear* (pronounced 'criffir'), which is the very earliest Irish word for a priest, coming as it does from the Latin *presbyter*, earlier than the word *sagart*, from the Latin *sacerdos*. This underlines the fact that he belonged to the earliest generation of Christians in Ulster. Since he baptised Colm Cille, he must have been born before 490. It was to become not uncommon for clerics to foster children, but this is one of the earliest examples. Even if we accept that Cruithneachán was married – some accounts give him three daughters as nuns – it remains an unlikely beginning for the son of kings, unless we posit that Cruithneachán was best placed to provide the sort of education Féilimí and Eithne considered essential for their son. It is important to remember that up to this time education was oral, a feat of memory, conducted by the *filí* (or poetic profession) and their pre-Christian predecessors, the *draoithe* (druids).

The only reasonable suggestion is that the priest was in a position to introduce the boy to international learning, religious and secular, through the medium of Latin. Ireland was outside the Roman Empire looking in and increasingly aware through contacts in trade, in piracy, in religion, of the power, wealth, cultural expression, even the written culture, to which Latin provided the key. The idea that Féilimí and Eithne had 'predestined' their oldest son for the Church does not make sense, and relies on the infallibility of hindsight. They sought up-to-the-minute education for their son, obviously in a progressive and Christian context or ethos. Native balance was to be provided later by the *file* Gemmán (pronounce with a hard 'g').

Cruithneachán, if we are to go by the literal meaning of his name, was a 'little Pict'. The people called the *Cruithnigh* in Irish and *Picti*

---

9. The daughter of a small farmer (*óg-aire*) learnt to use the quern, kneading-trough and sieve, while his son was taught to care for lambs, calves, kids, piglets, and to dry corn, comb wool and chop firewood.

('painted ones') by the Romans were the original inhabitants of Scotland, north of the Lowlands. However the *Ulaidh*, the original inhabitants of Ulster (to which they gave their name), were also known as Cruithnigh. Their kingdom had been reduced by the time of Colm Cille to the present counties of Derry, Antrim and Down. It may be from these that Cruithneachán descended. All we are told is that his father was called Ceallachán, of Gaelic stock then. Cruithneachán may have been a byname.

Cruithneachán was the priest at the church of *Tulach Dubhghlaise* (now Templedouglas) between Gartán and Letterkenny. To discharge this important trust he sought advice from an unidentified wise person (perhaps a *saoi litre* or expert in ecclesiastical learning and the Laws) about when to teach the boy to read in Latin, of course, since Irish was not yet written at the time. On another occasion he took him on a visit to St Brughach mac Déga, bishop at *Ráth Maighe Éanaigh* (Raymochy) in Tír Éinne, near modern Manorcunningham. The bishop invited them back for Christmas. When the old priest became unwell as he was singing the psalms with the bishop, Colm stepped into the breach and sang alternate verses of the long Psalm 88 along with Brughach.

On another occasion Cruithneachán took Colm with him when he went on a sick call. On the way home the old priest collapsed as he was crossing an obstacle on the road. He fell in such a way that the boy Colm thought he was sleeping. He put his cloak under the old man's head, and spent the time singing while he waited for Cruithneachán to restart the journey. The nuns in a convent nearby heard him sing and came to investigate, Cruithneachán's daughters among them, and found that the priest was dead. Legend then takes over for Colm to restore him to life at the request of the nuns. Columba's youth was over. Tradition of course recalls Colm Cille as a gifted singer and poet.

He was sent then to a Christian *file* called Gemmán who, like Eithne, was from Leinster. The *filí* were the custodians of native history, genealogy and *seanchas*, as well as poetry. If we accept the descent of Eithne from Cairbre *file* it would indicate that Colm's mother had a parallel interest in secular learning. The poet Gemmán may even have been a relative.

To the Monastery

Our view of monks and monasteries has been coloured by Benedictines and Cistercians, by Augustinians and Dominicans and Franciscans, by habits and cowls and cloisters. The Irish system was ascetically tougher and at the same time more free and easy, coming as it did from Coptic Egypt by way of Spain, Gaul and Britain. First of all, we need to recognise that, while the early saints like Éanna of Aran, Finnian of Clonard, Mobhí of Glasnevin and so on, educated a second generation like Colm Cille, Comhghall of Bangor, Ciarán of Clonmacnoise, Cainneach of Aghaboe, and that the influence of all of them helped shape the view we have of the early Irish Church as dominated by monasticism, all of these monastic founders grew up in a church with local priests and bishops. Thus we meet Cruithneachán as tutor of Colm Cille, or Lurach tutor of Cainneach. The early Irish Church had an insufficient number of priests and an inadequate system of sustenance for those it had. To christianise the *pagani* ('country-dwellers') in similar circumstances in Gaul, St Martin of Tours had developed a patchwork of small monasteries and the Irish adopted both him and his approach, even to the extent of making him out to be the uncle of St Patrick!

This was the system into which Colm Cille went to continue his education. He is said to have studied, particularly the Scriptures – the Bible was usually the only book that was reasonably accessible before the printing press – with Finnian of Moville (in Co. Down) and Finnian of Clonard (in Co. Meath), amongst whose students he is named as one of the so-called *twelve apostles of Ireland*. Professor Pádraig Ó Riain maintains that there was only one Finnian, venerated in the two places. Adhamhnán states that Colm was ordained deacon while with Finnian. Mánas Ó Dónaill, in his *Beatha Cholm Cille*, says he was ordained priest at Clonard, and that the reason he did not become an archbishop was that the bishop, whom he does not or cannot name, refused to ordain him on the proper day. It seems likely that the written word in Scripture and the practice of penmanship may be seen ostensibly as at the source of St Columba's vocation to monastic life.

To Derry

The saint is said to have also studied with St Mobhí (pronounced 'movee') of Glasnevin. Now Mobhí, we are told, had a premonition that he himself would die of a threatening epidemic of bubonic plague and told his students to disperse. He instructed Colm Cille that he was not to accept land or establish a religious house without express permission from himself (something that might indicate reservations about his character and perhaps a question about how this scion of the royal house of Uí Néill might use authority).

Colm headed back north by quite a roundabout route to his own people. When he reached *Doire Chalgaigh*, his royal cousin Aodh Mac Ainmhireach, king of the northern Uí Néill, greeted him with the offer of the island at Derry for his first religious foundation. While still hesitating because of Mobhí's command to him, two of the community of Glasnevin reached him bearing the crios or belt of St Mobhí. Mobhí had died and was now signifying that Colm was free to establish his own house if he wished. So he accepted the king's gift; the year was 546; he was twenty-five years of age. Such at any rate is the traditional account of the founding of Derry.

It is an account that Dr Brian Lacey and others have dismissed, insisting that Colm was not the real founder of Derry at all. Doctor Lacy goes on, on the basis of entries in some of the annals, to state that the true founder of Derry was Fiachra, son of Ciarán (d. 620), the nephew of Aodh Mac Ainmhireach.[10] These entries were copied much later from an earlier source, and it is recognised that they originate at Clonmacnoise, not in the north, that they are scarcely more reliable than those objected to, and at best do not show evidence of a necessary connection between Fiachra and the *monastic* establishment, which is Derry's main claim to importance for most of its history.[11] Richard Sharpe, in the Penguin Classic *Life of St Columba* (1995), asserts that the account of the donation could not be accurate because Aodh's father Ainmhire did not die until 569 and he himself did not become high king until the 580s.

While Adhamhnan's *Vita Columbae* does not make the connection between the saint and Derry, it is clear that it views Derry as a long-standing port of call or staging-post for monastic travellers to and from Iona. It also records that Colm's nephews *Cobhrán* and *Aodhán* were buried in the immediate environs of Derry. While one cannot state definitively that Colm Cille founded Derry, no compelling evidence has been adduced thus far that would warrant setting aside what poetry, tradition and folk-belief have united to support for centuries. One of the factors that leads to a certain reluctance to accept the

---

10. Cf. *Siege City: The Story of Derry and Londonderry*, Brian Lacey (Belfast: Blackstaff, 1990), p. 18. *Chronicum Scotorum/Annals of Tighearnach*.

11. The only reason to connect Fiachra with the monastery as 'the other founder' is that the entry is in Latin. But Fiachra does not occur in any other document or genealogy, secular or sanctoral. He was probably not king of the northern Uí Néill. It seems to make better sense to connect him with the *military* problem of holding on to Derry.

connection with Colm Cille is the unquestioned belief that Derry was always a substantial religious centre. Hindsight gives the donation an importance it almost certainly did not have at the time. Derry would seem to have become significant only in the twelfth century. Why this should have been so is perhaps more puzzling than is the controverted Columban connection.

There are problems with the tradition of course. The island of Derry has been and is highly prized. It is scenically commanding, compact and easy to defend, with access to fresh water and with enough land for some cultivation. Why then did it become a religious rather than a political centre? Father John R. Walsh perceptively suggests that it had already been a pagan religious centre, but this was scarcely a guarantee of political immunity in later times.

There is one further factor that must be borne in mind. After the capture of Derry the English decided on two separate occasions to fortify the 'island', doubtless because they immediately saw its defensive possibilities. It must be asked why no local potentate saw its potential for this purpose. Dónall mac Ardghair Mac Lochlainn, for example, made himself High King of Ireland with Derry as his capital, but he chose to live at Enagh. Ó Dochartaigh lived at Aileach Mór. Ó Dónaill had a residence at Derry but it was built by Ó Dochartaigh for him on land that was bought from the Church erenagh. Ó Dónaill's (Aodh Rua) mother chose to live in retirement at Carrigans. It would seem that Derry was an open city, a religious site which leaders like Ó Catháin, Ó Gormlaigh, Ó Cairealláin and others were free to visit (even when not on the best of terms, with the result that carnage ensued from time to time), that it was a place where people came, as we might say, 'to make their sowl'.

Aodh Mac Ainmhireach, although head of the three branches of the northern Uí Néill, belonged to Cineál Chonaill whose homelands were to the south and west of Barnesmore Gap. Inis Eoghain belonged to Cineál Eoghain. In between lay the lands of Cineál Éinne (what is now the Lagan or east Donegal), land coveted by both neighbours who were, in time, to overrun it. In fact, Derry was then, as now, a border town.

On the eastern bank of the Foyle was the territory of the Cruithnigh (or Ulaidh). In 562/3 the battle took place of *Móin Mór Doire Lothair* (now probably Loughermore[12] in north Derry) in which

---

12.   The common identification as *Moneymore* in south Co. Derry is much too far from the scene of the action.

the Uí Néill, acting as mercenaries in a civil war amongst the Ulaidh, received, as a reward, possession of the east bank of the Foyle as far as Benevenagh. It is highly probable that the capture of Derry by Aodh Mac Ainmhireach marks an earlier stage in the long process by which the Uí Néill were eventually to push the Ulaidh east of the Bann. It seems reasonable to suggest that, having captured it, Aodh was unsure that it could be held, so he gave it to the Church in the person of his young cousin, who might also have been seen as a future threat, since he was eligible to be king. In similar circumstances, Downpatrick was initially given to the Church to keep out rivals, just as far to the south the *Eoghanacht* did with their capital Cashel. It would be unsurprising if Aodh did this without the agreement of his father, High King Ainmhire, who may indeed have left 'home affairs' in the hands of his son and in any case would have approved of ensuring succession for his son.

Mánas Ó Dónaill records that, after Colm Cille had accepted the gift of Derry, it was set on fire. It is such an unlikely thing to do that the event must have a basis in fact and probably authenticates Fr Walsh's suggestion of a pagan religious centre. Mánas Ó Dónaill sees it as proof of the efficacy of Colm's intercession against fire and lightning when he composed the hymn *Noli Pater indulgere* to save the *doire*, the original oakgrove, from the conflagration. Subsequent reporting in the annals shows that the *doire* was in fact quite an extensive wood, not just a grove. Whatever else, it shows that Derry was already inhabited, that the inhabitants did not belong to the Uí Néill, and that Aodh did not consider their wellbeing to be his concern. A further problem in the whole context is the paucity of information about what Colm actually did in Derry, other than the activities described in the wonder tales given by Mánas Ó Dónaill.

Exile
Apart from these stories and the disputed evidence about his part in the battle of Cúl Dreimhne, there is no evidence of the saint's involvement with his own people. The connection with the battle and his subsequent exile arises in the first instance from Adhamhnán's way of dating events by other important events. He dates the arrival in Iona from Cúl Dreimhne. It is not of course beyond belief that Colm might have

copied Finnian's psalter, particularly if it contained the new Vulgate text.[13]

It is quite possible too that Curnán, the son of the King of Connacht – a hostage with High King Diarmaid Mac Cearbhaill and protégé of Colm Cille – was put to death by Diarmaid. That this should provoke outrage in Colm Cille is understandable, but there is no evidence that he took part in the battle (although a noticeable scar – *colm* – was found on his body after his death). War between the northern and southern branches of the Uí Néill was likely enough anyway and it is not unlikely that Colm should have given moral or even public support to the northern branch, his own relatives.

He was excommunicated, the story goes, for his contribution to the war. The sanction was withdrawn by a synod at *Tailteann* (Teltown in Co. Meath) held during Diarmaid's *aonach* or Assembly in the kingdom of Meath and a sentence of exile was substituted. Diarmaid was probably a pagan, although all this is no more than hearsay. The whole episode is quite confused and Adhamhnán does not refer to it.

The Island of Í – which became Í Cholm Cille (Iona)

The insignificant island of Í,[14] off the coast of another island, Mull, in the Hebrides off the west coast of Scotland, would later be famous as *Í Cholm Cille* (or because of the miscopying of a tired scribe, *Iona*). According to the *New History of Ireland VIII*, the saint left Ireland in AD 561 and arrived on Iona in 563. Early evidence suggests that he went first to the island of *Hinba*, unidentified but perhaps Jura, Oronsay or Elachnave (where it was later believed that his mother was buried). In the tradition, he left Derry and landed on Iona on 13 May 563, Pentecost Sunday. He travelled with twelve disciples, including his uncle, Earnán,

---

13. The saint's love of the Scriptures is a constantly recurring theme. He was one of the great scribes of his time. The *Cathach*, or copy of the Psalter, used as a battle halidom by Cineál Chonaill (whence its name *the battler*), was written by a contemporary if not by Colmcille himself. It can be seen in the Royal Irish Academy. The episode of Cúl Dreimhne may even have been invented to explain the name *Cathach*. Finnian of Moville is said to have introduced a version of the Scriptures from Rome, possibly St Jerome's Vulgate. Incidentally, it was Irish scribes who first separated words from one another in their copying, and who first provided margins. Did they thus invent the book as we know it?

14. *Í* originally meant a tree, probably a *bile*, or sacred tree, and came eventually to mean a yew. The genitive plural was *eo*, which gives *Maigh Eo* (Mayo). *Iúr* is also a yew, as in Altinure and Newry. The English version of the name *Iona* results from the error of a scribe who was supposed to write *Ioua* (in Latin), but turned the 'u' upside down.

perhaps a brother of his mother. Colm was to spend thirty-four years on the island at the centre of the network of religious houses that were to be established.

No contemporary rule of these Columban monasteries exists, in the later sense, of a collection of directives such as that created by St Benedict. The early Irish monastery was governed by the inspiration and spiritual testament, what we might call the *charism*, of its founder. What is clear is that the regime was very strict, much stricter than that evolved and codified by St Benedict, but also allowing much more freedom, for example, to the monk who chose to live as an anchorite, alone in his *díseart* or hermitage. On Iona, there was a rath or *vallum* that enclosed about twenty acres. Inside stood a church with at least one side-chapel, as well as a guest-house and a spacious building, which provided community facilities and housing for most of the monks. Some individual cells or huts existed too, including the *both* where Colm himself slept on bare rock. The kitchen was a separate building because of the danger from its large fire, as was the all-important *scriptorium* for the copying of manuscripts. There were storehouses (a shed and a barn). Around them lay an open area, possibly paved, crosses set up at different points, a garden for the growing of medicinal herbs (the monastery provided a medical service to the surrounding population). Most of these buildings would have been made of timber (as are many churches in Scandinavia today), probably brought from a considerable distance. Later too there were to be workshops for leather and woodworking. And there was to be a cemetery, *Reilig Óráin*, named after Órán (*Odhrán, Otteranus*), the first monk to die on the island.

Everyday Life

The monks met to chant the canonical hours of the Office at midday for the Eucharist on Sundays and feast days, though not on weekdays, to all of which the monks were summoned by a bell struck by a hammer in the early Irish fashion, rather than having a clapper. The founder, too, would have them summoned to pray for special reasons. The monks fasted on Wednesday and Friday, and had a special meal on Sundays and feast days and on other days when the saint thought it appropriate. Work was part of the routine: copying the Scriptures, books for services in church (including 'the week's hymns') and other manuscripts, preparing the inks and pens; agricultural work in the fields, harvesting, building farm walls, tending cattle for milk and meat, fishing, blacksmithing, wood-turning, milling, shoemaking. The island had its own port, and since travel was easier and safer on water than on land at the time, visitors were frequent.

Colm Cille as He Was

We get a picture of Colm from Adhamhnán's biography as a monk amongst monks, always busy, copying, working in the hayfield, at the harvest, milking the cows, welcoming guests. We see him, almost like a parish priest, visiting people on their farms, performing baptisms, hearing confessions, celebrating Sunday Mass (concelebrating with a visiting bishop on one occasion), praying on his own in the church. And we see the ecclesiastical leader planning buildings in Durrow, counselling a delegation from the King of Strathclyde, becoming involved in the succession to the kingship of Dál Riada, crossing 'the spine of Scotland' along the Great Glen to negotiate mission openings with Bruide, King of the Picts (for which he needed an interpreter). Although he met the king on at least two occasions, there is no evidence that Bruide became a Christian. (If we believe the story, the saint was also the first to put manners on the Loch Ness monster.)

There is little evidence that Colm had great personal success as a missionary, or indeed that he may have considered this as his primary duty. He did, however, set in place a pastoral system for the benefit of the people of Dál Riada, that Gaelic bridgehead across the Sea of Moyle, and in the long term for the people of all Scotland, to which they had no access before he came and which brought much of the country to Christianity. It is for this reason that he may rightly be considered 'the apostle of Scotland'.

The Convention of Droim Ceat

In 574, Colm consecrated Aedán mac Gabhráin as King of Dál Riada, the territory of which lay partly in Scotland, partly in Ireland. At Droim Ceat (now the *Mullach,* south of Limavady) was held the Convention of Kings, recorded as happening in 575 (a date which appears to be too early), when the status of the Irish territory of Dál Riada was at issue. Aodh mac Ainmhireach of the northern Uí Néill represented a sea power that could have been a deadly threat to the sea-divided Dál Riada. The question to be settled was to whom did the kingdom owe its taxes and military service. With the help of Colm Cille they agreed that the men of Irish Dál Riada would render their military service to

Uí Néill overlords, but their taxes to 'the men of Alba'.[15] Also settled was the position of the *filí*, the hereditary caste of poet-chroniclers and guardians of tradition. Because of pagan associations and their demand for ever-greater privileges – and 'because they had become too numerous' – they were threatened with expulsion from the country. Due to his former tutor, the *file* Gemmán, and his maternal family background, Colm appreciated the value of the bardic heritage and traditionally was reputed to have shared in their art. His eloquent defence preserved them from expulsion and effected a reconciliation between them and Aodh (who seems to have viewed them with considerable *hauteur*). Ever afterwards, the poetic profession vowed a great reverence to the memory of their saviour, and the poetry attributed to him for that reason would constitute a separate chapter in the history of Gaelic literature.

The Death of the Saint
Colm Cille died on Sunday, 9 June 597 in his seventy-seventh year, a very old man for his day. Adhamhnán's elegiac account of his last day of life makes compelling reading even at this distance in time. Still at his daily work in the *scriptorium*, the last words he copied were Psalm 33:11, *Those who seek the Lord shall not want for anything that is good*, and his last words to his monks were that *they should have unfeigned love for one another with peace*. He was buried on the storm-bound island in the middle of a gale, although centuries later the enterprising Normans were fortunate enough to find his unaccompanied, sea-borne coffin, and were able to inter it at the centre of their new earldom at Downpatrick, along with Patrick and Brighid!

The Legacy of Colm Cille
a) In Scotland
The original founders of the kingdom of Dál Riada were Irish who were known to the Roman world as *Scoti*. In the course of time this kingdom extended its power and influence to the whole of the country to which they gave their name, Scotland. Until the time of the Vikings, Iona was the great religious centre that held the mausoleum of the kings

---

15. *Alba* in Irish is Scotland; *Albanach* is a Scot, and in unreconstructed days meant also a Presbyterian. The Scots (or *Scoit*) descend from Eibhear Scot, the great-grandson of Gael Glas, great-great-great-grandson of Magog, grandson of Noah. This is according to the medieval genealogies that wanted to link the peoples of Ireland with the people of the Bible.

of Scotland. Duncan (actually *Donncha*), Macbeth and Kenneth Mac Ailpín are buried there. With the devastating attacks of the Vikings there could be only a token presence of monks on Iona, and the religious centre of Scotland shifted first to Dunkeld and then to St Andrews. Eventually the islands were ceded to the Vikings. Norman and continental influence led to the appointment of St Andrew as national patron. Gradually Lallans replaced Gaelic as the language of the Scottish court. In the course of time the Vikings too became Christian and deeply attached to the island their ancestors had ravaged. It was a viking who introduced the cult of Columba to Iceland, bringing wood with him to build a church in his honour. They in turn became Gaelic-speaking. Their descendants – *Mac Dónaill* (Mac Donald/Mc Connell), *Mac Giolla Iain* (Mc Lean) – with others in the hinterland of Iona like *Caimbeul* (Campbell), *Camshrón* (Cameron) and so on were the people from whom Carmichael gathered his *Carmina Gadelica* in the nineteenth century, his collection of prayers and blessings that is nowadays one of the safer foundations of that enigmatic entity 'Celtic Spirituality'. The Scots are rediscovering the relevance of Iona to their sense of history and national consciousness, as the growth of its Community and the burial there of the British Labour leader John Smith gives witness.

b) In Ireland

The monks of Iona made the fateful decision not to move to the new monastery in Dunkeld dedicated to St Columba. Iona's relics were divided and some brought back to Ireland, first to *Ceanannas* (Kells), then to Raphoe. Eventually, in the twelfth century, Derry became the head of the *paruchia* of Colm Cille. The monastery was in the forefront of Church reform in that century, giving two leaders to Armagh, St *Giolla Mac Liag* (Gelasius) *Mac Ruairí* and St *Conchúr Mac Con Choille* (Conor Mc Enhill) and having its own energetic abbot, *Flaitheartach Ó Brolcháin*. The Norman invasion resulted in the loss of their monastic lands in Meath and Leinster. By the end of the century, the Columban Order itself disappeared when it accepted the rule of the order of the Canons Regular of St Augustine of *Arrouaise*, which had its Irish headquarters at Armagh.

In the course of the thirteenth century, as parishes came to be formed, Colm Cille became patron of many churches under the aegis of the descendants of the original Uí Néill, the Mac Lochlainn kings of Cineál Eoghain (including south Derry). Hence we find Ballinascreen,

39

Desertmartin, Kilcronaghan, Desertoghill dedicated to Colm Cille, whereas Errigal and Dunboe are dedicated to St Adhamhnán (Adamnán or Eunan), reflecting the Cineál Chonaill connection, when Ó Dónaill and Ó Dochartaigh had extended their power to Inis Eoghain. West Tyrone, the former kingdom of Ard Sratha, remained faithful to St Eoghan, and Badoney to St Patrick, while Droim Rátha (Omagh) in Derry diocese and Termonmaguirk (Carrickmore) in Armagh gave their allegiance to Colm Cille. No proper examination of this process has as yet taken place. In the thirteenth century, Derry itself, from being the monastic city of Cineál Eoghain (under Mac Lochlainn), became a Cineál Chonaill capital, ruled by Ó Dónaill and Ó Dochartaigh.

Quite apart from this background, Colm Cille has become part of folklore in most parts of Ireland, often for the most unlikely reasons. There is a well dedicated to St Colm Cille on the seashore at Cill Chiaráin, on the western tip of Connemara. Loch Bradán near Fintown in Co. Donegal has in fact no salmon, 'because Colm Cille cursed it'. For similar reasons the mouth of Mulroy Bay will not yield you a fish. In Glenelly you will learn that a fleeing Colm Cille cursed anyone who puts on a shoe and a sock before both socks. His patronage against lightning was invoked not only in Derry but also in Britain, France and Germany. Not that people were naively superstitious; rather they lent the power of his name to wise advice, or recognised that even if what they perceived was beyond explanation or beyond their control, Colm Cille was their ally. In the process he sometimes became more of a druid than a saint. We must not judge the myth of Colm Cille in the perspective of our own times, failing to see the force of his personality, the scope of his achievements and the courage of his choices. We may also fail to recognise the power of the hope that his career illustrates.

THE BISHOP EOGHAN

Ardstraw, as an ecclesiastical centre, was founded by St Eoghan (now anglicised 'Eugene') who was always referred to as *Eoghan easpag* ('the bishop Eoghan'). The nearby parish of Badoney claims to have been founded by St Patrick, and Tírechán, biographer of St Patrick, claims that the saint ordained Mac Erca as Bishop of Ard Sratha, thus making Ardstraw subject to Armagh. As a result, the *Calendar of Aenghus* suggests that Eoghan/Eugene was the son of Bishop Erc of Sláine. This is of course fanciful, but it is not the only fancy that has been foisted on St Eoghan. The name Eoghan itself means 'born under the yew-tree', that is 'under the protection of the sacred yew-tree', an inherited pagan totem-name such as many early saints bore in Ireland. The name has no connection with 'Eugene' except in appearance, the original Greek *Eugenios* meaning 'well-born'. Eoghan was born of a south Leinster father, while his mother belonged to the Mugdorna (modern Irish *Muórna*) of south Down/Monaghan, although it has been suggested that the family she actually belonged to was a branch whose name is traceable in the placenames Mourne and Glenmornan.

Seventh-century bishop Tíreachán was writing out of the situation at his own time when Armagh was trying to build up its prestige and authority in the Church in Ireland, which would mean that the church of Ardstraw was then an independent foundation. This independence is underlined by the way authors stress the friendship between St Eoghan, St Cairbre of Coleraine and St Tiarnach of Clones, starting when they were educated together by St Ninian of Rosnat/Whithorn in Scotland, as were a number of early Irish saints. Despite the claim that they arrived there after being kidnapped, it is in fact more likely that they went there to discover the civilisation of the Roman Empire, which included not merely Christianity and the legal and economic system but, sometimes overlooked, the use of an alphabet to read and write – a civilisation of the book – the equivalent in our time maybe of learning 'to surf the net'. According to his biography he was kidnapped twice and taken the second time to *Armorica*, now Brittany, which may mean no more than that he was caught up in some of the invasions which helped break up the Roman Empire in Britain.

This Latin life of St Eoghan was written long after his time and has little historical value, but some probable facts do emerge from it. He returned to Leinster from Whithorn to found the monastery of *Cill na Manach*, south of Dublin, where he became well known for educating a number of bishops and priests. The author of the *Life* includes amongst them as his nephew St Kevin of Glendalough. According to the genealogies, however, Kevin seems to have been a younger cousin. The *Life* places Eoghan in a monastic setting, even in Ard Sratha, but in the genealogies he is almost always *Eoghan easpag*, 'Eoghan the bishop'.

When Eoghan came north, it is reasonable to assume that he came not just as a missionary, but also 'as a pilgrim for the sake of Christ' in exile. While it is usually assumed that this meant leaving Ireland, it was not necessarily so. Due to the division of the country into a grid of independent states or *tuatha*, exile meant leaving one's own and taking one's chances in another *tuath*. Without personal resources, one had no honour, personal standing, or legal protection outside one's own *tuath*. When Eoghan came to Ardstraw then, he came as an exile, but bearing with him the aura of a seasoned monastic founder in the new Christian religion that had swept the Roman Empire and was now spreading in Ireland also. His perceived expertise in Roman language, religion, law, economics and power made him as attractive to the Irish of the time (who had never been within the Empire) as European civilisation, including Christianity, was to prove in Africa in the nineteenth and twentieth centuries. Grace, after all, builds on nature. Since Christianity spread first to south-east Ireland, it is not surprising that a missionary effort in the north should begin from Cill na Manach. After all, St Colm Cille's mother was a Christian from south Leinster. We must not forget that the careers of Colm Cille and Eoghan overlapped – with Eoghan having much the greater impact at that stage on west Ulster.

The Church in Ireland had begun with a system of bishops and priests as in other countries, but became markedly more monastic in character. This process no doubt had many causes: shortage of secular priests; difficulty in establishing a system of maintenance for a new body of clergy in a society without coinage and where one's position in society depended on one's 'honour-price'; the fact that the learned professions were passed on within kin-groups and limited to them; and the remarkable attraction shown by so many of the Irish towards monastic community life.

A Comrade of St Patrick

The roots of Christianity in what is now the diocese of Derry go far back in the Christian story. It is well known that the element in Irish placenames which is nowadays written 'Donagh' or 'Doney' represents the Gaelic term *domhnach*, from the Latin *dominicum* or 'house of the Lord', a term used to denote a Christian place of worship only down to the sixth century AD. The fact, then, that this element occurs in Carndonagh, Donaghmore, Donagheady and Badoney demonstrates that the Christian Faith was preached in these places more than fifteen hundred years ago. By comparison, it is only a short few years since Poland was commemorating the thousandth anniversary of its conversion in the tenth century. The conversion of Germany may be said to have begun with the missions of Irish and Anglo-Saxon monks from AD 592. The Anglo-Saxons themselves first heard the Good News of the Gospel from Iona with St Aidan's coming to Lindisfarne in 634. Even the French, who like their country to be seen as 'the eldest daughter of the Church', date that distinction from the conversion to Catholicism of the Frankish King Clovis in 497. Patrick had by then already begun his work in Ireland in 432, and these placenames of ours still record those ancient origins.

One of these names in particular is still associated directly and personally with the preaching of the national apostle. This is the parish of Badoney – in Irish *Both Domhnaigh* – indicating a temporary or makeshift place of worship from the Patrician era. Not only that but both tradition and written record have preserved the name of the first of Patrick's fellow-missionaries to work there. This was the saint *Cormac Athghin*.

On the face of it, Cormac Aithghin means Cormac 'the re-born, *renatus, rené*'. Professor Pádraig Ó Riain suggests that the name Cormac may be a scribal misreading of the job description in his genealogy in the *Leabhar Breac*, 'Aithghin .i. cóic Pátraic' (i.e. Patrick's cook), and that, as a result, the actual name of the saint is simply Aithghin. In his *Dictionary of Irish Saints*, Professor Ó Riain seems to have somewhat modified his position on the question of the scribal misreading. He considers the name Aithghin to be a variant of Aodhghin, meaning 'born of fire'. Since Aithghin points to Baptism ('re-born') while Aodhghin would indicate a pagan origin, the former might seem to suit the case better.

The name Athghin occurs only once in the historical annals, in the year 650, where AFM records the death of Aithchen, Abbot of Tír Dá Ghlas (Terryglass, Co. Tipperary); the same person, one must presume, is named Maelaichthin in AU (+656). Athghin is in fact found in genealogies and annals only in this compound form: Maelaichthin of Tír Dá Ghlas (+656: AU);[16] Maelaithgen, Abbot of Cluain Eidhneach (+767 AFM: AU 772) and Maelaithghin, Bishop of Armagh (+890: AFM). The prefix 'mael/maol' refers to tonsure and indicates a name taken out of respect for the charism of the original bearer. We have no evidence about where these men came from but the compound suggests that the name Athghin was quite well known by the seventh and eighth centuries.

---

16. Also 'Aidbe (i.e. Aidben) tuathach Tíre', Whitley Stokes, ed., *The Martyrology of Oengus the Culdee* (London: Harrison and Sons, 1905), 24 May, pp. 126, 137.

In their genealogies of the saints and kings,[17] the Four Masters repeat the nomenclature that is in question: *Aithghen .i. Corbmac Boithe Domhnaigh* (Cormac of Badoney). They repeat this in the Table of the Martyrology given at the end of their *Martyrology of Donegal:*[18] Aithghein .i. Corbmac Bhotha Domhnaigh, without any reference to *cóic Phádraig.* Both entries may be traceable to the same original, but the entry in GRSH is filled out to include the saint's pedigree: *Aithghen .i. Corbmac Boithe Domhnaigh mac Daoil mac Maisine m Fearghosa m Duaich m Breasail m Colla Menn m Eathach Doimhlen.* The book also gives him a sister Curcach, with feast day 8 November, and a brother *Cruimhthear Ciarán,* with suggested feast day 11 November. They are the only descendants of Colla Meann found in the genealogies of the saints, whereas there are many amongst the descendants of Colla Meann's brothers. Triplicate entries for a single saint can occur, but it is uncommon that one of the trio should be female. The brevity of the list of descendants of Colla Meann,[19] both in numbers and generations, and the vagueness of the associations would point to the antiquity of the original list, and thus, paradoxically, to its authenticity, although its contemporaneity with St Patrick may bear investigation. The actual format of the genealogical reference 'Cormac Boithe Domhnaigh', however, is in the Irish of a much later age, since early references speak of 'Both Domhnach'.

The title 'cruimhthear',[20] applied to his brother Ciarán, reminds us once again of how early a period in the history of the Christian Church we are faced with. This title is the earliest form taken in Ireland by the Latin *presbyter* (which in English became 'priest'), so early indeed that it takes us right back to the system of bishops and priests set up at the beginning but which was to prove unworkable in very early missionary Ireland. As a result, the Church in Ireland made its own the system developed by St Martin of Tours to convert rural Gaul, which involved the establishment of small monasteries on land given by benefactors to provide sustenance in its mission for a clergy without the status

17. Paul Walsh, ed., *Genealogiae Regum et Sanctorum Hiberniae* (GRSH) (Dublin: Maynooth Record Society, St Patrick's College, 1918), p. 73.
18. J.H. Todd/W. Reeves, eds, John O'Donovan, trans., *Calendar of the Saints of Ireland* (Dublin: Irish Archaeological Society, 1864), p. 361.
19. Colla Meann 'the stammerer', one of three mythic brothers who raised havoc in early Ireland, if it is all to be believed, and who were the progenitors of the Airghialla, tribal groupings who carved territories for themselves out of the south of the kingdom of the Ulaidh, extending from what is now south Down to the valley of the Faughan. Colla Meann is reputed to have died young.
20. Pronounced 'criffer'.

or means to hold property. Since it was in monasteries that records of events were later kept, it follows that records are sparse for earlier times. This has had the result that the century after the death of St Patrick has left us an almost silent Church. Much of what we can say about Cormac Aithghin, then, can only be discovered by deduction and inference from what was eventually recorded.

Because of the dual name Cormac Athghin, there is always an outside chance that we are dealing with two different persons. However, since the surviving evidence seems to leave no room for that hypothesis, it is proposed to accept that there was one person whose name was simply Cormac Athghin, and for a number of reasons:

i.   The sobriquet Athghin does not seem to have become a recognised name on its own in Irish, unlike its continental equivalents, René or Renato;

ii. The epithet 'reborn' suggests an early convert;

iii. It suggests furthermore that he was baptised in adult life;

iv. He was a very early convert, since the theological implications of the name would have become less specific as time passed;

v.   He is associated with a domhnach, the earliest word for a church in Irish;

vi. If Athghin is such a byname, he must have had some other name before his conversion and 'Cormac' is the obvious candidate.

The Company of Patrick

What we are told of Cormac, then, does not seem to amount to much: that he was probably an early convert; that, allegedly, he was St Patrick's cook (.i. cóic Phádraig); and that Patrick left him behind to care for the newly established Church of Badoney – hardly an exacting task in the sparsely populated Ireland of the time and not such an important mission station at any time, one might think.

Nonetheless, to understand what these facts imply, it is necessary to replace them in the social and political context of the times. Ireland, in the days of St Patrick, was divided into about 150 tuatha or states. Each one, it is estimated, would have had an average population of no more than 3,000 men, women and children, and it has been speculated that the population of the whole country may have been under half a million. Each tuath was ruled by a king and claimed independence, although some recognised the overlordship of a more powerful neighbouring *tuath*.[21] All, however, accepted the *Féineachas*, the civil legal system governing the whole country. This system did not see the need for the principle of the equality of citizens before the law. Society was strictly hierarchical and in the eyes of the law each person's status was determined by his *lógh n-enech/luach einigh* (literally the value of his 'face'), therefore his honour or dignity. This indicated what had to be paid in case of injury, theft, murder and so forth committed against his person. The honour-price of a freeman ranged from fourteen *cumhala* ('female slaves') – the equivalent of forty-two milch cows – for a provincial king down to a yearling heifer for a *fear midboth* (a youth living on his father's land). Remember that we are talking of a pagan, cattle-farming and pre-monetary society. The privileges of rank were accorded to the *rí* (king), *flaith* (lord) and *file* (poet), to be joined only in later Christian times by the cleric.

Clearly, the *flaith* would have been the most common individual of rank. The position of the *flaith* resulted from the number of *céilí*, or clients, that he had. The *flaith* advanced a *rath* or fief of land, livestock or farm implements to his *céilí*, in return for rent in the form of food, winter-hospitality,[22] manual labour and military duties.[23] There were in turn various grades of *flaith*, whose honour-price was stated in terms of *séit* (modern Irish *séada/seoda*). One *sét* was the equivalent of half a milch cow (*bó bleachta*) or of one *sámhaisc*, a three-year-old dry heifer, in those days before currencies. The lowest rank of *flaith*, the *aire déso*, had a price of ten *séts* and was entitled to a retinue of six persons. The *aire ard* was worth fifteen *séts* and had twenty clients as retinue; the *aire tuiseo* was worth twenty *séts* and had twenty-seven *céilí*; and the *aire forgill* bore a price of thirty *séts* and had forty *céilí*. (*Aire* – in modern Irish a government minister – originally meant freeman or lord.)

As already mentioned, the borders of each *tuath* were jealously guarded so that crossing such a frontier could be fraught with problems or even danger, for each person would be received according to his status in law. This raised a serious problem for the *ambue*, the non-native or outsider, especially if he came from a *tuath* that had no

21. Fergus Kelly, *A Guide to Early Irish Law* (Dublin: Dublin Institute for Advanced Studies, 1988), pp. 3–6.
22. Namely a feast for between twenty and sixty persons (depending on the rank of the *flaith*) between New Year and Shrove.
23. Patrolling the borders, hunting thieves and wolves, escort duties, maintenance for military personnel, active service and so on.

agreement or treaty with the one he now entered. He would seem in this case to have been excluded from all legal agreements and rights, so that he could even be killed with impunity.

A serious difficulty then faced Patrick or any other foreign missionary in Ireland, coming from God knows where with a strange and outlandish message. With no status in law how could he gain access across borders? Knowing the country from his youthful exile there, he solved the problem by travelling with a retinue of rank, since the retinue at least would be received according to their status. In the *Annals of the Four Masters* we find the names of '*Muintir Phádraig na pater ag a raibh ro-Laidin*', 'the household of Patrick of the prayers who had good Latin', followed by the names of thirty-eight people, male and female. The list is clearly confected since it includes St Martin of Tours, described as Patrick's mother's brother, five of his aunts and his nephew.[24] There is another list in CGSH of the *ceathrar ar fichead batar in urd la Pádraig* – 'the twenty-four who were in religious community with Patrick', which does not include Patrick's alleged relations.[25] The list is also given in DF,[26] which agrees with CGSH but omits two names, and in VT.[27] Finally, there is an expanded poetic listing given in CGSH. Interestingly, if we exclude all those in the AFM list whose occupation is not stated, we arrive at a total of twenty-four, the same as that of CGSH 671 and VT.

Does it Matter?

It matters in that this digression may clarify for us how St Patrick managed to travel with some measure of safety and was able to cross *tuath* frontiers as a person of some substance. It shows clearly that he travelled as flaith of intermediate rank, either as an *aire tuiseo* or as an *aire forgill*, together with his *céilí*. As a result he would have appeared strong but not threatening. Furthermore, his *muintir* included members like Cormac who laid claim to being of royal descent so that he was entitled to be received with a further degree of respect. As we know from his *Confessio*, the reception Patrick received was not always favourable, but given that his work in Ireland seems to have been accomplished without martyrs, it was clearly effective.

---

24. AFM ad ann., 448: I, 134–141.
25. CGSH 671; 672.
26. Dubhaltach Mac Fhirbhisigh, *Great Book of Irish Genealogies*, N. Ó Muraile, ed. (Dublin: Edmund Burke Publisher, 2004), 695.1; II, 698–9.
27. Whitley Stokes, ed., *Vita Tripartita/Tripartite Life of Saint Patrick* (London, 1887), I, 264–8.

We know that the Christian Church in the neighbouring island financed Patrick's mission and that British missionaries may have accompanied him. Since there is no evidence of the use of coinage in contemporary Ireland and since Ireland was outside the Roman Empire, the finance probably took the form of silver or gold. This would give him a further reason for a strong retinue, and that in turn must have eaten into his finances.

To return to Cormac Athghin: as a descendant of Colla Meann, he would have been a native of south Down. It is accepted that Patrick's first port of call as a missionary was at Saul in that area. It would make sense then that Cormac, as an early convert, should also belong to the retinue. In addition, as a descendant of Colla Meann he would have been *persona grata* with the rulers of the *tuath* of *Uí Mic Cairthinn* in the Faughan valley and the *Uí Fiachrach Ard Sratha*, who claimed descent from Colla Uais.

The church at Both Domhnaigh is numbered amongst the seven churches said to have been founded in the Faughan valley by St Patrick. Glenelly, however, where the site of that original church is, may well have been in an independent *tuath* of its own, called *Daigurt*, a name found still on the mountain Dart. It is also on the borders of the kingdom of *Ard Sratha*, of course. No trace remains of the other six churches; even their whereabouts is a matter for conjecture. Badoney alone can lay claim to a connection with St Patrick that makes historical sense. Even though many modern historians suggest that Patrick's work was mainly in Connacht, the region he had known as a slave, it is not unreasonable to posit that a journey through the area we are considering makes good sense, coming from his original starting point in south Down. The other factor that needs explanation is the importance accorded Badoney in the view of the church of Armagh in the early Middle Ages, culminating in the unusual appointment of Muireagán of Both Domhnaigh as *Comharba Phádraig*/Successor of St Patrick at the start of the second millennium.

We have, of course, little idea of how *Gleann Aichle* or *Gleann Fhoichle* (Glenelly) may have been seen in those distant days. The places that people of the time wished to visit differed from the places important to us nowadays and the obstacles to travel were different as well: extensive forests, impassable marsh and bog. Early Ireland had indeed different grades of road, the maintenance of which was the responsibility of the local landowner, but the main roads that we follow connect towns that would not come into existence for another thousand years. It is probable, for example, that the area now opened up by the Ballygawley–Omagh road was a windswept, inhospitable mountain plateau. A glance at the topography of mid-Ulster would suggest that the Glenelly valley may have been quite a practical, less exposed, less wooded and safer way to travel through central Ulster on horseback or on foot from places in the Foyle basin, via Lough Fea, to important centres like *Tulach Óg* (Tullyhog) in east Tyrone, and on to *Eamhain Macha*, capital of the Ulaidh. Inhabitants of the kingdom of *Uí Fiachrach Ard Sratha* would have travelled that route and *via* the Moyola valley to meet up with their relatives in the *tuath* of *Uí Tuirtre* in south Derry, and thence onwards to the Bann, joining at Toome the *Slí Mhíluachra*, the main road south to Tara.

An illustration of this, perhaps, from later times is that, when Ó Néill (Aodh Mór), Earl of Tyrone, wished to escape hurriedly from the threats building up around him in 1607, he made his way from *an Chraobh* (now Stewartstown) through Glenelly and on to take ship at Rathmullan, stopping overnight at *Loch Beigfhine* (probably near the old Six Towns church in Ballinascreen). The church of Badoney, furthermore, stands at a crossroads where this east-west axis meets the north-south link, which skirts Dart on its way from north Co. Derry, as it now is, and continues through Barnes into west Tyrone/Fermanagh. The siting of a church there may make more sense than would appear at first sight.

Centuries afterwards, by the time it came about to record the names of Patrick's retinue, those who recorded the names, no longer aware of the original political purpose, presumed that a retinue must have functions of personal service to be invited to be of the company, and they may have imagined it on the model of an important ecclesiastic's household of their own time. As a result, each member of *Muintir Phádraig* was allotted an office: Seachnall his bishop, Mochta his priest, Órán his charioteer, Sinell his bellringer, Benen his psalmist, Béascna his chaplain, Caomhán his valet, Meascán his 'friend and brewer', Cadán his waiter, and so on. Athghin is said to have been his 'true cook'. Most of them became patrons of early churches, the last five in west Ulster. Benen, we are told, succeeded St Patrick himself at Armagh. In Badoney, the feast day of our St Cormac Athghin is 3 May.

At the medieval churches of the Roe valley there stands next to each church building another church in miniature, said to be the grave of the patron saint. There is no such structure at Badoney. Was it never built or was it swept away, as tradition asserts about the headstones of the medieval graveyard there, that they were broken up and used to make French drains in a nearby farm?

What then do these bald historical facts tell us of the beginnings of the Christian gospel in Badoney? Without departing radically from the little that fifteen centuries of passing time have left us, we can discern the outlines of that first mission. Coming from the success of his Christian bridgehead in south Down and from his foundation at Armagh, Patrick continues his mission through central Ulster on his way to the west where he had lived the life of a slave and turned again to the Christian faith of his childhood. Accompanied by a retinue of men of rank, one of them at least of royal blood, he successfully crosses the frontier into the lands of dynasties related to that prince. He is received there with sufficient respect to be allowed to explain the new faith. To do so, he and some of his fellow missionaries, probably of Welsh language like himself, are obliged to construct a new Christian vocabulary in Irish.

This process we can see in the example of the Irish term for the Trinity, *Trionóid*, adopted from the Welsh term *Trindodd*. Gradually, he is able to assemble a nucleus of Christian converts who at first gather to worship in a modest building on the Christian Sunday. It therefore comes to be called *Both Domhnaigh*, 'the Sunday shelter'. Passing on, Patrick leaves behind – to lead and develop the little community – his aristocratic disciple Cormac, whose Christian convictions have led him to take the name that proclaims his baptism and his new life in the faith, Athghin. He had such success that his faith and something of his memory has subsisted in his missionfield down to our own day.

MURA OF FATHAN

In spite of the towering figure of Colm Cille in the history, mythology and folklore of the north west of Ireland, and of his being acclaimed in medieval times as patron saint of the ruling dynasties of Cineál Eoghain and Cineál Chonaill, there is evidence of an earlier patron of Cineál Eoghain and of Inis Eoghain in particular. This was St Mura of Fathan, clearly a figure of great prominence at one stage in the story of Inis Eoghain, as his surviving personal relics demonstrate, but whose historical lineaments have to be teased out painfully from the overlay of political and dynastic preoccupations and rivalries that the annals reflect.

To understand this background, we must go over – at some risk of repetition – the dynastic conflicts of the early north west. Inis Eoghain, as it is known, takes its name from Eoghan, son of Niall Naoighiallach (of the Nine Hostages), who died in AD 453 and is described as High King of Ireland, though he may well have been little more than the leader of a successful war-band of the kind that kidnapped St Patrick. In any event, he is subsequently portrayed as leader and King of the Connachta. This was the name of a western dynasty where they left their name on the province of Connacht. Aggressive and expansionist by nature, they claimed descent from Conn Céadchathach, also said to be high king but much more likely their ancestor-god.

Bursting out of the west, they spread into Leinster where they provided the kings at *Teamhair* (Tara) and ultimately under three of the sons of Niall captured much of what is now Co. Donegal from the Ulaidh: Conall giving his name to Tír Chonaill, originally south Donegal, Éanna calling his domain Tír Éinne and Eoghan making his own of Inis Eoghain or Inishowen.

Eoghan is said to have met and been converted by St Patrick, who baptised him at Iskaheen, where he is said to be buried. It would look as if part of the placename has been lost, since *Uisce Chaoin* is in the genitive case and would presume a word like *Tobar* (a well) before it, on the face of it a not unlikely place to be baptised. While the descendants of Niall, the Uí Néill, took some time to dislodge the Ulaidh from the island at Derry, they were soon in control of access to Inis Eoghain. Eoghan's son Muireadhach extended their power across the south of the *inis, Críoch Mhuireadhaigh* – the territory of Muireadhach – which included Fahan.

These lands between the two loughs are dominated by the prehistoric sacred site of *Aileach: Aileach Neid* as it was at first known. Aileach was to be for centuries the spiritual and political home of Cineál Eoghain. Kings of the kindred would bear the name 'King of Aileach', though it had been prominent long before their time. In all probability, Críoch Mhuireadhaigh had similar boundaries to the parish of Fahan, Upper and Lower together, and perhaps including Desertegny as far as Mamore Gap. Such then are the historical stage and actors among whom the Christian missionary Mura appears.

Mura, the Man

Although Eoghan was allegedly baptised by St Patrick, and although it would be claimed in later times that 'the descendants of Niall are under the protection of Colm Cille,'[28] the patron of early Cineál Eoghain was, as

---

28. *Book of Leinster* VI, 1661.

we have said, St Mura.[29] To make him less of an outsider, he was fitted out by propaganda with a genealogy that tied him closely to the royal house of Eoghan. He was said to be the son of Fearadhach, son of Rónán, son of Eoghan Méarchroim ('bent-finger'), son of Muireadhach, son of Eoghan.[30] The same genealogy is given in *Corpus Genealogiarum Sanctorum Hiberniae* and in the Laud Collection, except that they both omit Eoghan Méarchroim. Muireadhach, according to all other genealogical tracts, had five sons, none of them called Eoghan Méarchroim.

However, in another recension of genealogies, the *Recensio Minor*, we find that Mura is said to belong to *Sliocht Fiatach Finn*, adding that his mother Deirinill Ceatharchíochach was also the mother of Saints Domhanghart, Ailleán, Aodhán, Mochumma of Droim Bó and Cilleán of Achadh Caol in Lecale on the shore of Dún Droma.[31] Saint Domhanghart is associated with Maghera, Co. Down, also near Dundrum Bay. Dál Fiatach was the area in south-east Down with which all of these were connected, and when we examine the genealogy of Dál Fiatach, sure enough, we find there that Eoghan Méarchroim was in fact the son of Muireadhach Muindearg ('the red-backed') 'whom St Patrick blessed in the kingdom of Ireland'.[32] There can be little doubt then that Mura belonged to the royal house of Dál Fiatach. The genealogists, wittingly or unwittingly, confused the two ancestors named Muireadhach. It is probable then that Mura was born in the area where tradition claims that St Patrick started his mission to Ireland.

If as seems likely, Mura belonged to Dál Fiatach, he came to Inis Eoghain as an outsider and missionary. He is said to have died in 645, which would suggest a date for his arrival at Fahan around 600, around the time of St Colm Cille's death. The annals tell us that there were two Fahans: Othain Mhór and Othain Bheag.[33] Othain Bheag may have been a hermitage or *díseart* in the Buncrana area, perhaps even Desertegny, as its name implies, although we know nothing of St Éigneach whose name it bears.

---

29. There seems to be no evidence for a long 'u' in the pronunciation of his name. It seems to rhyme with 'fur' and 'purr', rather than 'moor' and 'poor'.
30. *Genealogiae Regum et Sanctorum Hiberniae* (GRSH) 47, by the Four Masters, Paul Walsh, ed., 1918.
31. P. Ó Riain, ed., CGSH (*Corpus Genealogiarum Sanctorum Hiberniae*) (Dublin, 1985), 557; 722.27.
32. Mac Fhirbhisigh, *Book of Genealogies* II, p. 494.
33. It is not uncommon to find a prosthetic 'f' obtruded into words beginning with a vowel. Not far from Fahan, Faughanvale, for example, has nothing to do with the nearby River Faughan; it is *Uachongbháil* – 'new (monastic) foundation'.

Mura, the Myth

In the *Fragmentary Annals of Ireland*, we find an amusing story of Mura which illustrates the way in which the hostility of the annal to Cineál Eoghain rarely loses an opportunity to poke fun at the northerners, suggesting either that they were pious ignoramuses or uncouth in the extreme. Reading it, one could plausibly be at *Snámh Dhá Éan/Swim Two Birds* in the company of a ribald Flann O'Brien.

According to the story then, Aodh Uairíonach, great-great-grandson of Niall, probably King of Aileach at the time and soon to be high king, 'came through Othan Muru [*sic*] and washed his hands in the river which flows through the middle of the town. (Othan is the name of the river and from it the town is named.) He took a handful of water to put on his face. One of his men stopped him:

"O king," he said, "do not put that water on your face."

"Why?" asked the king.

"I am ashamed to say," said he.

"What shame do you have at telling the truth?" asked the king.

"This is it," he replied, "the clergy's privy is over that water."

"Is it there," asked the king, "that the cleric himself goes to relieve himself?"

"It is indeed," said the youth.

"Not only," said the king, "shall I put it on my face, but I shall also put it in my mouth and drink it (*drinking three mouthfuls of it*) for that water is a sacrament to me."

This was related to Mura, and he thanked God that Aedh Allán[34] had such faith. Then he summoned Aedh Allán to him (Aedh Uairíonach was another of his names), and Mura said to him: "Dear son," he said, "as reward for that reverence you have shown the church, I promise, as God is my witness, that you shall have the kingship of Ireland shortly, and that you will gain victory and the overthrow of your enemies, and that you will not be taken by sudden death, and you will receive the Body of the Lord from my hand, and I shall pray to the Lord on your behalf that it may be old age that will take you from the world."

It was not long afterwards that Aedh Allán took the kingship of Ireland and he granted fertile lands to Mura of Othan.[35] Moreover he won many victories over the *Laighin* (Leinster lords) and over his other

---

34. There were two high kings called Aedh Allán.
35. At the Inquisition held at the time of the Plantation of Ulster there were four quarters (sixteen bailte bó) in the churchlands of the parish of Fahan.

enemies. He was eight years in the kingship of Ireland and then mortal illness seized him and he sent for Mura. Mura came and the king said to him: "Cleric," he said, "you have deceived me, for I have neglected to do penance, because I expected, through your word, that I would grow old in my lifetime, and it seems to me that death is near me."

"True," said the cleric, "death is near you, and your life has been cut short, and you have incurred the Lord's anger, so explain all that you have done to offend the Lord.'"

The two then embark on a ridiculous examination of the king's conscience to find out where he has sinned: his attempt to build a house on Carrleagh Mountain whose fire would be visible from Britain and Argyle, his effort to acquire everlasting fame by building a marvellous bridge at Cluain Ioraird (Clonard, Co. Meath). But his particular offence in the view of this southern source was that his hatred had led him to slay the men of Leinster and force their women and slaves north to serve the Uí Néill. Mura points out that in hating Leinster he had brought down on his head the prayers of the saints of Leinster, especially St Brighid/Bríd whose prayers are more powerful than his (Mura's). The king does penance, is anointed and goes off to heaven.[36] Elsewhere it is suggested that Aedh Uairíonach did not in fact enjoy good health; his byname seems to mean 'of the cold pangs', which might imply some long-term stomach ailment.

Leaving aside the *burlesque* treatment, the annalist does seem less than impressed here with the powers of Mura. The story has clearly been re-worked, history re-told as prophecy, probably in sympathy with Leinster interests (although John O'Donovan thought this fragment was of Ulster origin). Anyhow, in its attitudes and language it is much later than the events it claims to depict. It gestures in the direction of popular piety by recalling the *trí bolgaim uisce*, the three mouthfuls of water, originating in paganism but traditionally taken by the devout after Holy Communion.

It also gives confusing hints at the start of the episode. Mura is so important that he can send for the king, yet the king does not know where exactly Mura resides. It allows Mura a pardon for getting it all wrong by stressing the national importance of St Bríd. The somewhat *ersatz* and ill-judged piety of the king and the limits of the power of Mura cannot defeat the great St Bríd whom it is more heinous to offend

36. Joan N. Radner, ed., *Fragmentary Annals of Ireland* (Dublin: Dublin Institute for Advanced Studies, 1978), pp. 4–9.

than it is to hate the men of Leinster or to enslave their womenfolk. The original purpose may well have been to account for St Mura's position as patron of Cineál Eoghain (as against St Colm Cille perhaps), as suggested by the fertile lands given him, yet as a patron he could not guarantee long life to his protégé, finding himself with the problem of having to account for the brevity of Aedh Uairíonach's reign. Aedh Uairíonach was high king from 604 to 612, while his descendant, the king more usually known as Aedh Allán, was high king from 734 to 743.

It is clear at least from the story that Mura had arrived at Fahan a little before Aedh Uairíonach's time. He chose his location well, near the royal seat of power at Aileach – which may or may not have been the fortification at Aileach itself – but not too near. His monastic site was known to the king's attendants but not to the king who knew him, at best, only by reputation. The annal is dated 605, but the initial event is clearly earlier than that, which would confirm what one would surmise from the date of his death (645). Unfortunately our story presumes too much on our knowledge of St Mura and adds nothing of any significance. Elsewhere we are told that he was known as *Muran, Gnia* (his pet-name – many early Irish saints seem to have received pet-names) and *Dimma*, his baptismal name. There is a further question involved here in that the latter two are usually diminutives of *Diarmaid*. Saint Mura's feast day is given in the martyrologies as 12 March.

The Reputation of St Mura

The career of St Mura overlapped with that of Colm Cille and he wrote a verse life of the saint which is no longer extant, although the *Martyrology of Donegal* quotes a verse of poetry about him, attributed to Mura by Mánas Ó Dónaill in his sixteenth century *Beatha Cholm Cille*:

Rugadh i nGartán dá dheoin;	He was born in Gartán by God's will;
oileadh i gCill Mhic Neoin;	he was reared at Cill Mhic Réanáin;
baisteadh mac na maise	the comely young man was baptised
i dTulaigh Dé Dubhghlaise.	at godly Tulach Dubhghlaise.[37]

Abbé Mac Geoghegan refers to the exalted veneration in which the monastery at Fahan was held 'on account of St Mura its patron, but

---

37. O'Donovan/Todd, eds, *The Martyrology of Donegal* (Dublin: Printed for the Irish Archaeological and Celtic Society, 1864). Irish original modernised.

also for the valuable monuments of antiquity which were preserved in it for many centuries; amongst others there was a small volume of Gaelic verse by St Mura and a large book of chronology, filled with many historical passages, concerning the nation in general. This work was much esteemed, and is frequently quoted by the antiquarians of the country. There still remain some fragments of it, Colgan says, which have escaped the fury of the reformers of latter ages.'[38]

Few of 'those valuable monuments of antiquity', relics of the age of St Mura, are left to us; *Bachall Mhura*, (his pastoral staff or crozier) is in the Royal Irish Academy, his bell in the Wallace Collection in London, the great St Mura's Cross in the cemetery at Fahan. This fine example of early stone decoration was probably created in the mid to late seventh century, shortly after the saint's death. Although inevitably there is scholarly discussion about its dating, some preferring to describe it as a minor and imitative work of the tenth century. One remarkable feature of it is that it is the only such stone monument in Ireland to have an inscription in Greek. It bears a doxology or invocation to the Trinity apparently derived from the Acts of the Council of Toledo in AD 633, which would argue for a date earlier than that of the insertion of *Filioque* ('and of the Son') into the Nicene Creed by the Church in Spain. If so, this would predicate a fairly close, ongoing connection between Spain and the north of Ireland at the time.[39] In which case the cross would possibly date to shortly after Mura's death.

The Inheritance of Mura

Prominent among the successors of St Mura at Fahan were Cillín Ó Colla, abbot and saint, who died in 724 on 3 January (his feast day) and Fotha na Canóine (who died in 818), one of the pioneers of the reform of the Church in the eighth century associated with the *Céile Dé* movement. He too is recognised as a saint with his feast day on

---

38. Abbé Mac Geoghegan, *History of Ireland*, Patrick O'Kelly, trans. (Dublin: 1844), I, 171. Largely based on John Colgan, B. Jennings, eds, *Acta Sanctorum Hiberniae* (Dublin: Stationery Office, 1948), I, 587.

39. A. Rowan, *North-West Ulster* (London: Yale University Press, 1979), pp. 289–90. Although not a 'high cross' as such, it has some of their typical features: the base of the cross is said to represent the hill of Calvary, and the 'house' at its head may be the shrine which the Emperor Constantine erected over the tomb of the risen Christ, which is copied in Adhamhnán's *De Locis Sanctis*. The circle is believed to derive from the *trophaeum* of Roman military achievement, the laurel wreath, here representing the triumph of the Christian Cross over sun worship. The panels on such crosses were used as catechetical visual aids.

3 February. He was a man of poetry and intellect with a reputation throughout Ireland, consulted on matters of moral, political and even military importance by the high king and by his colleagues, and credited with writing a metrical monastic rule himself.

Some idea of his standing, and perhaps by implication that of the monastery at Fahan, may be derived from the role he played at a difficult moment in the history of the country. In 804, the High King Aodh Oirnidhe had called a great assembly at Dún Cuair in Meath. Connmach of Armagh and representatives of the clergy of the north of Ireland came as they were legally bound to do, but they complained to the king that their attendance at such political and military hostings was burdensome and inappropriate. The king's reaction was to suggest that the problem be put to Fotha na Canóine and that they abide by whatever judgement he made. Since Aodh Oirnidhe belonged to Cineál Eoghain of Aileach, it is not improbable that he and Fotha of nearby Fathain had discussed the subject at some time and that Aodh already knew what decision he would receive. Fotha's decision was that the clergy should not have to attend, and he is credited with a poem on the subject (important statements were often set down in verse form) – perhaps one of our earliest statements on the relationship between civil and religious authority:

Eaglais De Bhí, lig di gach atá ag dul di;
bíodh a ceart ar leith mar is maith a bhí.
Gach fíormhanach bíodh ar a choinsias glan:
don Eaglais ar dual di déanadh amhail gach mogh.
Gach díolúnach mar sin gan reacht gan réir,
cead cé théas le cath Aodha náir mhic Néill.
Is í sin an riail cheart seach ní mór ní beag;
fónadh gach mogh gan chion gan locht.[40]

The Church of the Living God, leave her what is hers;
let her right be separate as has been best.
Every true monk, then, let it be on his pure conscience
for the Church to which it is due let him work like any slave.
Every freeman then, who follows no (*monastic*) rule of life

---

40. Whitley Stokes, ed., *Martyrology of Oengus the Culdee* (London: Harrison and Sons, 1905), pp. 10–11. See also corrected version in Best/O'Brien, eds, *Book of Leinster* (Dublin: Dublin Institute for Advanced Studies, 1967), III, 621.

is allowed to go to battle with noble Aodh son of Niall.
It is the right regulation, neither great nor small,
let every slave of God serve without sin and without fault.

Although he composed a rule and was a friend of Aonghas Céile Dé, we cannot be certain that Fotha was himself a *céile Dé*, but there can be no doubt that he shared their reformist enthusiasm. Posterity promoted him to sainthood, according to the genealogies.[41] He died at Fahan, which gives rise to the inference that he belonged to the community there and that Fahan may thus have become a house of *céilí Dé* itself. It may well be however that there were monks and hermits and *céilí Dé* in the same community, and that he may only have retired there towards the end of his days. His authorship of a monastic rule and his connection with Fahan would suggest that it was written for that community and it is only fair to number him among the spiritual and intellectual heirs of St Mura.

According to his genealogy, Fotha belonged to that branch of Cineál Eoghain, Cineál Binnigh, whose ancestor was Eochaidh Binneach, son of Eoghan.[42] They have perhaps the fullest genealogy of any of the lateral branches of Cineál Eoghain, but unfortunately had lost their political importance by the time the annals were put together and hence their names rarely appear there. We can establish two things about them: that they were prominent in the advance of Cineál Eoghain power across modern Co. Derry, to which area they brought with them devotion to St Colm Cille their patron; and that some of their leading families (like Ó Duimhin/Devine and Mac Conchoille/Mc Enhill) were prominent in the affairs of the Columban monastery at Derry. Fotha's particular genealogy suggests a close connection between Cineál Binnigh and the monastery at Fahan and between Derry and Fahan. Two members of Cineál Binnigh are even numbered among the *principes* (abbots or erenaghs) of Fahan.

It is debatable which of the two monasteries was the more important at that stage, the beginning of the ninth century, since we have no record of any cleric of Derry (except the scribe St Caochscoile, died 720; and St Dácuailén, undated), until sixty years after Fotha's death. If we can take it that the Greek inscription at Fahan church dates from this

41. *Genealogiae Regum et Sanctorum Hiberniae* 46 (21); see also Mac Fhirbhisigh, op. cit., I, 142.4; p. 334.
42. He belonged to Cineál Binnigh of Tulach Óg (Tullyhogue), as did families associated later in the Middle Ages with *Teach na Coimirce* at Clonleigh (Lifford): Ó Tomhrair (Toner), Ó Braoin, Ó Bogáin and Ó Brolaigh.

period and when we consider that the *rífhile* (chief poet) Maolmhura Othna[43] (whose name suggests some attachment to the community) died at Fahan in 884, we must see it as evidence of a vibrant religious and intellectual community of national importance there.

Two centuries later, a further adornment to the religious tradition of St Mura and Fahan was the Benedictine *beatus*, Blessed Marianus Scotus (as he was known in Latin), *Muireadhach Mac Rabhartaigh*, who died in 1088. He founded the Benedictine monastery, the *Schottenkloster* (or Irish monastery) at Regensburg in Germany and initiated a Benedictine revival in southern Germany and Austria. His story is perhaps best presented as reflecting the vitality and instinct for survival of the medieval ecclesiastical families we know as the erenaghs, exemplified in the next two essays by Mac Conchoille (McEnhill) and Mac Rabhartaigh (McGroarty).

BÉBHINN, A WOMAN IN MONASTIC DERRY

In studying the history of the remarkable twelfth century, which saw the reform of the entire organisation of the Church in Ireland and, to our particular purpose, the renewal of the Church in Derry, we come across in the annals two or three entries which exemplify in a quite exceptional way, and in one family, the upheaval which reform must have represented. These brief accounts in the *Annals of Ulster* read as follows:

AD 1112   Conghalach, son of Mac Conchoille, airchinneach of Derry, died, having performed exemplary penance, in the ninety-fourth year of his age.

AD 1134   Bébhinn, daughter of Mac Conchoille, female airchinneach of Derry, died on 22 December.

AD 1175   Conchúr Mac Conchoille, abbot of the church of Saints Peter and Paul, and afterwards successor of St Patrick, died at Rome, having gone to confer with the successor of St Peter.

---

43. The name means 'devotee of St Mura at Fahan'. There is a long poem by him in *Book of Leinster* III, pp. 516–23.

In these brief annalistic entries, it is noticeable that the titular head of the erenagh family at Derry was referred to simply by his surname, Mac Conchoille, as was the case with all the major families of the nobility; thus Ó Néill, Ó Dónaill and so forth. It points up the fact that these erenagh families were prominent members of the society of their time with a long history and no doubt the professional pride to go with it. It is therefore a matter of some interest to look a little more closely at the above three entries, spanning as they do a period of sixty odd years during one of the most dramatic moments in Irish ecclesiastical history.

Conghalach, we are told, son of the titular Mac Conchoille and erenagh at Derry, died at the advanced age of ninety-four years in AD 1112. This means that he was born around 1018, just four years after the great battle at Clontarf at which Brian Bóraimhe ended the Viking threat for good and constrained the Viking cities to settle down into the Irish political system. Most of his life, then, was spent in that older Ireland where the provincial dynasties warred towards the establishment of a unitary high kingship. Aged already over fifty in 1073, would he have taken note of the news from distant Rome of the accession of the monk Hildebrand to the throne of St Peter as Pope Gregory VII? Could he have guessed that the Europe-wide reform that the new pope would launch would have the most profound repercussions on his family and on the institution that they had embodied for generations?

Fifteen years later in 1088, already an old man, would they have brought him tidings of the death of that member of the erenagh family of neighbouring Fahan, Muireadhach Mac Rabhartaigh? Marianus Scotus, as they called him in Germany, where he had founded the Benedictine monastery at Regensburg, the *Schottenkloster*, and thereby launched a trail of such monasteries and a renewal of religious life in Franconia and Austria. Similar stirrings of religious life in his own country produced the national Synod of Rath Breasail in the last year of his life, ushering in the long period of negotiation and uncertainty that would culminate in the Synod of Kells in 1152 and a changed ecclesiastical landscape.

Conghalach did not live to see it, but during that interim for over twenty years his family's charge appears to have been exercised, exceptionally for those times, by a female member of the kindred,

Bébhinn,[44] styled by the annalist, *banairchinneach*, female erenagh, of Derry. The entry is tantalising in the questions it raises. Had the lady been helping Conghalach (her father or perhaps grandfather) in his duties as erenagh and had she in a male-dominated society nonetheless impressed by her character and competence? And had she continued in the administration at a time of uncertainty and confusion?

Anyhow her term of office seems to have continued for over twenty years, and during that time momentous events transpired in Derry. As head of temporalities, she would have had a prominent role in the funeral arrangements and interment of the High King Dónall Mac Lochlainn in the royal mausoleum in Derry in 1121. Nine years after her accession, Giolla Mac Liag Mac Ruairí became Abbot of Derry and subsequently in 1137, three years after the death of Bébhinn, Archbishop of Armagh. But he was succeeded in the primatial see by another member of the Mac Conchoille kindred, Conchúr, who made it one of his first cares to go on pilgrimage to Rome to establish relationships there. He died on the return journey in south-eastern France where he is still venerated under the name of St Concord, interestingly enough invoked when the inhabitants pray for rain!

Family Background

The Mac Conchoille kindred were, in that aristocratic society, of the very best blood. The descendants of Eoghan, son of Niall Naoighiallach – or Cineál Eoghain, retained political power in central Ulster for some 1,000 years. In that time they divided into various branches or septs, of which one was Cineál Binnigh, descended from Eoghan's son Eochaidh Binneach, whose members settled in what is now Co. Derry. They were never of paramount importance among the governing classes, but could make their presence felt on occasion, often militarily.

It was frequently the case that a sept who found real political distinction beyond them or who had been ousted from power found that they had no option but to take on another role in society. In this

---

44. (Pronounced as *bay* and *vin*.) Originally meaning 'woman' or 'wife', *bé* later became a literary term for 'maiden'. *Binn* means 'sweet-sounding', 'harmonious'. Irish distinguishes between *binn* 'sweet-sounding'; *milis* 'sweet-tasting' and *cumhra* 'sweet-smelling'. Mac Conchoille, 'son of the hound of the wood', one of many surnames reflecting admiration for the qualities of the hound, such as McCullagh (Cú Uladh), McNamara (Cú Mara), McNamee (Cú Mí), Conway (Cú Maighe). Such names date from the totems of pagan times but were conserved into Christian times by aristocratic families.

way, *Mac Doinnshléibhe/Ó hEochadha* (Dunleavy/Haughey) of the royal house of the Ulaidh (in Antrim and Down) became a medical family in Cineál Chonaill (Donegal), where they brought their Ulster origins with them in their new surname Mac an Ultaigh (McNulty). One of the solutions to this problem of social positioning was to become involved in Church affairs. An example of this is the clann of Mac Conchoille, who found Church employment as erenaghs in Derry. Fourteen generations down their genealogy we come across one Conghalach Mac Conchoille.

The New Status of Mac Conchoille
Erenagh, or *airchinneach*, is a technical ecclesiastical term in the early Irish Church that changed its function after the reform of the twelfth century. The difficulty we are faced with at this point is that Bébhinn Nic Conchoille died while that reform was in its earlier stages.

Originally the equivalent of *ab* or 'abbot', the term came to describe the person charged with the management of monastic property. Originally also this person might have even been a bishop. But by the tenth century, the position had become what one might call quasi-clerical – perhaps the incumbent had received tonsure, since tonsure was evidence of entry into the clerical state – but eventually the *airchinneach* was essentially lay. The importance of the position depended on the importance of the monastery and when many monasteries were federated into a *paruchia*, as were those following the rule of St Colm Cille for example, the position of *comharba*, or successor, of the saintly founder at the mother house of the order was a very powerful one indeed. Each subsidiary house as well would have had its own *airchinneach*, or erenagh, as the term has been anglicised.

After the reform of the twelfth century, the upkeep of parish buildings and the sustenance of the clergy came to be entrusted to the office of *airchinneach*, of which there was one in each parish with land set aside for him to administer for that purpose. The *airchinneach* was to be appointed by the bishop of the diocese. The office, like any other major avocation in medieval Ireland (poetic or legal or medical) was passed on within the sept. Thus, for example, the *airchinneach* of the parish of Langfield in Co. Tyrone was always Ó Baoill (O'Boyle).

We can then reasonably state, even from the scant entries in the annals, that Mac Conchoille were the erenaghs of the *monastery* of Derry. For Derry would not become the seat of a bishop for over a hundred years after the time of Bébhinn, in 1254.

The Enigma of Bébhinn

Accepting the fact that Mac Conchoille was hereditary erenagh of monastic Derry –therefore being in the role of successor of the founding family – what are we to make of the term *banairchinneach* or 'female erenagh', which is that of Bébhinn.

Banairchinneach is a very rare term. It is to be found in the early glosses or marginal notes written into the manuscript of Priscian in the library of Sankt Gallen in Switzerland by an Irish student making up his Latin grammar and is quoted in *Thesaurus Palaeohibernicus* as the equivalent of *antistessa*, meaning simply 'abbess'. It is found in a similar sense in the *Yellow Book of Lecan*, but the example in the annal that we are considering is the only example of its use in later medieval times. Any modern scholar who refers to the issue takes the term to mean 'erenagh of the nunnery of Derry'. Unfortunately this seems to sidestep the problem since there is no evidence of the existence of such a convent in twelfth-century Derry. (Neither can one prove that there was not one.)

The well-attested presence of Cistercian nuns in the city came after this period. Nonetheless, two placenames would argue for convent lands near the city, if not necessarily for a convent: Ballynagalliagh (nowadays unfortunately commuted to Galliagh) and Rosnagalliagh, or in Irish *Baile na gCailleach* and *Ros na gCailleach*. *Cailleach*, deriving from the Latin *pallium* meaning 'a veil', is a very early word in Irish for a nun. What evidence exists would tend to show that in the early Church in Ireland it was men who controlled the lands attached to convents, in spite of the eminence and initial authority of women like St Brighid in Kildare, St Ita in Limerick, or St Sáfann in Urney in the diocese of Derry.

The annals, however, refer to Bébhinn in exactly the same way as to Conghalach or any other erenagh except for the use of the feminine prefix to describe the office. The fact that the entry refers so precisely to the date of her death means that the entry was taken from an ecclesiastical chronicle kept in Derry or perhaps in another Columban monastery. Her death was noted with the same care as the advanced age of Conghalach.

In addition, the entry dealing with Conchúr Mac Conchoille, abbot of the house of Saints Peter and Paul of Augustinian Canons Regular of Arrouaise in Armagh proves that the family was in good standing. The monastery of Derry, which up to then had followed the Rule of Colm Cille, was to become a house of the same Canons Regular of Arrouaise, perhaps because Conchúr (or Conor) was the head of the

63

order, being abbot in Armagh (to which other Augustinian houses were subordinate).

Régine Pernoud, in her book *Women in the Days of the Cathedrals* (Ignatius Press, 1998), has shown that women of a certain social rank could aspire to considerable power and influence in the Middle Ages, and that their role regressed in early modern times. There would seem to be good reason for considering that Bébhinn, who was born to a certain family responsibility, achieved a position that put her in control of the economy of monastic Derry, whether she came to it by force of personality, or held on to it after perhaps assisting the aging Conghalach, or came to it because her father had no sons.

Postscript

The break in tradition, which the Twelfth-Century Reform brought, did not see the end of the connection of the Mac Conchoille family with the Church. As we have seen, St Conchúr Mac Conchoille (Conor McEnhill) went on to become Archbishop of Armagh and contrary to what the annals say, did not die in Rome but in France. The family was obliged to leave Derry when it became part of the kingdom of Cineál Chonaill under Ó Dónaill after 1200. They moved to Tyrone, where in Omagh they were custodians of the Black Bell of Drumragh (still preserved in the parish church there), a relic that they had perhaps brought with them from Derry.

It must be noted too that we tend to take for granted the importance of Derry as an ecclesiastical centre from early times. Derry was in fact a house of lesser importance in the Columban *paruchia* or federation until Dónall mac Ardghair Mac Lochlainn became High King of Ireland. He died and was buried there in 1121. He had his main residence at *Eanach* (Enagh), and had given his support to the Twelfth-Century Reform and to the establishment of territorial dioceses (as much because it fitted in with his dynastic planning as for any other reason). One effect of his influence was to increase the number of erenaghs, in that one was set up in each parish. Being his contemporary, Bébhinn may have been involved in the Reform also, although those in an equivalent position in Armagh were hostile to change.

The monastery of Derry long retained its own erenaghs, a role which became even more important towards mid-century when Derry's abbot St Giolla Mac Liag Mac Ruairí (St Gelasius) became Archbishop of Armagh and was succeeded as abbot by Flaitheartach Ó Brolcháin (a surname now transmogrified everywhere into Bradley). Under

Flaitheartach's energetic leadership, Derry became the motherhouse of the Columban Order and an important national religious centre. The Columban Order later accepted the rule of the Canons Regular of Arrouaise, who followed the Rule of St Augustine, and became subordinate to the priory of Saints Peter and Paul in Armagh. Derry receded in ecclesiastical importance until the bishop's see was moved there from Maghera in 1254.

Giolla Mac Liag Mac Ruairí, probably a native of what became the archdiocese of Armagh, and in later centuries Bishop Michael O'Reilly (from the Diocese of Kilmore) have been the only office holders of the bishopric of Derry to become Primate of All Ireland.

The Emergence of Clann Rabhartaigh

At the point at which we left the vibrant community of St Mura and Fahan at the beginning of the ninth century, it disappears from the historical record for almost 200 years. We can only suspect that its vulnerable geographic situation, and presumably its wealth due to the patronage of Cineál Eoghain, attracted the attentions of the Vikings. By the time it reappears, Inis Eoghain was no longer the prime base of Cineál Eoghain. They had moved steadily forward on their conquering way across what is now Counties Tyrone and Derry. In the process they had begun to divide into two factions competing for the leadership, one of them still based on Derry and Inis Eoghain headed by Mac Lochlainn and that moving on Dungannon commanded by Ó Néill. The various septs and family groupings within the Cineál Eoghain system would have to declare which side they were on in an episodic internecine contention that would last for two centuries. As far as can be seen, one particular kindred or sept, Cineál Binnigh, the one which is central to this essay, sided with and became as it were the shock troops of the eastern leadership, commanded by Ó Néill. While they had earlier perhaps the fullest genealogy of any of the septs of Cineál Eoghain, as we have said, by the time the annals were being written they had lost much of their political importance and therefore their prominence in the record. Let us recall, however, that their advance in the service of Cineál Eoghain power can be discerned firstly in their clear involvement in the affairs of the Columban monasteries at Derry and Fahan and thereafter in the traces of devotion to St Colm Cille, which they brought with them to their new homes.

By the end of the first millennium Derry was the capital of Mac Lochlainn's Inis Eoghain. Its monastery and church suddenly find new prominence in the annals. Fahan reappears in 1070 to record the death of Fearghal Ó Laidhgnén, its abbot or erenagh (The *Annals of Ulster* say *princeps*). Significantly, he belonged to Cineál Binnigh, now referred to as 'of Tulach Óg', in the sphere of influence of Ó Néill. (The surname may well have been transmuted in south Derry into Ó Lagáin). More to our purpose, a new surname figures on the Fahan list in 1075, that of Ó Ceallaigh, when the annals record the death of Cú Carraige Ó Ceallaigh, described as *comharba Mhura*, successor of St Mura. He is succeeded in turn as *comharba Mhura* by Maolmhártain Ó Ceallaigh, who died in 1098. In 1119 Ruairí Ó Tomhrair (Toner) died, described as *airchinneach Othna* ('of Fahan'), as is his successor in turn presumably, Rabhartach Ó Ceallaigh, *airchinneach* of Othain Mhór, who died in 1136. The recurrence of that unusual name 'Rabhartach' indicates that it was a traditional name in the family, and it signals the emergence of the Mac Rabhartaigh branch of Ó Ceallaigh, who became the most important sept of *Muintir Cheallaigh*, themselves a branch of *Cineál Fhearghasa* and in turn of Cineál Eoghain. Indeed one person of that name Rabhartach Ó Ceallaigh whom we know of died in 762, a century and more before the *airchinneach*. They belonged to the *Cineál Chaolbhadh mac Fhearghasa* branch of the descendants of Eoghan, perhaps based in north-western Inis Eoghain and centred on Carraig Brachaí.

At this point in time, we find ourselves in that period of the late eleventh and early twelfth centuries, which is a time of movement towards Church reform and of rapid change. In the record we are confronted by a profusion of titles, each describing what seems to be the same job, and it is difficult to be sure what exact authority lay behind any of them at any given time. With the title of *comharba Mhura* above, we may be tempted to wonder if we have here an attempt to assert a power that is no longer what it was. We know of course that it was a title of honour, whose holder, by reason of his relationship to the saint, had the right to be addressed by his surname alone, as did the head of any aristocratic *clann*. The title occurs in conjunction with places that had retained some continuity with the venerable past, like Termoncanice, but not as far as we can tell in the case of Ardstraw or Coleraine.

At any rate, it is becoming clear by the 1200s that in the process of reform the office of *aircheannach* has acquired a new dimension, that of administrator or farmer of lands being set aside for the upkeep of the newly forming parishes.

By that same time, however, an entirely new political situation had come about. The advance of the Anglo-Normans into northwest Ulster had fallen primarily upon Mac Lochlainn, dealing a severe blow to his power. The invaders occupied Derry in some fashion for most of a century, building fortifications like Northburgh or Greencastle, but they proved to be too far from any large Norman back-up base to exploit their advantage and create a permanent presence.

Nonetheless, their arrival created a temporary power vacuum in the Derry–Inis Eoghain area, and into it rushed Cineál Chonaill, in the shape of Ó Dónaill and Ó Dochartaigh. This it was which marked the real end of Cineál Eoghain power over Inis Eoghain. Mac Lochlainn was left dependent on his allies and on what lands he had left in north Derry and, perhaps on sufferance, in eastern Inis Eoghain. The important result for our theme was that Cineál Binnigh left the Derry area: Mac Conchoille retreated from Derry to Drumragh; Ó Tomhrair, Ó Brolaigh, Ó Bogáin and others would find their way eventually to the Lifford area. Fahan and its lands were taken over gradually by branches of the Ó Dochartaigh, and the resident erenaghs, Mac Rabhartaigh, belonging as they did to Cineál Binnigh, were faced with a crisis.

The details of how they did so escape us but face it they did, not only with success but with triumph even. What we do know is that it became the privilege of Mac Rabhartaigh to be the custodian of the sacred halidom of Ó Dónaill, *Cathach Cholm Cille* ('the battle-book of Columba', his Psalter). For centuries, Mac Rabhartaigh would carry this talisman into battle at the head of the Cineál Chonaill armies. The idea of being led to war by a sacred relic may seem outlandish to us, but it was not at all uncommon in the Middle Ages; Ó Néill for example followed the *Soiscéal Mhártain* (the gospel-book of St Martin) until it was lost to the Normans at the disastrous battle of Down. A similar privilege was that of Ó Muireasáin (Morrison/Bryson) of Clonmany, who wore special vestments when carrying the *Míosach Cholm Cille* (Columba's calendar), and it is more than likely that Mac Rabhartaigh were similarly privileged.

The remarkable part is that what evidence we have of a connection between Ó Dónaill and the *Cathach* comes from later than their conquest of the lands of Inis Eoghain and occupation of Derry. It may well be then that Mac Rabhartaigh were already the hereditary custodians of the *Cathach* in however different a context. How, if they were, did a sept belonging to Cineál Binnigh and ultimately Cineál Eoghain and seemingly dispossessed by Cineál Chonaill accomplish this? The answer might be that the *Cathach* had been placed in the custody of the erenaghs of Fahan, Ó Ceallaigh/Mac Rabhartaigh, when the *mionna* of Colm Cille came north from Ceanannas, first to Raphoe and finally to Derry. This in turn would suggest a closer connection between Derry and Fahan than we have posited up to this. The *Cathach* may have been regarded as an integral part of the *mionna* of Fahan[45] just as the *Míosach* was seen as that of Ó Muireasáin.[46]

Thus, at this major change of power, in a religiously conservative age, Mac Rabhartaigh's office as closely associated with the *Cathach* may have been viewed as too sacred to breach – given that he was not unwilling to transfer his allegiance. It would seem reasonable to postulate too that at this juncture the lands of Baile Mhic Rabhartaigh/Ballymagroarty were set aside to support the custodian of the *Cathach*, maybe after he had been ousted from his original endowment, all the more since there is some evidence that the word 'baile' occurs in placenames which are relatively late, as is evidenced in lands reconquered from the Normans in south Down in the late Middle Ages. The other Ballymagroarty in south Donegal would in that case have been a later addition still, by then in the gift of Ó Dónaill.

A Saintly Member of the Family

Not all the members of *Clann Rabhartaigh* settled into comfortable possession of their new lands and privilege under Cineál Chonaill. One of them, named Muireadhach, left Ireland about 1067 with two companions.[47] They arrived in Regensburg in south Germany about 1070 on their way to Rome and there they met another Irishman by the name of Muircheartach who was living as an *inclusus* in the city.[48] He persuaded them to stay in Regensburg where Muireadhach settled down to his writing and the study of Sacred Scripture, his two

---

45. *Mionna* were the sacred relics of a church. Oaths were sworn on them – which is the origin of modern Irish *mionna* meaning 'oath'.
46. It is not possible to trace the genealogy of Ó Muireasáin, so we cannot be certain of their connections.
47. The number of companions varies. Mac Geoghegan, following Colgan, speaks of Muireadhach plus six others.
48. *Inclusus*: 'shut in'; a hermit who lived in an enclosed space as a form of penance and to avoid distraction, near a cathedral or church where he had access to sacramental life and liturgy; a kind of traditional Gaelic *díseart* but in an urban setting.

companions preparing the vellum and inks for his active programme of copying manuscripts. In 1076 the Benedictine abbess Emma, with the approval of the Emperor Henry IV, gave him the church of St Peter and a citizen of Regensburg built him a monastery and cloister on an adjoining plot of ground. So began the great monastery of St Peter at Regensburg. From this start, eight other *Schottenklöster*[49] were set up in Germany and Austria, which eventually came together as an independent branch of the Benedictines. They even sent a monk to Russia to bring back a consignment of bear and wolf skins to pay for the church roof. Perhaps at this monk-merchant's suggestion, the house in Vienna established a new foundation in Kiev at the end of the twelfth century, but they had to withdraw in the face of the invading armies of the Mongol Golden Horde. The motherhouse of the federation was that of St James, also in Regensburg.

Muireadhach Mac Rabhartaigh[50] had brought with him to Germany his great skill as a scribe and calligrapher which he had learned at home – the talent which had first attracted the attention of Mother Emma, Abbess of that Benedictine convent. His companions, known to us as Joannes (John) and Candidus, prepared the vellum on which he wrote and the inks with which he embellished books of Sacred Scripture and added commentaries to them, often as gifts for the sisters and for poor clerics. He was the abbot and was the originator of what became a centre for the creation of beautiful manuscripts, of which at least two written by his own hand survive. This renaissance of Irish monasticism on the continent attracted many – not by any means all from Ireland – to join their ranks.

Ironically, due to a later incomprehension of who these *Scoti* were, some of their houses were claimed by and committed to the care of the Scottish Church, but that was when Ireland was no longer a fertile source for novices.

A charming medieval legend has it that the woman whose duty it was to prepare the lamps for Muireadhach once overslept. She woke others to help her make up time. When they went to Muireadhach's room, there he sat without lamp or candle, writing with his right

---

49. 'Monastery of the *Scoti*', the Latin name by which the Irish were known on the continent at that time.
50. Muireadhach Mac Rabhartaigh is known by the Latin name Marianus Scotus. He is to be distinguished from his famous contemporary Marianus Scotus (the First), 1028–83. His name in Irish was Maolbhríde. He was an *inclusus* at Fulda and Mainz and a chronicler.

hand, holding the other in the air. A light shone from his left hand, illuminating his work. We are told that they left him in peace.

The manuscript of St Paul's letters by the hand of Muireadhach, which is to be found in the Imperial Library in Vienna, ends with the words: *In honorem individuae Trinitatis Marianus Scotus scripsit hunc librum suis fratribus peregrinis.*[51] ('In honour of the persons of the Trinity Marianus Scotus wrote this book for his expatriate brethren.') It was written on 16 May 1078, and above them is the marginal note: *murdach trog mac robartaig* – in modern Irish 'Muireadhach trua Mac Rabhartaigh', and in Latin *Marianus miser filius Robartaci.*[52] He died on 10 February 1088 and is recognised as a *beatus*[53] by the Benedictines with feast day on 9 February. He is believed to have been interred in St Peter's church, but all traces of the saint and of his monastery were destroyed in the turmoil of the sixteenth century.

Such was the final flowering of the ancient tradition of St Mura at Fahan.

---

51. 'In honour of the indivisible Trinity, Muireadhach the Irishman wrote this book for his brothers who are living abroad'. *Peregrini* refers to those who had undertaken *peregrinari pro Christi nomine*: 'to wander abroad for the name of Christ.'
52. Marianus the wretched, son of Rabhartach.
53. *Beatus* = 'beatified'; i.e. Blessed Muireadhach Mac Rabhartaigh OSB.

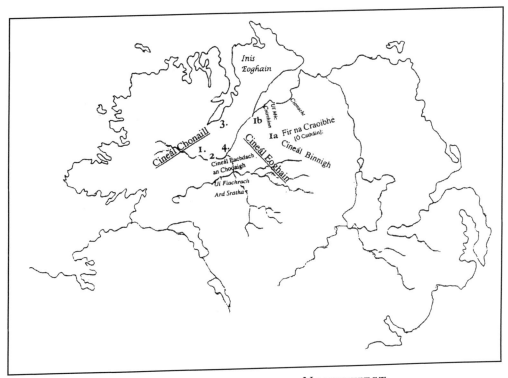

KIN-GROUPS IN THE EARLY NORTHWEST

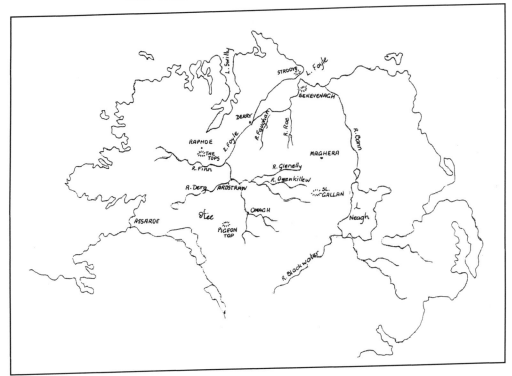

BOUNDARY MARKS OF DIOCESE, SYNOD OF RÁTH BREASAIL

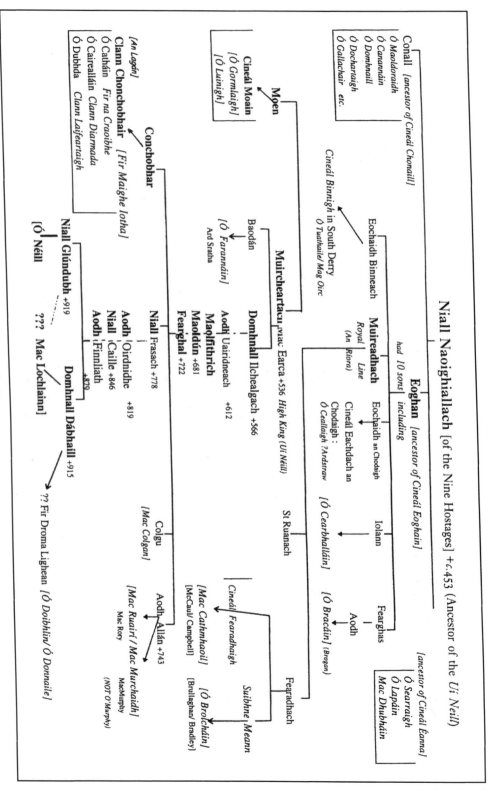

CINEÁL EOGHAIN

3
The Making of the Diocese

THE ORGANISATION OF THE EARLY CHRISTIAN CHURCH

N ITS FIRST FIVE HUNDRED YEARS OF EXISTENCE, THE Christian Church in Ireland developed an organisation that was different from the normal pattern in the rest of western Europe. This, to a large extent, was because Ireland was the first country in the region to be Christianised while never having been part of the Roman Empire. That empire was divided politically into administrative areas that were governed from local urban centres and the early Christian Church naturally organised itself on similar lines with bishops governing a religious unit called a diocese from a cathedral city where in the imperial administration a prefect governed his region politically from the same city.

When the early missionaries came to Ireland they were faced with a society that was rural and had no cities in the Roman sense. Instead, they found the island organised politically into over a hundred small kingdoms (about the size of a modern barony), reflecting a landscape divided into small areas of settlement by mountains, lakes and vast stretches of forest, bog and marsh. Each of these kingdoms was called a *tuath* and the missionaries sensibly based their churches on the *tuath*, just as in Europe they had used the Roman city, itself often a development of an earlier Celtic tribal centre. This succeeded so well that one of the laws of early Christian Ireland could state: 'A *tuath* without a scholar, a church, a poet and a king is not a *tuath*.'

However, together with this – from the very beginning – as we can see from St Patrick's own *Confession*, the Christianising of the countryside was helped along, as St Martin of Tours had already done in the Loire valley in France, by the founding of communities dedicated

73

to living perfectly the Christian message or monasteries, and even more particularly in Patrick's own case, monasteries of women or nunneries, to provide the new converts with spiritual example and guidance. A hundred years after St Patrick's death, by around AD 600, it is clear that the monastic system was so successful that it had gained a predominant position in the Irish Church at the expense of the role of the bishop.

This influence was increased by the tendency of monasteries to come together in a kind of league called a *paruchia*, especially through the prestige of great monastic saints like Colm Cille. Five hundred years later, however, by around AD 1100, this monastic system had fallen into decay, and the necessity of a return to the diocesan system normal in the rest of Christian Europe became one of the major objectives of reforming churchmen like St Malachy Ó Morgair in their effort to restore the Church in Ireland to its earlier vigour.

THE DIOCESE OF DERRY IN AN AGE OF REFORM

In the long history of Europe, moments of crisis and anguish have repeatedly been the harbingers of renewal, of the emergence of a radically changed society. The chaos into which the Roman Empire collapsed under the shock of barbarian invasions (including the Scoti or Irish), was painfully shaped into an early draft of European cultural unity in the empire of Charlemagne after AD 800, a draft to which Irish missionaries and scholars from Columbanus to John Scotus Eriugena, had made a fundamental contribution. In vastly changed circumstances, the discouragement and fear and religious disquiet of the dying Middle Ages in the sixteenth century threw up the effort towards religious renewal of the Protestant and Catholic Reformations. Much later again, similar upheavals like that of the French Revolution or the horrors of the two World Wars of the twentieth century generated fresh energies and fresh inspiration.

One of the most dramatic of these resurgences occurred around the year AD 1000 at a moment of external deadly menace and of internal terror and pessimism. Christian Europe in the tenth century felt threatened on all sides. Along its northern coasts, and nowhere more than in Ireland, it was attacked by the Viking raiders who were beginning to establish themselves as pagan colonists; in the south by Islam which had conquered almost the whole of Spain, pushed its outriders deep into France and turned Sicily into a Mediterranean base; and on its eastern borders by yet more pagan invaders, Prussians, Magyars, Slavs.

As the year 1000 approached, whole populations were haunted by apocalyptic prophecies of the end of the world that year; in Ireland it took the shape of a coming deadly plague, the *Scuab as Fánaid*, which was to devastate the land from north west to south east. And yet as the fateful year passed, an unlooked-for surge of hope and energy came upon western Europe that would produce a rebirth of all human endeavours. The moment is evoked in a frequently quoted passage from the chronicler and monk of the monastery of Cluny in Burgundy, Radulf Glaber:

> With the approach of the third year after the year 1000, church buildings all over the earth, but especially in Italy and Gaul, were seen being rebuilt ... One would have thought that the world itself was shaking off its old decrepitude and everywhere clothing itself anew in a white mantle of churches.

Such was the most striking outward sign of that blossoming of Christianity after the year 1000, which was to eventually produce what the French call 'the age of the cathedrals', the age not only of cathedrals but of the first universities, of the new learning of scholasticism, of Gothic art and architecture, of what is referred to as 'the twelfth-century renaissance'.

Even militarily, the resurgence showed itself in the defeat of the Vikings in 1014 by Brian Bóramha at Clontarf and again by Harald of England at Stamford Bridge in 1066; by the Norman conquest of Sicily under Robert Guiscard in 1060–1; and by the retaking of Toledo in 1085, a major success in the Reconquista of Spain. The victory of Otto I over the pagan Hungarians in 955, the foundation by the Ottonian kings of the Holy Roman Empire and the subsequent Norman conquest of England in 1066 settled the political outlines of what would soon be called European 'Christendom'. It was within this new ordering of things and in relationship with its monarchs, sometimes cordial, sometimes hostile, that there began the most far-reaching example of the renewed energies of Christendom, the reform of the Christian Church.

There was no doubt that the Church, and primarily the clergy, were in urgent need of reform in order to permit the spiritual renewal that was ardently desired in the aftermath of the fears of the year 1000. The fundamental problem was that ever since Charlemagne had made bishops and ecclesiastics part of the administration of his empire, these offices had gradually fallen under the control of local lay powers. Bishops were appointed by princes and barons, their authority signalled by the feudal ceremony of investiture. Offices and spiritual powers were bought and sold with scant account taken of the suitability of candidates. The consequent decline in the religious life of the Church can be imagined. The movement of reform to remedy this state of affairs reached its peak with the elevation to the Papacy in 1073 of one of its most determined pioneers, the Roman monk Hildebrand, under the name of Gregory VII.

The situation of the Church in Ireland at the end of the tenth century presents many parallels with the abuses and general need of renewal in the European Church, but there are a number of distinctive dissimilarities as well. While, for example, lay control of Church affairs was similarly a problem, the roots of it were less due to the encroachment of aristocratic patrons than to a social system which encouraged monastic lands to fall under the control of lay members of the family of the original saintly founder and to be transmitted by inheritance, with bishops often fulfilling a purely spiritual and sacramental role and exercising no jurisdiction over Church temporalities or over a defined territory. However different the causes, the effects were very similar and the need for reform equally pressing. Furthermore, just as the Ottonian emperors had instituted the Holy Roman Empire to the admiration of Christendom, Irish kings were groping their own way towards turning the ancient theory of the *ardrí* into a functioning national monarchy, though with little practical effect until the coming of Brian Bóramha.[1] Brian was probably influenced by the immense prestige in Ireland of the Empire under Otto III, and he did not hesitate to sign himself *Imperator Scotorum* in the *Book of Armagh* on the occasion of his formal alliance with this Patrician and soon to be primatial see.[2]

The century and a half between the death of King Brian at Clontarf and the Anglo-Norman Invasion saw the rise to power of rival provincial dynasties, *Ó Maoleachlainn na Mí* (Meath) and *Ó Ruairc in Mí/Breifne*, *Ó Briain* in Munster, *Mac Lochlainn* in Ulster and *Ó*

---

1. Cf. F.J. Byrne, *Irish Kings and High-Kings* (London: Batsford, 1973), pp. 264–70.
2. *Imperator Scotorum* – Emperor of the Irish. At the time the Irish were commonly known in Latin as the *Scoti*. The *Scoti* or Irish of the kingdom of Dál Riada, on either side of *Sruth na Maoile* (now the North Channel) gave their name to Scotland, and a *Schottenkloster* in Germany was a monastery founded by Irish monks.

Conchúir in Connacht, the last three contending with each other to become *ardrí*, supreme king of the entire country, but all reducing the smaller tuatha (kingdoms) to some degree of subjection.

It is against this background that we must try to consider the great movement of reform in the Irish Church that was to produce the organisation of Ireland into territorial dioceses, including what we now call the diocese of Derry. It perhaps needs to be said that while bishops are necessary to the spiritual and sacramental life of the Church, it is not necessary that this ministry should apply to a defined territory, or that the power to govern should be in itself essential to episcopacy. It is possible to describe a number of models of how the relationship of bishop and people might be worked out. As a result, the concept of the bishop having a jurisdictional rôle in the life of the Church developed much later than that of his sacramental one.[3] Such distinctions result from practical solutions to the problems summed up in the adage: *Ecclesia semper reformanda*: 'The Church is always in need of reform.'

Church Reform

We have become so inured to controversy about clericalism in the Church that we may forget the danger involved in its opposite. In Ireland as in the rest of Europe, any reform movement had to address itself, in the first instance, to the central problem of the Church having fallen under the control of a local aristocracy whose concern for its spiritual mission came a poor second to their desire to exploit its lands and influence for their own benefit. In Ireland there was the added complication that Church organisation had, since the days of St Patrick, developed on different lines from those that were the norm in continental Europe. There, in the lands that had been part of the Roman Empire, the post-apostolic Church had initially spread from city to city, and it was from the city that the surrounding countryside was gradually Christianised. Indeed the very word 'pagan' came from the Latin *paganus*, a dweller in the countryside. Not surprisingly, this

---

3. The development of a theology of episcopal orders and of the authority to be accorded to the bishop owed a great deal to the controversies resulting from the Hildebrandine reform and from the reflection of theologians and teachers like Peter Abelard, St Bernard of Clairvaux, Peter Lombard and St Peter Damian. See Patrick J. Corish, 'The Early Irish Church and the Western Patriarchate', *Irland und Europa: Die Kirche im Frühmittelalter*, Próinséas Ní Chatháin und Michael Richter, eds (Stuttgart: Klett–Cotta, 1984), pp. 9–14. Cf. A.Fliche, *La Réforme Grégorienne et la Reconquête Chrétienne*, Vol. 8 of Fliche et Martin: *Histoire de l'Église* (Paris, 1950), pp. 95–130; 198.

surrounding area continued to be governed – from an ecclesiastical point of view – from the city, and by the officer known since the earliest times as *episcopus*, the 'overseer' or bishop, in Irish *easpag*. The name applied to these units was 'diocese', a term derived from that of the political divisions (*diocesis*), which the Emperor Diocletian had established to make the Roman Empire easier to govern.

An Irish 'Federal' Church

In Ireland, however, in the time of St Patrick and for long afterwards there were no cities. The country was divided into about 150 *tuatha*, each ruled by a *rí* or king, elected from the *deirbhfhine* (or extended family) of the hereditary ruling kindred. To fit the new Christian clergy into the legal pecking order of the time the logical solution was for each *tuath* to have its own bishop – a system which at first glance might seem to produce remarkable opportunities for clerical promotion. The countryside was Christianised by missionaries who set up a local *domhnach*, the earliest word for a church, and subsequently *cill*, which were the forerunners of parishes much later.[4]

However, within a century or so of the time of Patrick, monastic religious life met with such success amongst the Irish that Church organisation came to be dominated, and finally based on, a network of great monasteries and their abbots, rather than on bishops as elsewhere. Just as the stronger kings were building up over-kingdoms of groups of *tuatha*, monasteries began, by force of the fame of their founder's sanctity and no doubt as a result of their abbots' enterprise, to build up federations of local churches which constituted their *paruchia* or sphere of influence. The *paruchia* was ruled by the *ab* or abbot, and his number two, the *seachnab*, who between them ran the administration of temporal affairs, while the rôle of the *easpag* or bishop was purely spiritual, confirming, ordaining priests, consecrating churches, providing spiritual direction. Often the bishop was actually a member of the monastic community.

In what would later be constituted as the diocese of Derry, many local churches were claimed for the *paruchia* of the great monastery of Armagh – which claimed authority over all churches not already

---

4. *Domhnach*, from Latin *dominicum* from *dominus*, lord, as church comes from Greek 'kurios', lord. *Cill* comes from Latin *cella*. Placenames starting with 'Kil-' often preserve the name of the original Christian priest/founder, or perhaps the name of the saint to whom he dedicated the church – when it is not *coill* 'a wood' or *coll* 'hazel' of course.

absorbed into a monastic *paruchia*[5] – parishes which still have Patrician connections, like Badoney, Donaghedy, the churches of the Faughan valley, Tamlaghtard and perhaps Kilrea. On the other hand, Termonmaguirk – still firmly associated with the memory of St Colm Cille – is now nonetheless in the archdiocese of Armagh, and Ballinascreen is in Derry, although it could be claimed that it was Patrician before it became Columban. Much farther from Armagh, the churches of Carndonagh and Donaghmore have Patrician associations.

It can be seen, then, that the organisation of the Church in Ireland down to the end of the first millennium had as its basis a sort of 'federal' system wherein local churches belonging to different *tuatha* were joined in a community of interests, a monastically-organised *paruchia*, sometimes perhaps as much to withstand powerful neighbours as for any spiritual purpose. Now and again this is obvious, as in the case of the medieval parishes of Cappagh and Langfield, dedicated to St Eoghan, which originated in the *paruchia* of Ardstraw. Sometimes medieval traditions reflected in the lives of the saints portray a close friendship, as for example between St Eoghan and St Cairbre, indicating a relationship between Ardstraw and Coleraine, perhaps making common cause to withstand the hegemony of a powerful neighbour, possibly Bangor or Derry. By the time that Ardstraw eventually fell into the Columban ambit, any monastery at Coleraine had disappeared or had been supplanted by Camus in the paruchia of Bangor.

In another example, the *Annals of Ulster* recount that one Muireacán of *Both Domhnaigh* (Badoney), from what would now be hardly thought of as in the centre of the action, was *comharba Phádraig* ('successor of Patrick') at Armagh in 993 (AU), and well enough established there to make, in his rôle of *comharba*, the usual 'circuit' or visitation, of his *paruchia* and 'confer kingly orders on Aedh, son of Domhnall, in the presence of the community of Patrick'.[6] This is surely an indication of the standing of Both Domhnaigh within the Armagh *paruchia*, and perhaps even of a personal relationship to the powerful family which controlled Armagh, Clann Síonaigh, who were to become the principal

---

5. See P.J. Corish, 'The Christian Mission', *History of Irish Catholicism III* (Dublin: Gill & Macmillan, 1971), p. 27. Armagh seems to have claimed any church with *domhnach* in its name. Donaghanie, now on the diocesan border, should have been a Patrician magnet for Termonmaguirk, one would have thought.
6. Aodh Ó Néill, known as Aodh *Craoibhe Tulcha* +1004, son of Dónall *Ard Macha*, rí Éireann +980. Cf. Tomás Ó Fiaich, 'The Church of Armagh under Lay Control', *Seanchas Ard Mhacha* 5,1 (1969), p. 91.

targets of the new reform, and of the great saint whose name is forever linked to it, St Malachy, or *Maolmhóg Ó Morgair* (an unusual surname).

Continental Influences

On a European scale, the movement for reform began in Germany when the successors of Otto I[7] were called on to establish order in Rome between warring factions which sought to control the papacy and the Papal States and to have popes elected who were not always chosen for the virtue of their lives. Once this problem had been overcome, the consequences of the solution then had to be faced: the fact that the Holy Roman Emperor in Germany now exercised political domination over the papacy and interfered in elections. Down the scale, kings and lords regarded it as their right to appoint their own protégés to episcopal office and this resulted in simoniacal appointments where office in the Church was bought and sold. Obviously, any programme of reform ran counter to the political interests of the kings and yet needed their cooperation and support, at least in part, to be successful.

It is perhaps useful to interject at this point and state that the understanding of Pope Gregory and his reformers – and no doubt of St Malachy and St Bernard – was not that of a Church separated from State and society such as is our concept today, but rather the concept of an *ecclesia universalis* inherited from the earlier Middle Ages. They held to the idea of a unity of Church and world with the aim of bringing the worldly dimension of that unity to its full potential. Thus too, just as the clergy had jurisdiction over religious matters, so the *sacerdotium* (the priestly power) in the person of its hierarchical superior, the Pope, should command the Christian world. Not that the theory had been thought through at that stage; that would be the achievement of the Roman canon lawyers of the thirteenth century, with the unforeseen result that their exaltation of the Papacy, if anything, tended to weaken the authority of bishops.

In neighbouring England, the reforming process worked relatively efficaciously, at least in its early stages, because it was applied after 1066 by the incoming Norman invaders of William the Conqueror, who was supported in his claim to the English throne by Pope Alexander II, educated at the abbey of Bec in Normandy by Lanfranc, himself William's adviser and his first Archbishop of Canterbury. The

---

7. Anointed/crowned (962) by Pope John XII to re-inaugurate the Holy Roman Empire, which lasted until 1806.

monasteries of William's dukedom of Normandy were the spiritual powerhouses of Northern Europe. It was mindful of William's success perhaps that, a century later, Pope Hadrian IV, the English cardinal Nicholas Breakspear, felt that something similar might be accomplished through the Anglo-Norman invasion of Ireland and the Irish submission to Henry II Plantagenet.

The Irish Church had not waited for reform to arrive on the mailed chargers of Norman knights. More than half a century before 1170, Irish contacts with the Church in Rome and the courts of the Holy Roman Empire had already launched a reform movement. In the eleventh century it had become common for ordinary Irish people and their rulers once more to go on pilgrimage to Rome, particularly after the agreement to protect pilgrims brokered by Emperor Conrad II in 1028. A certain Giolla Mhíchil, for example, though disabled, had been to Rome six times when he called seeking a cure at the hands of Edward the Confessor (+1066).[8] Flaitheartach Ó Néill, grandson of Dónall Ard Macha and King of Cineál Eoghain, had returned from pilgrimage with the *trostán* or pilgrim's staff forever associated with his name. At the same time there was a resurgence of interest amongst monks in the idea of *peregrinari pro Christo*. Marianus Scotus II (*Muireadhach Mac Rabhartaigh* +1088, of the erenagh family of Fahan) had, with two others, established a Benedictine monastery at Regensburg which became well known in Germany and beyond, with a number of daughter houses. If we also consider the monk of Glendalough whose notes of the lectures of Peter Lombard in Paris are still extant it would be inadvisable for us to think of an Irish Church cut off from and unaware of the ways events were shaping on the continent. So we find *Muircheartach Ó Briain*, king of Munster, legislating in his own domain in support of the Truce of God decreed at the Synod of Piacenza in 1095 under Urban II (+1099).

Scotland, Iona and Derry

Malcolm III, *Ceann Mór* of Scotland[9] had been recently widowed when his court gave refuge to an Anglo-Saxon princess fleeing the Norman Conquest. The chance to further annoy the Normans was more than

8. Cf. Denis Bethell, 'English Monks and Irish Reform in the Eleventh and Twelfth Centuries', *Historical Studies* VIII (1969), pp. 111–35. It was from late in this century too that the type of learning, on which the centuries-old Irish reputation for scholarship had been based, began to seem dated.
9. Son of Donnchadh I, the *Duncan* of Shakespeare's *Macbeth*. Maol Choluim means *devotee of St Columba*, 'maol' being originally someone 'tonsured'.

likely not one to be missed, but it seems that the king was swept off his feet by the beauty, intelligence and fashion sense of his guest and married her. She is perhaps better known to us as St Margaret of Scotland (1046–93). Malcolm could not read, like most of his royal contemporaries, and he gave Margaret a free hand in reorganising the Church in Scotland, merely acting as her interpreter in his bilingual kingdom. Although *persona non grata* with the Norman rulers, Margaret sought advice from Lanfranc and St Anselm, both formerly of the abbey of Bec and consecutive archbishops of Canterbury. In Scotland she held a series of Church councils. Religious practice in Scotland and the north of Ireland must have been broadly similar, and we find her councils dealing with matters like working on Sundays, marrying within the forbidden degrees (third cousins or closer) and reform of their liturgical rite at Mass. (There is some evidence that the so-called 'Celtic' rite continued in use after her time). She founded monasteries like Dunfermline Abbey and re-founded others including Iona.

Although King Magnus III, Bareleg of Norway, forced her son Edgar to cede the western Isles including Iona in 1102, there were Irish clergy at the court of her other sons, Alexander and David I, for they were commissioned there to write verses in Gaelic in honour of St Columba. We know that King David I received St Malachy at least once. Clearly the leaders of Ireland, lay and clerical, and especially of Cineál Eoghain who controlled Derry with its ties with Iona, would have been aware of all such developments.

The Aim of Reform

Like its counterparts in Scotland, England and on the continent, the reform movement aimed at freeing the Church from domination by the great families. In Ireland, however, it had the added challenge of introducing a new and unfamiliar concept – that of a bishop ruling with spiritual jurisdiction a specified geographical area, the diocese. It comes as no surprise for us to learn that the great Irish dynasties like Ó Briain, Mac Lochlainn, Ó Conchúir, Ó Cearúill were to be intimately involved in the process, or that the eventual layout of the new dioceses as arranged at the synods of Rath Breasail (1111) and Ceanannas/Kells (1152) would closely mirror the political boundaries of the time.[10]

---

10. The first reform synod with an all-clerical roll call seems to have been Inis Phádraig (1148). (AFM) Cf. Edward Rogan, Dissertation: *Synods and Catechesis in Ireland* (Rome: Pontificia Unversità Gregoriana, 1987), Appendix p. 9.

Centralising Power

While the movement for reform has been personalised as a confrontation between St Maolmhóg Ó Morgair (St Malachy) and the Clann Síonaigh, lay abbots of Armagh, it was in fact a many-sided affair, driven as much by laymen as churchmen, at least in its earlier stages. As the *tuatha* or small kingdoms lost their independence of action and coalesced into larger groups for self-preservation or were forced into submission by the more powerful, the ecclesiastical arrangements that had served them thus far lost their bearings. As the over-kingdoms sought to become at least province-wide, the desire to centralise and control must have grown. When these kings saw this modern Church being shaped by their royal confrères in Germany, England and Scotland (with strong support from Irish monks abroad, like those in Germany who supported the emperor against Pope Gregory VII), it must have seemed that reforming churchmen and centralising monarchs had broadly the same ends in view. Time would show how they differed.

The Rise of Cineál Eoghain

The typical founding myth of Cineál Eoghain since before the twelfth century was that of the inexorable progression of the dynasty from its homeland of Inis Eoghain to control of Ulster 'from Boyne to Drowes'. We are presented with a picture where, one by one, the smaller kingdoms fell before the various branches of the Cineál descended from the ten sons of Eoghan. With *Ó Duídhíorma* (McDermott), *Ó Maolfhábhaill* (McFaul/Lavelle) left to control their homeland in Inis Eoghain,[11] *Clann Chonchúir* and *Cineál Moain* were free to roll up *Cineál Éinne* in east Donegal; *Cineál Eachdach an Chodaigh* could attend to *Uí Mic Cairthinn* (Tirkeeran) in the Faughan valley and to *Uí Fiachrach Ard Sratha* (Ardstraw), and *Cineál Binnigh* could swoop on *Uí Tuirtre* and *Fir Lí* in south Derry. Ó Dónaill and Cineál Chonaill would accept second place, and *Mac Doinnshléibhe Ó hEochadha* (Mac Donleavy O'Haughey – later *Mac an Ultaigh*) in north Antrim, relic of the kingdom of the Ulaidh defeated at the time of St Patrick, would acknowledge final defeat. Over all these would rule the descendants of Niall Glúndubh – Mac Lochlainn and Ó Néill from Aileach and Tullyhogue. Reality, however, does not quite match the myth.

---

11. See *Ceart Uí Néill # 6* in Eamon Ó Doibhlin, *O'Neill's 'Own Country' and its Families* (Donaghmore: Donaghmore Historical Society, 1998), pp. 46–7.

Cineál Eoghain Invade Derry and West Tyrone

The area from Magilligan to the Bann had been ceded to Cineál Eoghain long before for their help as mercenaries in a conflict within the Ulaidh, which ended in the battle of *Móin Mór Doire Lóthair*[12] in 557, giving them a taste for conquest, perhaps. All we know about Cineál Eachdach an Chodaigh comes from the genealogies which allude to a battle with Uí Mic Cairthinn of the Faughan valley at *Ath Goirt an Chatha*, and although they claim one king who was king also of all *Uí Fiachrach* of Ardstraw, the surnames which originate in their pedigree have left no impression on the records or else are common to other septs.[13]

They lost out to more important groupings in their turn. Séamus Ó Ceallaigh has documented the progression of Cineál Binnigh into south Derry, where they eventually brought about the weakening of Ó Flainn of Uí Tuirtre and squeezed them over the Bann into what was to become the diocese of Connor. *Mac Con Choille* (McEnhill) and *Ó Fearáin* (custodians of St Dácuailén's shrine) who belonged genealogically to Cineál Binnigh, had connections with the monastery in Derry.[14] It was the turn of the Cianacht of Dungiven and the Roe valley to fall to Cineál Eoghain, defeated by Fir Maighe Iotha in 1076 at the battle of Belat.[15]

---

12. Móin Mór Doire Lóthair has been identified as Moneymore, Co. Derry, which is too far away from the action. The great moor of Loughermore would seem more likely. The *Ulaidh* originally ruled all of Cúige Uladh (Ulster), but their reduced kingdom after St Patrick's time was east of the Bann. Cineál Eoghain and the Ulaidh harboured a mutual hostility for centuries, which frequently erupted into aggression.

13. Kuno Meyer, ed., 'Laud Genealogies and Tribal Histories', *Zeitschrift für celtische Philologie* (ZCP) VIII, p. 295. According to the genealogy, two of the ten sons of Eoghan, son of Niall Naoighiallach, were named Eochaidh, Eochaidh *Binneach* – whence Cineál Binnigh – and Eochaidh an Chodaigh (*codach* seems to mean 'covenant'– what it was in this case has not seemingly been recorded). *Ath Goirt an Chatha* may be Gortica near Drumahoe. Amongst surnames said to originate here is Ó Ceallaigh (*Kelly*) – Ó Ceallaigh, lord of Uí Fiachrach Ard Sratha, died at Loch Laoghaire (Baronscourt) in 1150 (AFM). The name *Ó Ceallaigh* has many origins, since Ceallach was a common Christian name.

14. Séamus Ó Ceallaigh, *Gleanings from Ulster History* (1951/94), pp. 49, 52, 87 end paper Genealogy. Dácuailén was Abbot of Derry.

15. AU ad ann. The name Belat has disappeared but must be the same as the townland *Belud* of Plantation maps, near Drumahoe. Cf. *Londonderry and the London Companies* HMSO, 1928. Plate 7, pp. 32/151. The late Fr Jack Gallagher suggested that the last trace of the name is Belt Road, at Altnagelvin Hospital.

East Donegal

In our own time we have learnt, sometimes painfully, that what people believe to have happened is at least as important as what actually happened. Maigh Iotha (the Lagán) now east Donegal, according to the founding myth of the Uí Néill,[16] had been the short-lived possession of Éanna, brother of Conall and Eoghan, but he willingly gave it up to one or other of his brothers, according to which story you choose to believe. Obviously, giving up perhaps the best land the Uí Néill had captured is the stuff of fantasy. If Éanna had ever possessed the Lagán, by the time of recorded history the lands of his descendants were much reduced. Cineál Éinne still retained an existence of some sort for they had their own sub-kings in the eleventh century. Where their territory was then is unclear, but by c.1608 its boundaries were well known,[17] probably in the area between Inis Eoghain and Raphoe.

By the time the annalists focus on Maigh Iotha it is divided between minor dynasties of Cineál Eoghain: *Cineál Moain, Clann Chonchúir,* and *Fir Droma Lighean*. Fir Droma Lighean or *Men of Dromleen,* near Lifford (Ó *Donnaile* [Donnelly] and Ó *Doibhlin* [Devlin]) seem to have migrated quite soon to east Tyrone. Moan was a grandson of Eoghan, son of Niall Naoighiallach (Niall of the Nine Hostages), and his line gives rise to names like Ó Gormlaigh, Ó Luinigh, etc. Conchobhar (*Conor*) was one of the four sons of Feargal, son of Maeldún, High King of the Uí Néill, who died in 722 and he is the origin of names like Ó *Catháin* (O Kane), Ó *Caireallán* (Kerlin), Ó *Dubhda* (Duddy), Ó *Maoláin* (Mullan), etc. Their descendants settled in east Donegal but mostly to live in settled animosity, for their rivalry made them amongst the main players in the long civil war that divided Cineál Eoghain and was eventually to produce one of our diocesan borders.[18]

---

16. *Uí Néill* up to around the year 1000 are the descendants of Niall Naoighiallach (+c.453). They are to be distinguished from the surname Ó Néill (plural: Uí Néill) descended from Niall Glúndubh (+919), who are also a constituent part of the earlier Uí Néill.

17. These are unfortunately unclear, at least to me, 'from the streamlet of Tamhnach Fada unto Béal Átha Trona'. Cf. CSPI (1606–8), pp. 342–3. It borders on Ardmire, where Muintir Dhochartaigh originated.

18. Conchobhar is called in the genealogy *taoiseach ógthiarn Éireann*. Ógthiarna 'young lord' was on the lowest level of lordship, and was presumably dependent on his wits and his sword. See Meyer, ed., *Laud Genealogies*, p. 295; Fergus Kelly, *Guide to Early Irish Law* (Dublin: Dublin Institute for Advanced Studies, 1988), p. 26n.

The main stem of Cineál Eoghain divided in the tenth and eleventh centuries into two increasingly hostile branches. There is confusion about the genealogical relationship between them. The descendants of Niall Glúndubh (+919) took their surname from him, Ó Néill. Niall's brother, Dónall Dábhaill (+915), is said to have been the progenitor of Mac Lochlainn.[19] The trouble is that the genealogists got themselves confused and in different recensions trace Lochlann (+1023) back both to Niall and to Dónall. There is reason to be suspicious of the Ó Néill genealogy also. As throughout medieval Europe, the nobility, who had others to do the work for them, had little else left to do but worry about their honour, vie for power and fight.

The hostilities lasted until the battle of Caméirí, near Omagh, in 1241, when the power of Mac Lochlainn was finally broken, but for a century and a half before that Clann Lochlainn had been much the stronger. The struggle was really between two alliances. The main groups of interest to us were: with Mac Lochlainn were *Clann Diarmada* (who belonged to Clann Chonchúir), *Cineál Binnigh* in modern Co. Derry and the original Mac Lochlainn home base in Inis Eoghain; and with Ó Néill were Cineál Moain (Ó Gormlaigh), and Ó Catháin and Fir Droma Lighean, who kept a lower profile.

THE BOUNDARIES OF THE DIOCESE

Political: High King Ruairí Ó Conchúir

Without following the actual vagaries of the struggle for all that time we can focus on the uneasy truce established in 1176 by *fir Éireann* ('the Men of Ireland')[20] – under High King Ruairí Ó Conchúir, an assembly of other leading kings from Munster, Meath and Ulster and no doubt of unnamed leading ecclesiastics. They divided Tír Eoghain between Niall Mac Lochlainn and Aodh Ó Néill. The division centred on Sliabh gCalann (*Slieve Gallan*) on the modern Tyrone/Derry county march

---

19. *Niall Glúndubh* 'Niall Black-knee'; Dónall *Dábhaill*; 'Dábhall' was the name of the River Blackwater. Cf. M.A. O'Brien, *Corpus Genealogiarum Hiberniae* (Dublin: Dublin Institute for Advanced Studies, 1976), pp. 175–6.

20. The expression *Fir Éireann* 'Men of Ireland' expresses a broadly based coalition of dynasties of wider significance than a single province – not necessarily All-Ireland. It was *Fir Éireann* who commanded the consecration of Ceallach as reforming bishop of Armagh in 1106 (AU). Tír Eoghain was larger than the present county, of course.

at Desertmartin/Moneymore/Lissan. North of the mountain was to be the kingdom of Mac Lochlainn, and south of it was to go to Aodh Ó Néill, the *Macaomh Tóinleasc* who was to begin the recovery of Ó Néill fortunes.[21] For the ecclesiastics at least this must have involved some politicking, because, as we have seen, it separated Badoney from Armagh, Ballinascreen from Termonmaguirk (both belonging to the Mac Oirc patrimony) and Termonmaguirk from its Columban centre. It must have been in the nature of a trade-off. Apart from that one can say it followed the Foyle basin watershed through country that must have been largely uninhabited at the time.

Religious: The Synod of Ráth Breasail (1111)

The settlement arrived at in 1176 would seem to have drawn the final line in a process that had begun earlier in the century. The drawing of diocesan boundaries began in 1111 at the Synod of Ráth Breasail in Munster, which set as its aim to have twelve diocesan bishoprics in *Leath Choinn*, the northern half of the country or province of Ard Macha, and twelve in *Leath Mhogha*, the southern half or province of Caiseal, in imitation of England where a similar division had been made. Ulster was to have six, Ard Macha, Clochar, Ard Sratha, Doire or Ráth Bhoth, Coinnire and Dún.[22]

The limits of each diocese are given by naming locations at opposing ends of each territory, more or less, and those relevant to (modern) Derry were:

Armagh	From Sliabh Breagh to Cuaille Cianachta; from the Bior to the Abhainn Mhór. *Sliabh Breagh: hills (near Slane) to Cuaille Cianachta(?);* from the Moyola to the Blackwater.
Clochar	From the Abhainn Mhór to Gabhal Liúin from Sliabh Beatha to Sliabh Larga; *From the Blackwater to Galloon (Coole);*

---

21. AFM ad ann. 1167 *An Macaomh Tóinleasc* 'the lazy-bottomed youth' who would not stand up in his foster-father Ó Flainn's house to greet the hostile Mac Lochlainn king who had come searching for him.
22. John McErlean SJ, ed., *Synod of Ráith Breasail*, with notes, *Archiv. Hib.* III (1914), pp. 1–33.

from Slieve Beagh (where Tyrone, Fermanagh,
Monaghan meet) to Pigeon Top (near Omagh).

Ard Sratha	From Sliabh Larga to Carn Glas;
	from Loch Craoi to Beann Fhoibhne.
	From Pigeon Top to the Tops (three miles
	north of Castlefin);
	from Lough Lee (near Drumquin) to
	Benevenagh.
Doire *or*	From Eas Rua to Srubh Broin;
Ráth Bhoth	from Carn Glas to Srubh Broin.
	From Assaroe (Ballyshannon) to Stroove;
	from the Tops to Stroove.
Coinnire	From Beann Fhoibhne to Torbhuirg, etc.
	From Benevenagh to Torr Head, etc.

The area that we now regard as the diocese of Derry was part of the areas allocated to three dioceses by Ráth Breasail: Connor, Ardstraw, and a diocese with its centre unagreed, Derry or Raphoe. The boundary points that would seem to concern us are *Cuaille Cianachta* on Armagh's northern border, *Beann Fhoibhne* on the Ardstraw/Connor border; *Sliabh Larga*: Clogher/Ardstraw; *Carn Glas*: Ardstraw/Derry or Raphoe; and *Loch Craoi.*

Benevenagh is the most straightforward, majestic as ever above the Foyle. *Sliabh Larga* seems to be the Pigeon Top, near Omagh.[23] *Carn Glas* was identified as the Tops between Donaghmore and Raphoe.[24] *Loch Craoi* was identified as Lough Lee by the late Fr Pádraig Ó Gallachair.[25] *Cuaille Cianachta* has provoked the most argument. The intriguing thing about this point is that, while it marks the boundary of Armagh, it is not put forward as a border point for either Ardstraw or Connor. *Cuaille* just means a post or stake, and *Cianacht* was the territory of the Cianachta, roughly the Roe valley, now the barony of Keenaught. Sure enough, there is the townland of Coolkeenaght on the edge of the barony on the bank of Lough Foyle, but this could not have

---

23. Patrick Mulligan, *The Diocese of Clogher* (Monaghan: Clogher Historical Society, 1986), p. 8.
24. Neachtan Ó Dónaill had a strongpoint there in later times. AFM ad ann. 1417.
25. Cf. *Clogher Record* VII, 3 (1975), pp. 336–7.

been the location in question since the diocese of Ardstraw goes past this point to its boundary with Connor at Benevenagh.

Reeves suggested Foremass on the borders of Errigal Keeroge, Termonmaguirk and Clogherny.[26] Pádraig Ó Maolagáin suggested Stick Hill in the townland of Finglen, parish of Banagher. Séamus Ó Ceallaigh walked the ground to suggest the worth of Mullaghacoula (the 'Coolyes') on the Broaghderg/Davagh and Lissan/Ballinascreen/ Badoney borders.[27] Breandán Ó Cíobháin opts for Oughtmore at the junction of the baronies of Keenaught, Loughinsholin and Strabane Upper.[28]

The argument turns to a great extent on the location as noted in three documents: *Quollykenaght* in a survey of mountainous lands in the *Ulster Inquisitions*; *Coolechenaught* in a list of mountains in the patent rolls of James I; and *Collecknaught* on the borders of the barony of Loughinsholin in the *Civil Survey*.[29] The names on these lists are confused because of scribes unfamiliar with language and terrain, although it is possible that someone armed with great patience and a glass might unravel it all over the course of a dark winter.

It would seem that the place in question must have been on an existing border when it was chosen – perhaps of Uí Tuirtre – and be sufficiently remarkable in its own right. A *cuaille* or post is by its nature ephemeral. Ó Cíobháin mentions only to reject the townland of Keenaught in the parish of Kilcronaghan, diocese of Derry. It threads its way, according to local knowledge, between Cullion and Iniscarn in the parish of Desertmartin and Attyneal in Ballinascreen to meet the archdiocese of Armagh where the parish of Lissan crosses Slieve Gallan to *Lag an Cheo* on the uninhabited northwest face of the mountain behind the Windy Gap. Although written 'Keenaught' in civil documents and still a recognised ecclesiastical division of the parish of Desertmartin and Kilcronaghan, the local pronunciation is *Keen-agh* and the final 't' is often missing in the Plantation Papers, etc. It is hard to see what connection it might have had with the

---

26. W. Reeves, ed., *Acts of Archbishop Colton in his Metropolitan Visitation of Derry* (Dublin: Irish Archaeological Society, 1850), pp. 126–7.

27. S. Ó Ceallaigh, 'Northern Boundary of the Archdiocese of Armagh', *Seanchas Ardmhacha* I, i (1954), p. 58–62.

28. B. Ó Cíobháin, 'Deoise Ard Mhacha sa Dara Céad Déag', *Seanchas Ardmhacha* IX, 1 (1978), pp. 61–9.

29. *Inquisitionum Cancellariae Hiberniae Repertorium* II, Appendix 2, 11. *Irish Patent Rolls of James I* (LXXI 38), p. 257. R. Simington, ed., *Civil Survey AD 1654–6 Counties of Donegal, Londonderry and Tyrone* III, p. 168.

Cianacht who lived near the Roe. It has one advantage, however, for being *Cuaille Cianachta*, its location. Keenaught is in the right place still, at the present northern edge of the archdiocese of Armagh[30] and on *Sliabh gCalann* (Slieve Gallan), which is one of the frequently mentioned mountains in the history of mid-Ulster. The other is Sliabh Troim or Toadh ('Bessy Bell') near Newtownstewart. It is possible that the Ráth Breasail plan was no more than a tentative, preliminary sketch. It has been suggested that the reason for the vagueness of some of the boundaries is that the fathers of the Synod of Rath Breasail were unfamiliar with Ulster and its internal politics. Since Primate Ceallach was there, no doubt with an entourage, such an assumption would be incautious. Neither would those present have been so disingenuous as to be unaware of the internal politics of Cineál Eoghain. Unfortunately we have few details, but to underestimate the astuteness of political leaders of the time where their interests were concerned would be rash in the extreme.

Why Ardstraw at all?

From our perspective it may seem bizarre that Ráth Breasail should have fixed on Ardstraw at all, the former centre of a declining sub-lordship, and in so doing, overlooked the prestige of Colmcille and Derry, of which we would be more aware, as the episcopal centre for the whole region – or indeed Fahan. The real importance of Derry as the great Columban centre would seem to have developed after Ráth Breasail, and may indeed have been a consequence of the decisions of the synod (which left its leaders free to assert supremacy in the Columban 'order'). The fathers of Ráth Breasail seem to have been uncomfortable with the idea of Derry as an episcopal as well as a monastic centre, perhaps anxious that it should not rival Armagh, especially since Derry was the Mac Lochlainn 'capital' in the kingdom of Cineál Eoghain. After all it seems to have been renamed *Doire Cholm Cille* only later in the twelfth century. What we may also overlook is the prestige of St Eoghan (Eugene) at the time. He is usually described as 'the bishop', which must have left his patronage more suited to the new era. Ardstraw, its church and its bridge occur frequently in the annals, and of course it

---

30. Note that lower down and still on the Ardtrea/Desertmartin border is the Windy Castle, a high rocky point in the townland of Tirgan (Toireagán), which means a 'little tower' according to G. Toner, ed., *Placenames of Northern Ireland* V, Co. Derry: I (Moyola Valley) (Belfast: The Queen's University of Belfast, 1996), pp. 106–7.

pre-dates by a long time most of the modern population centres of the area. Presumably also it had enough resources to maintain a bishop and a suitable church building.

The Ambitions of High King Dónall

Dónall mac Ardghair Mac Lochlainn was at the height of his powers at the time of the Synod of Ráth Breasail. He had defied the power of the Ó Canannáin and Ó Maoldoraidh kings to instal his son Niall in 1101 as King of Cineál Chonaill (Donegal).[31] In 1113 he was to banish the King of the Ulaidh, divide the kingdom between two contenders and keep Dál nAraidhe (north and east of Lough Neagh) and Uibh Eathach (Iveagh, now the diocese of Dromore) for himself. It has been said that Muircheartach Ó Briain, King of Munster, drew the Ulster boundaries with a view to making things as difficult as possible for his rival. In fact, the diocese of Derry/Raphoe looks to have been created to mirror the kingdom of Dónall's son, since it would have included the homeland of Cineál Eoghain in Inis Eoghain, as well as Derry and Cineál Chonaill (basically most of modern Co. Donegal). The diocese laid out as Connor could be seen to be in line with King Dónall's imperialist ambitions in north Antrim, and, if it went to *Cuaille Cianachta*, included most of south Derry, the former lands of Uí Tuirtre at Slieve Gallan, on the Armagh diocesan border.

How the diocese of Ardstraw might have fitted into such plans is a difficulty. Dónall mac Ardghair Mac Lochlainn became King of Cineál Eoghain in 1083. His early actions show him establishing control of the west bank of the Foyle: over Cineál Éinne (1078), over Ó Gormlaigh of Cineál Moain (1084), over Ó Cairealláin of Clann Diarmada (a branch of Clann Chonchúir) and Ó Luinigh of Cineál Moain (1090). In 1080 he led the Fir Maighe Iotha, who could well have included those mentioned (whom he was later to slay), and defeated the Fir Manach, including the 'persecutors of Armagh' (unexplained in the annal). In 1076 the King of Uí Fiachrach Ard Sratha was slain in a battle with the Uí Tuirtre and Cineál Binnigh Glinne, both based in south Derry.[32] Cineál Binnigh Glinne seem to have been the shock troops of Mac Lochlainn, and so we find them at war with Uí Fiachrach Ard Sratha (who did not belong to Cineál Eoghain). It is worth bearing in mind

---

31. Killed by Cineál Moain in 1119 at the age of twenty-eight (AFM).
32. Uí Tuirtre seem to be anachronistic in this context, since they would seem to have been forced across the Bann into Dál nAraidhe a hundred years before this. Cf. James Hogan, 'Ua Briain kingship', p. 416. Mercenaries, perhaps?

that it was probably Dónall or one of his own kindred who installed Conchúr Ó Briain (+1078) of the royal Munster dynasty as short-lived King of Telach Óg in east Tyrone to muzzle the hostility of Ó Néill.[33] Putting all these entries from the annals together one would suggest that King Dónall Mac Lochlainn was breaking up the area of Ulster that he controlled into manageable areas and the idea of dioceses fitted into his strategy to divide and rule Ulster, using the Church as one pillar. His division did not long outlast him.

Dónall mac Ardghair Mac Lochlainn lived at Eanach (Enagh) outside Derry. He died on 9 February 1121, aged seventy-three (AU), and was buried in Derry, unlike his father Ardghar who had been buried in the royal mausoleum at Armagh.

Who were the Bishops?

No Bishop of Ardstraw is named in the annals at this time. The late Fr Aubrey Gwynn maintained that Maol Choluim Ó Brolcháin,[34] who was consecrated at Armagh in 1107 (AU) and died in 1122 and Maol Bhríde Ó Brolcháin (+1139), were both described as bishops of Armagh by a scribal error. They were in fact bishops of Ardstraw, Fr Gwynn suggested, because they belonged to a Cineál Eoghain family prominent in Church life.[35] A similar case, however, could be made for Maol Choluim's predecessor, Caoincomhrac Ó Baoill (O Boyle), Bishop of Ard Macha from 1099 to 1106, because the Ó Baoill name is connected with the church of Leamhchoill (*Langfield*) in the diocese of Ardstraw in medieval times. A necessary corrective to Fr Gwynn's view is that, although indeed members of Cineál Eoghain, the *Uí Bhrolcháin* were also related by *marriage* to Clann Síonaigh of Armagh: Mór, daughter of Duibhinse and great-granddaughter of the original progenitor Brolchán, was the mother of Maolmhuire, who succeeded Muireacán of Both Domhnaigh as *Comharba Phádraig* (1001–20). Because of this relationship, on balance, one must consider them as monastic bishops in Armagh in the less-reformed Clann Síonaigh, although Cineál Eoghain may have figured in their sacramental responsibilities.[36]

---

33. See James Hogan, 'The Ua Briain Kingship in Telach Óg', *Féil-Scríbhinn Eoin Mhic Néill* (Dublin, 1940/1995), pp. 431–4.
34. The name has been transmogrified into 'Bradley', itself a name of English origin.
35. Aubrey Gwynn, Gerard O'Brien, eds, *The Irish Church in the 11th and 12th Centuries* (Dublin: Four Courts Press, 1992), p. 259.
36. Cf. Meyer, 'Laud Genealogies', ZCP VIII, p. 300.

After Dónall

Dónall Mac Lochlainn was succeeded by his son Conchúr (Conor) who was deposed in favour of his brother Mánas in 1128 and restored the next year. Much of his career falls in the lost section of the *Annals of Ulster*. He is described as 'Lord of Aileach, and King of all the north, both Cineál Chonaill and Cineál Eoghain, Ulaidh, Airghialla and possible King of Ireland', when he was killed 'in treachery' by the Fir Maighe Iotha in 1136 (AFM). It was during his time that the assassination attempt was made on St Malachy. Gwynn suggests that Clann Mhic Lochlainn were responsible, but the preciseness of the annal entry would suggest rather that it was the other branch of Cineál Eoghain (who took a proprietary interest in Armagh), led by Ó Néill, later of Dungannon,[37] perhaps in alliance with the turbulent Dónall Ó Gormlaigh, briefly King of Cineál Eoghain (1143–5).

High King Muircheartach Mac Lochlainn

Three years afterwards, his nephew took revenge for Conor's murder by killing the chief men of Clann Laifeartaigh, a branch of Clann Chonchúir of east Donegal. This nephew was Muircheartach Mac Lochlainn, son of Niall, who was to become second-last King of Ireland, a man who would have delighted the heart of Machiavelli. That he played a prominent part in the reform process is clear, but what purpose he had in mind is less certain. The piety he showed on some occasions[38] does not seem to have inhibited his ruthlessness on others. He was a ruler of talent in many ways but, while in as complete control of the country as anyone of his time could be, he threw it all away in an act of *hubris* worthy of Greek theatre, and found himself abandoned by all save the thirteen who died with him in what was, in a way, a formal execution. In another outburst of their age-old animosity, Cineál Eoghain had gone to war in 1165 with the Ulaidh and banished Ulster King Eochaidh Mac

37. Aubrey Gwynn, op. cit., p. 213. He refers to an entry in AT which records the Cineál Eoghain of *Tealach Óg* as conspiring against St Maolmhóg (Malachy), but the Mac Lochlainn name rarely occurs in clear connection with Tullyhogue in the twelfth century.

38. In 1157 at Mellifont he gave 160 cows, sixty ounces of gold and one townland to 'the Lord and the clergy'. He was present in 1161 at the Synod of Ath na Dairbhrí in Meath, when he confirmed the jurisdiction of Comharba Cholm Cille, Flaitheartach Ó Brolcháin, over Columban churches of Meath and Leinster (AU). The *teampall mór* of Derry built in stone by Flaitheartach Ó Brolcháin *mac an easpaig*, the community of Derry and by Muircheartach Mac Lochlainn, *Ardrí Éireann* (High King of Ireland) in 1164 (AU).

Doinnshléibhe Ó hEochadha. At the request of Donncha Ó Cearúill, King of Airghialla, Muircheartach restored him again, after he gave hostages, jewels and the 'Sword of the Earl' as sureties. The agreement was sworn to before the primate, in front of Donncha and the laity and clergy, and on the 'Bachall Íosa' and 'all the relics of the north of Ireland'. In 1166, Muircheartach seized and blinded Eochaidh in spite of all these oaths, causing all the witnesses on earth and in heaven to lose face, so that all but a handful of his supporters turned against him.

Muircheartach had succeeded in 1136 but was deposed by Dónall Ó Gormlaigh, who became King of Cineál Eoghain by 'agreement' in 1143. In 1145 Muircheartach was restored by Cineál Chonaill and King Donncha Ó Cearúill (O Carroll), the great supporter of St Malachy's programme. In 1137, the year after Muircheartach's first accession, St Malachy resigned from Armagh and was succeeded by Giolla Mac Liag Mac Ruairí (St Gelasius Mac Ruairí), *comharba Cholm Cille* and Abbot of Derry since 1121, who was of Cineál Eoghain descent, but of a collateral branch, being descended from Aodh Allán.[39]

A Derry–Armagh Compromise?

If my contention is correct that the two Ó Brolcháin bishops, related by marriage to Clann Síonaigh, were attached to the Armagh *paruchia* and to the unreformed *Comharbacht*, it is probable that a deal was struck. Because Derry sent its *Comharba Cholm Cille* to Armagh as archbishop, Armagh sent to Derry one of its own, Flaitheartach Ó Brolcháin, son of the Bishop Ó Brolcháin, belonging to Cineál Eoghain yet representative of Clann Síonaigh, as successor and inheritor of the prestige of Colm Cille. His family connections with Clann Síonaigh might have made him something of an embarrassment in the new Armagh, and it would seem reasonable that Clann Síonaigh must have been given some recognition, since saving face and honour was a matter of life and death in medieval Ireland. It may well be also that a place as small as Armagh of the time had not enough room for two men of such energy as Giolla Mac Liag and Flaitheartach.

No date is given for Flaitheartach's succession to Derry. He is already active and in possession by 1150. Whether there was a deal or not, both appointments were remarkably successful in what must have begun

---

39. Aodh Allán (+743) was High King of the Uí Néill, brother of Niall Frasach, also high king, and of the Conchúr who was the ancestor of Clann Chonchúir of east Donegal, whom we have met and will meet again – Ó Catháin, Ó Cairealláin, Ó Dubhda, etc.

as a particularly delicate situation. In this context, the importance of these positions in contemporary society may be gauged from the way the appointment in 1164 of Flaitheartach Ó Brolcháin to the abbacy of Iona was blocked by 'the successor of Patrick, the King of Ireland (Muircheartach Mac Lochlainn) and the principal people of Cineál Eoghain' (AU). Flaitheartach himself seemed willing to accept.

According to the annals, at the Synod of *Brí mhic Thaidhg* near Trim in 1159, 'the clergy of Ireland with the successor of St Patrick, ordered a chair, like every bishop, for the successor of Colm Cille, Flaitheartach Ó Brolcháin, and the arch-abbacy of the churches of Ireland in general (*go coiteann*)' (AFM). O'Donovan translates 'like every other bishop', but the Irish reads *cathaoir amhail gach n-easpag*, with no word for other. He received a seat but not as a bishop. Was he made a mitred abbot? The promotion to 'arch-abbacy of all the churches of Ireland' must have meant more than just the churches dedicated to Colm Cille, but those in Ireland – with no mention of Iona. It sounds as if it was something like an inspector-general of religious life in the whole country (or most of it, since the bishops of Connacht had been prevented from attending the synod).

Also present at the synod was the papal legate, legate of Hadrian IV, the English Pope Nicholas Breakspear, who, as Eamon Duffy puts it, 'granted the English King Henry II the right to incorporate Ireland into his realm' by his decree *Laudabiliter*, two years before Brí mhic Thaidhg. Was there pressure from Rome to reform religious life in Ireland? The last remaining native order may have come into the firing line and perhaps Flaitheartach illustrates the adage: *Promoveatur ut amoveatur*. To get him out of the way of reform he may have been promoted to a position that sounded great but may have been little more than honorific. One could hardly imagine Cistercian or Benedictine monks with the mentality they were to demonstrate in the next century taking instruction from him.

It is worth bearing in mind also that St Conchúr Mac Con Choille, Archbishop of Armagh +1175, had been prior of the house of canons in Armagh and was almost certainly a member of the erenagh family at the monastery in Derry. He succeeded Giolla Mac Liag Mac Ruairí (or St Gelasius as he is often known) in Armagh. The Mac Con Choille family included the intriguing 'Bébhinn, iníon Mhic Con Choille, *banairchinneach Dhoire*, d'éag 22 December 1134' (AFM) – (Bébhinn, daughter of Mac Con Choille [McEnhill], *female erenagh* of Derry died, etc.). Conghalach Mac Con Choille, perhaps her grandfather, had died in 1112 at the age of ninety-four. Saint Conor McEnhill was prior of the Augustinian canons of St Peter and Paul's, Armagh, before his short career as archbishop.[40] It was around this time that the *Dubhreglés* of Derry became a house of Augustinian canons of *Arrouaise*, filial to St Peter and St Paul's, Armagh, perhaps earlier in fact than was thought.

Father Gwynn suggests that the first Bishop of Cineál Eoghain was Ó Gorm(gh)aile, who died in 1149 (AFM). The annalist mentions no diocese or other location in the notice of his death. Father Gwynn says that he must have been of Cineál Eoghain because Dónall Ó Gormlaigh, of Cineál Eoghain, was King of Cineál Eoghain in 1143–5. It is unlikely that a contemporary scribe would confuse two such quite different surnames (and in any case there is scant evidence of any ecclesiastical ambition amongst the Uí Ghormlaigh of that time).

It is probable that Fr Gwynn indeed got it right, but on different grounds. The Four Masters record the death on pilgrimage in 1218 of Giolla na Naomh Ó Gormaile, priest of Ráth Luraigh.[41] The surname Ó *Gormghala* occurs in the genealogical tree of Cineál Binnigh[42] of south Derry, so priest and bishop may have been native to the area and would have belonged to Cineál Eoghain. Ó Gormaile could well have been Bishop of Cineál Eoghain, which would rule out the possibility that he might have been bishop of a Derry/Ardstraw diocese separate from the diocese of Cineál Eoghain, as adumbrated by way of explanation of the anomaly by that most perceptive analyst of the polity of medieval Ulster, Katharine Simms.[43] The name may have become confused in English with Ó Gormlaigh/Gormley since then.

The twelfth-century synods were more at ease with Derry as a monastic centre, anxious perhaps that the fame of its patron might cause it to rival Armagh. Although he built the *Teampall Mór* in Derry, Flaitheartach Ó Brolcháin was not to be in episcopal orders but he did become the equivalent of a mitred abbot at the synod of

---

40. Saint Conor's successor in turn, Giolla an Choimdhe Ó Caráin, was Bishop of Raphoe before Armagh. See ref. 'O Caran' erenagh at Coolkeeragh in *The Bishopric of Derry and the Irish Society of London* I (1968), p. 216.
41. Ráth Luraigh or Machaire Rátha Luraigh, now Maghera, Co. Derry, was founded by St Lurach, brother of Bec, King of Uí Tuirtre; Bishop of Cineál Eoghain, was titular of Rathlury. It was presumably as the cathedral of this diocese that the church in Maghera with its celebrated medieval lintel was constructed. Cf. J.R. Walsh, *History of the Parish of Maghera*, 1973; Oilibhéar Ó Croiligh, *Rún Ardchrosa Éireann*, 2011.
42. See Séamus Ó Ceallaigh, op. cit., genealogy, end paper.
43. See 'The Origins of the Diocese of Clogher', *Clogher Record* X, 2 (1980), p. 197.

Brí Mhic Thaidhg in 1158. His contemporary bishop, described as 'Bishop of *Cineál Eoghain*' in the annals, was Muireadhach Ó Cofaigh (+1173) who is said to have transferred the see at his own volition from Ardstraw to Maghera,[44] and perhaps also because Ardstraw had become a dangerous place to live for a bishop in the Cineál Eoghain (Mac Lochlainn) interest.

What area was he bishop of? It must have included Inis Eoghain, simply because Cineál Eoghain would not have permitted anything else, and no one at that time was in any position to force them. Clann Chonchúir had spread, with one branch, Ó Catháin, now described as Fir na Craoibhe, indicating that they had control of north Derry as far as the 'Cutts' on the Bann. Their relatives Clann Diarmada (Ó Cairealláin–Kerlin) were still competing with Cineál Moain (Ó Gormlaigh) in east Donegal. All of these belonged to Cineál Eoghain. West Tyrone, the old lands of the Uí Fiachrach Ard Sratha, had long since been conquered, and Uí Tuirtre (Ó Flainn) had been banished from south Derry across the Bann. Thus it is that the diocese attained the shape it still has in spite of the fact that the dynasty of Cineál Eoghain were to lose control of Inis Eoghain and east Donegal in the following century.

Obviously the monastic city of Derry in the twelfth century was dominated by Cineál Eoghain, civilly in the persons of Mac Lochlainn monarchs, and religiously in its erenaghs and abbots. When Muircheartach Mac Lochlainn died, after his breach of sworn agreement and his cruelty had led to what was in effect his execution in battle in south Armagh, he was buried at Armagh. Flaitheartach Ó Brolcháin and the community of Derry felt the dishonour to St Colm Cille so keenly that the *taoiseach mhac léinn Dhoire*, the head of the students of Derry, fasted against his being brought to that cemetery (AU). The AU editor suggests that they objected to his being given Christian burial in view of his broken oath, sworn before *Comharba Cholm Cille* on the *Soiscéal Mhártain* (Gospel of St Martin), the halidom of Cineál Eoghain, but it is more probable that their objection was to the burial of one they saw as their own at Armagh rather than Derry. It marked a downgrading of monastic Derry after its blaze of glory.

---

44. *Illectus natalis soli dulcedine*, 'seduced by the charm of his native earth' as the bull of Innocent IV put it in 1247 at the time of removal to Derry. See an Ó Cofaigh sept as tenants in: Michael Glancy, 'The Church lands of Co. Armagh', *Seanchas Ardmhacha* I (1954), p. 79.

Confusion in West Tyrone

The tangle here has to do with the kingdom of Uí Fiachrach Ard Sratha. The Uí Fiachrach was one of the kingdoms making up the Airghialla. The kingdom of the Airghialla under Donncha Ó Cearúill became the diocese of Clochar with the brother of St Malachy as its bishop. Initially in the centre of the present diocese, Clochar came to embrace the whole Erne basin, and laid claim to any place of Airghialla provenance. Clochar was to claim that Derry took what is now west Tyrone from Clochar by main force, annexed by the military might of bishop Giolla an Choimdhe Ó Cearbhalláin ('Servant of the Lord' – *latine* 'Germanus' – O Carolan) around 1240.[45] It became part of the Derry deanery of Maigh Iotha.

The date 'around 1240' prompts the question as to whether it had anything to do with the disastrous defeat of Mac Lochlainn at Caméirí near Omagh in 1241,[46] and with the projected transfer of the seat of the diocese from Ráth Luraigh to the former monastic city of Derry, which was finally agreed in 1254. Derry by then was well on the way to becoming the Ó Dochartaigh/Ó Domhnaill city which the 'spin doctors' say it always was.

Was Ard Sratha ever part of an Airghialla diocese that included Clogher? The obvious answer must be no, if it is meant in any pre-reform sense. The last Bishop of Ard Sratha who was clearly a native was Aonghas who died in 878, and by 921 Ard Sratha would seem to have become part of the Columban *paruchia* with Droim Cliabh (Drumcliff). When King Muircheartach Ó Briain invaded through Eas Rua (Assaroe), attacked Inis Eoghain, demolished Grianán Ailigh and burnt forts and churches including Fathain Mhura and Ard Sratha in 1101 (AFM), he was attacking the buildings of Cineál Eoghain and the self-esteem of Dónall mac Ardghair Mac Lochlainn who was shown to be unable to protect even his churches. Ard Sratha was clearly within Dónall's bailiwick.

The actual kingdom of *Uí Fiachrach Ard Sratha* came to an end in the twelfth century. The last king mentioned, Murchadh Ó Críocháin, is merely named as King of Uí Fiachrach (without the *Ard Sratha*) in a

---

45. K.W. Nicholls, 'The Register of Clogher', *Clogher Record* VII, 3 (1971/2), p. 408.
46. The incursion of Norman power into their home base must have weakened Mac Lochlainn enormously, losing as they did the city of Derry and eastern Inis Eoghain. The location of *Caméirí* has been much controverted. See N.J.A. Williams, ed., *Poems of Giolla Brighde Mac Con Midhe* (Dublin: Irish Texts Society, 1980), p. 268.

curious and obscure entry in the *Annals of Ulster*, when he died at the hands of Conchúr Beag Mac Lochlainn in 1201 'through a miracle'. In the twelfth-century entries they are usually found in contention with Fir Loirg and Uí Chinnéidigh[47] (who have given their names to baronies of Fermanagh). Ó Críocháin are found also as kings of Farney. This looks like the case of a ruling group (perhaps quite small) who have been forced out of their own lands and are seeking space with their related neighbours. They would also have retained the appellation of Uí Fiachrach after they had moved elsewhere.

By the mid-twelfth century, the sub-kingdom of Uí Fiachrach Ard Sratha had ceased to exist, and with it one would have thought any chance of an *Airghialla* diocese in the area in the terms demanded by Ráth Breasail and Kells.

Earlier in this essay, in discussing the rise of Cineál Eoghain, the division of Maigh Iotha (the Lagán) between Cineál Moain and Clann Chonchúir was referred to. In the course of the twelfth century the rivalry between them became as internecine as that of any Italian city-state. It is complicated by the use of descriptive titles that are ambiguous, or the same names applied to different groups, and sometimes by the groups changing sides. To give a full account of the relevance of their quarrel to the boundary disputes of Derry would require an essay in itself. It may provide a further reason for Muireadhach Ó Cofaigh electing to move his seat to Ráth Luraigh – it must have been much safer there. Katharine Simms is clearly right in suggesting a connection between the locating of a diocese of Ardstraw and the activities of Dónall Ó Gormlaigh of Cineál Moain.[48] Cineál Moain were determined to take over the former kingdom of Uí Fiachrach – and seem eventually to have succeeded – but at this stage their aims were, I would suggest, more dynastic and territorial than ecclesiastical. It seems to me that they were content to ensure that there would be no resident bishop in the Mac Lochlainn scheme of things in Ardstraw, but I see no evidence that they planned a diocese and bishop of their own.

To recall the groups in question in Maigh Iotha: *Clann Chonchúir* which divided into *Clann Diarmada* (Ó Cairealláin), *Clann Laifeartaigh* (Ó Dúda), *Fir na Craoibhe* (Ó Catháin); *Cineál Moain* divided into *Uachtarach* (upper) and *Íochtarach* (lower) and by surname into Ó

---

47. See AU/AFM/ALC 1076, 1103, 1118, 1129, 1150, 1160, 1164.
48. Katharine Simms, op. cit., in *Clogher Record* (1980), pp. 196–8. It may have been relevant that Domhnall Ó Gormlaigh possibly had a hand in the death of Niall, father of Muircheartach Mac Lochlainn.

Gormlaigh and Ó Luinigh. It is unclear why exactly Ó Catháin moved to Cianacht (Roe valley), leaving Clann Diarmada in the original location, basically the parish of Donaghmore. The parting seems less than amicable because Ó Catháin is often found fighting in conjunction with Ó Gormlaigh. Clann Laifeartaigh may have pushed out the *Fir Droma Lighean*, Ó Donnaile/Ó Doibhlin (Donnelly/Devlin) to become the basis of the parish of Clonleigh. Urney seems to have resulted from the success of Ó Gormlaigh, an Urney that included the area around Strabane – at least the present parishes of Mourne and Camus. By 1178 Ó Gormlaigh was King of Maigh Iotha and Cineál Éinne, and was well on the way to forcing Clann Diarmada (Ó Cairealláin–Kerlin) out of the Lagán. The latter moved closer to the leader of their alliance, Mac Lochlainn, at Derry, and gave their name to the parish across from Derry city, *Clann Diarmada* (Clon- or Glen-dermott). Many times in the course of their struggles they met at the bridge of Ardstraw and made peace in its church.

On one such occasion, in 1179, the leaders met in the church of Ardstraw to make peace and swear by the relics of Donaghmore, Urney and Ardstraw to keep it. The next day Amhlaimh Ó Gormlaigh, Lord of Cineál Moain, went to the house of Donncha Ó Cairealláin of Clann Diarmada to seek further guarantees but was killed at the doorway of the house in the middle of the *oireacht* (the formal assembly of leaders to discuss important matters)[49] 'in inhospitable treachery' in front of Donncha's own wife, who was Amhlaimh's sister, along with two of Amhlaimh's people: Cinaeth, son of Art Ó Bracáin (Brogan), and Giolla Chríost Mac Reodáin (McCrudden), Donncha's own foster-brother (AFM).

What is of interest here is the name of one of those killed with Ó Gormlaigh – Ó Bracáin – because the bishops of Clochar who protested at Bishop Ó Cearbhalláin's stealing of their lands were brothers named 'O Bragan'.[50] There were three consecutive Bishops of Derry named Ó Cearbhalláin (Carolan, a different name from Kerlin/Ó Cairealláin), one of whom, Fógartach I, succeeded Amhlaimh Ó Muireadhaigh in 1185. They belonged to Cineál Iollanna, a branch of Cineál Eoghain na hInse – those who are said to have stayed behind at Bréadach (Moville) in

---

49. For *oireacht* see Katharine Simms, *From Kings to Warlords* (Suffolk: Boydell & Brewer Ltd, 1987), p. 176.
50. Both Cistercians of Mellifont: Nehemias bishop 1227–40; David 1245–67. Ó Bracáin were descended perhaps from Cineál Aodha Mhic Fhearghasa branch of Cineál Eoghain *na hInse*.

Inishowen when the subsequently more prominent left[51] – and filled the see of Derry for over 100 years. This raises the question: was the suggested raid of Germanus O Carolan (Giolla an Choimdhe Ó Cearbhalláin) on Clochar in the first instance a row between branches of Cineál Eoghain, tied in with the cataclysmic defeat of Mac Lochlainn in 1241?

However, if the late Fr Ó Gallachair's identification of Loch Craoi with Lough Lee near the Langfield/Termonamongan border is correct, there may well be grounds for the complaint in the separation of the latter from indubitable union with Termonmagrath. Definite identification of Loch Craoi would settle the matter. On any map the projection of Termonamongan into Donegal is noticeable.

The position of Drumragh, whose medieval patronage of St Columba looks like a later addition, may bear examination, but the church there seems on the proper side of the Ráth Breasail border.

The Raphoe/Derry border in the Ballybofey/Stranorlar/Barnesmore region may have something to do with those shadowy tuatha mentioned in *Ceart Uí Néill* and in the State Papers, the exact location and boundaries of which have not been worked out. We note them here with their one-time ruling 'families':

Gleann Fhinne [*Mac Loinseacháin–McGlinchey*]; Tír Bhreasail [*Mac Fhearghail–McGarrigle*]; Magh Caorainn [*Ó Maolagáin–Mulligan*] and two mentioned earlier, Gleann Shneidhghile/Cluain Eidhile [*Ó Taircheirt*] and Ard Miodhair [*Ardmire, originally Ó Dochartaigh*].[52]

Parishes

Parishes in our sense of the word began to be developed in the lee of the organisation of the territorial diocese. This is a slower process, more difficult to follow because it is hard to document due to the catastrophic destruction of records in this much fought over diocese. The first parishes must also have followed the boundaries of the various *clanna* and related sub-groups within the larger polities. We have seen how they began to emerge in east Donegal in Maigh Iotha in the bounds separating Urney

---

51. Cf. S. Pender, ed., *O'Clery Book of Genealogies* in *Anal. Hib.* 18 (1951), pp. 53, 54–5. K. Meyer, ed., 'Laud Genealogies', ZCP VIII, p. 299. Ó Muireadhaigh belonged to the Clann Diarmada (Ó Caireallláin) branch of Clann Chonchúir, and later dominated the priory of Augustinian canons at Dungiven – to which the rectory of Badoney came to belong. The central house of the canons regular was, as we saw, in Armagh.

52. Cf. E.Ó Doibhlin, 'Ceart Uí Néill #1', op. cit., pp. 30–5.

(Cineál Moain [Ó Gormlaigh]), Donaghmore (Clann Diarmada – before re-locating at Derry) and Clonleigh (perhaps Clann Laifeartaigh or the other branch of Cineál Moain [Ó Luinigh – Lunny]). It will call, however, for patient detective work comparing common local surnames with the genealogies and placenames to decipher the process at all adequately.

Financing the Operation

More immediately accessible to our investigation of the origin of the territorial diocese is the question of how these leaders envisaged the maintenance of the new order, now that it could no longer depend on the monastic system. As the *paruchiae* came to be divided by diocesan boundaries and as a parochial system began to break up their earlier links, it obviously must have been a pressing problem – of interest to any young man intending to pursue a clerical career.

The only recognised form of wealth at the time was land, so the solution arrived at in this new diocese had to be found in the *baile bó*, or 'townland' as it became known in English. A number of *bailte bó* was set aside for the upkeep of church and clergy. This must have been organised centrally, because the striking fact about the medieval churchlands of the parishes of the diocese is that they very often include the best land in the parish – often, as a result, the most thoroughly 'planted' at the Plantation of Ulster subsequently.

The amount of land varies from parish to parish, but as a general rule, there are at least four townlands. More important parishes had more. Ballinascreen had 'Six Towns'. Tamlaghtard was entirely churchland, much of it mensal, as was the case with the churchlands of Fahan, supporting both bishop and monastery of Derry. Another indication that the system was centrally organised is that often the churchlands of different parishes 'lie into one another', as is the case with Maghera and Termoneeny, and the parishes which belonged to *Comharba Chainnigh* in later years – Termoncanice (Limavady): Drumachose, Tamlaghtfinlagan and Aghanloo, or the *plebaniae* of Inis Eoghain (which seem to mean permanently combined parishes, as e.g. Moville-Culdaff).[53]

In the monastic *paruchia*, the temporalities were administered by the erstwhile monastic superior or *aircheannach* (which became erenagh in English), who belonged to the *fine* (or extended family)

---

53. Might *plebania* from Latin *plebs* 'people' have something to do with that curious Irish version given to Má Bhile – Bun an Phobail – *pobal* being a Church term for the people, from populus. Interestingly the *comharba*, like the lord of a sept or clann, was addressed by his surname.

into whose hands the monastic possessions had come. This title was now given to the person who administered these churchlands (thus relieving the clergy of the worry of worldly matters!). He was obliged to maintain the church, sustain the clergy, pay tithes to the bishop, receive him hospitably on visitation, and welcome travellers, etc. On the face of it this looks like an astute compromise, because it seems to have not merely reconciled the monastic system with the episcopal/parochial one, but did so within the context of the professions as the preserve in Ireland of the hereditary extended *clanna*. Just as poetry or medicine or the clergy had a defined legal status and role, so too would the lay administrators, taking over the old monastic title, and no doubt prestige, of the *aircheannach*.

If one thinks of the 'levitical families' of our own day, producing priests in each generation without institutional support, one would surmise that, in the course of time, the *airchinnigh* must have become involved at some level in the education of the clergy, from the expertise inevitably built up in matters clerical, in those pre-seminary days where the training of the priest was by apprenticeship. One must posit some sort of Latin school, and perhaps theological training or monastic/cathedral schools in conjunction with the new status of the *fir léinn* of Armagh. Perhaps as the *filí* had their schools, the *airchinnigh* may have developed something similar. Later on, as Montgomery's *Survey* demonstrates, there was some access to the university of Glasgow, and maybe even to those of Oxford and Paris.

Changing Fortunes of the Erenaghs

In the *Plantation Inquisitions*, it was claimed that the holder of the office of erenagh took his title from the founder of the church, but many of them were of much later provenance. Thus we find Ó Catháin in Termoncanice about 1400 muscling in on Mac Thaidhg, who belonged, as we can deduce from his name, to the pre-Ó Catháin *Cianachta* of Glengiven. Other Cineál Eoghain *clanna* trade in their political friendships for an ecclesiastical base. Ó hÉanna, given a spurious authority in Inis Eoghain according to *Leabhar Chlann Aodha Bhuí*, seem to be trading on the similarity to Ó hÉanaigh of Banagher – who were to have a lasting sideline in sand. Ó Cearbhalláin, also of Inis Eoghain, were able to produce bishops from their base in Clonleigh. Ó Farannáin of Ardstraw were descended from a grandson of Muircheartach Mac Earca (+536), first high king from Cineál Eoghain. Ó Doiréidh and Ó Galáin came to Donaghmore, Ó Braoin (Breen) to

Lifford, and Ó Ceallaigh in Urney could be the same as the erenagh of Fahan, or perhaps the compensation Ó Ceallaigh of Cineál Eachdach *an Chodaigh* exacted for their failed pretensions in Ardstraw. The descendants of that other Eochaidh, son of Eoghan, *Cineál Binnigh*, produced Ó Tuathaile (Tohill) in Desertoghill (who might hide Ó Dubhghaill of Desertmartin)[54] and also a group of families associated with 'transparochial ministries':

- *Muintir Tighe na Comairce* in Clonleigh (Ó Brolaigh, Ó Bogáin, Ó Tomhrair – O Brolly, O Bogan, O Toner) seem to have had responsibility for a collegiate church or 'college', which was the ultimate responsibility of the Derry chapter, and may well, for that reason, have been a house of *Céilí Dé* since before the time of the reform.
- *Mac Con Choille*, associated with the monastery in Derry, who may have had to change location with the advent of Cineál Chonaill (Ó Dónaill/Ó Dochartaigh) to Derry and move to Drumragh with St Colm's 'black bell'.
- *Mac Oirc* (McGurk), keepers of the *Dé Diongbhálta*, the Columban bell associated, it would appear, both with Ballinascreen and Termonmaguirk.
- *Ó Fearáin*, as we have seen, with their responsibility for St Dácuailén's Shrine.
- *Ó hÉigeartaigh*[55] appear in close association with places having a strong relationship with St Columba – although as nativi or dúchasaigh, perhaps, rather than as erenaghs – Fahan, Donaghedy (Grange), Ballinascreen, etc.
- *Mac Cathmhaoil* (McCawell/McCaul), of Cineál Fearadhaigh, who were to become prominent later in the church of Clogher, turn up as erenaghs at Dunboe, the parish reserved for the Archdeacon of Derry.

---

54. 'Patrick Odoell, last erenagh of Desertmartin', *Bishopric of Derry and Irish Society of London* I, p. 182.
55. One of the intriguing questions of the history of Cineál Chonaill is the fate of the families who lost out at the rise of Ó Dónaill/Ó Dochartaigh. The royal line of Ó Maoldoraidh seems to have moved to Fermanagh to become Mac Giolla Fhinnéin. The last of the name Ó Taircheirt, lords of Clann Shneidhghile (Clanelly, which seems to have been between Ardmire of Ó Dochartaigh and Cineál Éinne) gets a brief mention in 1232. Their lord, Éigeartach Ó Taircheirt, fell at Fearsat Súilí in 1098. Did some of the *clann* take their name from him, become Ó hÉigeartaigh and discover a new ecclesiastical role?

It seems clear then that many of the erenagh families do not have the antiquity that was to be claimed for them at the time of the Plantation of Ulster, but nonetheless they represent the profound ramifications of the restructuring of the diocese that began in the twelfth century. In addition, although the office of erenagh – like other offices in medieval Ireland – was passed on in the family, it became the prerogative of the bishop in the new system to appoint a new erenagh, probably from another branch of the *clann*, if the holder's family died out – which, if we are to judge from continuity in modern family businesses, might have happened more often than we would suppose at first sight, or if the proposed candidate was thought unworthy.

It is a further indication of the effectiveness of the system introduced by the reform and of the way that the position of the bishop caught hold. As Kenneth Nicholls has pointed out, the medieval Irish *clann* has more in common with the modern concept of the limited company than it has with what the word 'family' conveys to us. The reform actually put the administration of local temporalities in the hands of local *clanna*, whom it was the role of the bishop to monitor. (As a result the bishop also had the power, at least in theory, to guard against alienation of church property.) This would seem to indicate that the Irish Church was more comfortable with laity having a quasi-clerical responsibility (the *ceann fine*, the head of the erenagh *fine* or extended *clann*, received tonsure in the early days, it seems) than was the Church in England or on the continent. The system was effective and remained in place in west Ulster until the Plantation. One result, it would seem, was that anti-clericalism in late Gaelic Ulster seems mainly to have been of the *ceathrar sagart gan a bheith santach* or *bráthair bocht brúite ó fhíon* type, as lampooned in Mánas Ó Dónaill's well-known verses, but as against that there was a determination on the part of these *clanna* to provide their own clergy, mostly from their own ranks – not necessarily a recipe for moral rectitude.[56] We have no clear picture of what was the practice at popular level, in poetry or prayer, but the vigour of inventive intellectual life began to decline, it would seem, from the twelfth century onwards – perhaps the result of living in a society unable, because of foreign intrusion, to control its own destiny.

56. See K. Nicholls, *Gaelic and Gaelicised Ireland in the Middle Ages* (Dublin: Gill & MacMillan, 1972), pp. 8–12; 111–113. Lists of the names of late medieval clergy and erenaghs may be found in *O'Kane Papers* in *Anal. Hib.* 12 (1943), pp. 81–111, A.F. O'D Alexander, ed.; and in *Seanchas Ardmhacha* 1996–7, pp. 44–76, Henry A. Jefferies, ed., *Clerics of Derry, Annates of Derry re-examined* in *Derriana* (1976), pp. 18–52.

It was unfortunate that the reform of the Irish Church, already well advanced by the European standards of the time, was interrupted so early through the invasion of the Anglo-Normans in 1172. While Henry II, King of England, came under the dubious banner of reform, he was rather more inspired by his own political preoccupations, and the irruption of the feudal world was to have ambiguous consequences, not only for religion but also for the cultural history of the Irish.

The basic cultural inheritance of that feudal world was a mixture of memories of Ancient Rome (from the Latin language to the network of cities and roads in the lands of the ancient Empire), of Christianity based on the Scriptures and a sacramental system, with the pope, Bishop of Rome, at its head, as well as a substratum of Germanic and even Celtic customs, myths and ceremonies. In the development of that culture in the lands subject to Charlemagne, Irish monks and scholars had played a notable part two hundred years before; it might then have been anticipated that a considerable degree of mutual understanding and respect would have been the result.

However, this new civilisation, which by then was becoming dominant everywhere from its origins in northern France to most of western Europe, had only recently, since AD 1000, become a self-conscious culture with a corresponding sense of its own worth. It saw itself as the legitimate heir of Ancient Rome. Its members liked to speak of their world as *latinitas* and of those who spoke and thought like themselves as the *gens latina*. As it spread north, east, west and south, borne by armies, ecclesiastics, merchants and colonists, it became the norm of the 'civilised' world. Its triumph was due primarily, of course, to military technology. Its leaders were trained warriors, equipped with special armour and weapons and skilled in new tactics. Their system was a combination of mailed cavalry charge supported by longbowmen or crossbowmen, accompanied by the practice of immediately fortifying territory won with impressive castles. For a hundred years no Irish army could withstand a charge of Norman knights. The poet Giolla Bhríde Mac Con Mí explained the bloody defeat at the battle of Down in 1260:

> Unequal they came to the battle ...
> Fine linen shirts on the sons of Conn,
> the Gaill one mass of iron.

Perhaps then it is not surprising that the attitude of the new invaders to the indigenous population was one of contempt, particularly on the part of the social élites. And even though a gradual Gaelicisation took place, for long it was an attitude that the authorities of the new colony or Pale would retain, as is evidenced in the Statutes of Kilkenny of 1310. Even St Bernard could say in the twelfth century of the Irish, that they were 'Christians in name, but really pagans.' Saint Maolmhóg (or Malachy) too in his reforming zeal was just as severe on his countrymen, even though he must have been well aware that theirs was a Christian culture going back for seven centuries. The aim of Maolmhóg (or Malachy) and his fellow-reformers, cleric and lay, was to remodel Church and culture more closely on the model of the continent, the customs of which were for them the norm. The Anglo-Normans saw the Gaeil as 'pagans', not because they were not Christians and Catholics, but because they did not live according to the same social customs as the feudal society they knew.

The end result was a tragic division in the Irish Church which lasted throughout the Middle Ages, with even the primatial see of Armagh divided into Armagh *inter Anglos* and Armagh *inter Hibernos* and generally occupied by bishops without sympathy for or even knowledge of the culture of their flock. Soon the new monasteries of Norman-dominated Ireland would refuse to accept Irish postulants as monks, and theologians would debate whether it was a sin to kill an Irishman. The long history of native Irish monasteries as foyers of Gaelic literature comes to an end. No more do anchorites celebrate in Irish the joys of nature or the glory of God, or hero-tales be transcribed or reworked. Henceforth, these functions pass to the reconstructed lay schools of poetry, history and law. The reformed monastic inspiration demanded that monks hew more closely to their religious business, perhaps an understandable purity of intention for a reformer, but an undeniable cultural impoverishment all the same. Not until the Catholic Reformation of the seventeenth century would clergy return to the forefront of literary creation.

In Conclusion

The external boundaries of the modern diocese of Derry relate to the expansion of Cineál Eoghain, with Ó Catháin reaching the Bann, Cineál Binnigh investing south Derry,[57] Ó Gormlaigh/Ó Cairealláin coming to power in east Donegal/west Tyrone, and all within the kingdom

---

57. Cineál Binnigh gave its medieval name, *Binneach*, to the diocesan deanery, which included most of Co. Derry. The deaneries were *Inis Eoghain, Maigh Iotha, Binneach* and later *Ráth Luraigh*. See William Reeves, ed., *Archbishop Colton's Visitation of Derry* (Dublin, 1850), p. 74.

created and held by Mac Lochlainn for about a century and a half. Had the Reform happened at a different time the boundaries of Derry would have been significantly different.[58]

Difficult though it may be to follow and understand the ebb and flow of political rivalries and alliances, and the rise and fall of dynasties and lords in these medieval centuries, study of this kind is essential to any comprehension of the emergence of the modern ecclesiastical unit we know as the Diocese of Derry. The tragedies of its later history and the subsequent massive loss of written documents, architectural monuments and even oral religious traditions enshrined in our lost language, all make for an incomplete and often confusing picture. It is also our loss that we are not aware of the personalities of those who created what we take for granted – kings like Dónall mac Ardghair Mac Lochlainn, whose persistence and determination in building up his dynasty gives the feel of one who has stepped straight out of the succession lists of the French Capetian kings, or the curiously modern character of Flaitheartach Ó Brolcháin with his flair for publicity and genius for raising money, talents that have stood some members of the clergy in good stead since his time.

The spiritual gifts of the bishops – Ó Cofaigh, Ó Muireadhaigh, Mac Ruairí, Mac Con Choille (three of them acclaimed as saints by popular veneration) – are stressed in their obituaries. One cannot but be struck by the number of the main actors in these events who died on the eve of the Anglo-Norman/Mac Murchadha Invasion. One great 'if only' of the time must be that, had Muircheartach Mac Lochlainn had his grandfather Dónall's self-discipline, it might have been he – with a different relationship with Diarmaid Mac Murchadha – rather than the dithering High King Ruairí Ó Conchúir, who would have had to work out a *modus vivendi* with the Norman barons. On the other hand the annalists seem to feel a greater affection for Niall, Muircheartach's father, than they do for him.

One can only guess at the force of character that has made Bébhinn Nic Chon Choille (McEnhill) stand out from the page of history as a woman to be reckoned with as these events unfolded.

---

58. It is perhaps worth restating that when a *clann* moved or were moved elsewhere it was the ruling group at the top who moved. The *biataigh* and *bó-airí* and those who ran the *caoraíocht* were affected only in that the political change was probably just another source of attack (to gather taxes or out of revenge) on them. Not everybody in the territory ruled by such a lord belonged to the ruling *clann*, nor did they all share its surname or ancestry.

What such historic figures created is still writ large on our landscape in diocese, deanery and parish. The available records force us to operate at the level of kings and the great lords who surrounded them, but there is hardly a surname mentioned that is not numerous still in its ancient territory. These people managed parish temporalities, provided the priests and the educational establishments. Their descendants still live in those parishes and continue the same living Christian community. In unravelling their history we unravel our own age-old inheritance.

A Turbulent Boundary – Medieval West Tyrone

The area of the diocese of Derry, now recognised as west Tyrone, is one of the blanker spaces on the map of late medieval Ireland. That this is so is mainly due to deficiencies in such records as have survived the vicissitudes of time, particularly in the various collections of annals. It is clear that the sources available to the annalists were also quite deficient, either because local chronicles had already been lost, or perhaps had not been kept at all, for reasons we can no longer discover. It is possible, for example, to put together a fuller account of the diocese of Derry in the twelfth than in the thirteenth or fourteenth century. We can only guess, to take a case in point, at the process *relying on temporal power* by which Richard de Burgo, the Anglo-Norman 'red' Earl of Ulster, and his heirs came to claim rights of Church patronage in Derry by 1327. Some catastrophic upheaval had obviously disturbed the routine recording of events.

From the point of view of ecclesiastical organisation, most of west Tyrone, now made up of the baronies of Omagh and Strabane, is in the diocese of Derry, but its diocesan history is quite complicated. Much of it had originally been in the *paruchia* of Ardstraw, which served the Uí Fiachrach kindred, themselves belonging to the Airghialla rivals of Cineál Eoghain. Traces of this can still be seen in the parishes of Cappagh (*Ceapach*) and Langfield (*Leamhchoill*), whose medieval patron was St Eoghan of Ardstraw. The church of Badoney (*Both Domhnaigh*) now in Derry, and that of Donaghanie (*Domhnach an Eich*), now in Armagh, both looked to St Patrick and to Armagh, while Drumragh (*Droim Rátha*) in the diocese of Derry and Termonmaguirk (*Tearmann Mhic Oirc*) in the archdiocese of Armagh came to share the patronage of St Columba and presumably looked to monastic Derry. The diocesan boundary was drawn between them in the twelfth century, probably after some 'horse-trading', and presumably before areas now in the north of the diocese of Clogher (*Clochar*) were drawn into the Ó Néill hegemony.

The present Armagh/Derry diocesan boundary came from the political frontier agreed eventually between two federations – one led by Mac Lochlainn and the other by Ó Néill, vying for supremacy within the Cineál Eoghain dynasty. When Clann Lochlainn disappeared from view as a political force, first as a result of the inroads made by the Anglo-Normans and secondly by their defeat at the battle of Caméirí (Cummery) near Omagh in 1241 by the alliance of Maoleachlainn Ó Dónaill and Brian Ó Néill, other groupings sought prominence in the area that Mac Lochlainn had controlled before the Anglo-Normans had intervened. Clann Diarmada (*Ó Cairealláin*), who had been ousted by Cineál Moain (*Ó Gormlaigh/Ó Luinigh*) from their lands in east Donegal (now the parish of *Domhnach Mór Mhaigh Iotha* or Donaghmore), moved closer to their Mac Lochlainn allies around Derry and left their name on the parish of Clann Diarmada (now Clon- or Glen-dermot) on the east bank of the Foyle. Clann Diarmada were a branch of Clann Chonchúir. However it was another kindred descended from Conchúr, made up of Ó Catháin, Ó Maoláin and others, who were to have the greater sway in north Derry, and for the next three hundred years the Foyle was to be the frontier they shared with Cineál Chonaill, who from about 1200 were led by Ó Dónaill and Ó Dochartaigh.[59]

It is perhaps in this process of shifting leadership that there lies the origin of the claim that Bishop Giolla an Choimdhe (*Germanus* in Latin) Ó Cearbhalláin of Derry (+ 1279) wrested by military force what had been the Airghialla diocese of Ardstraw in west Tyrone from the main Airghialla diocese of Clochar. The synods of the twelfth century do not include all of the present west Tyrone in Clochar. The diocesan (and barony) boundary does, however, have every appearance of being more political than religious in significance, since it includes most of the Derg basin, and on any map, whether of counties or dioceses, it has the appearance of a protrusion.

One of the boundary points of the diocese of Ardstraw, according to the Synod of Rath Breasail (1111), was *Loch Craoi*. The late Fr Pádraig Ó Gallachair has given what seems to be the most plausible identification

---

59. Cf. Henry A. Jefferies and Ciarán Devlin, eds, *History of the Diocese of Derry from Earliest Times* (Dublin: Four Courts Press, 2000).

of the place thus far, as *Lough Lee* near Drumquin.[60] If he was right, it would tilt the balance of the boundary argument, suggesting that what had been the ancient *tearmann* of Loch Derg was divided between Termonmagrath, which is still in Clochar, and Termonamongan now in Derry.

Nonetheless, while the annexation may have happened during the episcopate of Bishop Ó Cearbhalláin, the annexing forces could only have been those permitted by the political leaders of Cineál Moain. There is no contemporary example in Cineál Eoghain of an ecclesiastic being allowed to act as a military leader while remaining an ecclesiastic. (The one such whose name might suggest otherwise is Dónall Cléireach Ó Catháin, who may originally have been a cleric at some minor level.) Muintir Chearbhalláin became erenaghs[61] at Clonleigh (Lifford) and belonged to Cineál Iolanna, a minor sept of Cineal Eoghain *na hInse*. In fact, there is reason to believe that all the main ecclesiastical protagonists in this episode belonged to Cineál Eoghain *na hInse*,[62] including the Ó Bragáin[63] brothers, both Cistercians of Mellifont and bishops of Clochar, said to have been on the losing side to Bishop Ó Cearbhalláin.

Apart from the names which one would expect to find in the annals in this contentious area (like Ó Néill, Ó Dónaill or Ó Catháin), the only sept given much prominence in the contemporary record is Ó Gormlaigh of Cineál Moain, the deaths of whose leaders figure quite frequently there, indicating that they were the early local beneficiaries of the fall of the kingdom of the Uí Fiachrach of Ard Sratha, especially since they had been firm allies of Ó Néill, and on the winning side in the long civil strife with Mac Lochlainn. This would help to explain that 'special intimacy with the O'Gormleys of Cineál Moain', which Nicholas Williams detects in the poetry of Giolla Bhríde Mac Con Mí (died c. 1272),[64] since the Mac Con Mí lands centred on Loch Uí Mhaoldubháin

---

60. See *Clogher Record* VII, 3 (1975), pp. 336–7.
61. Administrators of churchlands, responsible for upkeep of church buildings and sustenance of the clergy.
62. These were the branches of the Cineál who remained on in Inis Eoghain, or left only later when the Uí Néill moved out. Ó Cearbhalláin belonged to the *Bréadach* (Moville) and Ó Bracáin to Cineál Aodh Mhic Fhearghasa. Note that the names Ó Cearbhalláin (O'Carolan) and Ó Cairealláin (Carlin/Kerlin) differ in origin and are quite separate names.
63. Cf. AU 1179, where Cinaeth, son of Art Ó Bragáin, is described as belonging to 'the people (*muintir*) of Amhlaidh Ó Gormlaigh', killed treacherously by Donnchadh Ó Cairealláin.
64. Cf. N.J.A. Williams, *The Poetry of Giolla Brighde Mac Con Midhe* (Dublin: Irish Texts Society, 1980), p. 3.

(now in the Baronscourt demesne). The Ó Gormlaigh lordship, the origin of the parish of Urney – included Strabane and the area around it – must have reached well up the Derg valley, since in *Ceart Uí Néill* Cineál Moain is responsible for Killeter.[65]

Given the infrequency of entries in the annals, one could be forgiven for thinking that otherwise nothing much happened in Tír Eoghain for most of the fourteenth century. This may perhaps have been due to the decline of Ardstraw as an ecclesiastical centre, since it is noticeable that entries from the Foyle basin tail off after about 1220. One might posit the existence of a Book of Ardstraw as a source for the annalists before that date.

When local entries do resume, the power of Ó Gormlaigh in turn had waned as Ó Dónaill ingerence increased and they established themselves in Maigh Iotha, calling themselves now lords of Cineál Moain, which was by this time descriptive of the area around the Finn River rather than denoting the kindred of that name. Cineál Moain – the kindred – lost the western part of their lands and were moved away from the Finn and Mourne valleys. Some pushed up Glenelly and the Owenkillew and Owenreagh glens, to which they gave the alternative name by which the sept is known, *Muintir Luinigh* (Munterlony). The Mourne/Derg system became a contentious frontier between Ó Dónaill and Ó Néill. Older population centres, of religious significance, gave way to strong defensive points. It is interesting that only at this stage of their history did these lords feel the need to construct castles and tower houses. The castles were to become the focus for what later became the main towns of the area: Castlefin (built before 1434, the town of Neachtán Ó Dónaill) and Lifford, later fortified by Mánas Ó Dónaill. Over against them Omagh, Fintona, Dromore, Castlederg (before 1497), Strabane and Newtownstewart (which is already called 'an Baile Nua' by the Four Masters and known as 'the Newtown' to Sir Henry Docwra in 1600), were all initiated by branches of the Uí Néill.

The attention that they paid to their western frontier is exemplified by the entry in the annals, which tells us that Dónall Caol Ó Néill died at storied Loch Laoghaire (now *Lough Mary* in Baronscourt demesne) in 1325. This was sixty-five years after the death of his father, Brian Rua, *Brian Chath an Dúin* as he was called after his bloody defeat at the hands of the Anglo-Normans at Downpatrick. The poet Giolla Bhríde

---

65. E. Ó Doibhlin, *O'Neill's 'Own Country' and its Families*, D.Ó Doibhlin, ed. (Donaghmore: Donaghmore Historical Society, 1998), p. 51.

Mac Con Mi, however, also refers to him as *Brian Locha Laoghaire*.[66] Dónall Caol, unlike his father, would appear to have died in his bed after returning from a pilgrimage to Rome.[67] Dónall's son Seán had been slain by an Ó Dónaill (Aodh, son of Dónall Óg) in Derry seven years earlier while his father's attention was absorbed by the devastating invasion of Edward the Bruce. Éamon Ó Doibhlin asserts that it was Dónall Caol who built the first Ó Neill castle at Dungannon,[68] but his son Aodh Ramhar (d. 1364) is described in the *Leabhar Eoghanach* as *Aodh an Fhraochmhaighe. An Fraochmhaigh* is believed to be the castle at Augher[69] where he had his main residence and a separate banqueting-hall in a town of some sixty houses (with, arguably then, about 200 fighting-men as garrison).[70] What this information implies about the size and importance of contemporary Dungannon is an open question. It would seem obvious that Dónall and Aodh Ramhar should retain at least a defensive presence near their western border, although in that difficult century of famine, disease and political instability there may well have been other preoccupations.

Rivalry between various branches of Ó Dónaill in the 1340s and 1350s allowed Aodh Ramhar Ó Néill to intervene in the affairs of Cineál Chonaill, but after Aodh's death in 1364 the dynastic dispute between his own sons, Niall and Dónall, must have led to the situation being reversed. In 1370, Niall and Dónall divided *Tír Eoghain* between them and Dónall recognised Niall, soon to be styled Niall Mór, as lord and gave him hostages. What the division was is unstated, and there is no further mention of Dónall, son of Aodh Ramhar.

Niall Mór reserved east Tír Eoghain for himself, it would appear, since he is stated to have built a house at *Eamhain Macha* to host a convention for the poetic order in 1387. He must also have made a further departure of policy for it was at this time that his son, and intended successor, Anraí Aimhréidh, takes up residence on the western borders. The name of Anraí has lived on in folk tradition and in the ruined stonework of the so-called 'Harry Avery's Castle' near Newtownstewart, so that he is one of the best-known of the medieval Ó Néills. The *Leabhar Eoghanach* gives him six years as Ó Néill but in

---

66. Cf. Williams, op. cit., pp. 151, 317.
67. Cf. Tadhg Ó Donnchadha, ed., *Leabhar Cloinne Aodha Buidhe* (Dublin, 1931), p. 32.
68. Ó Doibhlin E., op. cit., p. 62.
69. *Onomasticon Gadelicum* identifies *An Fraochmhaigh* as Augher.
70. *Leabhar Chloinne Aodha Buí*, p. 32: *dúnárus agus baile bunaidh ... trí fichid teach ... teach uaigneach óla.*

fact he died before his father. He was given the sobriquet *aimhréidh* (meaning, 'uneven, difficult, contentious'). According to the *Annals of Loch Cé*, it was given to him 'per antiphrasim' because he was in fact quite the opposite. His wife, Aifric, was daughter of Aodh *na Fiodhbhaighe* Ó Néill of Clann Aodha Buí (Clandeboye) and died three years before him. Anraí had at least seven sons, it would seem.

The annalistic entries about him are perhaps of ecclesiastical provenance, since they record unusually accurately the date of his death, the feast of St Brendan (16 May 1392) and go into some detail about the manner of it. The tone is deeply respectful, describing him as *rídhamhna Éireann* de jure (*Annals of Loch Cé* and *Annals of Connacht*), as *dea-ábhar ardrí* (*Annals of the Four Masters, Annals of Ulster*),[71] adding that he would have been King of Ulster if he had lived, and listing many of his virtues. *Miscellaneous Annals*, however, refer to him as 'a perverse, corrupt, wicked man',[72] which is in accord with tradition if not with most of the historical sources. (From our distance, it might seem a description rather more in keeping with what we know of the character of his son Dónall Bog.)It is remarkable that he has lived on in tradition, even if only in caricature. He is said to have donated lands free of tithe to the friary of the Third Order Regular of St Francis at *Comhrac* (Corick 'Abbey'), but his dates make him seem perhaps too early to have been involved with this foundation.[73] Furthermore, the friary at *Pobal* (near Newtownstewart) would have been much nearer his keep.

Most of the rest of Anraí's career occurs during the lost section of our annals. In 1380 his support tilted the balance in favour of Tarlach an Fhíona, son of Niall Garbh the First, who had just seized the position of Ó Dónaill.[74] This would indicate that he was the power in west Tyrone by this date, the time at which presumably he built the imposing castle named after him. In fact, the number of strong points mentioned in association with the Ardstraw/Newtownstewart

71. Although this kind of editorial comment is common in the annals, it is rarely so fulsome. On the question of the position within the lordship and succession rights of *rídhamhna* (royal heir) or *ábhar rí* (one eligible to be king), see Katharine Simms, *From Kings to Warlords* (Suffolk: Boydell & Brewer Ltd, 1987), pp. 55–8.
72. Ad ann., 'Claon coirpthe colach' – the epithets would seem to point to some sexual irregularity.
73. See J.K. O'Doherty, *Derriana: Essays and Occasional Verses* (Dublin: Sealy, Bryers and Walker, 1902), pp. 64–8, for history, tradition and folklore about him.
74. *Annals of Ulster*, ad ann.

area may be confusing, but they certainly underline the importance at that time of controlling it: *Loch Laoghaire, an Caisleán Maol, an Seanchaisleán, an Carraigín,*[75] *an Baile Nua,* clearly not all of them operative at the same time, or indeed mutually exclusive. A working hypothesis might be that in time Anraí's castle became known as *an Seanchaisleán* (the 'Old Castle').[76]

As already noted, Anraí is mentioned only once in the annals apart from his obituary, but in the year his wife died (1389), his son – unnamed, but probably Brian or Dónall – went raiding in Magh Ene, between Erne and Drowes. In the year that Anraí died, Tarlach an Fhíona Ó Dónaill returned the compliment by raiding Clann Anraí and taking Dónall captive, probably as a way of controlling his unruly neighbours. Dónall's brothers figured in the 'great army' led by their grandfather Niall Mór Ó Néill to overawe Cineál Chonaill in 1392. A Connacht force moved simultaneously north until it was eventually thrown back by Cineál Chonaill, while at the other end of the lordship Cineál Eoghain plundered Ó Dochartaigh's lands 'both civil and religious'. Ó Néill and Ó Dónaill finally came face to face at Fearsaid Mhór on Loch Swilly, but the outcome was a peace agreement, no doubt with Dónall, son of Anraí, being released as part of the bargain.

If that was the case, it is fair to say that making peace was not often to be the distinguishing mark of his career. In the power politics of the time Dónall was a ruthless operator. He is known to history as *Dónall Bog,* not improbably because he was far from 'soft'. In 1395 Ó Dónaill despoiled the lands of Clann Anraí again and were too much for the forces that had pursued them. In the defeat Brian, Dónall's brother, and thirteen of their stalwarts were captured and held for ransom. Perhaps because they had not been supported by their cousins in east *Tír Eoghain,* Dónall turned on them, plundered and took captive Brian, son of the ageing Niall Mór first of all, and then returned to Ó Néill's own town where he carried off Ó Neill's wife and some other prominent figures and took them to the English, just about the time that Niall

---

75. The editor of the *Annals of Ulster* identifies *an Carraigín* as Carrigans (Co. Donegal), whereas in fact it denotes a hill close to Newtownstewart (now known as 'Mary Gray').

76. For *an Seanchaisleán,* see the note of Micheál Ó Cléirigh quoted by Fr Paul Walsh, '*I mbaile an tSeanchaisleáin de leataoibh Sléibhe Troim*' – 'on the side of Sliabh Troim.' Sliabh Troim is now known as 'Bessy Bell'. Cf. P. Walsh, *Irish Men of Learning,* Ó Lochlainn, ed. (Dublin: At the Sign of Three Candles Press, 1947), p. 179n.

Óg, Niall Mór's son and successor, was submitting to English King Richard II in Dundalk. It may be guessed from such manoeuvres just how statesmanlike the 'wars' of these aristocrats were. The result of all this *Realpolitik* was that Niall Mór ransomed Brian, son of Anraí and brother of Dónall Bog, from Tarlach an Fhíona Ó Dónaill for horses, armour and other valuables and delivered him to Dónall Bog, who in his turn released Brian, son of Niall Mór.

If Anraí Aimhréidh had been installed to protect the western boundary of Cineál Eoghain, his sons on the other hand used their proximity to Cineál Chonaill to seek allies in their attempt to wrest the supreme power from the eastern branch of the O'Neills led by Niall Óg, son of Niall Mór, the main obstacle to their progression to leadership of the Cineál (to which they had at least a legal entitlement on foot of the *deirbhfhine* principle).

Níall Mór's last military foray was that of 1397 against Tarlach an Fhíona Ó Dónaill, by now in alliance with Sliocht Anraí. It was an invasion that ended unusually in that Ó Néill and his forces grew weary and slipped off homewards almost unnoticed by the Conallaigh and Sliocht Anraí, apart from a few skirmishes and the capture of some horses. The weariness was undoubtedly that of the old man Niall Mór who retired and died shortly afterwards.

For practically the following century, we can only guess at the difficulties which must have assailed any ecclesiastical administration amid the welter of changing alliances, raid and counter-raid among the petty lords on what was becoming politically the most unstable border region of the diocese of Derry. How were the parish boundaries maintained, granted that they originated often in the domain of a local family? Was the economic basis of that administration deeply affected, or was all this aristocratic agitation just another manifestation of what the Church faced in many a medieval society? What of everyday life? Could a parish priest or a Franciscan friar go about his business with some degree of security?

Unfortunately, the nobility occupy too great a prominence on the historical scene for the annals to provide answers to such 'ordinary' questions. At any rate, to begin to consider these matters, we are obliged to detail the fortunes of the petty lords in order to be clear on the background against which Church life was lived.

What becomes clear is that the fortunes of Sliocht Anraí Aimhréidh become, with the death of Niall Mór, closely involved with Cineál Chonaill on the other side of this unstable boundary. Indeed, in an entry in the *Annals of Ulster* for 1398, they would even seem to be numbered among the lords and the assembly (*taoisigh agus oireacht*) who turned against the Ó Dónaill of the time. They are listed there with another family, *Clann tSeáin* (Ó Dónaill), whose father Seán had been ousted by Tarlach an Fhíona (with their own father's help!). Their aim of course was to profit from his difficulties, but the same Tarlach an Fhíona was not so easily daunted; in that year he was the only leader in Ulster – *Gall* or *Gael* – not to submit to Niall Óg Ó Néill.

When Niall Óg succeeded his father Niall Mór as Ó Néill, he marked his succession in the customary way, by an inauguration raid or *creach* on south Tír Chonaill – *Tír Aodha* as it was called – and the lands of the Abbey of Eas Rua. It seems to have been as inconclusive as most of these ritual encounters were, but an important political aspect of it was that Sliocht Anraí were prominent in support of Niall Óg against Ó Dónaill. In 1399, Sliocht Anraí attacked the English of Dundalk (*Gaill an tSráidbhaile*). The annals give no reason. It was probably just another ritual raid, but the outcome must have surprised them: Sliocht Anraí were heavily defeated, some of them were even killed, Dónall Bog was taken prisoner, an offer of ransom was refused and Dónall was packed off to England.

Two years later, in 1401, Niall Óg, the new *taoiseach* of Cineál Eoghain, made another raid on Ó Dónaill without obvious success. They later concluded an alliance at Caoluisce on the Erne and Ó Dónaill submitted to Ó Néill (*Annals of Ulster*, 1402). Brian, son of Anraí, did not consider himself bound by any such agreement and attacked Cineál Chonaill. He seemed to have won the day and, buoyed by success, decided to raid Anraí Ó Gormlaigh on the way home. They killed Ó Gormlaigh and were driving off their booty with Brian and a small force acting as rearguard, when Ó Dónaill caught up with them. Brian was killed in the ensuing skirmish. At this stage, Dónall Bog was finally ransomed from the English, perhaps with a view to disrupting the entente between Ó Néill and Ó Dónaill.

Sure enough, his spell in captivity had taught him nothing, for the next year Ó Néill and Sliocht Anraí were at daggers drawn again and 'destroyed the country in every direction between them', in the typical way of the nobility of medieval Europe, kept in style by others who had to pick up the pieces after them. Perhaps, to get some idea of what 'Christendom' was like in that age one has only to glance through Shakespeare's historical plays, or recall the French serial novel *Les Rois maudits*, broadcast as a television series, *The Accursed Kings*, some years ago, or even reflect again on the relationships between those most 'civilised' of political entities in that period, the Italian city-states of the Renaissance.

Fate took a hand in this tangled tale later in 1402. Niall Óg died of natural causes 'after anointing and penance', to be followed by his son and successor Brian Óg as a result of smallpox, and in the next year by his brother Brian. Dónall Bog, son of Anraí, became Ó Néill, the legalities being fulfilled as events seem to indicate, although he was to face the abiding hostility of Eoghan Mór, son of Niall Óg. In 1410, Eoghan's brother-in-law, probably by arrangement, made Dónall Bog captive – 'which was not fitting', comment the *Annals of the Four Masters* – and handed him over to Eoghan, who in turn sent him on to Mag Uír with instructions for him to be kept in close confinement (*imchoimeád*). Two years later Aodh, Dónall's brother, escaped from custody in Dublin after ten years there and immediately demanded Donall's release, but without success. He bided his time, and in 1414 caught Eoghan by surprise and took him hostage. In an exchange both Eoghan and Dónall Bog were released and Dónall reassumed the lordship.

Over the next years, alliances alter with confusing regularity. In 1417 Ó Néill (Dónall) attacked Neachtán, son of Tarlach an Fhíona Ó Dónaill at Carn Glas (*Tops*) between Raphoe and Donaghmore. In 1448 Niall Garbh, son of Tarlach an Fhíona, harried Dónall Ó Néill into exile with Mac Uílín (Mac Quillan) in Co. Antrim, while Dónall's nephew, Brian Óg, son of Brian, son of Anraí Aimhréidh, was involved in the capture of Tomás Óg Mag Uír – probably in retaliation for Dónall Bog's captivity in Fermanagh in 1410. In 1419 Dónall is back at war with Eoghan, and probably in exasperation 'all the Gaeil of Ulster' – Ó Dónaill, Eoghan Ó Neill,[77] Mag Uír, Mac Mathúna come together to banish him to internment among the *Gaill* of Ulster, probably at Carrickfergus, 'with great dishonour', say the annals. Even Clann Aodha Buí (Ó Néill), for once on the same side as Dungannon, raided the

---

77. It was perhaps relevant that Tarlach an Fhíona Ó Dónaill was Eoghan Mór's uncle by marriage. His first (?) wife was a daughter of Niall Mór and therefore a sister of Anraí Aimhréidh and of Niall Óg Ó Néill, and mother of Niall Garbh and Neachtán, who both succeeded their father in turn as Ó Dónaill. Anraí Aimhréidh's sons seem to have allied themselves with the opposition within Cineál Chonaill, the descendants of Seán Ó Dónaill, son of Conchúr, whom Tarlach had removed as lord, and who was married to another daughter of Niall Mór.

flocks of his *caoraíocht*[78] in the Glens of Antrim. Another attempted comeback in 1420 leads to him being banished once more, this time to Ó Conchúir of Sligo. By 1423 he was back in the fold again, still Ó Néill (the legalities of his position must have been unassailable), now in alliance with Eoghan Mór and 'all the Gaeil of Ulster', forcing the *Gaill* of Dundalk and Meath to pay their tribute.

Subsequently, during negotiations with the said *Gaill*, when the Earl of March died, the Irish leaders were imprisoned by Lord Furnival. Amongst them was Ó Mealláin, custodian of *Clog an Uachta*, St Patrick's Bell, who was probably there as a surety, and which would seem to argue a breach of faith. The leaders – Ó Néill, Neachtán Ó Dónaill, Eoghan Ó Néill, Ó Néill Buí, Mac Uílín – were taken to Dublin. Ó Néill and the last two accepted English terms and were released forthwith, but it was later, in 1425, before Eoghan Mór and in 1426 before Neachtán were ransomed, the latter having to leave his son Tarlach (presumably his son Tarlach Cairbreach) as a hostage in his stead. Needless to say, this policy led to further dissension in Ulster. In 1427 Ó Dónaill attacked Mac Uílín, the ally of Ó Néill, in support of Ó Néill Buí, the head of the Clandeboye O'Neills. Apart from a successful intervention as Ó Néill on the side of Ó Raghailligh in a power struggle with Ó Ruairc in Breifne in 1429, the annals make no further mention of Dónall.[79] Presumably he retained his legal title as Ó Néill while real power had passed to his rival Eoghan, son of Niall Óg, a much more energetic figure.

The end of Dónall Bog came in 1432; he was done to death, we are told, in *Oireacht Uí Chatháin* by Dónall and Aibhne, sons of Diarmaid Ó Catháin. Also killed on that occasion were Dónall, son of Ó Néill, Pádraig Ó Maolchalainn and the son of Ó Mealláin, while Eoghan Mór was inaugurated Ó Neill in his place. This is a most interesting incident, even if we could have done with more information. As joint custodians of *Clog an Uachta*, St Patrick's Bell, Ó Maolchalainn and Ó Mealláin's son must have been there in an official capacity. Were they there to keep the peace

---

78. The *caoraíocht* – a herd of livestock together with the body of herdsmen and their families attached to it, accompanied military expeditions outside home territory to provide supplies for the fighting men. Since these were used as a weapon of war at times (to graze down and thus set back the enemies' crops), it is probable that Clann Aodha Buí did not welcome the competition Dónall Bog had brought. See A.T. Lucas, *Cattle in Ancient Ireland* (Kilkenny: Boethius Press, 1989), pp. 88–102.

79. Katharine Simms, op. cit., p. 53, suggests that Eoghan was the real leader of this expedition.

or to warn? The entry in the *Annals of the Four Masters* does not say who killed them, but it goes on to make an unusually solemn statement about the status of the inauguration of his successor. The *righeadh*[80] of Eoghan Mór was done on Leac na Rí at Tulach Óg unanimously, 'by the will of God and men, bishops and *ollúna*'. It was Ó Catháin, of course, who had the right to inaugurate the new Ó Néill. All this gives Dónall's death something of the appearance of a ritual execution for non-fulfilment of duty, perhaps after due warning by the custodians of the shrine. Intriguingly, which is perhaps the right word in this context, Dónall Bog seems to have gone willingly to Muintir Chatháin, which might indicate that the joint custodians (whom the *Annals of Ulster* do not mention) went along to provide a safe conduct. The *Annals of Loch Cé* add that the killing took place at Eanach (Enagh), near Derry.

Whatever about his position as Ó Néill, by 1431 Dónall Bog and his family seem at best to have been clinging perilously to their west Tyrone homeland because in that year Neachtán Ó Dónaill attacked and captured the castle of Loch Laoghaire from one Tarlach Ó Dónaill and ransacked it of all its valuables. Tarlach was such a common name amongst the Ó Dónaill family that one can only guess at who he was or what his role might have been.[81] But this had been an Ó Néill residence. Was he there in the interests of Sliocht Anraí Aimhréidh as ward of the castle or some such, and did his expulsion result from a conference Neachtán and Eoghan Mór had had earlier that year? The entry may however indicate that Cineál Chonaill had expanded the area under their control to include not merely the Finn but the Derg valley as well.

In 1435, a year in the winter of which MagUír was able to escape the invading Ó Néill forces by bringing all his valuables, his pack-horses and his cattle away to safety across a frozen Loch Erne, Neachtán Ó Dónaill and Brian Óg Ó Néill (grandson of Anraí Aimhréidh) made a pact to attack Ó Néill (Eoghan) and his sons Anraí and Aodh. Ó Néill moved his *caoraíocht* swiftly into Cineál Moain (the Urney district not the sept which was in the Finn valley by this time), and made camp at *na Rasa* – probably 'the Raws' between Castlefin and Castlederg. Neachtán and Brian Óg attacked and captured Ó Neill's *longfort* or 'fortified encampment'. At this stage Anraí Ó Néill demonstrated the qualities that were to make him a most effective leader, for he persuaded his followers, including their

---

80. Inauguration as *rí* (king).
81. Seán Ó Dónaill had a grandson called Tarlach, son of Aodh, son of Seán (Ó Cléirigh 65).

THE MAKING OF THE DIOCESE

galloglass captain Mac Dónaill, to attack at night. In bitter hand-to-hand fighting Ó Néill's forces were victorious. Aodh (son of Eoghan) Ó Néill seriously wounded Brian Óg with his spear, and Neachtán Ó Dónaill and Brian Óg fled the field, leaving their followers and galloglasses, led by Mac Suibhne of Fanad, to extricate themselves as best they could. Mac Suibhne defended an orderly retreat down the Derg, perhaps the less happy recourse for him since it led farther and farther from his home base in Fanad, but towards the home base of his absent leader, Brian Óg. Mac Suibhne's defensive line was finally overcome at Sliabh Troim ('Bessy Bell') and they were made captive.

Brian Óg, recovered from his wound, was given command of the castle of Áth Seanaigh (Ballyshannon) by his ally, Neachtán Ó Dónaill. But he was to prove as unreliable in peace as he had been in war, for he defected again to Ó Néill (Eoghan) while retaining control of the castle. It was a mistake, for Eoghan was not prepared to forgive his past treachery, punishing him brutally by cutting off a hand and a foot, and mutilating two of his sons. The family of Brian Óg reacted to this by seizing the fortification at Loch Laoghaire, which was by now back in the hands of Cineál Eoghain. Ó Néill (Eoghan) and his son Anraí surrounded the lake and sent for Tomás Óg MagUír, Lord of Fermanagh, to put to use his skill in making *coití* ('cots') to row across to the strongpoint. Clann Bhriain Óg recognised the inevitable, handed back the *crannóg* and made peace.

Brian Óg died in 1449. The place of death is unknown, but subsequent entries in the annals seem to indicate that his descendants went east to the territory of Clann Aodha Buí (Clandeboye),[82] the inveterate enemies of the *ríora* of Dungannon. Eoghan, Brian Óg's son, was there to defend himself and slay Niall, a son of Anraí, son of Eoghan Mór, who in 1450 had launched yet another *creach* (or cattle foray). In 1482, his relatives are still to be found in south Derry in the company of Clann Aodha Buí (with *Clann Dónall Donn na Banna*, perhaps), warring with Féilimí Ó Neill, son of Eoghan Mór, of *Gleann Con Cadhain* and *An Fharachta* (nowadays Glanconkeyne – the parishes of Ballinascreen and Kilcronaghan – and Orritor).

The policy of Niall Mór Ó Néill of installing his probable successor in such a position as to control the western border of the Cineál Eoghain

---

82. Those who left were the group in leadership at the top of the clann, together with their clients and dependants. The bulk of the people would simply have learnt to live with a new élite.

state had led to rebellion, a weakening of the frontier and at best an uneasy peace. Anraí, son of Eoghan, was to prove perhaps the most able leader of the dynasty in his time, acting as king-maker in Cineál Chonaill and controlling Castlefin, Cineál Moain and the Derg valley. He or his father Eoghan may have had a blind spot where his brother Art was concerned. Art was to build a castle at Omagh and become a major figure in west Tyrone. In time his descendants, *Sliocht Airt na hÓmaighe*, were to cause even more problems for the Cineál than did those of Anraí Aimhréidh. By 1470, Sliocht Anraí Aimhréidh and Sliocht Airt had joined forces to raid the lands they had been forced out of by their relatives, around Omagh and Drumquin. *Sliocht Airt* faced up to the reality of their weak position and settled down in west Tyrone, if not in Omagh itself. *Sliocht Anraí* seem by then to have faded out of sight amongst Clann Aodha Buí (Clandeboye).

War in Medieval Ireland

The picture given by the annals of medieval Ireland that we have been following would seem to be one of almost uninterrupted warfare and one would be tempted to conclude that the entire country must have been a desert and religious life, in any real sense, a virtual impossibility. It would be wrong, however, to transfer to that time our contemporary experience of 'total war' with its wholesale destruction of cities or of vast stretches of countryside by 'scorched earth' policies. War generally in the Middle Ages, whether in Ireland or elsewhere, was primarily the business, even the pastime, of a military aristocracy. There is no doubt that, when waged in pursuit of political power or dynastic aggrandisement, battles could be bloody and ruthless, like the Ó Néill triumph at Caméirí in 1242, but in the ordinary course of events it was a much less impressive phenomenon. Only with the imperialism and religious hatreds of the sixteenth century were the tactics of methodic destruction and the killing and starvation of whole populations to become the tools of the Tudor conquest of the country.

Warfare between neighbouring *tuatha* or ruling families were usually raids by light cavalry, numbering no more than a few score horse. It permitted the demonstration of those personal qualities prized by an aristocracy: physical courage, inherited pride, skill in combat and generosity in handing out the plunder. In an agricultural economy, cattle were the main booty because they were moveable, and when successfully brought home were a welcome addition to the local food reserves as well as to the prestige of the local lord. Warfare in other words, as the renowned French historian Georges Duby puts it, was a form of harvesting.[83] It permitted leaders to demonstrate their military tactics, up-and-coming young noblemen to practice their swordsmanship and to live up to the norms demanded by family honour, to profit too from the division of the spoils or from the ransom of noble prisoners of war. Generally speaking, war did not involve the common people, farmers, tradesmen and so forth, the producers of wealth, except occasionally as what might now be called 'collateral damage'. It was certainly no purpose of the raiders to destroy an economy that would produce again for next year's expeditions. Rather it was to promote the reputation and influence of ruling families; and even political victory and aggrandisement rarely meant more than the right to collect taxes for a wider area of country.

While it is possible to follow from the annals, at least in outline, the complex and ever-changing political landscape of west Tyrone in the fifteenth century, down to within half a century of the cataclysm of foreign conquest and religious division – which began with the first of the Tudor monarchs in England, Henry VII – it is much more difficult to reconstruct the history of religious life and organisation in the same period. The doings of the local aristocracy practically monopolise the attention of the chroniclers. The consequences of that conquest at the end of the next century were to shed a ruthless light on at least the economic substructure of Church administration, if only with the purpose of alienating it for good. Paradoxically, by examining the records of confiscation a hundred years later, we can recover something at least of that organisation and that will be the subject of a later account in this volume. As far as religious life and faith are concerned, we can assure ourselves that it was vibrant and deeply-rooted enough to survive dispossession and persecution in the generations to come.

A Note on Genealogy

It may be a source of puzzlement to readers that genealogy plays such a prominent part in the study of medieval Irish history, as in the preceding essay. The reason is, as in the case of any military aristocracy, that the family origins of the Irish nobility were of the first importance in determining the legal and social status and the fame or influence of the lineage. This dual purpose was the responsibility of the learned class

---

83. See Georges Duby, *Le Dimanche de Bouvines* (Paris: Éditions Gallimard, 1973), p. 190.

of *seanchaithe* or historians, who discharged it so devotedly that they have left us a chronological framework, reliable at least as far back as the seventh century and probably unique in its kind in Europe.[84]

Their work presents itself in two forms: firstly the *ginealach* or pedigree, which aims to prove the blue blood of the contemporary lord by tracing his ancestry back to a historic or even prehistoric hero (like, say, Niall Naoighiallach), and in that way circulates that ancient heroism down to the living generation. The second form is the *craobhscaoileadh* (using the metaphor of the family tree), which begins with the ancient hero figure (like Míl or Milesius from whom all the Gaelic nobility claimed to be descended) and goes on to demonstrate at what stage a given lineage breaks off from the main royal stock or *ríora*, and consequently how closely or distantly they were related to it. Obviously, the legal and social consequences with regard to sharing in the heritage were all-important and the net result was a surprisingly well-preserved historical record.

Dynasties were intent on basing their legitimacy on distant and illustrious ancestors whose heroic qualities were passed down in direct descent from generation to generation. Only when the trail of remembered ancestors gave out would genealogists call up links with the mythical past, even back to pagan gods like Lugh and Nuada. Since as far back as the Twelfth-Century Reform and the new strictness imposed on Church schools, records were kept in the monasteries. The prime purpose of the first written genealogies in the seventh century may have been precisely to substitute a human ancestry for a pagan divine one. And so ancient Irish dynasties came to be traced back to Biblical origins, to Noah and the Flood and thence to Adam. The Christian subtext for this process was to demonstrate the common humanity of the nobility and therefore to remind them that they were all redeemed by Christ.

---

84. See Katharine Simms, *Medieval Gaelic Sources* (Dublin: Four Courts Press, 2009), pp. 39–56.

4

The Life of the Late Medieval Diocese

OUR PARISHES, THEIR PATRON SAINTS AND ERENAGHS

T
HE PARISH AS THE GEOGRAPHICAL CHURCH UNIT WE ARE
familiar with in Ireland originated in the thirteenth century,
following on from the creation of dioceses in the reform of
the Church in Ireland in the previous century. Until then the
focus was on the individual church as part of the *paruchia* claimed by
a monastic centre within which the bishop lived, responsible for the
sacramental charisms of his office but not necessarily with jurisdictional
authority. How the boundaries of individual parishes were arrived
at must be to a great extent a matter of conjecture. However, since
diocesan borders originated in political divisions, the same must be
true of parishes. Some of these seem to have been ancient divisions, like
Fahan – upper and lower— which may be commensurate with *Críoch
Mhuireadhaigh*, the area across the 'neck' of Inishowen, controlled by
Muireadhach, son of Eoghan, eponymous Lord of Inis Eoghain, in the
sixth century.

Conflict in the 1200s within the *Clann Chonchúir* branch of *Cineál
Eoghain* – the descendants of that same Eoghan – in what is now east
Co. Donegal, would seem to suggest that a temporary settlement led
to the creation of Donaghmore, territory of Ó Cairealláin (Kerlin) and
Urney, that of Ó Gormlaigh, while Ó Dónaill pushed on the Raphoe
frontier. The parish of Urney included the modern parishes of Mourne
and Castlederg (apart from Ardstraw West) and probably expanded
at a time to include Camus. The conflict was such that from around
Lifford Ó Catháin was forced away from the area to the Roe valley and
Ó Donnaile and Ó Doibhlin moved to east Tyrone. The ultimate result
in the area was that Ó Cairealláin and their *clann* also moved away from

Donaghmore towards Derry, where they would leave their name *Clann Diarmada* on Clondermott (somewhat more exact than Glendermott). Clonleigh may originate in the lands of Ó Laifeartaigh also at this time.

It is worth remembering that it was the *clann* leadership that moved. Most of the people stayed where they were. One should also be aware that a *clann* was more like a limited company, as Kenneth Nichols remarks, than a family grouping. Many surnames and occupations may have been involved. Thus, for example, one finds many Donegal surnames in west Tyrone as Ó Gormlaigh and their followers went east towards Badoney under pressure from Ó Dónaill. The power of Ó Dónaill encroached so much on the lands of Ó Néill at one stage that they occupied what is now Baronscourt (*Cúirt na Bairdne*) before being ousted. Imperialism is not a recent invention! There are then a number of matters that have to be borne in mind when considering how parishes came about, but it would seem that by the end of the thirteenth century parish boundaries were fairly settled. The process of causing an erstwhile ruling sept to move on need not have been violent. It could be done by turning them into 'clients', making them an offer of livestock, seed, etc., at a rent. If they were unable or unwilling to pay or repay in kind and in time they could be constrained as debtors to seek an alternative. The subject has not really been teased out.

It is proposed here to examine the name of each medieval parish to see what, if anything, that name tells us; to discuss its patrons and other saints; to take a look at its erenagh family, where known; and perhaps to uncover other relevant facts. We begin with a few general observations.

Airchinneach/**Erenagh**

The question of lay investiture in Church benefices and offices was very much a live issue in the twelfth century. The Church throughout Europe sought to put an end to simony and control of appointments that had had a deleterious effect on standards in Church life and preaching. After the Twelfth-Century Reform in Ireland, sustenance of clergy and maintenance of parish buildings in each parish became the responsibility of the *airchinneach*/erenagh. The country had been accustomed to a Church system based on the union of churches within a monastic alliance, where the abbot might be a layman or where the temporal affairs of a monastery were often in the hands of the *airchinneach*, said to be the successor (*an comharba*) of the founding saint and belonging among the descendants of the people who had originally granted its lands. In any new arrangement, where monastic establishments were to lose their importance, the interests of these people had to be taken into account.

The solution was a specifically Irish one. There would be an erenagh in each parish whose office would be hereditary, in the same way as *filíocht/* poetry, *seanchas/*history, etc., passed on generation by generation in the sept. To meet the legal requirements of the time, the job of erenagh was notionally a clerical one, in that at first the erenagh received tonsure. He was appointed by the bishop and was answerable only to him. If one thinks about a business rarely continuing in a family beyond the third generation, this appointment may have come about more often than one might think. Perhaps in keeping with custom, he was chosen from the *deirbhfhine* of his predecessor, although there are examples of erenagh clanna who were ousted completely, e.g. Mac Thaidhg by Ó Catháin at *Tearmann Chainnigh/*Termoncanice about 1400. When he came to Derry, Archbishop Colton examined the credentials of all Church personnel, including those of the erenaghs, an indication that the system was governed through law and documentation. Another essential role of the erenagh was to ensure that the tithes and taxes due to the bishop were collected and paid, and of course, the erenagh would have had tenants and workers.

Rather than being responsible for monastic lands, the erenagh became responsible within a new system of churchland tenure, *bailte bó* or townlands, set aside for the support of each parish.[1] The initial arrangement must have had the full support of civil power, because these lands are usually amongst the best land in any parish and are contiguous. According to the jurors at the pre-Plantation *Inquisitions for Coleraine County* (most of whom belonged to erenagh families):

> Donnell Mc Hugh O'Neale, kinge of Ireland, did, longe before busshops were made in the same Irelande, give unto certain holy men, whom they call *sancti patres*, severall portions of land and a third parte of all the tithes that they should say praiers and bear a third parte of the charge of repairing and maintaining the parishe church, thother two third parts being borne by the parson and the vicar to whom the rest of the tithes is yerely paied, and also for their owne honor and sustentation [*sic*].

1. Might it have been at this stage that that peculiarly Irish concept of the *baile bó* or *taite* was decided on? Many of them are named for things so ephemeral that one can only wonder if someone in authority asked: 'What do you call this place?' and was answered with the first thing that came into the local's head.

The only Dónall Ó Néill who was King of Ireland was Dónall Ard Macha (+980), but he was son of Muircheartach na gCochall Craicinn. The person the jurors had in mind must have been Dónall Dábhaill (RÉ 887–915), son of Aodh Finnliath, but he was Ó Néill only in the sense that he was one of the Uí Néill, descended distantly from Niall Naoighiallach (+c.453). The surname Ó Néill as we know it originated with the grandchildren of Dónall Dábhaill's brother Niall Glúndubh (RÉ 916–19). The purpose of the *Inquisitions* was to establish what lands belonged to the Church, so that they could be retained for the established Church. Most of the Coleraine jurors belonged to the erenagh families and their sworn description of the erenagh lands is more complete than are the *Inquisitions* for Tyrone or Donegal. Their historical perspective, however, is in need of some fine-tuning. Three of the fourteen jurors for the 'county of the city of Derry' were Irish: Éamann Óg Ó hÉigeartaigh, Mánas Mag Rabhartaigh and Donncha Ó Daighre (Deery), all with ecclesiastical positions. Incidentally, the sequestrated erenagh lands were to be tightly planted.

The role of erenagh had to be made an attractive proposition with the result that, in most parishes, four townlands/one quarter were set aside, but it could rise to six in Ballinascreen, to ten in Ardstraw and to all the parish as mensal lands in Tamlaghtard where the bishop had a residence. The reason for the larger number in some parishes is unclear, but one suspects that it had something to do with the education of the clergy, in which case greater resources would have been needed. Since the education of priests took place by apprenticeship to practising priests in those days before seminaries, one can probably also infer that the erenagh in such a parish had a serious contribution to make since his office would have represented continuity. Logic and common sense, one would think, would lead erenaghs to communicate with other erenaghs, as happens in any occupation, thus inevitably creating something of a joint policy.

As well as the erenagh, there was a *tearmannach* or 'termoner' who had a similar but more exalted position at a *tearmann*, a church which had rights of sanctuary, as at *Tearmann Chainnigh* (Limavady) or *Tearmann Uí Mhongáin* (Aghyaran) or *Tearmann Doire*/the Termonderry we read about in the Plantation Papers. Of lesser importance was the *dúchasach* or *nativus* whose role is unclear. Something like this may have been the role of *O Caran*, suggested as 'erenagh at Culkeeragh'.[2] There were, on occasion, a number of erenaghs in some parishes.

The erenagh also had an important social role since he had an obligation to provide for travellers, making him the successor – under Church auspices – of the *brughaidh* of earlier times with his obligation to hospitality. The implications of this role would seem to call for the makings of a township at each parish church. This would seem to be borne out by Archbishop Colton's Visitation in 1397 where Cappagh could not provide sufficient accommodation for a large party, but Ardstraw, Urney and Banagher could. Ardstraw, Urney and Banagher had horses readily available for such a party, but those of Leckpatrick were out grazing. Colton seems to have no difficulty communicating with curate and erenagh at Cappagh, which may mean that they were at home in Latin or, less likely, that he had learnt some Irish in Dublin. There were also clerics from Armagh in the company to interpret. Many of the bardic families became erenaghs, for example *Mac Con Mí* at Ardstraw or *Mac an Bhaird Uí Cheallaigh* at Urney.

One of the results of the system was that many of the clergy, not unexpectedly, came from the erenagh families, partly to ensure control of emoluments, partly because it would have gone with the erenagh's job to be concerned with provision of priests. It meant that there was no shortage of priests – some of whom succeeded their father in the occupation. This may demonstrate an irregularity about standards, how general one cannot be sure. Records of dispensation before ordination for illegitimacy or for being the son of a priest may be read as the exceptions or the norm, although, given the wider definition of consanguinity (to the third degree), difficulties about legitimacy at law due to invalid marriages were more likely to happen. It would seem that the rector of a parish (what we might call a parish priest) was sometimes a young man in training for priesthood who would be ordained later and only then become a curate. There may also have been another level of 'working' priests below those whose names occur in the records. Questions arise that we cannot answer: was there a

2. See T.W. Moody and J.G. Simms, eds, *The Bishopric of Derry and the Irish Society of London* (Dublin, 1968), I, 216. The name is indexed there as O'Cavan but spelled with an 'r' in the text. See also, 'Cormuk Corran of Grange in the Liberties, aged sixty-nine, fisherman … from his youth', II, 80; 'Owen O Corran, aged thirty-two, fisherman'. II, 81. Giolla an Choimdhe Ó Caráin was Bishop of Raphoe before succeeding Conchúr Mac Con Choille at Armagh c. 1175. The name may have been transmogrified to McCarron since.

school for erenaghs similar to those for the *filí* (poets)? Was there involvement of the theological school at Armagh? Does the name 'Mac Fhir Léinn' (McErlean) – son of the theologian – so common in south Derry, indicate a hereditary occupation or just the descendants of a particularly celebrated 'fear léinn'? Were the theologians laymen, as is found in Greece?

Saint

When Pope John Paul II was being buried, there were cries of 'santo subito', indicating that some people felt he should be canonised immediately. We have grown used to a canonical procedure before someone is recognised as being worthy of being venerated as a saint. For the first millennium, however, the recognition of sanctity was within the competence of local churches. The Church in the eighth to the tenth centuries was in such a state of crisis and the proliferation of devotions was approaching such anarchy that the process had to be controlled and centralised. The first occurrence of the word 'canonization' occurs in 1016 but it became customary for the papacy to declare saints only from the late twelfth century, to eliminate the risk of error and ensure that such figures proposed would be models of Christian behaviour. As a result, only a handful of those recognised as saints in Ireland have been canonized by Rome. They are, however, recognised as saints by reason of popular acclaim, the *sensus fidelium*, in theological terms. One feature noticeable in the annals, for example, is that certain personages are referred to in a way that indicates admiration for their lifestyle, whereas others who might seem to have been more active, even more effective, do not receive this accolade. The ordinary believer has had and still has the ability to notice the distinction. Canonisation must always have the *sensus fidelium* as a constitutive factor.

Déanacht Dhoire/Deanery of Derry

It is common knowledge that *Doire* means an 'oak-grove', from *dair*, an 'oak tree'. Accounts of the founding of Christian Derry by St Columba seem to indicate that the oak-grove was already there, which may well indicate that it was a *neimheadh* or pagan religious site. It was also inhabited because the account says that St Columba set fire to it, but relented and saved the oak-grove from the spreading fire by his hymn-prayer *Noli Pater indulgere*. Controversy has arisen in recent years about the account that has Colm Cille founding his monastery at Derry after the timely arrival of the *crios* of the dying St Mobhí set him free of his promise not to make any foundation without permission. St Mobhí's order surely indicates a certain doubt on his part about what this scion of royalty might set up if given his chance. After he left to pursue his studies with Gemmán the poet, on the death of his foster-father Cruithneachán the priest, the only evidence of any later contact on St Columba's part with the north west is his arrival at Derry.

The tradition that urges his connection with Derry is, in many ways, sounder than that of his birth at Gartan. One factor in the argument about his foundation of Derry would seem to result from a belief that it was a major Columban centre. However, the evidence would tend to show that Derry was more a sort of monastic port or staging post on the journey from Tír Chonaill to Í Cholm Cille, due to the close connection of Cineál Chonaill with Iona.[3] References to the monastery of Derry in the annals would indicate that it became important only in the twelfth century. The sea journey from Derry can be inferred from Adhamhnán and is suggested by the placename Iskaheen, which calls for Old Irish neuter 'uisce' to be grammatically in the genitive case, preceded by a word like *cúil* or *foinse* showing its importance to seafarers: 'cúil an uisce chaoin': the recess of the fresh water, which is also where Aodhán the monk, nephew of St Columba, was buried, according to Adamnán's Vita.[4]

Finally, the question of how it came about that Aodh mac Ainmhireach might have offered Columba the site of Derry. Derry has for much of its history been a border town. In the mid-sixth century it was on the borders between the lands seized by the sons of Niall Naoighiallach, modern Co. Donegal, and those of the Ulaidh (men of Ulster) from whom they had seized them. Furthermore, it lay on the edge of the land of Cineál Eoghain (Inis Eoghain), Cineál Éinne and at a distance from Cineál Chonaill farther south, to which Aodh belonged. It was not so long since the battle of Móin Doire Lóthair[5]

---

3. Evidenced by the two monks who had 'rowed across from Britain not long ago and today have come from Derry' to visit Colum Crag with news of the death of Colm Cille. Adomnán of Iona, *Life of St Columba*, Richard Sharpe, trans. (London: Penguin Classics, 1995), i, 2 p. 113.

4. Appendix to the *Vita* gives the burial place as *Cúl Uisce*, identified by John Colgan as Iskaheen. This is also where Eoghan (of Inis Eoghain) was buried, allegedly. AFM ad ann. 465.

5. The location of Móin Mór Doire Lóthair has been controverted: from Moneymore to near Coleraine. Loghermore near Limavady or Letterlogher near Claudy would seem more likely if we think of an army going to fight in hostile territory. The followers of Ainmhire had no land east of the Foyle, it would seem.

(c.563), when Ainmhire had led Cineál Chonaill and Cineál Eoghain to intervene successfully as mercenaries in an internal feud amongst the Cruithin and when they were rewarded with territory at Magilligan and across towards the Bann. If Aodh came into possession of the island of Derry he would have faced difficult choices. How was he to hold it for his father, High King Ainmhire, so far from his home base? He may even have been uncertain that he could hold it against attack from Uí Mhic Cairthinn, not long since arrived in the Faughan valley (who were to leave their name on the barony of Tirkeeran). Having taken it, presumably from the Ulaidh, he could not just give it back. Although his father was king of the united forces of Cineál Chonaill and Cineál Eoghain, there was tension between the two, with the result that he was unlikely to give it to Cineál Eoghain.

His solution was quite simple: give it to the Church, which effectively kept everybody else out of it, the same solution as was to be used at Downpatrick. In addition, he gave it to the Church in the person of his cousin and potential rival for kingship, a member of the *deirbhfhine* of the Uí Néill. For those reasons the connection of St Columba with the foundation of Derry is quite reasonable. The reference in the *Annals of Tighearnach* to Fiachra, son of Ciarán, son of Aodh, son of Ainmhire, who died in 620, 'Bass ... *alii fundatoris Dairi Chalgaigh*' – 'the death of another founder of Derry', does not have to invalidate the traditional belief that St Columba accepted the gift of his cousin and uncle of Fiachra. Unfortunately, Fiachra and his father Ciarán occur elsewhere only at the end of their line in the *Ó Cléirigh* Genealogy of Cineál Chonaill.[6]

Derry was a monastic centre until the thirteenth century. At the start of the twelfth century when dioceses were being created, it was agreed that there should be a diocese with its centre at either Derry or Raphoe, probably to accommodate the views of High King Dónall Mac Lochlainn, who saw himself as lord of all of what is now Co. Donegal with his son as king there. This plan did not work out, possibly due to Dónall's death in 1121. The diocesan see was created instead at

---

6. S. Pender, ed., *Anal. Hib.* 18 ed. (Dublin, 1951), pp. 4–25. The *Annals of Tighearnach* (AT) and the *Annals of Ulster* (AU) are closely related at this period but AT were compiled very much later, at Clonmacnoise, adding a further entry at some dates, not always accurately. AU give the death of Fiachra without mention of Derry. Did AU choose to omit *alii fundatoris* from a common source? Where did the AT late entry originate? See K. Grabowski & D. Dumville, *Chronicles and Annals of Medieval Ireland and Wales* (Suffolk: Boydell & Brewer, 1984), pp. 53–6, 111–24.

Ardstraw but was transferred to Machaire Ráth Luraigh (Maghera) by the bishop. A century later another bishop received permission to bring the diocesan centre to Derry. The Columban monastery had by this time become a house of Canons Regular of St Augustine of the Arrouaise obedience.

Much of what is now within the Liberties of Derry was part of Inishowen, including Ballymagroarty.

TEAMPALL MÓR/TEMPLEMORE

Name

In 1163, Flaitheartach Ó Brolcháin, *comharba Cholm Cille* (the successor of Columba), had a lime kiln built, seventy feet square, in preparation for the erection of a church. Over eighty houses were demolished creating *Caiseal an Urláir*, a wall and esplanade. The open space was created to lessen the ever-present danger of fire – most buildings were in wood – and to make room for the great church, while the wall was to mark out the cloister and separation of the monks 'with a curse on anyone who would climb over it'. Having, it would appear, cleared the site, Flaitheartach, son of the Bishop Ó Brolcháin, *sámhadh Cholm Cille* (community of St Columba) and Muircheartach Ó (*recte*, Mac) Lochlainn, High King of Ireland, erected *Teampall Mór* (great church), 'in which there are eighty feet and the stone of that great church was completed in the space of forty days'.[7] It is this *Teampall Mór*, built in 1164, that gives its name to the city parish of Templemore. The building of the church followed on from a series of events that culminated in the change of name for the city, from *Doire Chalgaigh* to *Doire Cholm Cille*. Dónall Mac Ardghair Mac Lochlainn, High King of Ireland +1121, had made Derry his capital and was buried at the monastery, to which the relics of St Columba had been brought after they had passed from Iona to Ceanannas to Raphoe.

Although the temple was familiar to the Irish since first acquaintance with the Bible, the evidence of placenames would show a huge growth in the popularity of *teampall* as a word for a church and in placenames at this time. There are, for example, 105 placenames in the *Onomasticon Goedelicum* beginning with the word 'teampall'. Referring originally, of

---

7. *Annals of the Kingdom of Ireland* (Four Masters) and *Annals of Ulster* ad ann.
   AU gives the dimension as ninety feet, presumably in length. Medieval churches in the area tended to be long and narrow, no doubt due to problems providing support for the roof. See those at Banagher, Tamlaghtfinlagan, Drumachose, etc.

course, to the Temple in Jerusalem, the word must have come back into fashion with the Crusades, the first preached by Pope Urban II in 1095, described as 'a pilgrimage in arms', a means of penance imposed on those who broke the 'Truce of God', to bring support to the Byzantine empire of Constantinople under pressure from the invading Turks and to put an end to reported persecution of Christians in the Holy Land. After St Bernard, the 'conscience of Europe', preached the second crusade at Vézelay in 1146, the idea of joining the crusade became a popular cause throughout what was being called 'Christendom'.

While there is little evidence of Irish political leaders taking up crusading, given the relationship between St Malachy and St Bernard through the Cistercians, it would not be unexpected for the course of events to have its influence in Ireland. They were not to foresee that the crusades would be so undisciplined and uncontrolled as to deepen the hostility between Latin and Orthodox and to make the epithet 'crusader' one of the worst insults a Moslem can hurl at a Christian. For St Bernard, a terrible truth dawned when he had to go to the Rhine valley to put an end to the massacre of Jews at the behest of a crazy monk. In the heady days of idealism for some and opportunism for others, the attention of many was focused by the imposition of the Saracen rent or tithe in 1188 to go towards paying for it all. Anyhow, from this time Derry would seem to have had two churches, the *Teampall Mór* and the *Dubhrégles* of the Canons Regular of St Augustine of the Arrouaise observance. Inch, Burt and Iskaheen were in Templemore. Inch (*Inis na nOisrí*) had a medieval chapel dedicated to Mary.

Saints Associated with Monastic Derry

- **Columba/Colm Cille** – feast day 9 June
- **Dácuailén, aka Dá Chua,**[8] an Abbot of Derry – feast day 12 March. He was later seen as a prophet. His name is made up of two terms of endearment *dá-* and *-én* around *-cua(il)* i.e. 'dear little cua(il. ?), but his full name is unclear. As befitted one associated with the monastery in Derry he belonged to Cineál Bínnigh. There was a shrine associated with his veneration but all we know about it is that Ó Feaháin were its custodians.

---

8. Anne O'Sullivan, ed., *Book of Leinster* VI (Dublin, 1983), p. 1595, l.48950. For the prophet, cf. W. Stokes, ed., *The Martyrology of Oengus the Culdee* (London: Harrison and Sons, 1905), 190 n.

- **Caochscoile**, scribe of Derry who died in 720. His name, caoch means 'one-eyed', 'partially sighted', or 'purblind', and *scoile* 'of the school': his ailment may have resulted from overworking in the manuscript school attached to the monastery.
- **Giolla Mac Liag Mac Ruairí** (Gelasius MacRory) – feast day 27 March; d.1166, Abbot of Derry; Archbishop of Armagh.
- **Conchúr Mac Con Choille** (Conor McEnhill) – feast day 4 June; d.1175 of the erenagh family of Derry and Drumragh, prior of St Peter and St Paul's, Armagh, Archbishop of Armagh.
- **Blessed Muireadhach Mag Rabhartaigh** (Marianus Scotus II) – feast day 9 February; d.1088, of the Mag Rabhartaigh family, custodians of *Cathach Cholm Cille* and for that reason, tenants at Ballymagroarty, scribe, founder of the Benedictine Schottenkloster of St Peter at Regensburg, Germany. A manuscript copy of the *Epistles of St Paul* written by Muireadhach is still to be seen in the Imperial Library, Vienna.

Buried at Derry

- **Bran** – nephew of St Columba.
- **Aodhán**, monk – nephew of St Columba, buried at Cúl Uisce.[9]
- **Dónall Mac Ardghair Mac Lochlainn** – High King of Ireland, +11.2.1121.
- **Saint Muireadhach Ó Cofaigh** – Bishop of Cineál Eoghain, + 10.2.1173.
- **Amhlaoibh Ó Muireadhaigh** – bishop, +1185.

Erenaghs at Derry (Monastic City)

Mensal Lands

The various documents detailing grants of erstwhile religious lands in Derry at the start of the Plantation of Ulster are confusing. The

---

9. Anderson and Anderson, eds, Adomnan's *Life of Columba* (London, 1961), Appendix: 546–8. Also in Stokes and Strachan, eds, *Thesaurus Palaeohibernicus* (Cambridge: Cambridge University Press), II, 281. Colgan, with local knowledge, says Cúl Uisce is Iskaheen.

lands attached to the bishopric were: Creggan/Creagán, Drumeneny (Drumiurny)/Droim an Aonaigh? and Cour(t)neglogh/Cúirt na gCloch to the north of the 'Island' of Derry, and included four acres of land where the bishop paid a rent to Lochlannach the erenagh for a house and large garden south of the cathedral, lying near the tower called 'Kellmuckellie's Tower', 'Colmcille's Tower'. 'Duncreggan' might pinpoint the location of Creagán. 'Dromineene and Courtneglogh were mensal lands or great demesnes ... of the bishops of Derry and so enjoyed by Bishop O Galloher, Bishop Montgomery, Bishop Babington and Bishop Hampton, who kept their dairies upon these grounds, depastured them with sheep and cattle for the provision of their houses, and horses for their stables, and tilled such parts they lived,' wrote Bishop John Bramhall, disconsolate that his immediate predecessor had leased it all to an uncooperative Sir Thomas Staples. Also leased by the bishop were three parcels of meadow near St Colmcille's Well for £1.13s.4d, and 'an acre of land in a place called the Bogg with buildings thereupon', possibly the site of the Dominican friary, at a yearly rent of twenty shillings.

Monastic Lands

The first list of the churchlands dates from 1604 and is at variance with the lists detailed by the Inquisition jury some ten years later. On the face of it, the latter should be more accurate since they were certainly delineated with the benefit of local knowledge. The 1604 list provides some interesting variants of nomenclature, e.g. another name for Ballougry would seem to have been Carrownasrady (*Ceathrú na Sráide*). The later lists give Termonbaccoe, Creevagh, Balliwirry (Baloughry?), Mallennan, Kellegh, Ardnomohill, Alt O'Derry, Corneshalgagh (Ballynashallog?), Granesholgillagh, Loluske (the name would seem to include '*uisce*': Springtown?), Ballinagarde, Clonemore and Dirgebroe. Dirgebroe is *Deargbhruach* at Gransha, across the river. The first seven lie west of the city and the first five of this seven together are called Termon Derrie/*Tearmann Doire*.[10] The next five lie to the north of the city.

Ardamohill and Altoderry together make up the 'quarter of land of Cargan', and Cargan can only be modern Creggan. Ard na mBuachaill would indicate height and pasture (*buachaill* is a herdsman), while *alt*,

---

10. Moody & Simms, eds, *Bishopric of Derry and the Irish Society of London, 1602–1705* (Dublin: Stationery Office for the Irish Manuscripts Commission, 1968–83), I, 213, although at I, 221–2 this is contradicted.

'a ravine', in Alt an Doire?/Alt Uí Dhoiréidh? would suggest a steep slope, a notable geographical feature of the area. It is noteworthy that some of these areas, like Killeigh, are in the diocese of Raphoe. Their erenagh was Ó Doiréidh (O Derry), who were also erenaghs at Donaghmore. To add to the confusion, Derry had two other erenaghs, Ó Daighre (O Deery) and Ó hÉigeartaigh (O Hegarty), the latter associated with the monastic lands to the north of the city, probably, with Ó Daighre perhaps sharing lands on the west with Ó Doiréidh. The similarity of the names Ó Doiréidh/Ó Daighre, the lack of clarity in the Plantation Papers and the complete destruction of native records invite someone's patient analysis on a wet winter night.

The 1604 list adds other lands of the canons regular outside Derry: Carrownowe, Suppocke, Drumhiert (Burt?), Cormackan, Derrivaghan, Tory Island, Grange Dennet and Inchcorrill (an island in the Foyle near Lifford).

The Dean and Others

The Dean of Derry, who was curate to the bishop at the cathedral, was Rector of Cluain Diarmada/Clondermott in his own right. Temple quarter (*Ceathrú an Teampaill*, at Enagh), Clonkey (Caw?), Coole(c) ronagh (Culkeeragh?) and two quarters of land at Ballyowen were in his demesne. An entry in *The Bishopric of Derry and the Irish Society* asks, 'if O Caran is the erenagh at Culkeeragh'. The erenagh at Enagh and Caw, we are told, was Mac an tSagairt/MacEntaggart.

The Grange of Burt belonged to the Cistercian Abbey of Macosquin; there the erenaghs were the 'Clanmagwories', *Clann Mhig Mhuirí* (*Mhuireadhaigh*).

There was also 'near the town of Illagh (Elagh) in the county of Donegal the half-quarter of land of Ballynacalliagh an old and ruined chapel with the half-quarter of Rossnecalliagh near the town of Donalonge (Dunalong) in the county of Coleraine', about the ownership of which there was uncertainty by 1600 but must represent lands given to support the convent of Cistercian nuns.[11] Cailleach meant a nun, but by 1600 the convent had gone into desuetude. Finally, there was the land attached to the Dominican friary to the 'north of the bog'. The Ó Dónaill castle in the 'lower fort of the city of Derry' was built on

---

11. 'Convent of Blessed Mary of Derry', founded in 1218. Little is known of its history, but the convent was in ruins, desolate, without abbess or sisters in 1512. See Flannan Hogan, 'Derry: the Cistercian Connection', *Hallel* (Roscrea) XXIII, 2 (1998), pp. 126–9. *Baile* /'bally' represents a relatively late placename.

churchland purchased by Ó Dónaill from Lochlannach the erenagh and built for Ó Dónaill by Ó Dochartaigh.

FATHAN MHURA/FAHAN

Name

Originally 'Othan', the parish takes its name, we are told, from its river beside which St Mura established his hermitage. In the course of time two places of the name developed, *Othan Mhór* and *Othan Bheag*. It is unclear where exactly *Othan Bheag* was. Perhaps as St Mura's foundation grew, it may have felt the need of another house or hermitage. It is common in Irish to find the letter 'f' obtruded into words beginning with a vowel, so that *Othan* became *Fothan* and later *Fathan*. The Bishop of Derry had one residence in the castle at Fahan and the Abbot of Derry was rector of the parish.

Saints

Mura
Cillín Ó Colla
Fothad na Canóine
Colmán Iomrámha
Ainmhire of Aileach – feast day 10 June.

Erenaghs

At *Litir*: Sliocht Mhic Néill Uí Dhónaill/sept of Niall Ó Dónaill.
At *Lisbannagh*: Sliocht Mhuireartaigh Uí Dhónaill/sept of Muireartach Ó Dónaill.
At *Sleane & Millquarter*: 'Mounterheiles'/Muintir Shiail (Ó Siail: Shields). Sleane = *Ceathrú an tSléibhe* (Mountain quarter); *Ceathrú an Mhuilinn* (Mill).
Erenaghs were immensely proud of the antiquity of their calling and their links with saintly founders, but here we have examples of a common complaint by churchmen in the Middle Ages – that of lay lords taking over churchlands, evidenced here by two septs of Ó Dónaill who clearly had muscled in on these lands. It might, of course, have been a swap. The original erenaghs at Fahan were Mag Rabhartaigh Ó Ceallaigh (McGroarty) who became the custodians of *Cathach Cholm Cille* and, bearing it, led Ó Dónaill into battle.

The parish included the bishop's mensal lands of Castlequarter (*Ceathrú an Chaisleáin*) and Machaire Beag, whose erenagh may have been Ó hÉigeartaigh. The granges of Inch and Drumheirt/Drumheard/ Drumheggerty belonged to the Abbey of Derry, while the grange of Burt belonged to the Cistercian Abbey at Macosquin.

DÍSEART ÉIGNIGH/DESERTEGNY

Name

Díseart comes to Irish through Latin from Egypt where St Antony and many others like him had gone out into the 'desert' to find solitude and peace to pray. Disciples joined them to form monastic establishments around them or to imitate them as anchorites or hermits. The *díseart* was a hermitage, usually an outpost of a monastery. Desertegny may have been attached to the monastery at Fahan, and may even have been *Othan Bheag* originally. That it was a separate entity from Fahan is recognised by those who refer to it as 'the parish'.

Saint

Éigneach – feast day 24 April: said to be the son of Cú Cathrach.

Erenagh

Mag Rodaigh was erenagh. Ballyannan and Tonduff were the erenagh lands.

CLUAIN MÁINE/CLONMANY

Name and Patron

Columba

Máine[12] – feast day 24 November.

Also known as *Cúl Máine*. *Cluain* means meadow or pasture land; *cúil* means a recess. DIL records examples of *cúl* meaning 'protection, keeping'.

Máine is a person's name, quite common in early Ireland, unfortunately for our search. The genealogy of the saints, the *Naomhsheanchas*, gives the name of Bishop Máine, son of Eichin, son of Eoghan, who belonged

---

12. There is another saint, Aodh Deochan, 'the Deacon', associated with a place called Cúil Máine, in this case said by an tOllamh Pádraig Ó Riain to be in Fermanagh. CGSH 10, 320.

to Cineál Eoghain na hInse (i.e. of Inishowen).[13] His feast day is 24 November. We cannot be certain but as a very early saint it would be not unexpected for his name to be recorded in association with a place, less likely if he had lived later on as the monastic Church developed and bishops became less prominent. If Eoghan was a contemporary of St Patrick, as is claimed, his grandson would be early sixth century and a missionary.

The original church may have been built near Carraig Brachaí, centre of the kingdom ruled later by Ó Maolfhábhaill (McFaul/Lavelle).

Erenagh

Ó Muireasáin/O Morrison/Bryson was custodian of *Míosach Cholmcille*, St Columba's Calendar. As custodian, he wore special vestments when he carried the halidom, when leading an army into war and carrying the relic *deiseal* (right-hand-wise) around the force; described as *comharba* (successor) to the abbot, which probably reflects its coming within the *paruchia* of Colm Cille and Derry.

The erenagh lands were extensive but the areas as stated in the Appendix to the *Inquisitions* do not add up: five and a half ballibetaghs (*baile biataigh* was the equivalent of sixteen *bailte bó*; one baile bó equalled sixty acres in west Ulster). Each *baile biataigh* was the equivalent of four quarters (*ceathrú*) and one quarter, therefore, was four *bailte bó*. The erenagh held two quarters as erenagh to the bishop, to whom he paid rents. He had one quarter free, Donally – the best quarter in Inishowen, thought Bishop Bramhall – and held three others in his capacity as custodian of the *Míosach*, land 'given by Ó Dochartaigh and Ó Dónaill as a dedication towards his vestments when he went to war'. 'In the said parish are six *gorts* of glebe, whereof three *gorts* belong to the vicar and the other four *gorts* to the keeper of the missagh or ornaments left by Columkill'. Ó Muireasáin paid the bishop the yearly rent of ten shillings English, and was the collector of bishop's rents and duties in Inishowen. Apart from Donally the erenagh lands are not named in the *Inquisitions*, but the survey of 1608 names Carrowne strady (*Ceathrú na Sráide*, 'sráid' indicates a *clachán* or village), and Carrowne hannagh (*Ceathrú na hAdhnachta?*) The *Civil Survey* (1654–6) gives Carro Sradd and Anaught. About the time of the

---

13. John Colgan, B. Jennings OFM, eds, *Acta Sanctorum Hibernae* (Dublin: Dublin Stationery Office, 1948), 399.

Plantation, Clonmany had six stone houses (three with roofs), a bridge and two castles.

DOMHNACH MÓR MAIGHE (GLINNE) TÓCHAIR/ CARNDONAGH

Name
Domhnach, as already mentioned, is the earliest word in Irish for a church and comes from the Latin *dominus* meaning 'lord'. *Domhnach Mór* the 'great church', of *Má Tóchair* 'the plain of the causeway'/'*Gleann Tóchair*'; 'the valley of the causeway or passage'; 'tóchar' usually refers to a roadway made through marshy ground. Here it might reflect the narrow entrance to the glen.

Patrons
Patrick – said to have visited and founded the *domhnach* on land given him by Aodh, son of Fergus, son of Eoghan, where he left in charge Mac Cairthinn, brother of St Mac Cairthinn of Clogher. When the brothers disagreed about an ordination, St Patrick foretold poverty for the church of the culprit, *Dómhnach Mór Maighe Tóchair*. Whether this is a late attempt to explain two members of Patrick's household with the same name, or associated with different churches, or an indication of an importance that *Domhnach Mór* had lost at a later time, is a matter for further investigation. Saint Patrick is said to have wished to found a *díseart* at Achadh Drumman,[14] perhaps the other church there may have been such if the first was called *mór*.

Erenagh
Mac Colgan – possibly descended from Colgu, two of whose brothers, Aodh Allán and Niall Frasach, were high kings in the eighth century. Dónall Mac Colgan was erenagh at the time of the *Inquisitions* and may have been 'the parson O Colgan who lives at Donaght in Enishowen', who revealed that Niall Garbh Ó Dónaill was conspiring to betray Derry or Lifford to Ó Néill and Ó Dónaill. This was obviously the sept to which Joannes Colganus OFM, the noted historian, belonged.

---

14. Whitley Stokes, ed., *Tripartite Life of Patrick* (London: 1887), I , 156–7.

Erenagh lands

There were three quarters of land, unnamed in the *Inquisitions*, but named in the 1604 list as: Carneballybranegan, Carrowintemple and Moydoony, while the *Civil Survey* names Carrowtemple, Ballibranigan and Carreck.[15]

After the Nine Years War there were 'four stone houses, three in ruins, one habitable with a yard enclosed by a stone wall'.

CÚIL DABHCHA/CULDAFF

Name

Cúil – 'a recess'; *dabhach* – 'a vat, a hollow, a collection of sandhills near the sea' (DIL). Culdaff formed a *plebania* with Moville, with a rector in common.

Patron

Saint Buadán – identified with St Baoithín, Abbot of Iona. Feast day 9 June.

Erenagh

Ó Dufaigh – custodian of St Buadán's Bell, perhaps descended from Caolbhadh, son of Fergus, son of Eoghan.

Erenagh lands

Carrowtemple, Carrowmoidgheldoagh, Towahenny (1604). Knockquarter, Church Quarter, Crancor (CS).

CLUAIN CHATHA/CLONCHA

Name

Cluain – 'a meadow'.
Cath/catha – 'of a battle, of a company of soldiers' (DIL).
It was a parish made up of two permanently combined parishes: Cloncha and Grillagh.

---

15. Rawlinson A., 237, *Bodleian* in *Anal. Hib.* III (Dublin, 1931), 170. Robert C. Simington, ed., *Civil Survey 1654–56* (Dublin: The Stationery Office, 1945), p. 15.

Patrons
The Seven Bishops. Neither their names nor why they were venerated together are recorded. They are found again at Clonleigh.
Saint Columba – feast day 8 June.
Saint Adhamhnán/Eunan at Grillagh.
Saint Muirdhealach at Malin – feast day 3 November.

Erenaghs
Lochlannach at Grillagh
Ó Maolmhochéirí (Loughrey/Early)
Ó hEarcáin

Erenagh lands
Towne Rosse, Carrow in temple, Lackdromen, Larragh Kirrell, Carrow temple grillagh, Dromvilley (1604).
Carrow Temple, Doncass, Lawsechrill, Glacknedromon, Drom ballicoslin, Templemoyle, Dromnaville (CS).

MÁ BHILE/MOVILLE

Name
Má – 'an extensive stretch of open ground'.
Bile – 'a large tree, especially an ancient and venerated one'.

Such a tree was often the focus of an inauguration site for king or chieftain. In this case it may have served Ó Duídhíorma (the name has become McDermott), King of *An Bréadach* of east Inishowen. That the church would be located near such a site would make sense, probably at Cooley. This parish formed a *plebania* with Culdaff, permanently united with a common rector. *Plebania*, presumably, comes from *plebs*, 'the common people'. Might this be the origin of '*Bun an Phobail*', the name on the signposts, since that seems to refer to area rather than people, its true meaning?

Plebania might now be translated as 'cluster'. At the Plantation there was one stone house.

Such sacred trees were known elsewhere in Europe. For example, when the city-state of Florence was at war with Siena in the thirteenth century, one of the first objectives was to cut down Siena's sacred tree.

Patrons

Saint Finnan, as recorded by Montgomery,[16] cited by Sir James Ware.[17] Whether this is 'Fionnán' of Derry as venerated at Kilfennan, or Maelfinnen, who died on 9 February 948, 'learned Bishop of Doire Chalgaigh/blessed Maelfinnen, Abbot of Derry' or St Finnian of Movilla (Co. Down) and/or Clonard is unclear. The last named must be considered unlikely for that time. The other two may be two versions of the same person's name.

Saint Mary at Northburgh (Greencastle), the Anglo-Norman foundation.

Erenaghs

Sliocht (sept of) Uilliam Duibh Uí Dhochartaigh.

Manus MacMelaghlin at Cooley.

MacLaughlin at Taivennagallen (which looks like *taobh an ghallain*, 'beside the standing stone', and may be descriptive rather than an actual placename).

MacMelaghlin is Mac Maoleachlainn rather than Mac Lochlainn. Maoleachlann was a common Christian name among the Mac Lochlainns. The usual version as a surname is Ó Maoleachlainn, and its anglified version may be Melaugh.

Erenagh lands

Grange Magh, Bally mc Rowarty, Carrowne naph, Clonetrogh, Carrowne, Tirrorovan (1604).

Carronaugh, Tirgovane, Cooly, Clancree (CS).

CLANN DIARMADA/CLONDERMOTT/GLENDERMOTT

Name

Clann Chonchúir, a branch of *Cineál Eoghain*, were also known as the *Fir Maighe Iotha* ('men of the plain of Ioth'– the area round the River Finn). *Maigh Iotha* was known for its fertility and its corn, which attracted covetous eyes, and resulted in intermittent hostilities between Clann Chonchúir and Cineál Moain (Ó Gormlaigh/Ó Luinigh-Lunney).

---

16. See Henry A. Jefferies, 'Bishop George Montgomery's Survey', *Seanchas Ard Mhacha*, 17,1 (1996/7), 52.
17. *Bishopric of Derry and the Irish Society of London* I, 405.

In the long struggle for supremacy within Cineál Eoghain between Mac Lochlainn and Ó Néill, Cineál Moain sided with Ó Néill and Clann Chonchúir split. Part of Clann Chonchúir (Ó Catháin/Ó Maoláin, etc.) moved away to the Roe valley and sided with Ó Néill. The branch descended from Diarmaid, son of Conchúr (Ó Cairealláin-Kerlin), took the part of Mac Lochlainn and, when ousted from Maigh Iotha in the 1200s, went to live near Mac Lochlainn, whose main residence was at Enagh, and they gave their patronymic as name for the area: *Clann Diarmada*, which much later became the name of the parish.

Patrons
Saint Columba at Clooney – feast day 9 June.
Saint Breacán at Clooney – feast day 16 July.
Saint Fionnán at Kilfennan.
Saint Colm Crag at Enagh, *not* Colm Cille – feast day 22 September.
Cobhrán, nephew of Colm Cille – status unclear.

Erenaghs
Mac an tSagairt/Taggart at Eanach/Enagh and Caw (*Cluain Catha?*).
Ó Caráin at Culkeeragh/Cúil Caorach: *nativus*/*dúchasach*?

Sept of 'Nealportcloney', *dúchasach*/'dowsager' of four ballyboes at Clooney[18] where they also had the fishing rights.

The *Inquisitions* state that there were two parishes in the 'county of the city of Derry: the parish of Derry, where the bishop was parson (from Latin, *persona*) or rector and the dean of the diocesan chapter was vicar or curate; and the parish of Clandermot where the dean was rector and vicar, although he had to keep a curate (who had a garden of glebe)'. The dean got a third of the tithes of Derry and all of the tithes of Clandermot except for those of Enagh, a third of which went to the bishop: 8d (pence) for every cow and calf and the rest in kind. The dean had two quarters (eight balliboes) of land at Ballyowen: Lisneele, Lisreely, Broccagh, Lisnagalloglie, Ardolagh, Kilfennan, Crachbreedy and Karnee. The balliboes of Clooney were Lusdreenagh, Ballintemple, Ballymulley and Rossedony. Ballintemple suggests a medieval church, while Rossdowney suggests a *domhnach*, a very early 'Patrician' church. Uilliam Mac an tSagairt was Dean of Derry at the Plantation of Ulster.

---

18. Nealportcloney: *Niall Port Cluaine* (?). Clearly a surname is missing. The original Irish for Clooney is unclear. There were a number of places along the Foyle whose names began with *port* 'a harbour or landing-place'. *The Bishopric of Derry and the Irish Society* II, 471. *Inquisitions*, Appendix.

He conformed to the established Church and ended his days as Rector of Termoneeny and Kilcronaghan.

Before the time of Shane Ó Néill, we are told, the Archbishop of Armagh received two marks (13/4d x 2) per annum from the lands and fishing of Clooney, and when Archbishop Colton visited Derry in 1397 he said Mass for 'thousands of people' at Clooney, knowing he had a right to be there. Where did that right originate? Perhaps not in the seven churches St Patrick is said to have founded near the River Faughan, including *Domhnach Mín-chluaine*, which Brian Lacey suggested was Clooney and who identified *Domhnach Dola* as Templemoyle towards Muff, Eglinton, which was known as 'the Moigh' in the 1600s. It was there that 'St Patrick' left his *sagart méise*, his chaplain, the priest Béascna. Worth considering also are Rossdowney and Templetown at Enagh.[19]

NUACHONGBHÁIL/FAUGHANVALE

Name

The name of this parish has nothing to do with the River Faughan. In an ecclesiastical context *congbháil* means 'a monastic foundation or establishment', and *nua* means 'new'. With the article *an* before it, the word sounds as if it begins with the vowel u, and in such a position it is not unusual for the letter 'f' to be obtruded, as happened in the name 'Fahan', coming from *Othan*. The townland of Faughanvale with its old cemeteries presumably holds the 'new foundation' right in the middle of the erenagh lands of the parish, 'new' perhaps in comparison with the 'old' at 'the Moigh'. In the 1,000 years from St Patrick to the end of the Middle Ages – given the life span of most buildings – there may have been many 'new foundations'.

Patron

Saint Cainneach (Canice).

---

19. B. Lacey, *The Uí Meic Cairthinn of Lough Foyle in Derriana* (1979), pp. 10–11. Má Dula/Domhnach Dula are sometimes equated with Moyola in south Derry, but Séamus O'Kelly and Éamon Devlin have shown that Moyola is *Má Dhá Loch* 'the plain of the two lakes'. Domhnach is the earliest word for a church in Irish. While the name cannot indicate a Patrician foundation everywhere it occurs it may well indicate a claim on that church by the *paruchia* of Armagh. The established Church built its church more conveniently for its worshippers at 'the Moigh'. *Bishopric of Derry*, etc., I, 397–8.

Erenagh

Mac Bhloscaidh (McCloskey), who are a branch of Ó Catháin.

Erenagh lands

Tullyvarrie, Killywily, Goolagh, Kemlitter (BD & ISL I, 58).
Tullederry, Killewilly, Callowe, Killeitra (*Inquisitions*, Appendix).
Tullevenry, Killewilly, Cullow, Killeytra (Ware in BD & ISL I, 404).
Killeitra/Killeytra must be the townland of Faughanvale whose name
must come from the new foundation. Killeytra looks like *cill íochtarach*
'lower church' or *coill íochtarach* 'lower wood'. As a branch of Ó Catháin
the sept of Mac Bhloscaidh must have come late to the erenaghship and
may have brought in St Cainneach as patron with them. The Dean of
Derry was rector here. The lands of the dean were to be found in each
of three rural deaneries of the diocese: at Derry, at Lifford and here at
Faughanvale. This led to continuous jousting in the later Middle Ages
between candidates from each deanery: Ó Cearbhalláin from Lifford,
Mac Giolla Bhríde Ó Dochartaigh from Derry and Mac Bhloscaidh
from Faughanvale, with frequent trips to Rome by one or other to have
someone else displaced. Seán Mac Giolla Bhríde, for example, went to
Rome five times on business in the mid-fifteenth century.

CUMAR/CUMBER

Name

Cumar means a 'confluence of rivers' and, occasionally, the additional
notion of a 'meeting place'. In the Catholic system, part of the original
medieval parish is now included in the parish of Faughanvale. The
parish is in the barony of Tirkeeran, which takes its name from the
Uí Mic Cairthinn, descended from Cairthinn, grandson of Colla
Uais whose sept, the *Uí Tuirtre*, belonged to the *Airghialla* and ruled
south Derry/east Tyrone. They expanded into the Faughan valley. The
surnames arising in the *Uí Mic Cairthinn* are Ó Colgan and Ó Conaill.[20]
Defeated at the battle of *Áth Ghort an Chatha* (probably Gortica near
Drumahoe), they retreated up the valley and into obscurity. That they
were masters in their own bailiwick beyond that defeat is to be seen in
the name of the medieval patron of Cumber, St Eoghan/Eugene, now a
patron of the diocese. A native of Leinster, he was missionary founder

---

20. Ó Dubhagáin, James Carney, eds, *Topographical Poems* (Dublin: Dublin Institute
for Advanced Studies, 1943), 14/361–4.

and patron of the church in Ardstraw, centre of the *Airghialla* kingdom of *Uí Fiachrach Ard Sratha*, descended from Fiachra, a brother of Cairthinn. It was at the east wall of the medieval church of Cumber that the martyred Bishop Réamann Ó Gallachair was buried in March 1601.

Patron

Saint Eoghan/Eugene – feast day 23 August.
Kilcalton may originate with St Catán, a disciple of St Patrick.
It has been suggested that the Miskan Stone may be a relic of the passage of St Meascán, another disciple of St Patrick.

Erenagh

Those given by Montgomery are Milerus et Jacobus Mc Innie/Maolmhuire (Miler) and Séamas (James), but the surname is not clear. A note endorsed by James O Devin in 1671 draws attention to an oath sworn about the use of churchland of Alla and Cumber in the 1620s. The testimony was given by Bryan McIllnie, who describes himself as a herd at the time.[21] Obviously his involvement was important in the matter, partly because of his age, and, partly one might suggest, because his standing in the matter was more than that of a herd. He might be a member of the erenagh family. One of the few north Derry names that might fit would be McElhinney, but there is no evidence from elsewhere of any Mac Giolla Chainnigh involvement in the medieval Church. The name might also be Mac an Airchinnigh/son of the erenagh, which adds little more.

Erenagh lands

Claydagh, Owenbeg, Bankinderry, Arran (*Inquisitions,* Appendix).
Cladogh, Clegg, Ballintemple, Binhenry (*Civil Survey,* 243).
These two lists do not quite match. Claudy, Cregg and Binn are clear enough. Arran in the first list must be an error for Alla, since Stradarran is in the parish of Banagher. Ballintemple can only be Cumber itself since the ruins of the medieval church are there. Alla, Tullintrain and Teenaght were 'gorts of glebe', according to the *Civil Survey.*[22]

---

21. *Bishopric of Derry and the Irish Society of London* II, 4.
22. Pp. 243, 244.

BEANNCHAR/BANAGHER

Name

There are the remains of three medieval churches in the parish, Templemoyle, Banagher and Stradarran. *Teampall maol* usually means a roofless church, a ruin, probably indicating that it was replaced by the building at Banagher. *Sráid Uí Aráin* would indicate a village on the lands of Ó hAráin/Harron. The old church there was dedicated to St Constans (or Cuana), a priest. It is of interest that it is situated near Cleggan, an ancient cemetery. Much of the medieval parish is in the barony of Tirkeeran and much of the Foreglen/Ballymoney part of the modern parish was in the medieval parish of Bovevagh. Some derive the word *Beannchar* from *beann* 'peak' or 'point', so that it may refer to some configuration of the church roof, but it is more likely to be connected with *beannaigh* 'to bless', underlining the sanctity of the site, perhaps in imitation of the great religious houses of Bangor in Co. Down and Bangor in Wales. The building itself is worth visiting as an example of a medieval church. The site is exceptional also for the building beside it. It must have been larger at one time, with a surrounding complex of other buildings, since it was clearly the site that Archbishop Colton kept in mind for the culmination of his visit to the diocese in 1397. It is notable that Banagher was able to accommodate his large retinue quite easily, while Dungiven Priory could not. Dungiven may indeed have been part of Banagher before Ó Catháin founded the priory of Canons Regular.

Patrons

Saint Muireadhach Ó hÉanaigh.
Saint Constans (Cuana) at Stradarran – feast day 14 November.
Muireadhach Ó hÉanaigh/O'Heaney is known only from folklore and tradition, yet it is remarkable how defined and lasting that has been. Some of what is told about him is typical of folktale, e.g. his encounter with (at *Creig an Iúir*) and victory over the *péist* ('serpent'), but after all St Colm Cille encountered the Lough Ness monster. It is part of the process of storytelling. Unusually, there was a *turas* (pilgrimage) associated with him, from Slanagh Well in Magheramore to, in the long version, Boveva Well.

Since there are no records, he is impossible to date, but since he has a surname he must belong to medieval times, perhaps the eleventh or twelfth century. He may have been responsible for Banagher church in Magheramore, which would seem to have been built before 1121, when Giolla Easpaig Eoghain Ó hAiniaraidh (probably Ó hInnéirí/ O'Henry), King of Cianachta, was killed in its cemetery. Cemeteries were open, common ground at the time unlike today, used for markets, negotiations, etc., so that bloodshed there was not unknown.

Saint Constans was a native of the area, belonging by descent to *Uí Mic Cairthinn*, the dynasty who gave their name to the barony of Tirkeeran (of the Faughan valley). Constans spent much of his life as an anchorite and learned man at *Eoinis* on Lough Uachtar, Co. Cavan, and died in 777.

Erenagh

Ó hÉanaigh were important in the parish until just beyond memory. 'Banagher sand', when lifted by an *Ó hÉanaigh* and thrown against an opponent in a lawsuit, guaranteed judgment in favour of the thrower. Lest anyone is tempted, it had to be lifted by a member of the erenagh family and they are no longer extant there. Despite their importance they do not occur in the genealogies, so their origin is uncertain. LCAB suggests that *Ó hÉanna* had a role in the defence of Inishowen, appointed by Ó Néill on leaving, but this looks like a contrived attempt to avoid mentioning Mac Lochlainn, the real power at the time.[23] Anyhow this is not the same name.

Erenagh lands

Tianan, Templemoile, Carnanban, Derechrier, Naloske (BD & ISL I, 104). Tiavan, Carnanbane, Templemore, Derry Tryer, Aughluske, Machumore, Killmaght, Raleagh (*gort* of glebe) (CS 215).

DÚN GEIMHIN/DUNGIVEN

Name

In Old Irish the word *dún* was usually applied to the main residence of a lord or dignitary, consisting of an earthen rampart, the *ráth*, within which the house or houses were erected. Sometimes the rath was made up of three ramparts and at times included a moat. It was usually called after the builder or owner. Bishop Reeves, borne out by Dinneen, suggested that *geimhean* means 'hide or skin'. Its diminutive *geimnen* means 'a hide used as a shroud or winding-

---

23. T. Ó Donnchadha, ed., *Leabhar Cloinne Aodha Buidhe* (Dublin, 1931), 43.

sheet for the dead'. A verse lament for Maol Fothartaigh, King of Uí Tuirtre (south Derry/east Tyrone now), + 669, says he was taken in his *geimhnín/gaimhnen* to be buried at Doire.[24] Bishop Reeves was perhaps swayed by the irony of the fact that Dungiven was fated to become part of the lands allotted to the London Company of Skinners at the Plantation.

On the other hand, the name may suggest the centre of a tanning or hides 'industry'. Cattle hides were used as a surface on which food was placed, as a bed-covering, as a surface on which corn was flailed, as a source of vellum for manuscripts, a covering on the inside of a chariot, as well as what we would see as the more common uses of hide: shoes, bags, belts, halters, dog-muzzles, and of course, as St Brendan demonstrated, for covering the framework of a boat. Since numbers of cattle were seen as an indication of wealth and importance, and since few bull calves were allowed grow to maturity (to save milk for humans), there must have been a real turnover in hides.[25] It is unlikely that everyone would have been able, or even wanted, to provide all or any of these artefacts. Ireland also had a substantial export market in hides.[26]

Dungiven was clearly the centre of Gleann Geimhin/Glengiven, the area given to the *Cianachta* after a band of them came north from Leinster to fight as mercenaries in the conquest of Ulaidh of west Ulster by the sons of Niall Naoighiallach, Conall, Éanna and Eoghan.[27] The *Cianachta Glinne Geimhin*, the descendants of *Cian*, gave their name to the barony of Keenaught, but may initially have received the upper reaches of the Roe valley. The royal house/lords of *Cianacht* were *Ó Conchobhair*, now *Ó Conchúir*.[28] At the start of the second millennium, Ó Conchúir were defeated with *deargár* 'great slaughter' at the battle of Belat in 1076 by Aodh Ó Maol Sheachlainn, probably of Aileach, and *Fir Maighe Iotha* and lost their kingdom to Ó Catháin. *Maigh Iotha* was the Finn valley, a hotbed of war at the time, which may have forced Ó Catháin and his allies away from the Lifford-Castlefinn

---

24. O'Donovan in AFM I, 280n identifies *Doire* as Derry; more probably it is Derryloran (Cookstown).
25. A.T. Lucas, *Cattle in Ancient Ireland* (Kilkenny: Boethius Press, 1989), 223 sqq.
26. Fergus Kelly, *Early Irish Farming* (Dublin: Dublin Institute for Advanced Studies, 1997), pp. 54–5.
27. T.F. O'Rahilly, *Early Irish History and Mythology* (Dublin: Dublin Institute for Advanced Studies, 1946), 95n.
28. Unrelated to the Ó Conchúir/Ó Connor kings of Connacht.

area. Amongst the septs associated with Ó Catháin were Ó Loingsigh/ Lynch, Ó Maoláin/Mullan, Ó Godáin, Ó Coinn, Ó Doibhleacháin (now subsumed into Devlin), Ó Muireadhaigh/Ó Muirí/Murray. Some of these have left their names on places in the area: Ballymullan (the area round Park), Ballygudden, Ballyquinn, Lisnagelvin (Ó Doibhleacháin), etc.

Of these septs the most involved in Church affairs was Ó Muireadhaigh/Ó Muirí. For a very considerable period in the later Middle Ages they provided the priors of the independent house of Canons Regular of St Augustine founded in Dungiven by Ó Catháin. Cú Maighe na nGall Ó Catháin, who died after 1264, lies buried in the priory church. *Cú Maighe* 'hound of the plain' was a common name only amongst *Muintir Chatháin*. From Cú Maighe comes the surname *Mac Con Mhaighe*/Conway or MacConomy, which is quite common in the Glenelly valley where the priory of Dungiven annexed the rectorship of Badoney. Such a dispossession would only have been accepted with vigorous civil power behind it. Surmise then would suggest that Glenelly became part of the lands of Ó Catháin in the time of *Cú Maighe na Coille* 'of the wood' Ó Catháin, lord of *Oireacht Uí Chatháin*, who died in 1385.

There is no evidence of the existence of a parish of Dungiven in the Middle Ages. The Appendix to the *Ulster Inquisitions* includes the word parish as a sort of afterthought. The purpose of the *Inquisitions* was to discover the parish lands that would provide income to the bishop of the established Church. Since the churchlands of Dungiven were priory lands, the dissolution of the monasteries by Henry VIII meant that all such lands were at the disposal of King James I, and the lands of Dungiven disappeared into the maw of the London Companies – in this case to the Company of Skinners – whose lands stretched from Dungiven to Draperstown.

Since the bishopric had no interest in these lands, the information we have about them is sparse. There were eight balliboes of land, 'with their tithes and of the whole parish belonging to the priory', and obviously they were the townlands near the priory. Their names were not recorded in any of the sources. Séamus Hassan tells me that the patron of the priory was Mary.

Patron

Saint Neachtán Néir, died 679. *Nér* is an ancient word for 'a boar' – probably irrelevant. He was involved in the mission to western Scotland.

There was a church and early parish dedicated to him, Kilnaughton on the island of Islay, although the parish there may date from ecclesiastical reorganisation after the conversion of the Norse.[29]

Monastic lands
One quarter: Tiremeely; one quarter: Mayherydungevyn; one quarter: Ballywully; one quarter: Ownebegg near said monastery; plus tithes of +two quarters of Leighvallychuiyg, of three quarters of Ballyassoone, and of two quarters of Bennade; plus the rectory of Boydony in Cormac O Neill's territory, now devastated.[30]

BOTH MHÉABHA/BOVEVAGH

Name
This parish has one of the more intriguing names. *Both* is the received translation for the Hebrew *ōhel*, the nomad tent which included the Tent of Meeting of the Lord. The Latin equivalent was *tabernaculum*, which gives us 'tabernacle', of course. It is an early Irish word for a church. It is not clear if it differed from *domhnach* in size alone or perhaps in permanency. It is a relatively common word for an early church. What is more difficult to understand is the second part of the name, which seemingly refers to the pagan goddess *Méabha*. The only other local placename that includes the name Méabha is that of Sawel, the mountain, *Samhail Phite Mhéabha*, perhaps to describe its topographical features. The martyrologies show no sign of any saint called Méabha. They do include saints' mothers of the name, but none from Ulster. But then, confusingly, Méabha's associations are not with Ulster either.

The parish includes Templemoyle, showing evidence of an even earlier church. Templemoyle had the alias Ballymcklosky according to BD & ISL I, 259, giving us the location of the MacCloskey/Mac Bhloscaidh branch of Ó Catháin, descended from Bloscadh Ó Catháin, whose son Donnchadh – the first *Mac Bhloscaidh* – died in 1196.[31]

---

29. David H. Caldwell, *Islay: The Lord of Lordship* (Edinburgh: Berlinn Ltd, 2008), pp. 29, 147, 318.
30. *Inquisitions: Londonderry: Tempore Jac I* (James I), 10 November 1603, Annagh/ Enagh. See Badoney (infra).
31. Note the *baile biataigh*/ballybetagh of Ballymaclostie: twelve ballyboes in Rawlinson A. *Anal. Hib.* 3, 163.

Saints

Saint Adhamhnán (Eunan) was patron, according to Colgan. Montgomery writes it as 'Eugani', but St Eoghan/Eugene's mission was to the *Airghialla* of Ardstraw. Saint Aodhán/Aidan of Both Mhéabha of the Cianachta was a native of the area.

Saint Ringan was patron, according to tradition. It has been suggested that Ringan is a local form of Aodhán. In Scotland, however, Ringan is another form of St Ninian,[32] founder of the monastery of Whithorn/Candida Casa where many early Irish saints were educated, including Cairbre of Coleraine and Eoghan of Ardstraw.

Erenagh

Mac Conghalaigh – perhaps descendants of Conghalach, who belonged to the Ó Conchúir royal house of *Cianacht Glinne Geimhin*.

Erenagh lands

Half of one quarter: Clouganabogh (Clonganabogh) and Ardnanerine. (BD & ISL I, 104) Ballytemple; Ardenecrisse; Inshconner (CS III, *215*).

Ballytemple/*Baile an Teampaill*: Bovevagh townland with its medieval church?

Ardenecrisse looks like *Ard na Croise*, 'the height of the cross'.

Clouganabogh, perhaps *Clochán na Botha*, being the 'village at the church'.

Inshconner/*Inis Chonchúir*: 'Conor's (O'Connor's?) milking meadow'.

TÁMHLEACHT FHIONNLUGHAN/TAMLAGHTFINLAGAN

Name

Támh means 'plague, pestilence' and *leacht* means 'gravemound' or 'memorial cairn'. Here we are faced with a very ancient grave site, probably reverenced before Christian times. It would not be unusual for Christians to set about Christianising such a site with a church.

Patron

Saint Fionnlugh or Fionnlú, *anglice* Finlagan (from the genitive case). According to the genealogies, the brothers Fionnlugh and Fiontán were

---

32. John MacQueen, *St Nynia* (Edinburgh: Polygon Books, 1990), 72. 'Sanct Ninian' pronounced *sanct rinian* (in a mixture of Scots and Scots Gaelic), in the way cnoc is pronounced *croc* in Ulster Irish. This is also the origin of Trinian.

descended from Caireall ('who believed in Christ'), son of Muireadhach Muindearg, King of the Ulaidh (*rí Uladh*) towards the close of the fifth century. The martyrologies give St Fionnlugh's feast day as 3 January. Fionnlugh was the monk 'Finluganus' of Adamnán's *Life of Saint Columba*, who saved the life of St Columba when he was attacked by the spear-wielding Lámh Dheas, one of the band of Conall, son of Dónall, whose family Columba had excommunicated for 'persecuting churches'. Finluganus stepped between Colm Cille and his attacker. He happened to be wearing Colm Cille's cowl, which the spear could not pierce. Fionnlugh is venerated in western Scotland, especially on the island of Islay where the MacDonalds, Lords of the Isles, centred their lordship on the island castle in Lough Finlaggan, named for him. It is not clear whether Fionnlugh came back to Ireland or whether he lived and died in Scotland. As the genealogy shows, he had no necessary connection with this area. So the question arises as to whether the church here was founded by St Fionnlugh in person, or whether it was dedicated to him after his death. There is no evidence that he came to the area. Like St Cainneach and St Columba, many of the saints in the Roe valley are connected with and spent time as missionaries in Scotland. Indeed some of the clergy of Tamlaght Finlagan in the fifteenth century bear surnames closely associated with religious sites in the west of Scotland, including Iona.

Erenagh

A branch of Ó Catháin seem to have officially taken erenagh lands in the area at the beginning of the fifteenth century. A continual complaint from Church sources throughout this period was of civil lords using churchlands, and paying little heed to the threats of excommunication and interdict that were hurled at them and indeed imposed at times.

Erenagh lands

Mulkeeragh (Maol Caorach/the rounded hilltop of the sheep).
Shanreagh (*Seanriabhach* formerly-cultivated, rough-grassed fallow ground).
Drumnacarney (originally *Tír Mhic Cheatharnaigh*/McKarney's area).
Tully(hilly) (*Tulach (Coille*?)/the hill of the wood, or simply Tulach – a hill).
Moneyrannel (*Muine Raghnaill*/Ranald's thicket or scrub, or Ranald's hill).
Cloghfin (*Cloch Fionn*/the white stone).
Glassdare (*Glas Darach*?/stream of the oak tree). (Also written Ghanereagh)

TEARMANN CHAINNIGH/TERMONCANICE

Name

Tearmann Chainnigh was made up of three parishes: Dromachose/ *Droim an Chuais*? 'ridge of the hollow'; Aghanloo/Áth Lugha? 'the ford of Lugh; Balteagh/Both Dhá Fhiach 'the little church of the two ravens'. Tamlaght Finlagan was not part of *Tearmann Chainnigh*. The combined parishes were known in Latin as a *corbania* because the rector was known as *Comharba Chainnigh* 'the successor of St Canice', recognised as a dignity of the diocese. The position of *comharba* was so important that the incumbent was addressed by his surname, like Ó Néill or Ó Dónaill, known in English as 'chief of his name', and the only one so addressed. Everyone else was spoken to by his patronymic.

Droim an Chuais is named *Droim Cóasa* in GRSH, not to be found in DIL. Aghanloo is written 'Allowa' in the *Inquisitions*. *Áthán*, as is suggested sometimes, is not commonly found in placenames: it is hard to see how a 'little ford' would differ from a 'large ford'. As well as being a ford in the river, *áth* can refer to a shallow spawning place for salmon. *Áith* is a kiln, *áith allais* 'a sweat-house'. Saint Lugh is said to be the parish patron, but the name might be *Áth Fhionnlugha*, although local pronunciation may rule that out. *Lugh* is prominent in history and mythology as a pagan god. In the name of Balteagh, the word *both* refers to a small church in early Irish, although nowadays it is a 'hut'. In fact *both* is the translation of 'tent' in the 'Tent of Meeting' used by the Israelites in the desert in the Book of Exodus, which was translated into Latin as *tabernaculum* and has come down in English as 'tabernacle'.

Patrons

Saint Cainneach/Canice at Drumachose and Balteagh – feast day 11 October.
Saint Eolach of Drumachose of the *Cianachta*, therefore a native.
Saint Lugh at Aghanloo – feast day 16 June.
Saint Dubhdúin of Aghanloo and perhaps of Iona.
Saint Colmán of Balteagh – feast day 23 December.

Erenagh

The Primates' Registers at Armagh bear witness to a continued campaign by Church authorities to keep control of churchlands in the face of recurrent inroads being made on them by local lords. Bishops used the full armoury of Church sanctions in the struggle, interdict, excommunication, etc., with, it would seem, a limited measure of success. The churchlands of *Tearmann Chainnigh* lay in the *tuath* or kingship of *Cianacht Glinne Geimhin*. Saints Eolach and Colmán belonged to the Cianachta. The erenagh at *Tearmann Chainnigh* was *Mac Thaidhg* (McKeague/McTague/Montague) and *Tadhg* was the name of the son of *Cian*, ancestor of the *Cianachta*. The *Ó Conchúir* Kings of *Cianacht* had been defeated and dislodged by *Ó Catháin*. About the year 1400 we can see in the Primate's Register a branch of Ó Catháin engaged in ousting Mac Thaidhg from their position. Eventually Ó Catháin achieved full recognition, so that by 1600 the family held the erenagh lands of the whole Termon.

Erenagh lands
In Aghanloo: Ballyshanoigh, Cooleaghy, Ballymanagh (BD & ISL I, 58).
In Balteagh: Trine, Cahary, Mullin, Drenagh, Downechomo (Dromechome), Banalhy, Altenagh, Carrownakilly, Trianagarke, Ballyvolley, Drumgess. (BD & ISL I, 58)
In Drumachose: two quarters and two ballyboes: Drumore and Mullane (*Inquisitions*, Appendix).
One ballyboe at Mullaghiecrosse (*1604 list: Anal. Hib. 3,164*).

The list is taken straight from the Plantation Papers, whose scribes seem to have been confused by the relationship between the three parishes. The termon included Droim Ceat and a main Ó Catháin castle, 'built on churchland after a grant in exchange with a certain bishop.'[33]

Maolpheadair Ó Colmáin, *comharba Chainnigh*, 'successor of Canice', died in 1207 – 'the tower of piety and hospitality of the North of Ireland' (AU).

TÁMHLEACHT ARD/TAMLAGHTARD/TEARMANN MHIC GHIOLLAGÁIN/MAGILLIGAN

Name
Támhleacht (Tamlaght), like Cleggan, indicates the presence of an ancient burial ground, originally opened to cope with plague victims. The parish was clearly a place of importance in early Ireland from the frequency of references to it. At 1603 the parish was made up of forty

---

33. H.A. Jeffries, ed., 'Bishop Montgomery's Survey of Derry', *Seanchas Ard Mhacha*, 17, 48, 61.

towns or balliboes. This is testified by the fact that it was a *tearmann* with rights of sanctuary, etc. The parish has come to be known by the name of its medieval erenagh, Magilligan. As well as Tamlaghtard there was a church at Duncrun, the ancient site of *Dún Cruithne*, strong point built by the *Cruithnigh* before they were forced back to north Antrim about the time of St Patrick. Most of the land seems to have been churchland, mostly belonging in the *mensa* of the bishop, though some of it was no doubt set aside for the support of the clergy and upkeep of the churches. There were two, if not three, erenaghs.

The bishop had one of his three residences here. It was from Tamlaghtard that Bishop Réamann Ó Gallachair, in his capacity of acting primate, wrote to Bishop Conchúr Ó Duibheanaigh of Down and Connor in 1588, delegating him for one year to dispense 'with salutary penance' in all cases where Ó Gallachair himself could, in virtue of his apostolic brief and primatial dignity, because he cannot visit the area 'due to imminent dangers and hazards to life'. It may even have been towards Tamlaghtard and hoped-for security that he was heading when martyred at Cumber by a band of marauding English soldiers in 1601. Bishop Amhlaí Ó Muireadhaigh/Muirí, buried at Derry, described as 'a shining light, illuminating both clergy and laity', died at Duncrun in 1185 aged eighty-six.

Patrons

Saint Patrick at *Dún Cruithne*/Duncrun.
Saint Patrick left Beo-Aodh, a bishop, at *Dún Cruithne*.[34]
Saint Catán (or Cadán), described as *cruimhthir*, from Latin *presbyter*, the early Irish word for 'a priest', said to be of Tamlaghtard and to belong to St Patrick's retinue, where he was given the job of attendant or waiter.[35]

At some subsequent time it has become accepted that the patron of Tamlaghtard was Saint Aodhán (Aidan), and it was agreed that the name Cadán probably underlay Aidan. Prescinding from the possibility that Aodhán might be a diminutive of *Beo-Aodh*, there is another complication to the question. Most of the patron saints of the Roe valley had some connection with Scotland: Cainneach, Fionnlugh, Neachtán and Ringán. Some of the fifteenth-century clergy of Tamlaght Finlagan were connected by surname with places in Scotland like Iona. There is also Adhamhnán (Eunan) as patron at Dunboe and Errigal. Saint Catán

---

34. Whitley Stokes, ed., *Tripartite Life of St Patrick* (London, 1887), I, p. 160.
35. CGSH # 671.15, p. 119. His name is given as 'Gedanus' by Montgomery and others.

was venerated on the west coast of Scotland from Bute to Skye.[36] In that pattern it may even have been Aidan of Iona and Lindisfarne who became patron in Tamlaghtard. It is also relevant that there is no trace near the Roe of veneration for St Cianán of Duleek, one of the great names of *Cianachta Glinne Geimhin*. The *Cianachta* were displaced by Ó Catháin. If we recall the involvement of some Ó Catháin leaders in support of the kings of Scotland in their struggle with the Norse (which resulted in names like Monroe and McCausland, as we are told), perhaps some of those displaced by the Norse found security in the Roe valley.

There was also 'Ballinascreen de Ardo', the *scrín* based at Magilligan. It was a shrine associated with St Columba, about which nothing else is known.

Erenaghs

Mac Giollagáin/Magilligan, tearmannach/termoner, of the bishop's lands. Ruairí Mac Giollagáin was tearmannach c.1609.[37]

Eoghan Gruama (Eoghan 'the morose') Mac Giollagáin was one of the jurors sworn in at the Inquisition at Limavady on 30 August 1609.[38]

Mánus Mac Giollagáin was convoked by Archbishop Colton in 1397 to defend himself against the accusation that he had divorced his lawful wife Caitríona Ó Dochartaigh and taken 'other women'.

Montgomery says the erenagh was 'Patrick O Luine', which is probably Ó Luain or Ó Luanáin, a name found occasionally amongst the clergy, now O'Lone. He was parish erenagh presumably. He spoke Irish, Latin and English.

The *Annals of Ulster* note the death in 1207 of Giolla Phádraig Ó Falachtaigh, erenagh of *Dún Cruithne*. Montgomery, by 1609 had 'demised a profitable quarter of land at the chapel of St Patrick to Patrick O Falaghtie', described as a bird catcher or fowler.[39]

---

36. G.F. Black, *The Surnames of Scotland* (New York: New York Public Library, 1946), 1999, 512
37. See p. 151, H.A. Jefferies, ed., 'Bishop Montgomery's Survey of Derry', *Seanchas Ard Macha*, 17, 1996/7, pp. 48, 61.
38. *Inquisitions*, Appendix III
39. In medieval Ireland, rather than naming someone after their patron saint directly, they often put *Giolla* 'servant of' before the saint's name, so that Patrick O Falaghtie was quite probably *Giolla Phádraig*. This custom may have originated in Gaelic Scotland. In Ireland it had been more usual to put maol ('devotee of') before the saint's name. See above the ballyboe 'Bally Imulfedder', from surname *Ó Maolpheadair* 'town of the descendant of the devotee of (St) Peter'. *Mac Giolla Pheadair* – 'Kilfether' and 'Feathers'.

Erenagh lands

Bally Imulfedder, Dowagh, Moy, Ballivagallery, Ballymaregan, Gortmore, Ballimckwellan, Dromon, Ughtamore, Ballyileghy, Bally Smulchallan, Dromanally, Droncrine, Ballyskellan, Tawlaghtard, Dremon, Ishaga, Ballymckvoltmore, Cloggan, Tolly, Anearny.

DÚN BÓ/DUNBOE

Name

Dún Bó – the fort, place of residence, place of security, of the cow. But this was no common or paddock ruminant. She was the *Glas Ghoibhneann* or *Ghaibhleann* of ancient myth, the 'Grey of Goibhniu', the smith, who earlier still was the pagan god of smithcraft. According to the legend, this cow yielded a stream of milk that would fill every container put under her. There are many tales told about her in folklore all over Ireland: how Balar the tyrant tried to steal her, how Balar's evil eye turned her and her calf to stone, how she came ashore from the sea to help a poor family and stayed till one of the family struck her, how she was milked at *Dun Bó* but lay at *Leaba na Glaise* 'the bed of the grey' (Labby, in Ballinascreen).

Dún Bó was the parish of the archdeacon of the diocesan chapter. Dunboe has the doubtful distinction of having its vicar and archdeacon Aodh Mac Bhloscaidh/MacCloskey reported to Rome in 1497 for dereliction of duty, in that the parish church is neglected, inhabited by lay people who cook and presumably eat there and keep their utensils in it. The one doing the reporting, Conchúr Mac Cathmhaoil, belonged to the erenagh family who should have had a say in the matter, but Rome could not be expected to know that there was more to it than appeared. But then they would have heard similar stories from elsewhere. It is impossible to know if this state of things was exceptional or common. Conchúr wanted him out.

Patron

Saint Adamnán/Adhamhnán/Eunan, Abbot of Iona, 'little Adam' – feast date 23 September.

Erenagh

Mac Cathmhaoil/McCaul/MacCawell/Campbell.

O'Doherty Castle at Burt, Co. Donegal
Photo: © Kenneth Allen, geograph.org.uk

Castle of Anraí Aimhréidh ('Harry Avery'), Newtownstewart
Photo: © Kenneth Allen, geograph.org.uk

CROSS OF SAINT MURA AT FAHAN

Photo: © Andreas F. Borchert

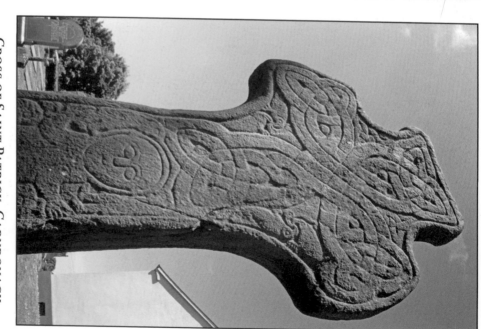

CROSS OF SAINT PATRICK, CARNDONAGH

Photo: © Paul Harris

TOMB OF CÚ MAIGHE NA NGALL ('COOEY-NA-GALL') AT DUNGIVEN

Photo: © David Lyons, Imagefile

Franciscan Friary, Corick Glen, Co. Tyrone
Photo: © Kenneth Allen, geograph.org.uk

O'Doherty Tower House, Derry City
Photo: © Derry City Council Heritage & Museum Service

Lintel, Church of Saint Lurach, Maghera

CROSS AT ALTAGHONY,
PARISH OF CLAUDY

TOMB OF SAINT MUIREADHACH Ó hÉANAIGH, BANAGHER

Photo: © John O'Kane, geograph.org.uk

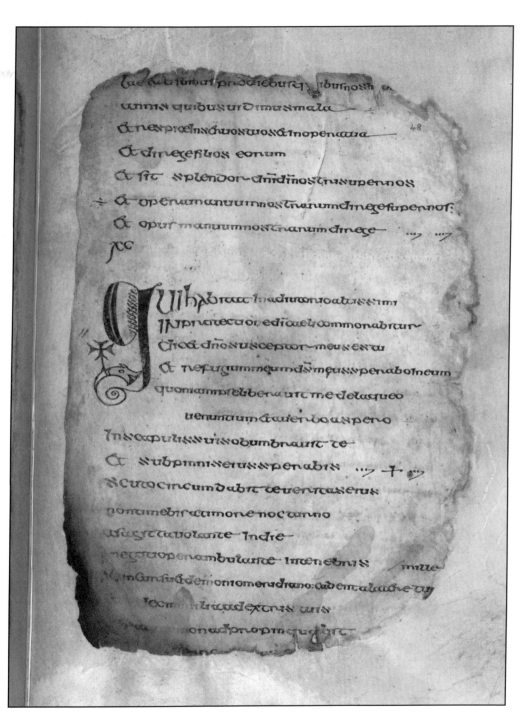

Page from the *Cathach* of Saint Colm Cille, fol. 48r
Photo: © Royal Irish Academy

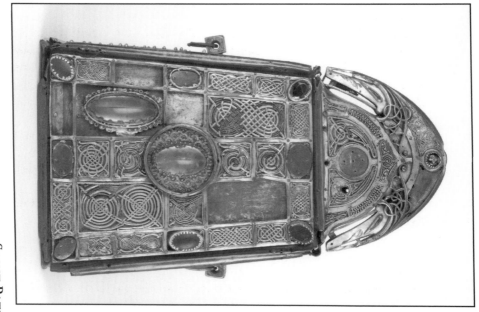

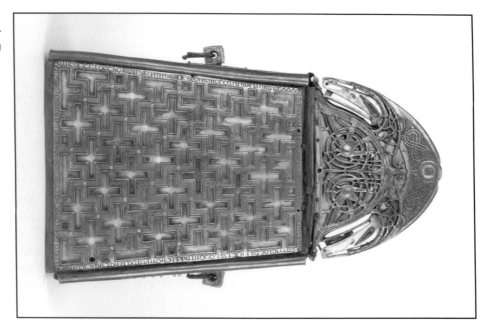

Erenagh lands

The erenagh lands are very extensive, running to eighteen townlands according to CS.

Three balliboes (i.e. Banreagh, Drominegully, Ballivowdage), over and above the two balliboes of Naburny and one ballyboe of Ballimaddy. Erenagh lands of Graungemore: Patoge, Mullane, Farranlegesserie, Masserigeny, Ballyeny, Quylly, Ballymullackaghbeg, Ballymullackaghmore, two balliboes of Graungemore, the half-balliboe of Ballynasse and the late weir near Ballinasse belonging to Camos.

Ballenemadigan, Balleruddducke, Drumnaquille, Banreagh, Burrenkill, Burrentwigh, half town of Dunboe, Pottagmore, Gortenagrane, Grangemore, Farrenlestre, Mulleagh, Balleane, Masregee, Quillemore, Quillebegg, Ballyblackbegg, Balleneblackmore (CS III, 159).

The garden of glebe was Tircurrinmore, Tircurrinbeg and half of Toberclare.

CÚIL RATHAIN/COLERAINE

Name

Cúil means 'a recess', a place set back from the highway. Arguably, *Rathain* fits in with that, meaning 'ferns', 'bracken'. However, in early times, pigs were sometimes left to fend for themselves, eating acorns and nuts and various roots, including roots of ferns. *Rathainmhá*, 'ferny plain' was reckoned amongst the types of valuable non-arable land.[40] It was especially useful beside the River Bann, for trout could be grilled on a spit over a fire of dry bracken.

While an out-of-the way place might seem to have been an ideal spot to site a monastery, it would not have been in keeping with the purpose of such foundations in early Ireland. Theirs was a missionary aim, with the result that the sites of such monasteries are usually found near some centre of population, for example, near a chieftain's *dún* where people would gather, and rarely far from a road. Early Ireland had a system of roads of different widths and differing in importance. The *Slí Mhíluachra* ran north from Tara to *Dún Sobhairce*/Dunseverick, branching at Connor to go to Derry and crossing the Bann at a ford south of Coleraine. A *slí* was a highway, usually royal, and wide enough to allow two chariots each drawn by two horses to pass. Roads were to be maintained by the farmers whose land they crossed, presumably

---

40. Fergus Kelly, *Early Irish Farming* (Dublin: Dublin Institute for Advanced Studies, 1997), pp. 338, 381, 385.

because they added greatly to the value of the land. Crossing a river at a ford could be made more secure by building up the riverbed at a shallow place with a firm bottom with stones or planks, or as at Dublin, with hurdles, *Áth Cliath*. The plain between Bann and Bush was known as *Maigh Éilne*.

Patrons

Saint Patrick is said to have visited and been offered a site for a church where some youths were engaged in setting fire to ferns. Although there was a medieval church dedicated to St Patrick,[41] it seems more likely that the first church in the area was that of St Cairbre. Saint Cairbre's genealogy is uncertain. GRSH claims him for Dál nAraí, which would indicate that he was more or less a native. However, Mac Fhir Bhisigh copies this entry only to delete it, and names three other saints Cairbre of uncertain ancestry. It was a common name, taking up almost four pages in Mac Fhirbhisigh.

Saint Eoghan/Eugene of Ardstraw was one of a large number of young people, also including St Tiarnach of Clones, captured by pirates and borne off to Britain. There he became a student at Candida Casa (Whithorn in Galloway) founded by St Ninian. The act of piracy is probably a literary conceit – the result of St Patrick having made abduction fashionable – but there seems no reason to doubt his education at Whithorn at St Ninian's school, although Ninian was probably dead by that stage. Other students there included Tiarnach of Clones. Pirates intervene again and bear Eoghan and Tiarnach, now joined by Cairbre of Coleraine, to Armorica where they are put to milling corn. The 'King of the Gauls' sent them back to Whithorn. It is possible that they were caught up in the aftermath of the Anglo-Saxon invasions, which led to that southward migration of Britons due to the Anglo-Saxon invasions, changing the name of Armorica to Brittany. Two kidnappings seem too good to be true, however. When St Eoghan/Eugene came north from Cill na Manach in Leinster to Ardstraw he maintained his friendship with Cairbre and Tiarnach. We are told that at Cairbre's request he provided him with a copy of the gospels, 'which was left on the altar at Ardstraw and was borne by angels to Coleraine'. Perhaps Ardstraw had a scribal school while Coleraine did not. Cairbre died about 560 and his feast day is 11 November.

41. Costello, *De Annatis Hiberniae: I Ulster* (Dublin, 1912), pp. 130, 138.

CILL EOGHAIN/CILL EOIN/KILLOWEN

Name

The Anglo-Norman effort to subdue Ulster led Bishop John de Grey, King's Justiciar, to invite the Scots Earl of Atholl, Thomas Fitz Roland, known as Tomás Mac Uchtraigh, and the descendants of Somerled – Norse in origin but who would become Mac Dónaill/Mac Donald – to settle on the northeast coast. In 1213–4 they built the castle at Coleraine and were confirmed there by King John in his capacity as Lord of Ireland.[42] Although the castle was taken in 1224 by Aodh Ó Néill, the castle builders had, according to the Four Masters, used the stone of all the cemeteries and buildings of the town – presumably those of the monastery – in the process. They seem to have left the church as it was, but it is presumed that it was at this stage that it was re-dedicated to St John/Eoin. Since then it has trembled between John the Baptist and John the Evangelist with a flutter towards Eoghan/ Eugene.

Erenagh

According to Bishop Montgomery, the erenagh was Éamonn Ó Catháin, who was also the vicar.[43]

Erenagh lands

According to Montgomery there were two quarters of profitable land, but which 'are being concealed by the same Éamonn or belong to the bishop'. The concealment works against us as it did Montgomery because the balliboes are not named at the time, although a survey of the bishop's lands in 1653 admits to two unnamed balliboes or half a quarter there.[44] Finally the names turn up in the *Civil Survey* (1654–6), Tullivenaghan and Knockenree, given in a contemporaneous note in BD & ISL as 'Tullirenaghan and Knockenree'. There was one 'garden of glebe'. In Killowen there was only a rector. The parish seems to have been joined to Camus in some way at 1610.

---

42. F.X. Martin in *New History of Ireland* II (Oxford: Oxford University Press, 1987), 147. AFM ad ann.
43. H.A. Jefferies in *Seanchas Ard Mhacha*, 1996–7, 48, 60.
44. BD & ISL I, 246, 333. CS III, 160

CAMAS CHOMHGHAILL/CAMUS-ON-THE-BANN
Name

Camas means a bend in a river. Saint Comhghall was the Abbot/ founder of the great monastery of Bangor. Comhghall (pronounced *Co'al*) belonged to the Dál nAraí kindred in north Antrim and was regarded as their heavenly patron and protector, which meant that the area belonged in Dál nAraí, and that the church belonged to the *paruchia* of Bangor. The importance of Camus can be measured from the fact that the name occurs frequently in early records.

Saints

Saint Comhghall, said to have died in 602. His feast day is 11 May. Saint Colmán, Abbot of Camas (or of Lann Mocholmóig?). Feast day is 30 October.
Saints Colma, Bogha and Laisre of the convent of Camas and/or of *Litir* in Antrim, described in one source as 'the daughters of Comhghall'. Feast day is 22 January.

Erenagh

Ó Dubhagáin/Ó Duagáin/O'Duggan, also erenaghs at Má Coscáin/ Macosquin Abbey.

Erenagh lands

One quarter of land, made up of two balliboes at Castlerowe, two balliboes at the church of Camus, and half a *baile bó* at Ballynass and 'a fishing weir'. There were also two 'gardens of glebe', one for the vicar and one for 'the curate to be kept there'. The half *baile bó* was held by Ó Néill, Hugh, Earl of Tyrone, presumably for the fishing, under what title is unclear, although it may have been given him by Ó Catháin. It was at Castleroe that he spent his fourth honeymoon, with *Caitríona Nic Aonasa*.

MÁ COSCÁIN/MACOSQUIN
Name

It is unclear what *Má Coscáin*, or perhaps *Má Coscráin*, might have meant originally. *Má* (earlier *Magh*) is an open stretch of land, a plain. *Coscán* means 'a brake' nowadays.

The Cistercian abbey *de Claro Fonte* 'of the clear fountain' at *Má Coscáin* was founded in 1218 at the request of Ó Catháin at much the same time as the Cistercian convent in Derry. The circumstances and the people involved are now unknown. The only thing known about the abbey is that it belonged to the Clairvaux line. It is surmised that it was founded from Mellifont by way of the abbey in Newry. The first person we hear of associated with it was Seán Ó Flannúra, abbot, who became Bishop of Derry in 1401. Since the surname is uncommon in Ulster he may have come from another house of the order. The abbey itself had a chequered if spasmodic history.

Erenagh

Ó Dubhagáin/O Duggan. This name may conceal the surname *Ó Dubh Dhúin*, which arises amongst *Cineál Binnigh*, a sept of the descendants of Eoghan (Cineál Eoghain) that left such a mark on the medieval church in Derry.

Erenagh lands

Eleven ballyboes, 'together with a free loope fishinge att the salmon leape of the river of the Banne'. The established Church amalgamated Camus and Macosquin (which was not a parish) and BD & ISL speaks only of the lands of the parish of Camus. The churchlands were in fact at the disposal of the king as a result of the dissolution of the monasteries. Not being parish lands they were not part of Bishop Montgomery's income and so are not named in his survey nor singled out for his attention. The *Civil Survey* indicates that they passed straight into the control of the London Company of Merchant Taylors,[45] as Dungiven Priory went to the Skinners. An inquisition in 1603 names the two quarters of Ferannnemonastragh, half a quarter of Sowlenemannagh; two quarters at Coolart in Inishowen and one quarter of Grange beside Burt Castle in Inishowen; plus tithes on fishing in the Bann, and a 'grange in the property of Mc Connell inside the kingdom of Scotland' (my translation from Latin). Mc Connell is Mac Dhónaill/MacDonald, who was lord of the Isles.

---

45. CS III, 148–9.

ACHADH DUBHTHAIGH/AGHADOWEY

Name

Achadh means a 'field'. *Dubhthach*, or *Dufach* nowadays is a personal name, based on *dubh*, black. From it comes the surname Ó *Dufaigh*, O'Duffy.

Patrons

The patrons of the parish were the two saints called Guaire:
Saint Guaire Beag 'little', and St Guaire Mór.
Guaire Beag and Guaire Mór's father, Colmán, were first cousins.
The feast day of Guaire Beag is 9 January, and of Guaire Mór 22 January.
They belonged to the *Uí Tuirtre*, descendants of Fiachra Tort, whose *tuath* was what is now south Derry – east Tyrone. Guaire Mór would seem from his genealogy to have been a contemporary of his distant relative St Lurach of Maghera whose brother Becc, King of Airghialla, died at the battle of Dún Bolg in Wicklow in 598.
The *Inquisitions* indicate a hospital or termon of Guaire with four quarters of land.[46]

Erenagh

English records have 'Mc Irridie', which may be Mac Riada. That the name seems to have four syllables may well indicate Mac Con Riada. In Ulster Irish the 'n' would have amalgamated with the 'r' after 'c' (as in *cnoc*, pronounced 'croc'), '*Mac e'ree-eda*'.

Erenagh lands

The erenagh lands of Aghadowey were extensive, consisting of one *baile biataigh*, which should mean sixteen *bailte bó*/ballyboes, named in BD & ISL (I, 57, 337) as:

Segnowry, Ballykally, Ballyginn, Monacarra, Dromnodoragh, Creveleagh, Ballybriam, Lismaghan, Killinlesemuscky, Givebegg, Balliedallie, Ardea;

Sydowny, Ballyeally, Balliquin, Monacarra, Dromnedoragh, Creweleagh, Ballibrittin, Lismoghan, Killin, Lissemucky, Givebegge, Ballydally, Ardea (BD & ISL I, 103).

Ballykillmore, Ballykillbeg, Balle Quin, Mollagh, Mullan, Ballebrittane, Ballewill, Monebronan, Arnsole, Lismorgh, Kiltene, Balledevitt, Ballimagerke, Ardragh, Clunrulla, Balledale (*fifteen and*

---

46. *Inquisitions (4): Londonderry: James I*, 10 Nov 1603.

one half townlands or balliboes); Moynecarne, half Mullenbrone, half Mullanard, Killakerragan, Sagore, half Lisboy, half Moynis, half Gortegorane, half Drumnagraniell, half Drumnadaragh, half Lage, half Dernatros, Lismuck (*eight and one half townlands*) (CS III, 161).

There was a garden of glebe for the vicar, perhaps Craglen and Corrascanle (CS 163).

ÁTH GEIMHE/AGIVEY

Name

In the parish of Aghadowey, but not of it, was a priory of Canons Regular of St Augustine under the auspices of the house of Canons Regular of Ss Peter and Paul, Armagh. Agivey Priory was a well-known place of pilgrimage in honour of the Blessed Virgin Mary and possessed a wooden statue of Our Lady, which established Church Bishop of Derry Brutus Babington, in an outburst of iconoclastic zeal, threw into the sea. The sea promptly returned it, so he burnt it. His death shortly afterwards was popularly regarded as the result.

At the Plantation of Ulster, Agivey Priory ceased to exist and was at the disposal of the king.

Patron

The patron was Mary.

Erenagh

Unknown, but probably *Mac Con Riada*. There were four ballyboes of erenagh land.

AIREAGAL ADHAMHNÁIN/ERRIGAL

Name

Aireagal derives from Latin *oraculum*, 'place of prayer', 'oratory'. Adhamhnán, which means 'little Adam', is of course St Adamnán/Eunan, Abbot of Iona, biographer of St Columba, social reformer and international statesman, who died in 703. How an *aireagal* might differ from the many other terms to denote a church is unclear.

Patron

Saint Adhamhnán/Eunan, abbot. Feast day 23 September.

Erenagh

O Margey, according to Montgomery. Ó Meargaigh/Markey is a south Ulster name. It may well be a version of Ó Muireadhaigh, associated with Dungiven Priory.

Erenagh lands

One quarter/four ballyboes: Templearregal, Owter, Brackagh, Gortemoyagh.[47]

Balletemple, Gortfadd, Gortnemoy, Brackagh (CS III 162) (in Irish *Baile an Teampaill, Gort Fada, Gort na Maighe, Breacmhagh*).

Gort and *breacmhá* indicate two uses of land: cultivation and rough pasture.

'Templearregal' may show that someone had forgotten what *aireagal* meant.

'Owter' is presumably *uachtar* 'upper'. Farrantemple nearby is *Fearann an Teampaill*: 'land of the church', probably the *gort* of glebe, 'ffarranteinell' (CS).

DÍSEART UÍ THUATHAIL/DESERTOGHILL

Name

Díseart, through Latin, brings us back to the Church in Egypt centuries ago when men and women went out into the desert to practise an eremitical (solitary) life. Eremitical gives us 'hermit', so *díseart* is 'a hermitage'. There are a number of other places in Co. Derry to remind us of hermits: Desertmartin, Brackadysart, Desertlyn, etc. Many of them are associated with St Columba. Ó Tuathghaile/Ó Tuathail/Tohill are one of the septs descended from Eochaidh Binneach, son of Eoghan (of Inis Eoghain). As well as being the military force of Cineál Eoghain in their expansion out of Inishowen, they became imbued with devotion to St Colmcille to the extent that he was made patron of any place they settled. One of the unforeseen consequences has been that their zeal created the belief that Columba had founded the Church in that area and so eradicated traces of any earlier evangelisation.

Patron

Saint Columba – feast day 9 June.

---

47. BD & ISL I, 58.

Erenagh

Ó Tuathail. As well as Desertohill, the name is found where Craigavole is popularly and in fact more accurately pronounced 'Craigyole': *Creig Uí Thuathail*. Tradition recorded Ruairí Mór Ó Tuathail as the last chief of the name.[48]

Erenagh lands

One quarter/four ballyboes; Templedisert, Cloghtegall, Drom Iferen, Moletraghkill.[49]
Moyletrakill, Drumnanarin, Drumnaduffe, Killanallo (CS).

Moyletraghkill looks like *maol íochtarach na cille* 'lower bare, round hill of the church' or perhaps *na coille* 'of the wood'. Templedisert is of course *Teampall an Dísirt* 'church of the hermitage'. The others names seem to have been lost, just as well perhaps, since Drom Iferen looks like *Droim Ifrinn* 'the ridge of hell'.

CILL RIADA/KILREA

Name

Riada occurs in ancient placenames like *Eiscir Riada*, the great esker running across the centre of the country, and *cill* is a church, from Latin *cella*, introduced to Ireland in monastic times. It has been suggested that the name is *Cill Riabhach, riabhach* is a sort of nondescript brown, or brown as the predominant colour with an admixture of others, hence 'brindle'. *Cill Riada* is the form given in the list of Patrick's disciples in the *Book of Lecan* which names a disciple of St Patrick, *Caomhán Chille Riada*, given the job of valet in Patrick's retinue when people had forgotten why he had a retinue. We cannot be certain he was the disciple left at the church of Kilrea, but it is a fair inference from the fact that St Patrick was the medieval patron, and that the church belonged in the *paruchia* of Armagh. In 1245 Innocent IV gave the protection of the Apostolic See to the church of Ss Peter and Paul of Armagh, confirming them in their rule, possessions, rights, privileges and immunities, including the church of Killreda with lands at Maguegraim, Tirculam, and three fishings on the Bann.[50] According

---

48. James B. Leslie, *Derry Clergy and Parishes* (Enniskillen: Leslie, 1937), p. 185
49. BD & ISL I, 58, 102; CS III, 162
50. M.P. Sheehy, *Pontificia Hibernica* II (Dublin: M.H. Gill, 1962–5), p. 273.
    Maguegraim = Moneygran?

to the Appendix to the *Ulster Inquisitions*, for the previous 170 years, the 'abbot [*recte*, prior] of Peter and Paul of Armagh had the right of prestation of parson and vicar and right of patronage, which is now come to the crown'.

Patron
Saint Patrick/Pádraig, bishop – feast day 17 March.
Saint Caomhán: There are two saints called Caomhán, one called Caomhán Breac, venerated on 12 June; a different name from St Kevin/Caoimhín of Glendaloch.

Erenagh
Ó Diamain/O'Diamond: *diamain* seems to mean 'clean', 'faultless', 'pure'.

Erenagh lands
One quarter/four ballyboes (unnamed). In the established Church system Kilrea was soon joined to Tamlaghtocrilly. The townland/ballyboe names were recorded as an indication of episcopal income, all native records being destroyed. Since income had gone to Armagh and monastic land fell to the king, the *Inquisitions* did not pursue the matter.

TÁMHLEACHT UÍ CHROILIGH/TAMLAGHTOCRILLY
Name
Támh means 'plague', 'pestilence', hence 'death'. *Leacht* is a 'grave monument', 'grave mound' or 'cairn' (of stones). The second part of the name comes from those who were the erenaghs: *Ó Croiligh*/O'Crilly.

The parish has another name in fifteenth-century Roman records, variously spelt: Tamlaghtmacneach, Tamlaghtmacineach, Tamlahtmatneach, Tawlaghtmacninaych.

The townland, Macknagh, may suggest an unlikely connection with root vegetables (*meacan*), even if hospitality was an erenagh's responsibility. The name will bear further research. The erenagh lands include Dromagarner now in the parish of Kilrea. Archbishop Colton, on his visit to Derry in 1397, appointed Dermitius Omolgan Rector of Dromogarvan. Reeves takes this to be Diarmaid Ó Maolagáin/Mulligan, but perhaps in south Derry Ó *Mothlacháin* is more likely. Like Ó *Catháin*, Ó *Maoláin* and others, they belonged to the *Clann Chonchúir* branch of *Cineál Eoghain*. The name was anglicised Mallaghan and often shortened to Mallon, although the latter had a different origin. However, the entry, whatever the name, shows that 'Dromagarvan' was where the parish church of Tamlaghtocrilly then was.

Patron

According to Montgomery's Survey the patron was St Coulie, which is most probably a scribal attempt at *Comhghall*, where in Irish the *mhgh* is almost silent, giving something like *co'al*. Whether St Comhghall of Bangor or St Comhghall, Abbot of Both Chonais in Gleneely in Inishowen, is meant is unclear. Given the influence of the Cineál Binnigh branch of Cineál Eoghain on the Church in medieval south Derry (as it now is) one would suggest the latter.

Erenagh

Ó Croiligh; Eoghan Ó Croiligh was rector and erenagh in 1607. The sept of *Muintir Chroiligh* are something of an enigma. The name does not appear in any of the genealogies, yet they were clearly prominent. There is a suggestion that they came from Munster, but that is a device often used to improve the credentials of a sept who were there all the time. Bishop Reeves suggests that the name comes from Connacht. He takes the original Irish to be *Ó Crualaoigh*, which is however a different name, usually anglified as Crowley.[51] The name may find its remote origin in words no longer in common use: *craidhleach*, 'one who proclaims' or *créidhleach*, 'trustful, devout'.

The importance of Muintir Chroiligh is testified to by the poem of Aonghas na nAor Ó Dálaigh, generally known as *an Bard Rua* or *Aonghas na nAor* 'of the satires' to distinguish him from several other members of *Muintir Dálaigh* of the name Aonghas. He lived in the reign of Elizabeth and is said to have been specially employed by the agents of Lord Mountjoy and Sir George Carew to write this poem, which is a bitter lampoon, satire, or burlesque, directed against the chiefs of the principal ancient Irish families, and such of the Anglo-Normans as had adopted their customs and formed alliances with them. This was in order by dint of assertion and bare-faced effrontery to stir up angry passions and discord so that the conquest of the country might be made easier. The boast of the Irish was hospitality: even their enemy acknowledges that they were recklessly hospitable. Where better to attack them, particularly those whose very occupation was

---

51. William Reeves, *Colton's Visitation of Derry 1397* (Dublin, 1850), p. 81.

concerned with hospitality, the erenaghs? Amongst those who come in for treatment (except for those he was afraid of) are:

Ó Croiligh beag na gciabh gcas   Wee Ó Croiligh of the curly locks,
fear nach ndearna riamh a leas   a man who never did what was for his
                                                        own good;
aghaidh an duine ar a bhráid   the fellow's face on his neck,
ag tarraingt a choire ar éigin as. producing his miserly cooking pot.

Erenagh lands

Five ballyboes: Drumacanany, Drumagarnan, Dromean, Moneyloghra, Dromlish. Droma Kanany, Dromegarnan, Dromeane, Moniloghgra, Dromlishy.[52]

Drumacanany looks like Droim an Chanónaigh 'the canon's ridge', which suggests the otherwise unknown presence of Canons Regular in the area.

Seven ballyboes: Dromarde, Drowlen, Dromnliss, Gortmᶜkreen, Dromegan, Dromigarnan (CS).

Glebe: Killmuck, Rillgulb, Bellimᶜpeck, Munysteghan/Monestahane (half townland) (CS).

BAILE UÍ SCOLLÁIN/INIS TAÍDE/BALLYSCULLION

Name

Like Ó Croiligh, Ó Scolláin is not found in any genealogy. Séamus Ó Ceallaigh suggests Ó Scuillín. *Baile* is a quite late arrival in placenames, yet there are more *Baile* – names in this parish – than in surrounding parishes: Ballynease/*Baile Aonasa*; Ballymacombs/*Baile Mhic Thomáis* (Ulster pronunciation of *Tomás* puts the stress on the *first* syllable); Ballymacpeake/*Baile Mhic Péice*, etc. *Baile* is cognate with Latin *villa* and later with Norman French *ville*. It meant a 'homestead' or 'farmstead' or 'a piece of land belonging to a person, family or group', indicative of a settled, organised community since many townland names are descriptive rather than personal. The parish corresponds to the civil territory of *Tuath Locha an Droichid* 'lake of the bridge'.

The civil lord of the area, under *Ó Néill* of *Clann Aodha Bhuí* (Clandeboy), was Ó Maol Chalainn/Mulholland, based at *Seanmhullach*

---

52. BD & ISL I 57, 102; II 334. CS III 186. The parish seems to have escaped the Inquisitions.

(now Castledawson). They would seem to belong to *Cineál Eoghain*, descended from Maol Chalann, brother of High King Niall Caille (+846). The greater claim to fame, perhaps, of Ó Maol Chalainn was that they were, along with Ó Mealláin of *Meallánacht* (Lissan), the custodians of St Patrick's Bell, *Clog an Uachta*. Séamus Ó Ceallaigh wrote a short account of their guardianship and faithfulness to the trust, even through penal times.[53]

Patron

Saint Taíd, who gave his name to the 'pattern' site on the island of *Inis Taíde* in *Loch Beic*. Taíd does not occur in martyrology or genealogy, but like St Muireadhach Ó hÉanaigh of Banagher, there is no doubt about the devotion inspired over the centuries in those who make the pilgrimage. The island site would suggest an anchorite or penitent in a hermitage. The island has given the parish its alternative name, *Inis Taíde* (or *Taoide*).

Erenagh

Montgomery gives the erenagh's name as O Finlune, which does not match any known Ulster name. It must be a transcription error. It is properly Ó Scoillín/Scullion. The name may originate in *scolaidhe* 'a scholar', with added diminutive *Ó Scolaidhín*. The *dh* being silent gives *Ó Scoillín*. A related word *scológ*, also meaning 'a student', 'a disciple', has the acquired meaning 'a tenant of (Church) land', a 'farmer'.

Erenagh lands

One ballyboe: unnamed, but presumably 'Ballyscullen more' and 'Ballyscullen begg'. CS says Ballyscullion borders on Tawlagh-due, Lawaghbegg, Bellaghy and Bellim^cillcony. *Támhlacht Dubh* and *Béal Eachaidh* are easily identifiable.

TEARMANN EANGA/TERMONENY

Name

Tearmann (from Latin, *terminus*, 'limit') indicated a protected area around a monastery where an offender could seek asylum. Church law fitted in with Irish civil law under which any freeman could give

---

53. Graham Mawhinney, ed., *Gleanings from Ulster History*, Second Edition (Draperstown: Ballinascreen Historical Society, 1994), pp. 66–72.

legal protection for a set period of time. It was a crime to injure anyone under such protection. Not all offences could benefit from sanctuary, however. Excluded in ancient Ireland were those of a fugitive killer, a son who fails to look after his father, a runaway wife or slave, anyone who absconds from his own kindred.

There were four *tearmainn* in the diocese: *Tearmann Chainnigh/* Termoncanice; *Tearmann Uí Mhongáin/*Termonamongan; *Tearmann Doire/*Termonderry (which included Termonbacca); *Tearmann Eanga/* Termoneeny. Támhleacht Ard/Magilligan is sometimes said to be a *tearmann*. What led to this special position is unclear. In the case of Termonderry and Termoncanice it is perhaps attributable to the prestige of the founder. Termonamongan could call on its connection with Lough Derg. Termoneeny is especially difficult since the meaning of *eang/eanga* is vague. The word *enncae* in DIL provides another possible avenue of investigation in the context of *tearmann*; it means 'innocence', 'guiltlessness of any action incurring penalty', but it would seem to undercut the need for sanctuary. The alternative name of the parish, Mullaghenry/Mullaghanry/*Mullach Eanadh* is not much help. The ancient church site is still pointed out on the original mullach near Maghera. The ending -anry/-eeny/-any is not Heaney, as Leslie suggests;[54] -anry/-enry is too ancient to be from Anraí/ Henry. It seems clear that the original sense has been lost over the years. The ending occurs elsewhere in the diocese: Tobereny, a well at Badoney; Killeeny, an ancient church in Donaghedy; Nadun-eny in the churchlands of Drumragh; Termoneeny here. Then there is the problem of the original of the surname McAneny.[55]

*Clog an Uachta/*St Patrick's Bell disappeared from written history in 1446. Nearly four hundred years later, at the beginning of the nineteenth century, an old man – a teacher – was on his deathbed at Shane's Castle in Co. Antrim. He sent for one of his pupils, a successful businessman in Belfast named Adam McClean, and bequeathed to him all he valued, which was buried in a box in the garden. The box was found to contain a Bedell's Bible and St Patrick's Bell in its ornate late eleventh-century shrine. The old man was Henry Mulholland, last of the Ó Maol Chalainn family who were hereditary custodians of the bell. From the title page of the Bible we learn that Henry Mulholland's grandfather,

54. James B. Leslie, *Derry Clergy and Parishes* (Enniskillen, 1937), p. 302.
55. Father Uaitéar Ó hÉigeartaigh devotes a section to the question in his notes but comes to no conclusion.

Brian, custodian no doubt in his turn, died in 1758 at Mayogall. The bell and shrine are now in the National Museum in Dublin.

Patron

Mac Nessan, according to Montgomery: Sons of Nessán. Nessán's seven sons are named in the Martyrology of Oengus. It says that four of them were 'in Enga': Muireadhach, Crónán Cráifeach (the pious), Caireall and Flann. They were *Laighin* (from Leinster), natives of Fingal, north of Dublin. No one offers an opinion on why they should be associated with Termoneny.

According to GRSH and CGSH, Muireadhach and Crónán are the same person. DF omits Flann, includes Dúcaill and counts Muireadhach and Crónán as distinct.[56] They must belong to a much earlier stratum of belief, predating the medieval influence of *Cineál Binnigh* in their travels and their zeal for spreading the patronage of St Columba.

Erenagh

Ó Caoilte/Kielt. The name is not found in the genealogies, annates and papal and primate's registers in the fifteenth and sixteenth centuries.

Erenagh lands

Ballicarigy, Knock Ichilty, Lisidroghell, Ballinetollagh.

Baile na Carraige means Rocktown, although the present Rocktown seems too far from the Mullagh. (Erenagh lands were usually contiguous.) It is perhaps Carricknakielt. *Cnoc Uí Chaoilte* is Knocknakielt. The Mullagh should be one of the others.

CS gives Bellimihowne, Carrogokillty, Knockokillty, Mullagh, with glebe lands at Bellinahownewoghteragh. (*Baile na hAbhann Uachtarach*/Ballinahone Upper.)

CILL AN LOCHA/KILLELAGH

Name

The 'church of the lake' in Carrowmena. The Appendix to the *Ulster Inquisitions* calls it 'Killologhan', which might suggest *Cill an Locháin* 'the church of the little lake', or Cill na Lachan, from the bothersome duck that interfered with the construction, or even with, as an outside

---

56. Whitley Stokes, ed., *The Martyrology of Oengus the Culdee* (London: Harrison and Sons, 1905), pp. 82, 90. CGSH 284.1. GRSH 87, 89, 90.

possibility, *Cill Uí Lachtnáin* 'O'Loughlin's Church'. A lake figures in Fiannaíocht tales having been dug by Bran, the hound of *Fionn Mac Cumhaill* in pursuit of a *fia draíochta*, 'an enchanted deer', which disappeared into the ground just as Bran was about to apprehend it, and of course we are not far from *Suí Finn*/Fionn's Seat, 'Seefin Hill'. Nearby in Tirnoney stands a dolmen, indicating an ancient and storied history; ancient, because the name Tirnoney dates from a time when *tír* (meaning 'land, country, territory') was a neuter noun, which eclipsed the following consonant. It is Old Irish, then, well over a thousand years old. This makes the pursuit of its meaning problematic. *Tír nOmhna* or *Tír an Oghma* 'land of the tree-trunk' has been suggested, perhaps used as a boundary-mark.

It is interesting that Carrowmena/*An Ceathrú Meánach*/'the middle quarter' lies between Tirkane, Tirnoney and Tullyherran, distinct territories, clearly. The temptation to equate Tirkane and *Tír Chatháin*, because O'Kane and *Ó Catháin* are the same name is perhaps just that, a temptation. It is well to recall that there was also a King of Cianacht, which was across Carntogher in the Roe valley, called *Ó Céin*, unconnected with *Ó Catháin*. *Tír Chéin*, 'territory of Cian' may be just as likely. The name *Cathánach* occurs in the *Cineál Binnigh* genealogy.

The parish originates in the Twelfth-Century Reform of the Church in Ireland when territorial dioceses and parishes were established. The area we know as the diocese of Derry was formed originally as the diocese of Ardstraw, but the diocesan see was transferred from Ardstraw to Maghera. It is probable that Killelagh was formed at this stage, perhaps as part of the episcopal *mensa* or as a benefice for some dignitary like the dean or archdeacon of the diocese.

Patron

Saint Muireadhach (Muiriach) Ó Cofaigh, bishop from before 1152 to 10 February 1175; buried at the Columban monastery in Derry (*Dubhreglés*). He or his predecessor Ó Gormaile transferred the seat of the diocese from Ardstraw to Maghera. He was known for his learning, chastity, humility and his generosity to the poor. He attended the Synod of Kells in 1152, building and renovating some seventy churches. As an old man along with other bishops he did fealty to English King Henry II who had come to Ireland to keep an eye on his Anglo-Norman barons.[57] The annals report that the night he died the sky was lit up from midnight to cockcrow by a moving ball of fire, which made it as bright as day.

Where the name Ó Cofaigh/Ó Cobhthaigh came from is less clear. It is a Munster name usually. For a possible northern point of origin in the genealogies there is Cobhthach, son of Meilghe, son of Éanna Boghaine, son of Conall Gulban, placing their origin in *Cineál Chonaill* (south Donegal), or Cobhthach, son of Brión of *Síol Ír*, many of whose branches belong in modern Antrim and Down. By 1609, 'the sept of Salamon Coffey/Solamh Ó Cofaigh were seized of ... one town', including Mullagh Brollaghan and Fearann Uí Chofaigh in the churchlands of Armagh.[58] These references might indicate that the sept of Ó Cofaigh were not natives. (See further discussion under Maghera, below.)

Possibly, in the zeal of early reform at the time, a different type of bishop was purposefully sought out. Muireadhach/Muiriach belonged, we are told, to the Canons Regular of St Augustine. If the parish was founded by him when bishop, as is suggested, it could not have been founded with him as patron. The name Montgomery gives, 'St Crom'urmori', has been corrupted in transmission, although 'mori' at the end may suggest *Muiríach*. On the strength of the townland name Tullyherran, seemingly, Leslie, following Reeves, suggests St Ciarán. None of the many St Ciaráns seems to have been associated with the area.

Erenagh lands

Name of erenagh not recorded.

Four balliboes: Tirnony, Tollikeran, Ballimeanagh, Treacheana (BD & ISL).

Tyronany, Tollykeran, Ballymeanagh, Tiercheana.

Tiranony, Tulloghkerran, Kerrumenagh, Tiraknogh; plus glebe: Gortinure (CS).

MACHAIRE RÁTHA LURAIGH/MAGHERA

Name

Machaire: 'a plain', 'a stretch of level ground'. In early Ireland the level, often 'cleared', space in front of a *dún* was to keep an eye on those

---

57. J.R. Walsh, *History of the Parish of Maghera* (1973), pp. 24–6; J. Blennerhassett Leslie, *Derry Clergy and Parishes* (Enniskillen, 1937), p. 239.
58. Mac Fhir Bhisigh 158, 7; 497.15; 1174. 4 (*Furadhrán Othna mac Fearadhach m Eochaidh 1174.4*).

approaching, as a green for grazing sheep (so that they could be brought in easily at night) and as an area for games.

Ráth: 'a rampart', 'an earthen embankment surrounding a king's residence', by transference, 'a fort'. The purpose of the embankment was to keep out wandering dogs, foxes, wolves, etc., rather than human enemies. Inside the *ráth* was the *lios*, where the dwelling and animal pens, etc., were built. Since wood was plentiful the buildings were relatively easily constructed. In this case the *ráth* would have surrounded the church buildings.

Lurach is the saint who founded Maghera. It would seem that the first syllable of his name 'Lur' rhymes with 'fur', 'purr', 'slur'. The usual spelling in the martyrologies is Lurach, usually without accent, although one suggests a variant reading 'Laurach/Luarach'.[59] Tradition assures that in English locally he was called 'St Loury' (as in 'now'). *Ráth Luraigh* became the seat of the diocese originally to be centred on Ardstraw. Why this was so is unclear. There is strong evidence of political instability in the area of the diocese that is now west Tyrone-east Donegal. This may have had the result that the bishop moved east for a quiet life.

The decision may have followed on from the efforts in south Derry of *Cineál Binnigh* as vanguard of expansionist *Cineál Eoghain*, adding to their military success a zeal for renewal through devotion to St Colmcille, making it a choice between carrying on the Reform in one area or coping with internecine strife in the other. The diocese changed name from Ardstraw to *Cineál Eoghain* and *Ráth Luraigh*. It may have helped that the first territorial bishop in the process belonged himself to *Cineál Binnigh*. Bishop Ó Gormala or Ó Gormghaile died in 1149, 'a noble and pious elder after penance and intense penitence'. This is definitely not the same name as Ó Gormlaigh of *Cineál Moain*, who were prime movers in the strife around Ardstraw. It is not stated where he was bishop, but since he belonged to *Cineál Binnigh Tuatha Rois Blaí*, which included the Maghera area, it is reasonable to say that he was bishop there. It might even lend some poignancy to the reason given for the transfer to Maghera that, when the time came for the see to be moved to Derry the bishop had been *illectus natalis soli dulcedine*, 'seduced by the charms of his native soil', according to Innocent VI

---

59. CGSH 13.

in 1247,[60] who gives a further reason for the transfer: Maghera was inaccessible because surrounded by mountains, woods and marshes, too barren and lacking in necessities so that bishop or canons cannot reside there nor the clergy come to the synod and other such events. The papal decree was hardly publicised in Maghera.

The pope writes that Muireadhach Ó Cofaigh was responsible for moving to Maghera in the first place, which would look conclusive. However, the fame of the saint clearly eclipsed Ó Gormaile, who would seem much more likely to have been 'seduced by the charms of his native soil' than Muireadhach Ó Cofaigh, his successor.[61] In addition, Innocent IV gave permission to the diocesan chapter in June 1247 to make use of all the privileges, indulgences and concessions that had been conceded by Rome to the Church of Maghera.

Patron

St Lurach, bishop – feast day 17 February.

Sixth century, brother of Becc, King of Uí Tuirtre. Legend has made him a nephew of St Patrick, son of Darerca – Patrick's sister – but there is no independent evidence of her existence. This may result from confusion with the claim that she was mother of St Lurán Duanaire of Derryloran. It is said that Lurach was a pupil of Lurán. It is quite possible that they are identical: Lurán is referred to as *duanaire* and one title given Lurach is Lurach *na ndán/*'of the poems'.[62] Tradition suggests that he was baptised by St Patrick and that he in turn baptised St Cainneach when his straying cow arrived at the home of the hungry child. Since even a saint's cow might not have had the stamina to stray over by the Roe valley, this should be seen as a sort of apostolic succession, from Patrick to Lurach to Cainneach. From the dates it is quite unlikely that he and Patrick could have met but if nothing else it shows that there was a strong Patrician tradition in south Derry, however weakened by subsequent devotion to St Colmcille. Lurach

---

60. Cf. M.P. Sheehy, ed., *Pontificia Hibernica* (Dublin: M.H. Gill, 1965), II, 292, p. 152; 294, p. 134.
61. Giolla na Naomh Ó Gormaile, priest of Ráth Luraigh, died in 1218 on pilgrimage, AFM ad ann.
62. According to Michael O'Clery, *The Martyrology of Donegal* (Dublin, 1864), 52/53, Lurach *na nDán*, son of Cuana, of *Doire Luráin*, in Ulaidh, of the race of Colla Uais, monarch of Éire. Son of Darerca. He was also a bishop. When Maol Fothartaigh, King of Uí Tuirtre, died in 669 he was buried at Doire, most probably Derryloran, again showing the importance of the Lurán/Lurach connection in Uí Tuirtre.

was of royal blood, being descended from Colla Uais, alleged King of Ireland, said to be buried at Carncose on the slopes of Sliabh gCallan Slievegallon.

Tradition asserts that the three Colla brothers carved out a series of kingdoms in the south and west of Ulaidh, the kingdom of the Ulstermen, in the process capturing and burning *Eamhain Macha* (Armagh) in 337. These were known as the Airghialla, one of them being the kingdom of the *Uí Tuirtre*, the descendants of Fiachra Tort, son of Colla Uais. Becc, brother of Lurach, was King of Uí Tuirtre and Overking of Airghialla. The kingdom of Uí Tuirtre included the territory between the Moyola and the Blackwater Rivers. Becc was killed in 594 at the Battle of Dún Bolg near Baltinglass (Wicklow) along with High King Aodh mac Ainmhireach (donor of Derry to St Columba) by Brandubh, King of Leinster. Lurach, his distant relative Trea at Ardtrea (Moneymore), and Taíde at Bellaghy alone of the early saints have maintained some presence in the area over the centuries. We can only wonder why they survived in local piety when others disappeared without trace.

Erenagh

Name of erenagh not recorded. This is surprising, given the prestige attached to the parish. It is possible that there were more than one. There are a number of names found amongst the clergy of the period, which should indicate that they belonged to erenagh families but are not recorded as such. There is one conundrum that has defeated everyone up to the present, the name common in the Church in south Derry and spelt variously as Otheagan, Otchegan, Ochegegan, Othoagan, Otehegron. As Séamus Ó Ceallaigh stressed, this name is not Ó hAgáin/O'Hagan. Any name that occurs as frequently as this shows the importance of the bearers. The names of most other erenaghs in south Derry are still to be found in large numbers in their area. Some Mac names became O names. This may be the case in Maghera where a similar name with 'Mac' instead of 'O' is found among the clergy of fifteenth-century Maghera: Meiceochagan, Macheoghogan, Meicroghan, Machcochoeran.

This is almost certainly Mac Eochagáin/MacGuckin, although it might be MacGuigan. MacGuigan is said to be *Mac Uiginn,* 'son of Viking', but *uiginn* is not found as a first name in the genealogies. Séamus Ó Ceallaigh drew attention to a name in the *Cineál Binnigh* genealogy, spelt Uididén and Uidegén, but takes it no further than that. Might that be the origin of MacGuigan: Mac Uidheagáin rather than Mac Uiginn? It would also help explain how such a common name escaped the attention of the genealogists and how it originally came to south Derry. With the name *Mac Eochagáin* in mind, we may consider that Otheagan, Otchegan, Ochegegan, Othoagan, Otehegron, etc., looks similar.

The most likely candidate is the name Ó hEachaidhéin/Ó hEocháin/ Haughian, that of a bardic family in the lordship of *Clann Aodha Buí* (Clandeboy) Ó Néill.[63] This area included much of south Derry, the domain of *Clann Dónall Donn na Banna*, a branch of Clann Aodha Bhuí, whose remit ran from the *Bráid*/Braide in Antrim to *Gleann Con Cadhain*/Glenconkeine in south Derry. Ó *hEachaidhén*/Ó hEochadháin descended from Eochaidh (+572), son of Dónall Ilchealgach, high king (+566), a sept of *Cineál Eoghain* known as the *Fir Droma Lighean*/Men of Drumleen (Lifford), which included Ó *Donnaile*/Donnelly and Ó *Doibhlin*/Devlin. Many bardic families had erenagh associations. The name Haughian may well have been melded with Haughey since then, as Devlihan merged with Devlin or Ó Caráin became MacCarron. *Mac Eocháin* or Ó *hEocháin* may well have been erenagh at Maghera, unless Tamneymullan is relevant to the quest.

Erenagh lands

Six-and-a-half ballyboes: Ballynacreeny, Tawnynymallan, Creggamore, Loraghgantagha, Cregada, Fultagartrewy, Ballywonmore, plus six acres of glebe.
Ballymacreeny, Tawnymullen, Cregganmore, Largagantaghy, Creggada, Fallagartreny, Ballyvonymore, plus six acres of glebe (for the vicar). (BD & ISL)
Maghera, Tawnimullan, Cregmore, Cregduff, Lergantagher, Fallgortreach, Minimore, Creeve (being eight towne land and a halfe: [CS]).

Ballynacreeny/Ballymacreeny is a misprint for Ballynacreevy: *Baile na Craoibhe*, Crew. This may indicate the importance of Maghera to the royal house of Uí Tuirtre. It was common for such septs, originally in pagan times, to have a sacred tree (*bile*) often known as *Craobh*. There was another such tree in adjoining Kilcronaghan at *Cnoc na*

---

63. For Ó hEachaidhéin poems see T. Ó Donnchadha, ed., *Leabhar Cloinne Aodhe Buidhe* (BÁC, 1931), pp. 82, 120, 135, 153, 190, 211, 240, 243, 249.

189

Daireóige Duibhe 'the hill of the black oak', now Black Hill, which was an assembly place (a sort of early democratic forum), according to John O'Donovan's letters.

Falgortreavy may indicate land used for cultivation, a *gort* within a *fál*, an enclosure, and *gort* often also meant the curate's glebe land in a parish, although not seemingly here.

Of Tamneymullan, the original *tamhnach*, a forest clearing, probably came to mean 'mountain grazing', similar to *léana* in Tyrone. The second part of the name '-mullen' is more difficult. Gregory Toner follows Séamus Ó Ceallaigh in positing *Tamhnach Uí Mhaoláin* as 'O'Mullan's field'.[64] Ó Maoláin country was a large area around Park in north Derry known as the 'Ballymullans', where they played an important role in the civil polity of *Oireacht Uí Chatháin*. It is highly unlikely that they lowered their aim at any time to settle for a parcel of churchland in an area where they would have been regarded as suspect by *Clann Dónall Donn na Banna*. Ó Ceallaigh submits that the Ó *Catháin* writ ran for a period in what is now south Derry. If it did it was ephemeral. So where does that leave us with Tamneymullen? The spelling of the first entry above allows for possible Ó Mealláin/Mallon, but they were strongest in *Meallánacht* around Cookstown. I would draw attention to Ó Mothlacháin, which has become Mallaghan and then Mallon in English. We do know that Ó Mothlacháin were prominent in the medieval Church in the area, but we can no longer trace their native parish. Wishful thinking?

The half-ballyboe was for the sustenance of the *officialis* of the diocese – nowadays more usually called the judicial vicar.[65] We can easily forget that the medieval Church had a full panoply of offices and officers. This draws attention to the large area of churchland in Maghera, twice the usual parish size; it must mean that parishes like Maghera had wider responsibilities than most. Unfortunately, with the destruction of native records, all we can do is guess what they might have been. They may have supported priests in training (by apprenticeship to senior priests, before seminaries were thought of), or students of canon law or theology at Armagh. There were of course many workers on erenagh lands, under the management of the erenagh.

---

64. *Gleanings* 57; *Placenames of NI* V, County Derry 1, QU (Belfast, 1996), 198–9.
65. The judicial vicar, qualified in canon law, forms a tribunal with the bishop and is empowered to act as judge in cases pertaining to canon law.

CILL CHRUITHNEACHÁIN/KILCRONAGHAN

Name

Cill, 'a church', dating from the second generation, monastic church, based on the Latin *cella*, originally a small, storage room. Like *díseart* in Desertmartin, *cill* here indicates a foundation from the larger community associated with St Columba at Ballinascreen.

The area was not always concerned for peace. A major meeting to plan war took place in the house of Lieutenant Crosby in Calmore in April 1642.

Patron

Saint Cruithneachán/Cronaghan, priest – feast day 7 March; foster father of St Columba. Said to be the son of Ceallachán, Cruithneachán is said to have been married and had three daughters before he became a priest. He is known as *an Cruimhthear Cruithneachán, cruimhthear* being the form the Latin 'presbyter' took in Irish, the earliest word for 'a priest'. Since he is said to have baptised Colm Cille and died when Colm Cille was a youngster, he belongs in the early sixth century. He is the only historical person who bears the name Cruithneachán, which makes one wonder if in fact it was a by-name.

The name means the 'little *Cruithin*' or Pict (the Picts were a group of late Iron Age and early medieval Celtic people living in ancient eastern and northern Scotland). By the time of Cruithneachán, the *Cruithnigh* had lost power over most of Ulaidh and were restricted to what is now Antrim and Down. He may have been a native of east Ulster or maybe he looked like a little Pict, however that might have been defined. Education was provided within a system, *altram*/fosterage, in which, between the ages of seven and seventeen boys and girls were given into the care of those who would educate them in the duties of the child's state in life. There was little social mobility. Fosterage could be done for a payment (greater for girls than for boys) or as an act of affection.

In the semi-pagan Ireland of the time it was unusual to choose a priest as foster-father, yet Féilimí and Eithne made this choice, probably because Cruithneachán could introduce their child – who might one day, remember, be high king – to the civilisation of the Roman Empire, including the quite uncommon gift of being able to read and write. The only script in use in Ireland before then was Ogham. Colm Cille was to prove an excellent pupil and like a son to the old man. In fact Cruithneachán died on the way back from a sick call. Colm Cille was with him and thought the old man asleep. To pass the time until the old man wakened he began to sing and the nuns in a nearby convent, including Cruithneachán's daughters, heard the beautiful singing and came out to find the old priest.

Erenagh

'Ohad', or Jacobus Towell, according to Montgomery.[66]

Séamus Ó Ceallaigh found the name Haddy/ÓhAideidh as lords of Uibh Eachach/Iveagh in Down before the Norman invasion, but that is probably too far away to allow for a fall-back position in south Derry, although not impossible. The other possibility is Ó hUid/Hood, a bardic family who lost their lands in the *Bráid*/Braide in Antrim.[67] This parish and the *Bráid* would have been within the control of *Clann Aodha Buí Ó Néill*/Clandeboy.

Jacobus Towell might be Séamas Ó Tuathail, as in Desertoghill, but is more probably Ó Dubhghaill/Ó Dúill/Doyle as in Desertmartin.

Erenagh lands

Four ballyboes: Ballintrolla, Derreskerden, Dirrygrinnagh, Kellynahawla. (BD & ISL)

Tillirnan, Tawneosker, Cranne, Mirrimeith (CS).

The scribes must have been in a rush home for their tea judging by the spelling of the foregoing!

DÍSEART MHÁRTAIN/DESERTMARTIN
Name

Díseart, from Latin *desertum*, means 'a hermitage', 'a retreat'.

Mártain (now *Máirtín*)/St Martin was Bishop of Tours in France. Born in Hungary, he was a Roman soldier who became the great apostle of rural France, using a system of small monasteries in the countryside. This was imitated in Ireland with similar success. Accordingly he was deeply venerated in this country, especially in a monastic context. This would apply to followers of St Columba, as in Ballinascreen. Incidentally, our ancestors were not all that keen on putting *naomh*/'saint' before the name of a saint.

Amongst the prize possessions and sacred halidoms of *Cineál Eoghain* was *Soiscéal Mhártain*/the Gospel of Martin, said to have

---

66. BD & ISL I, 211; H.A. Jefferies in *Seanchas Ardmhacha* (Armagh Diocesan Historical Society, 1996–7), 53.
67. Cf. *Leabhar Cloinne Aodha Buidhe* 127, where Séamus Ó hUid asks for their return.

been brought to Ireland by St Patrick and preserved at Derry. It was lost to the Anglo-Normans at the battle of Dunboe in 1182, when it disappeared from history.

Patron
Saint Martin, Bishop of Tours, +397, presumably the original patron – feast day 11 November.

Saint Covellus, according to Montgomery, or St Conellus, according to Ware.[68] It is an open question as to whether this is St Comhghall (*pronounced co'al*) of Bangor or St Comhghall of Both Chonais (Gleneely) in Inis Eoghain, more probably the latter due to the influence of *Cineál Binnigh* in south Derry – feast day 4 September.

Erenagh
Montgomery gives 'Nigellus Towell', but the name in fact was Ó Dubhghaill/Ó Dúill/Doyle.[69] The last erenagh Pádraig Ó Dúill was still around in 1634, when he testified that Art Ó hÁgáin, steward of Ó Néill (Aodh Mór: Earl of Tyrone) had dispossessed him violently from Ballenagawnagh because the land was needed for the horses of Ó Néill. His sons: Seinchín aged thirty-four, Ruairí aged thirty-two, Eoghan aged thirty and Patrick aged twenty-seven, also testified. In his letter to the Bishop of Derry (established Church), Rev. Oliver Mather also gives us the name of another witness, the last parson/rector of the parish, Peirce O Doell/Piaras Ó Dúill, 'son of Owen O Doell, *alias* Parson Odoell, the last parson of the same'. The ironic fact was that the land was now in the hands of the captain of the garrison in Desertmartin. It was not to be returned, of course.

Erenagh lands
Four ballyboes: Shra Inishnagardy, Moydrowne, Magheryvally Farsan, Ballinecorrow. Strafinshnagardy, Moydrowne, Magheraballifarson, Ballincorren.[70]

---

68. H.A. Jefferies, ed., SA (Armagh Diocesan Historical Society, 1996/7), 54; BD & ISL I, 405.
69. BD & ISL I, 182. See also I, 357, to discover that Ruairí Ó Dúill, unusually perhaps for a member of an erenagh family, signed as witness with his mark. The churchlands of Desertmartin would remain a bone of contention, as did those of Kilcronaghan, for the established Church Bishop of Derry: Cf. I, 355.
70. BD & ISL I, 57, 172

Srath Inis na nGardaí 'the holm of the island of the guards' probably reflects its position close to the island in the lake, an important place which gave its name to the barony of *Loch Inse Uí Fhloinn/* Loughinsholin, a strong point of Ó Floinn when lord of Uí Tuirtre and prized much later. A 'barony' is a post-Plantation division based on an earlier native one. The barony of Loughinsholin included Lissan, now in Co. Tyrone. The island fortress was one of the first seized and longest garrisoned in the 1642 war, even withstanding a siege.

Moydrone has become Knocknagin. It is possible that the name Moydrowne included Ballynagown, as Ó Dúill's testimony (see previous page) seems to show. Ballynagawnagh looks like *Baile na Gamhna*, 'the town of the calf'. The snag is that in Derry Irish that *amh* is nasalised, and pronounced as *am*, in neighbouring Drumsamney, Tamneymullen, Tamlaghtocrilly, Glengamna. It may well have been an area set aside for cows calving, since such an area would be necessary for protection from wolves, foxes, dogs on the loose and other threats. *Baile*, although viewed now as the quintessential component of Irish placenames, in fact came into use in such names relatively late.

Machaire Bhaile an Phearsain, 'the plain (level ground) of the town of the parson' indicates that this was land for the support of the parson. 'Parson' comes from Latin *persona*, 'person', someone of standing with rights and responsibilities. The usual medieval word was 'rector'.

Baile na Cora, no doubt from a weir on the stream, perhaps for fishing or to provide a mill race or to control water levels in Loch Inse Uí Fhloinn.

In addition to the parish erenagh lands, the priory of Saints Peter and Paul in Armagh received rents from the two townlands of *Aighiter* in Desertmartin. This name was created from '-each íochtar', the middle syllables of *Gráinseach Íochtarach*, Grange Lower. This may explain how Henry McGillmurray/*Anraí Mac Giolla Mhuire* came to be the priest in Desertmartin and Kilcronaghan in 1631, according to Sir Thomas Phillips. The *Mac Giolla Mhuire* family were amongst the erenaghs of the churchlands of Armagh.[71]

There were also three acres of glebe for the vicar (curate), probably at Dromore (CS), although the *Inquisitions* report only a rector there. (Cf. also BD & ISL I, 144)

---

71. Michael Glancy, 'The Church lands of Co. Armagh', SA I, 1 (1954), 79. Henry was changed to Drumragh where he was subsequently hanged on 7 May 1643 by the Donegal army of Sir Robert Stewart, 'Cín lae Ó Mealláin', *Anal. Hib.* 3, 19

BAILE NA SCRÍNE/BALLINASCREEN

Name

The 'town of the shrine', of *Scrín Cholm Cille*, associated with St Columba. How or if it differed from *Scrín Cholm Cille* preserved at *Baile na Scríne de Ardo*, the shrine of St Columba at Tamlaghtard Magilligan, is unknown. Said to have been made by Connla the craftsman for St Patrick for a newly-built church at Duncrun to 'safeguard the gospels and many relics of the saints', and completed by St Colm Cille, it is possible that the shrine which was created to house 'the gospels and many relics' contained *Soiscéal Mhártain*, the 'Gospel of Martin', said to have belonged to St Martin and to have been brought to Ireland by St Patrick. This *Soiscéal* was lost to the Anglo-Normans in 1282 at the battle of Dunboe and disappeared. John O'Donovan suggested that it was kept at Derry but gives no reference. The story of how it escaped Patrician Armagh to come to rest at Derry would have made interesting reading.

The tradition about Lough Patrick would suggest very early evangelisation around Slieve Gallan, but all traces seem to have disappeared. Sources agree that St Columba crossed the Bior when fleeing north from the outbreak of plague at Glasnevin.[72] The *Bior* is said to be the River Moyola, although *bior* just means 'water' or 'stream'. One could construe his returning to *Tír Chonaill* by way of south Derry as showing a certain lack of urgency. Perhaps he took the main road north, the *Slí Mhíluachra*. His return north over the *Bior* is credited with his making the Moyola a barrier to the spread of the plague, which must surely be a belief arrived at after the plague had ended.

The area is dominated by the charisma of St Columba. Even the mythological cow, the *Glas Ghaibhleann*, was pressed into service to ensure his supply of milk, even if it was a short trip from her resting place at Labby/*Leaba na Glaise* to Tullybrick, where she was tethered, or to pasture at *Buaile Cholm Cille* near Loch Patrick. Neither Colm Cille nor Patrick could have been to all the places they are credited with visiting. Modern research tends to limit the foundations made personally by St Columba to three or four: Iona, Durrow, Moone and Derry, and even the last two have been challenged. There seems little doubt that Columban associations in south Derry result from the arrival of *Cineál Binnigh*, a branch of *Cineál Eoghain*, leaving the trace of their

---

72. O'Kelleher and Schoepperle, eds, *Betha Colaim Chille* (Illinois: The University of Illinois, 1918), 1994, pp. 62–3, 148–9.

passage in the dedications of Desertoghill, Desertmartin, Kilcronaghan, Ballinascreen and possibly Errigal, before going to Termonmaguirk and Drumragh.

Saint Patrick is credited with founding seven churches in the Faughan valley, one of them Domhnach Dula, at Magh Dula, said to be the origin of the name Moyola. Magh Dula however is Muff, the older name for the Eglinton area, with its ancient church site at Templemoyle. Séamus Ó Ceallaigh was convinced, from versions of the name written down at the Plantation, that the original stress on the word Moyola was on the last syllable, not the second, which suggested to him that it hid the word *loch* and that the original was *Má Locha* 'the plain of the lake', deriving from the original of the Creagh Meadows at Toome.[73] This omits the middle long vowel. The late Fr Éamon Devlin suggested *Má Dhá Loch* 'the plain of the two lakes' (Neagh and Beg).

This may not fully solve the problem of the river's name. One of the reasons for the Magh nDula/Magh Dula/Moyola equivalence being attractive is that local pronunciation and the name of the river in the *Civil Survey* agree on Monola/Minola, giving an Irish version *Magh nDóla* or possibly *Magh nGabhla*. There is even a word *dulach*, meaning 'fast-running', which may have been one name of the river. All that is clear is the report that Patrick founded *Domhnach Dula*.

In his letters from south Derry, John O'Donovan drew attention to ancient manuscripts mouldering away in the damp conditions of nineteenth-century housing in Ballinascreen and to the level of native learning in the parish. He perhaps captured the end of a long tradition begun by Féilimí, son of Eoghan Mór, son of Niall Óg Ó Néill[74] who was made lord of *Arrachta*/Orritor, of whom at his death in 1461 AFM remarks that he was eminent for generosity and know-how, protector of the learned and the stranger, the person who bought most poetry and had the largest collection of poetry of his time. Féilimí died in his own bed as a result of a seizure 'having overcome the world and the devil'. Under his son Brian (+1482), Féilimí's family extended their power around Slieve Gallan into *Gleann Con Cadhain*/Glenconkeyne. Legend has it that the valley got its name from the massive hound of Cadhan Ó hInnéirí, or from Cú Chadhain Ó hInnéirí. *Cadhan* means

---

73. *Gleanings* 29. In Derry Irish *loch/locha* and *lacha* would have had the same sound.

74. Both Niall Óg and Eoghan Mór held the position of Ó *Néill*, head of *Cineál Eoghain*, and were in effect rulers of Ulster, east of the Foyle. The various sons of Eoghan Mór were given areas to control.

a 'brent goose'. Ó hInnéirí has become Henry but has a different origin from MacHenry, who are a branch of Ó Catháin/O'Kane. Ó hInnéirí was ruler of the area at a time, according to tradition, but if so, *Ó Néill* was his overlord.

Patron
Saint Columba/Colm Cille.

Erenagh
Unnamed in the Plantation Papers or elsewhere. Séamus Ó Ceallaigh suggests that the erenagh was *Mac Ruairí* /McCrory (Rogers) but may have changed his mind since he does not mention *Mac Ruairí* amongst the erenaghs of south Derry when he deals with the subject in his later work.[75] According to legend, St Columba set about building a church in the area several times but his efforts were always destroyed by a monster. Eventually he had recourse to prayer and God opened a window in heaven from which a bell descended melodiously. The saint told the people to spread their cloaks on the ground to catch it. The bell landed on the cloak of MacGillion but rebounded on to that of MacGurk. Where the bell landed the church was built. The tale has to do with the legitimacy of possession of the saint's bell, a notable *mionn/* relic on which oaths were sworn. It has not been possible to discover the genealogy of MacGillion, but *Mac Oirc*/MacGurk belong to *Cineál Binnigh*. The parish of Termonmaguirk (Carrickmore) takes its name from Mac Oirc/MacGurk and that parish has associations with St Columba and with his bell. The name Magallyn (Mag Aillín?) occurs once amongst the clergy of Ballinascreen in the early fifteenth century. Mac Oirc does not. Perhaps the bell had a different custodian in each parish, Mac Aillín in Ballinascreen and Mac Oirc in Termonmaguirk. It is worth noting that a name closely associated with the Columban monastery in Derry is found in Ballinascreen later at the end of the fifteenth century – Ó hÉigeartaigh/Hegarty. The exact relationship between the Columban parish churches and the monastery at Derry is unclear. Mac Oirc may have had to move on, taking the bell with him. Whether any of these was also erenagh is unknown.

---

75. 'Irish Christian Names', *Irisleabhar na Gaedhilge*, Nollaig 1901, 197.

Erenagh lands

Ballinetollabrick, Ballidonachony, Ballychanan, Ballinwey, Donaruan, Ballinehounreagh. Ballietullabrick, Ballyvounachony, Ballychane, Ballinvey, Dounarvan, Ballinehon'reagh plus three acres of glebe belonging to the vicar (BD & ISL II, 57, 103; *Inquisitions*, Appendix).

Belinitullibricke, Bellicronaghan, Bellinevay, Donarnon, Bellinecoragh plus Donaghran glebe (CS III, 190). (Some of these are reflected in the modern names of *Tullybrick, Moneyconey, Cavanreagh, Moyard, Glenviggan, Owenreagh, Bancran*.)

In most parishes there were four church townlands. Perhaps special provision was made for the custodian of the Bell. The above are the original 'Six Towns' given in medieval times to support parish clergy and church, obviously around the church. Although they are at the very southern end of the parish and seemingly out of the way, it is perhaps worth consideration that they are near a crossroads where roads from Lough Fea and east Tyrone towards Banagher and Derry, with branch down Glenelly, cross the north-south road. Most of the towns in the area, except Maghera, date from hundreds of years after the donation of the erenagh lands. When Ó Néill (Aodh Mór) and his party were engaged in their Flight of the Earls, which ended in Rome, they stopped overnight at *Loch Beigfhine*, according to Tadhg Ó Cianáin. *Loch Beigfhine* has to be close to Glenviggan, a narrow tongue of which reaches down between Tullybrick and Moyard to touch Moneyconey, where the church is. The only place that could have afforded accommodation to such a party there at the time would have been the buildings associated with the church. Hospitality was one of the duties of the erenagh. The erenagh lands, probably in part with hospitality in mind, were always amongst the best land in any parish (which means that the idea had to be initiated with strong backing from the civil power). Another interesting fact is that Loch Patrick is found on the erenagh lands, possibly another reason why the church was built in the area.

DÉANACHT MHAIGH IOTHA/DEANERY OF MOGHIE/MAHYA

Name

According to the Four Masters, the first battle fought in Ireland was at *Sleamhnaí Maighe Ithe* in the year 2530 of the age of the world, when Parthalán defeated the invading *Fómhóraigh*/Fomorians under *Ciocal*

Grigeanchosach. Towards the end of the rule of the *Tuatha Dé Danann*, on a clear winter's evening, Ioth, learned son of Breóghan, went to the top of the tower his father had built at Brigantia in Spain and saw the shadow of land in the distance. He told his brothers he was going to investigate it. Rejecting any suggestion that it was just a cloud, he set off and landed in Ireland at *Bréantrácht Maighe Ithe*. On learning that he was in *Inis Ealga* and what the names of its kings were he went to meet them at *Aileach Neid*. Unfortunately the three kings were in dispute and, thinking Ioth was a spy, they attacked and wounded him. His companions carried him off but he died on board ship on the way back to Spain. Éireamhón and Éibhear, sons of *Míl Easpáinne* (ancestor of the Milesians), returned in force, conquered Ireland between them and established the supremacy of the *Gaeil* 'in the year 3500 in the age of the world'.

The plain where Ioth was injured became Magh nIotha after him, modernised Maigh Iotha. One might point out perhaps that *ioth* also means 'grain, corn', and that the lands through which flows the river Finn have long been known for their fertility, something that has made them a focus for covetous eyes over the centuries. From the mid-twelfth century until the area passed under the rule of Ó Dónaill in the thirteenth it was the scene of internecine strife and cruelty. Its importance is shown in that the rural deanery now known as 'the Tyrone deanery' of the diocese was originally named after the plain. The fact that the name rings so few bells nowadays is a measure of its gradual loss of importance. The boundaries of the original *magh* are unclear. While the area came under the control of Ó Dónaill and was in the post-Plantation barony of Raphoe, it remained in the diocese of Derry, showing how profoundly the Twelfth-Century Reform had been accepted.

ARD SRATHA/ARDSTRAW

Name

Srath means 'a meadow or grassy area near a river, a holm' and *ard* means 'a height', pedestrian enough, one might say, for a place whose name and fame goes back two millennia. Mac Fhir Bhisigh may have wondered too since he records the alternative *Sreabh* 'a stream' instead of *srath*. Its perennial attraction has been the fertile land along the Derg, coupled with the easily defended lakes (for crannógs) in what is now the Baronscourt demesne, presumably *Cúirt na Bairdne* 'the Court of Poetry', since it has never been the centre of a barony. It has been suggested that Loch Laí, where Conchobhar mac Neasa went to drown the adulterous Aodh in the *Ulster Mythological Cycle,* was one of these lakes, Loch Laoire (now Lough Mary?), where lived Laoire Buach, one of the great warriors at Conchobhar's court.

At about the time of St Patrick, the kingdom of the Ulaidh was defeated by the Colla brothers who established a series of kingdoms from south Down to the Faughan valley called the *Airghialla.* Fiachra Tort, son of Colla Uais, established his kingdom in what is now south Derry – east Tyrone, named for his descendants *Uí Tuirtre.* Fiachra's nephew, also called Fiachra – son of Earc, son of Colla Uais – founded a kingdom at Ardstraw for his descendants known as *Uí Fiachrach Arda Sratha.*[76] The kingdom was to last some five hundred years, much of that time as a sub-kingdom under *Cineál Eoghain.* Its area cannot be determined, but it probably extended eastwards almost to Drumragh, since the parishes of *Leamhchoill/*Langfield and *Ceapach* had churches dedicated to St Eoghan (or Eugene), and perhaps west by Strabane to link up with their relatives *Uí Mic Cairthinn* in the Faughan valley.

Christianity came to Ard Sratha, we are told, with Eoghan, who was from Leinster, pupil of the great monastery of *Candida Casa/*Whithorn in Galloway, founder of the monastery at *Cill na Manach* in Wicklow.[77] He was a contemporary of St Columba and therefore a pioneer of monastic life in Ireland. One can only surmise that he may have come north as a way of doing penance – as it was put at the time *peregrinari pro Christi nomine* 'to wander (abroad) for the name of Christ', a form of self-imposed exile, which saw living in another *tuath* within the country as exile. Eoghan's mother belonged to the *Mughdorna,* a people associated with Monaghan, although we might be dealing with confusion regarding the less well-known *Modhairn* 'Mourne'.[78] While he had been an abbot at Kilnamanagh he was seen primarily in Ardstraw as a bishop, giving rise to the Christian name *Giolla Easpaig*

---

76. According to CGSH 338.20, Cairrtheann was nephew of Fiachra Tort and, according to GBIG, possibly great-grandson of Colla Uais, which posits an Eochaidh, son of Colla Uais and father of Fiachra Tort: 334. 7.

77. *Eoghan* means 'born [under the protection] of the yew', a tree regarded as sacred in pagan times. It has no connection in meaning with Eugene, which means 'well-born' in its original Greek.

78. *Loch Modhairn* is the lake near *Bearnas Mór,* and *Modhairn Bheag* the river, which leaves it to join the Strule and change its name to the Mourne. There is a shadowy people who appear in the *Annals of Ulster: Teallach Modharan,* neighbours, presumably, of Ó Gormlaigh of *Cineál Moain* on whom they inflict casualties in 1280. Typically the annal gives neither cause nor consequences. They may have been *Mac Fheargail/*MacGarrigle, lords of Tír Bhreasail. Whether their antecedents would have been around in St Eoghan's time is doubtful.

Eoghain, 'servant of Bishop Eoghan', perhaps the origin of the surname 'Gillespie'. His reputation seems to have been a determining factor when it came to choosing a site for the see of the bishopric in the area at the time of the Twelfth-Century Reform.

That the diocese named Ardstraw proved to be short-lived was probably due to political unrest in the area: Ó Dónaill looking with covetous eyes on the fertile Maigh Iotha/Lagan and coming up against Ó Caireálláin/Carlin at Domhnach Mór, Ó Gormlaigh at Urney, Ó Flaithbheartaigh/Laverty nearer Lifford and Ó Catháin/O'Kane. In the struggle the leadership of each of these septs was forced out of the area, one by one. In the process, what was left of *Uí Fiachrach Ard Sratha* was forced away towards their Airghialla relatives in Fermanagh/Monaghan.

The uncertainty of life around Ard Sratha can be seen in the various annals, where we find that between 1069 and 1150 there were four rulers, described as king in AU and lord in AFM: *Ó hAodha*/perhaps MacHugh now, *Ó Críocháin*/Creegan, *Mac Fothaigh*/Fahy and *Ó Ceallaigh*/Kelly. Ó hAodha was the only one of them to die in his bed. Two others called Ó Críocháin died in conflict with septs in Fermanagh, which probably means that by the early 1100s they were searching for a new base away from Ardstraw. Ó Ceallaigh was killed on Loch Laoire in 1150 by the *Uí Chomhaltáin*/Colton (who presumably gave their name to Magheracolton): all of whom probably belonged to Cineál Eoghain. Thus, when *Eochaidh Ó Baoill*/O'Boyle was killed by the men of Uí Fiachrach in 1193 it may have been the result of a border challenge since, according to Ó Dubhagáin, Ó Baoill was one of the septs of Clann Chonchúir of Cineál Eoghain appointed to 'keep the borders'. They later became erenaghs at *Leamhchoill*/Langfield. It is well to keep in mind that these conflicts involved almost exclusively the nobility, which was the pattern throughout medieval Europe, as Shakespeare's historical plays show about England. The work was being done by others, leaving the nobility ample time to test their courage and military prowess.

However, the resultant unrest may have provided reason for the transfer of the seat of the diocese from Ardstraw to Maghera. Even amongst these bellicose leaders there was still some evidence of faith. Enemies met at the bridge at Ardstraw to make peace, and, when reached, agreements were followed by oaths sworn on the *mionna* or relics of Ardstraw, Urney and Donaghmore. The church at Ardstraw was burned four times between 1069 and 1101, twice deliberately by invading forces, no doubt to show the local ruler that he was too ineffectual to protect his church. The church, too, was often the safe place where valuables were kept.

The fourteenth–fifteenth centuries saw the focus of population shift away from the area around the church with the building of 'castles' or tower houses, which subsequently became the towns of west Tyrone. *Anraí Aimhréidh Ó Néill* was probably the first, established by his father and *clann* in the area at what is now the Old Castle as a bulwark against the rising power of Ó Dónaill. Anraí was in line to become Ó Néill but died before his father Niall Mór. After his death his sons were often in rebellion against Dungannon, sometimes hand in hand with dissident groupings within the Ó Dónaill lordship. Thus we find Neachtán Ó Dónaill in 1431 ousting Tarlach Ó Dónaill from the castle on Loch Laoire.

Clann Aimhréidh still laid claim to the crannóg in Loch Laoire. In 1436 they seized the crannóg but were promptly surrounded by the forces of Ó Néill and surrendered when Ó Néill sent for Lough Erne cots to see the job through. Although Dónall Bog, Anraí Aimhréidh's son, became Ó Néill himself, they were eventually forced out of the area to the lands of the Clandeboy O'Neills/*Clann Aodha Bhuí*, to whom Anraí Aimhréidh's wife had belonged.

In the sixteenth century, Sliocht Airt Óig (Ó Néill) were established in west Tyrone, built the castle of Strabane, retained *Baile Nua*/Newtown (the '-stewart' was to come centuries later) and built Castlederg. Art Óg became Ó Néill in his time, but his descendants rebelled against the central power at Dungannon. Although Art Óg's grandson Tarlach Luineach became Ó Néill, his sons joined the English side at the end of the Nine Years War against Ó Néill (Aodh Mór). When the war ended their reward was to lose their lands and be resettled in east Tyrone. Tarlach Luineach was buried near St Eoghan, the patron, at Ard Sratha as was the medieval custom. *Note:* According to the *Book of Armagh* (18b), as quoted in the *Onomasticon*, there was a place near Ardstraw called Domhnach Comair.

Patrons

Saint Eoghan/Eugene, bishop, died c.550 – feast day 23 August.
Saint Coimdheánach, Bishop of Ardstraw, died 706 – feast day 26 November.[79]

---

79. According to the *Annals of Ulster* there were two earthquakes in the north of Ireland in a week in December 706.

The name presumably comes from *an Coimdhe*, meaning 'the Lord', although it is spelt Coibdenach in AU, which would seem to indicate 'a member of a band of marauders'. There was Coibdenach [*sic*], one of the three sons of Ecomris of the royal line of Uí Fiachrach, and uncle of Dónall, son of Flann Deirge (of the Derg), who died in 758.[80]

Erenagh
Ó Farannáin/O'Farnan.
Maolbhríde Ó Farannáin died in 1127 and Giolla Domhnaigh in 1179 (AU). AFM adds two more of the name to the list: Jacob who died in 742, described as a learned preacher, and Guaire, described as erenagh of Ardstraw, died 949. The latter two occur before the origin of surnames. The Christian name Forannán was relatively common, including, for example, Forannán, *comharba Phádraig* (successor of St Patrick) at Rockwallace in Clogher, scribe, bishop and anchorite, died 851 (AFM). The name probably suggests that they were descended from Forannán. Unfortunately, there are the descendants of Forannán, the royal line of *Uí Fiachrach Ard Sratha*, and the descendants of Forannán, son of Baodán +572, son of Muircheartach mac Earca +536, son of Muireadhach, son of Eoghan (progenitor of *Cineál Eoghain*). Both septs are known as Uí Fhorannáin, the latter spelt at times Uí Fhaireannáin. There seems no way of deciding which group we are dealing with in Ardstraw. Given the way the power of Cineál Eoghain advanced during the Middle Ages, the last named seem most likely.

Where the name has gone since that time is a mystery! Established Church Bishop Montgomery, in 1610, records 'Terentius O Farranan'/Tarlach O Farannan as vicar at Ardstraw and Denis O Farren as rector at Donaghedy (although a student at Trinity College, Dublin). The name is not the same as Farren/Ó Fearáin and is no longer common in west Tyrone, either as Farren or Farnan. Admittedly, the area was cleared methodically at the Plantation of Ulster, but it is rare for a surname to disappear so completely. It is possible that one branch chose to be named for an intermediate ancestor, as was the case with Ó Néill and Mac Lochlainn.

Amongst the possible resulting surnames of the area are MacNamee/Mac Con Mí and McHugh/Mac Aodha, whose genealogical descent is hard to trace. Aodh/Hugh has been a common Christian name for centuries. Cú Mí/'hound of Meath' was very rare, found only among Ó

---

80. CGSH I, 142: 141b1.

Floinn of Uí Tuirtre in south Derry/west Antrim. *Cú Mí* Ó Floinn had a brother, *Cú Maighe* Ó Floinn, whom he killed in 1176 and succeeded as lord. He defeated the invading John de Courcy and the Anglo-Normans in battle in 1177 but died at their hands in 1194. The name Cú Mí occurs three times in the Ó Floinn genealogy. The sept was eventually overrun by the Anglo-Normans. It would have been acceptable for them to move down the social scale into poetry, but, if so, their compositions show no memory of it.

By the sixteenth century, Mac Con Mí was in charge at Ardstraw of a *teach aoidhidh coitinn*, 'a house of general hospitality', which was part of the role of the erenagh. They were closely involved in Church matters: the Dean Mac Con Mí who died in 1525 was the son of Brian Rua, manager of the *teach aoidhidh*, as was Brian Dorcha, son of Solamh (Solomon), head of the sept at his time, an expert in *dán díreach* and poetry, a rich man, who died around the feast of St Colm Cille (9 June) in 1542 'through the miracles of God and Colm Cille and the curse of Ó Rabhartaigh for insulting and belittling the great cross at Ardstraw' by striking it. The reason for this burst of iconoclasm is not given but it may have been a first impact of Reformation theology. Ó Rabhartaigh were closely involved with St Colm Cille as comharba at the Columban church of Tory Island, as were Mac Rabhartaigh, custodian of *Cathach Cholm Cille*, St Columba's psalter, at Derry. There is no explanation as to why it was thought necessary to travel so far for a curse.

Erenagh lands

Four quarters; sixteen ballyboes (or fifteen ballyboes and two sessiaghs [*App.* UI])
Liscrie (Listry), Killen, Cooleraglas, Killshroglo, Lissafortie, Carnekenan, Proluske, Crossegoala, Burrinecreeny, Currenfarne, Coolegar, Doonynan (Doonienan), Cuvunescrine (Cananescrine), Bemelad (Bernelad), Laragh, Shanmullagh (BD & ISL 56, 106); glebes added 1626: Carrowcorkean, Lurgabeg (BD & ISL, 147).

These churchlands are given in the *Civil Survey* (1654) as: Tivenny, Killyn, Prushliske, Balllintain, Urbellreagh, Meaghey, Killstrull, Lettir, Carkenie, Mullaghlackey and Magheracoltan, Ballineleyne and Cavenehanna (CS 404–5). That there was so much churchland in the parish is testimony to its ancient status and probably to its being an important benefice or to a role in the education of the clergy.

Ardstraw had also the religious house of Franciscan Friars of the Third Order at Garrowekerne (Scarvagherin) with two ballyboes of land, and the other Third Order Franciscan House at Pobal with which went two ballyboes and one sessiagh of land. The *Inquisitions* Appendix asserts that the sessiagh of Shraghemere 'is not parcel of the said late abbey of Puble' (Srath Mór?). The Third Order had friaries, with both lay and clerical members, who specialised in education.

They arrived in west Tyrone from Dún na nGall under the aegis of Anraí Aimhréidh ('Harry Avery') Ó Néill and his family. Tradition records Anraí Aimhréidh as being generous to the Order at Corick, when the friars were in danger of dying of hunger. Tradition, of course – in the best Dracula manner – also turns him into a murderous tyrant with an unmarriageable daughter. The abbey of Ss Peter and Paul in Armagh had 'in their demesne, as of fee, in right of the said abbey, of and in the grange of Mourne and four sessiaghs of land', which should be around Strabane. This monastic land was declared forfeit to King James I because of the dissolution of the monasteries and therefore did not come within the ambit of the established Church.

BOTH DOMHNAIGH/BADONEY

Name

To account for the location of our early churches we must bear in mind that most of the places we tend to visit, and therefore the main roads that we follow, did not come into existence for about a thousand years after the time of St Patrick and the man he left in charge at Badoney – St Cormac Athghin. The obstacles to travel were different also: extensive woods, marsh and bog. Early Ireland had differing grades of road, the maintenance of which was the responsibility of the local landowner. A glance at the topography of mid-Ulster would suggest that the Glenelly valley may have been quite a more settled, less exposed, less wooded and safer way to travel on horseback or on foot from places in the Foyle basin, via Lough Fea, to important places like Tulach Óg (Tullyhog) in east Tyrone, and to Eamhain Macha, capital of the Ulaidh. Inhabitants of the kingdom of Uí Fiachrach Ard Sratha would have travelled that way and *via* the Moyola valley, to meet up with their relatives in the *tuath* of Uí Tuirtre in south Derry, and thence onwards to the Bann and the Slí Mhíluachra, the main road south. An illustration, perhaps, from later times is that, when Ó Néill (Aodh Mór), Earl of Tyrone, wished to escape in a hurry from the threats building up around him in 1607, he travelled from *An Chraobh* (Stewartstown) by way of Glenelly on his way to Rathmullan, stopping overnight at *Loch Beigfhine* (probably near the old Six Towns church in Ballinascreen). The church of Badoney, furthermore, stands close to a crossroads, where this east-west link meets the north-south road which skirts Dart on its way from north Co. Derry, as it now is, and continues through nearby Barnes into west Tyrone. The location of the church may make more sense than would appear at first sight.

This route through the glen became involved in international politics in the year 856 when a major battle was fought in the valley, which pitted an army led by Aodh Finnliath, King of Aileach and son of Niall Caille, the High King of Ireland, against the *Gall-Ghaeil*, who were defeated 'with great slaughter'. The placename Drumnaspar may well tell us where the battle took place. The word *sparr* had two linked meanings: it was a double-headed battle axe, the weapon favoured by the Vikings,[81] and it was also the name for the unit of fighting men, which comprised the *gallóglach* with his axe, the *ceithearnach* with a weapon like a pike for thrusting and cutting and a young horse boy who carried short throwing spears, tools to fix anything that might break and rudimentary medical supplies.

Right next to Drumnaspar is Glenga, perhaps the 'valley of the spears'. It seems an unlikely battlefield until one examines the geography. The *droim*[82] projects across from the southern side of the valley where it begins to broaden out, and almost blocks it, just allowing room for the river to squeeze through, perfect for ambush or defence. A similar formation, the *Casbhearna*, in the nearby Owenreagh valley was the scene of an Ó Néill ambush on an Ó Dónaill raiding-party. Local knowledge points out that there are in fact two ráths on the *droim*, which underlines the point.

We must digress to put the battle in context. Before the middle of the ninth century Scandinavian occupation of the western isles and north-west Scotland was complete. The Norse now had a secure base from which to turn their attention to Ireland and to sweep the Atlantic trade routes. In 833 Niall Caille and his nephew Murchadh defeated them at Derry. In 836 they were on Lough Erne. In 839 they were marauding from Lough Neagh towards Armagh and Louth, pillaging and taking captives as slaves, and were still active there in 841. In 843 Aodh Finnliath had to confront and defeat them in Maigh Iotha (the Finn valley).

---

81. G.A. Hayes-McCoy, *Scots Mercenary Forces in Ireland* (Dublin: Edmund Burke Publisher, 1937,1996), pp. 17–19.
82. The word *droim* means 'a back', 'a broad ridge', particularly one that forms a division or parting.

The Norse were ferocious enough, but the ultimate in terror came from these *Gall-Ghaeil*, the Norse-Irish or Scandinavian Irish, who came from west Scotland where Gael and Norse had got used to co-existence. Many of them were of mixed ancestry.[83] Some were pagan, some had been Christian. All were renegade freebooters who combined the worst qualities of both races and were guilty of even greater crimes against religious communities than the original Vikings. Led by Norwegian Ketil Flatnose who had made himself ruler of the Hebrides, they proved to be a menace not just to Gaelic rulers and people but to the Norse of Dublin led by Olaf (Amhlaibh), son of the King of Lochlann, who came in strength to Ireland in 853 to re-assert control over the Norse, including those of the Hebrides. The battle in Glenelly took place in 856. Olaf defeated Ketil Fionn and the *Gall-Ghaeil* in Munster in 857. Aodh Finnliath defeated them again at Lough Foyle in 866 for what seems the final time. It would seem that the remnants of the *Gall-Ghaeil* were forced eventually to leave the Hebrides for Iceland, to which, ironically, Orlygur Hrappsson, nephew of Ketil Flatnose, brought devotion to St Columba and wood to build a church in his honour.[84]

To return to Glenelly, we cannot tell what was the destination of the *Gall-Ghaeil* who were defeated in Glenelly. One of the reasons for attacking monasteries and religious centres was that people left their valuables in such places for safe keeping in times of danger. Whether Badoney was in their plans or if they had better information about greater prizes we cannot know. That Badoney might be considered in that context may seem surprising, but it seems to have had a greater importance in the early Middle Ages than we might think. By being marked out as a Patrician foundation it was clearly important in the perspective of the primatial Church of Armagh.

Armagh laid claim to the seven churches near the River Faughan, which St Patrick is alleged to have founded, one of them in Daigurt, still to be found in the name of the mountain Dart, but clearly the name of the area. This can only apply to *Both Domhnach*, which is the only one

83. The Irish of the time, *the Scotti*, gave their name to Scotland. *Gall-Ghaeil* gave Galloway its name.
84. See A.P. Smyth, *Warlords and Holy Men: Scotland AD 80–100* (Edinburgh: Edinburgh University Press, 1984), pp. 154–74. Just to confuse things still further: King Olaf of Dublin's first wife was Aud 'the deep-minded', daughter of Ketil Flatnose. Olaf put her away and married the sister of High King Aodh Finnliath, which scarcely improved relationships.

of the seven that can be identified with certainty and which remains to this day. It is in Daigurt, not in the Faughan valley, of course, but not far away, for the Faughan rises on the other side of the high mountains Sawel and Dart – not far as the raven flies, perhaps. From about the time of St Patrick the Faughan valley was the kingdom of the *Uí Mhic Carthainn* (who gave their name to the barony of Tirkeeran). They were closely related to the Uí Fiachrach of Ardstraw, belonging like them to the *Airghialla*, a congeries of small kingdoms in south and west Ulster, founded on the defeat of the Ulaidh (Ulstermen). Patrick is said to have left Cormac Athghin in charge when he left. By ancestry Cormac also belonged to the Airghialla, although from southwest Ulster.

The name of the church in Glenelly is proof of its ancient origin. Just as 'church' or 'kirk' originate in the Greek word for 'the Lord', the word *domhnach* comes from Latin *dominus*, also meaning 'the Lord'. It is now the Irish for 'Sunday', but, historically, it was the first word in Irish for a church. *Both* is a temporary dwelling or shed in Irish which was used to translate *tabernaculum*, the Latin for the biblical 'tent of meeting'. The antiquity of the placename in this case is proved by the version in the earliest documentation: *Both Domhnach*, which shows that the word *Domhnach* was still being treated as a foreign word without a genitive case. Only later did *Both Domhnaigh* become the recognised form. While the name does not prove that the church was founded by St Patrick, it certainly dates from not much later.

At the end of the first millennium the spotlight picks it out again when Muireagán of *Both Domhnaigh* is chosen as *comharba Phádraig* (successor of Patrick) or head of the Church of primatial Armagh in 998. Since the time of St Patrick the Church in Ireland had become monastic in character, based on a series of large monastic centres that had various smaller churches attached, which together made up its *paruchia*. There were no dioceses in the country, and the churches attached to a *paruchia* could be at some distance from each other. Thus the *paruchia* of Colm Cille's Derry included Ardstraw and Drumcliffe (Sligo). Bishops belonged in the monastery and performed the functions of a bishop but had no jurisdictional authority.

Badoney and the churches of the Faughan valley belonged in the *paruchia* of Armagh. While the *comharba Phádraig*/abbot in Armagh had originally been a cleric, by the tenth century succession in the post had passed down to Clann Síonaigh, whose representatives as *comharbaí* were laymen. Dubhdáléithe, who had been made *comharba* to Colm Cille as well as Patrick to make peace between Armagh and Iona in 989, was succeeded in Armagh by Muireagán of Both Domhnaigh in 993.

Dubhdáléithe was an old man by this stage (+997 aged eighty-three) and may have needed help since he may not have been able to manage a dual *comharbacht*, which involved travel, at least in theory. Muireagán may have been appointed as an interim *comharba*, perhaps because Maolmhuire, who was to succeed in due course, was too young. Muireagán had full support in the position because he performed the visitation of Tír Eoghain in his official capacity and ordained Aodh Ó Néill, known as *Aodh Craoibhe Tulcha*,[85] as King of Aileach in 993. Muireagán died in 1004 aged seventy-two. If he was called on to 'ordain' he must have been in orders, one would think. To be the agreed *comharba* in Armagh is an indication of high status within the Armagh *parruchia* and in the eyes of Clann Síonaigh. The name Muireagán is most common amongst the *Clann Chonchúir* branch of *Cineál Eoghain*, but it is unlikely that he belonged there. Interestingly, the name is found in the genealogy of Ó Brolcháin who belonged to *Cineál Fearadhaigh*, descended from Fearadhach, grandson of Eoghan, but are recognised as a separate grouping descended through Suibhne Meann (high king 615–28).[86] From Suibhne Meann's two brothers came the branches of Cineál Fearadhaigh, including eventually *Mac Cathmhaoil* (McCaul/Campbell), the leaders of the Cineál in later times, based in the Clogher area.

Tradition associates Uí Bhrolcháin with the monastery of Both Chonais near Clonmany. The origin of this link seems to be in Colgan's life of Maol Íosa Ó Brolcháin, the writer, sage and hymnodist (+1086), which states that he was educated at Both Chonais.[87] John O'Donovan records the tradition of their migration from Inishowen to Ballinascreen at the end of the sixteenth century.[88] On a cautionary note it might be well to remember Séamus Ó Ceallaigh's observation that the wistful *seanchaí* can be a peril to us all. It would seem to be clear that by the twelfth century some at least of Muintir Bhrolcháin had moved away from Inishowen. They would seem to have left their mark at some stage

---

85. Because he was killed in 1004 in winning the battle of Craobh Tulcha (Crew Hill near Glenavy). Craobh Tulcha was the sacred tree of the Ulaidh, a relic of ancient belief. He is the first person recorded as bearing the name Ó Néill as a descendant of Niall Glúndubh (+919).

86. O'Clery, *Genealogies*, Pender, ed., in *Anal. Hib.* 18,47. CGSH 146 d. 15, p. 180 actually gives the Ó Brolcháin genealogy as that of *Cineál Feradaich*. Cf. *Laud Genealogies* in ZCP viii, 300.

87. *Acta Sanctorum Hiberniae* (Dublin: Irish Stationery Office, 1948), 108.

88. M. O'Flanagan, ed., *Ordnance Survey Letters* (Bray: M. O'Flanagan, 1927), pp. 73–4.

on *Mollagh Brollaghane* in that portion of the churchlands of Armagh in the possession of Solamh Ó Cofaigh at the 1609 Inquisition.[89]

Their genealogy indicates a close connection with Clann Síonaigh. The mother of Maolmhuire (*comharba Phádraig*, 1001–20) was Mór, daughter of Duibhinse, who was the great-grandson of Brolchán, founder of the dynasty. Maolmhuire was the nephew of Dubhdáléithe who had been *comharba Phádraig* (abbot) from 965 until he was replaced by the unknown Muireagán of Both Domhnaigh. Muireagán was the only abbot between 965 and 1129 who was not a member of Clann Síonaigh and, therefore, the only outsider. The church of Both Domhnaigh/Badoney (in the Glenelly valley) belonged to the *paruchia* of Armagh. The name Ó Brolcháin/Bradley is even yet quite common in the surrounding area, in Tyrone and south Derry. The late Cardinal Ó Fiaich suggested that Muireagán had been brought in as abbot when Dubhdáleithe had assumed the burden of head of the Columban churches in his seventy-fourth year.[90]

Since Maolmhuire succeeded in 1001 aged only thirty-eight, perhaps someone reliable was needed to hold the post until he was ten or twelve years older and someone who would retire when asked. Since families tended to repeat forenames in succeeding generations, it is quite possible that Muireagán of Both Domhnaigh was related to Brolchán, and to Muireagán, son of Mór's brother Maolbhríde, brother of Maol Íosa *an cléireach* Ó Brolcháin, the hymnodist and Maelmhuire's first cousin. He may not have been as much of an outsider as would appear at first sight.

Both Domhnaigh disappears from view for another four hundred years except for a brief appearance in the record of income accruing to the bishop, made at Archbishop Colton's Visitation in 1397. This showed 'Botowny' paying ten shillings (50p) in rent and ten shillings (50p) in Episcopal Thirds, the same as most of the smaller parishes.[91] When it reappears in the Annates, the records of papal taxation on benefices reserved to Rome in the fifteenth century, its status has changed completely: the prior of the house of Augustinian canons, St Mary's, Dungiven, has become *ex-officio* Rector of Badoney.

How did this come about? It is, of course, impossible to document the reason for the change. However, one might suspect that it had

---

89. Michael Glancy, 'The Church lands of Co. Armagh', SA 1, i, 1954, 79.
90. Cf. 'Armagh Under Lay Control', SA 5, I, 1969, 91
91. W. Reeves, *Archbishop Colton's Visitation of Derry* (Dublin, 1850), pp. 71, 73.
    In a society pretty well without currency, this amount in silver, even if debased, was far from a paltry amount.

something to do with an expansion of Ó Catháin power from the lands of *Ó Maoláin*/Mullan in Tír Charthainn/Tirkeerin, the area around Altinure/Dreen/Park, up through Tamnagh, around Dart and into Glenelly. Even today there are noticeable affinities between the two areas. One might further surmise from the frequency of the name *Mac Con Mhaighe*/Conway in the area that this came about in the time of the energetic Cú Mhaighe na Coille Ó Catháin, King of Cianacht +1385, or by one of his four sons, since the transfer of rectorship to the priory must have happened no later than the late fourteenth century. No other sept made anything like the same use of the Christian name Cú Maighe 'hound of the plain' as did Muintir Chatháin.

In this context we should perhaps discuss the site pointed out at Barnas Gap at *Seaneaglais*/Shanaglash/'the old church'. It is generally considered that this was the place of worship built by Catholics when they lost the use of their parish church at Badoney after the Plantation of Ulster. That may indeed be the case, but it is worth noting that in the *Civil Survey* (1654–6) it is referred to as 'the old Mass house' and 'where the old Mass house was'.[92] Neither description suggests a building constructed within the previous thirty or forty years. There is no doubt that this church was used during penal times, perhaps even by St Oliver Plunkett, but might it have originated in an earlier time with people who also felt aggrieved at the loss of their church, even if held by a religious order? Of the vicars we know of in the 1400s one was Ó Muirí, a canon of Dungiven, one was Ó Baoill from Leamhchoill/Langfield, one was Machtananigh (Mac an tSionnaigh?/Fox?), one was Mac Giolla Shéanáin (now Nugent, Gilsenan or McElhennon). None was from Badoney, one would think.

There was also the house of Franciscans of the Third Order Secular at Corick, one of four such in west Tyrone. Both priests and lay brothers, they came together to live a life of self-sanctification and to cooperate in the pastoral work of the secular clergy and help in the Christian education of youth. Tradition records that Anraí Aimhréidh Ó Néill (*aka* now as 'Harry Avery') gave them a donation of land when they were in danger of starving. Anraí died in 1392 perhaps a little before their arrival. Their foundation would have needed support from him or from his descendants at Newtown.

---

92. R.C. Simington, ed., *Civil Survey 1654–1656* (Dublin: Stationery Office of Irish Manuscripts Commission, 1937), pp. 376, 406.

Erenagh

We have no record of the erenagh. It is probable that Ó Muirí/Murray came from Dungiven, as most priors there were of that name. The name Ó Muirgheasa/Ó Muiríosa/Morris is found amongst the clergy of Derry at this period, but it has not been possible to localise them. It is a relatively common name in Badoney. The other possibility is Ó Brolcháin/Bradley.

Erenagh lands

Barnes, Canaghy, Castledough, Dromesper (BD & ISL I, 56, 206).
Bearnish, Glenrone, Cashellduff, Drumnasparr (CS III, 406) 395 acres: arable 105; pasture 75; bog, mountain, rocks 215.
(*Bearnas, Gleann Ruáin, Caiseal Daimh, Droim na Sparr.*)
The word *damh* can mean 'house' and may refer to the church.
Another interesting placename is Landahussey. An older meaning of *lann* was that of a church or land pertaining to a church. The second part of the word looks like the surname Ó hEodhasa/O'Hussey, the name of a medieval poetic family in Fermanagh.

CAMAS NA MÓIRNE/CAMUS

Name

Coming from *cam* meaning 'curved', *Camas* means a bend in the river, which describes aptly the location of the old church as the River Mourne meanders around it. Until Art Óg Ó Néill built the castle at Strabane the area makes little impact on secular history either. This seems hard to understand given the quality of the land there but it may well be that we do not construe properly the information we have.

We are accustomed to regarding the Strabane area since the 1920s as border territory. It was equally so for much of the later middle ages, even if moving from time to time as Cineál Moain and Clann Chonchúir strove for territory and good land in the typical way of contemporary nobility all over Europe. Eventually Cineál Moain proved stronger than Ó Cairealláin/Kerlin and Ó Catháin/O'Kane of Clann Chonchúir, all of them originating in Inis Eoghain as descendants of Eoghan. As the invasion of the Anglo-Normans smashed the kingship of Mac Lochlainn in Tír Eoghain and Ó Maol Doraidh in Tír Chonaill, power was grasped in Tír Chonaill by the rising, and related, septs of Ó Dónaill and Ó Dochartaigh in the Kilmacrenan area.

Ó Dochartaigh took over Inis Eoghain and Ó Dónaill pushed down into the Lagan (or Maigh Iotha), moved Ó Gormlaigh over Finn and Mourne and for a time occupied part of Tír Eoghain. Ó Néill, who succeeded Mac Lochlainn as supreme lords of Cineál Eoghain, established branches of the family at various points in west Tyrone to control Ó Dónaill incursions. Thus, Anraí Aimhréidh (so-called 'Harry Avery'), son of Ó Néill (Niall Mór), built the Old Castle at *an Baile Nua*/Newtown in the late fourteenth century. Anraí died young and his family rebelled. After them came Art, son of Ó Néill (Eoghan Mór), who built Omagh in the fifteenth century; his descendants proved unreliable also. Finally in the early sixteenth century, Art Óg, son of Ó Néill (Conn Mór), built a castle at Strabane. Art Óg became Ó Néill himself, as did his grandson Tarlach Luineach. Niall Conallach, son of Art Óg and father of Tarlach Luineach,[93] gave the leadership at Dungannon some headaches as well. Ó Dónaill (Mánas) built his castle, *Port na dTrí Námhad*, 'the Fort of the Three Enemies', at Lifford[94] to contain Art Óg and his *sliocht*, strengthening the border between the two *tuatha* from above Clady to Derry, one that became permanent when the English shired the country (divided it into counties). The lands ruled over (but not owned) by Sliocht Airt Óig were commensurate with the barony of Strabane (including Badoney Lower and part of Cappagh).

In the thirteenth and fourteenth centuries, then, it is almost certain that the area we know as Camus was part of the kingdom of Ó Gormlaigh which centred on Urney. The soil in the area is too fertile and level to be ignored in a country where agriculture was practised right up the mountain valleys. Like the rest of the country it was divided into *bailte bó* (townlands) from around the year 1000, an indication of habitation and ownership, and where there is habitation there is movement of population and therefore roads.

The word 'road' itself, indeed, originally a seafarer's word, is said to have come from Norse into Irish and from there into English. In early Irish law the *Féineachas*, the maintenance of a road, was the duty of the owner through whose land the road passed. Thus, Archbishop Colton

---

93. The sobriquet after each name indicates where the person was fostered. Niall in Tír Chonaill and Tarlach in Muintir Luinigh (with Ó Gormlaigh). Education between the ages of seven and seventeen was by fosterage with a family who taught what would be the duties of the person's state in life. There was little mobility between the social strata.

94. It was there that Ó Dónaill (Mánas) wrote his celebrated *Beatha Cholm Cille*, 'Life of Colmcille'.

passed through the area, probably by carriage, from Ardstraw to Urney to Leckpatrick and was regally entertained, but there is no mention of him stopping at Camus and the parish leaves no record in the taxation list drawn up during his visit in 1397. It is perhaps the parish that has made the least impact on such historical documents from the Middle Ages that have survived to our time. The only reference we have to it would indicate that it was a curacy of Urney: a dispute in 1535 about possession of the vicarage without proper title drew in the Roman Curia, Archbishop Cromer of Armagh and Bishop Ruairí Ó Dónaill of Derry, the Dean of Derry and the Dean of Raphoe, plus the representative of the Bishop of Sodor and the Islands (of Scotland). *Aodh Mac An Bhaird*/Ward (O'Kelly) wished to oust *Mánas Ó Gormlaigh*, *Tarlach Mac Aodha*/McHugh and *Niall Ó Cearbhalláin*/O'Carolan, sharing together the vicarages of Camus and Ballinlinny, and be appointed himself in their stead. We do not know who won. Late seventeenth-century Strabane became a place of refuge for the Franciscans.

Patron

We are at somewhat of a loss as to who founded the church at Camus and when. Leslie suggests that the patron was St Conall.[95] The martyrologies give us some seven saints named Conall, including Conall Caol from Inis Caoil at Gaoth Barra, Glenties. We have no evidence unfortunately to connect him or any of the others with Camus. The other possibility is that it is a misunderstanding of *Co'al*, St Comhghall, founder and patron of Both Chonais (Gleneely) in Inishowen.

Erenagh

Montgomery gives Mulmoricus Maghinnie: Maol Mhuire/Myles, and perhaps the Tyrone surname McCanny in 'English', Mac Annaigh or Mac Cana (origin uncertain) or the surname that occurs just once in the annals, Mag Aithne. The name McCanny first appears in English records, borne by supporters of Sliocht Airt Óig Ó Néill around 1600. Native records do not survive, of course. Another possibility is deducible from

---

95. J.B. Leslie, *Derry Clergy and Parishes*, Enniskillen, 1937, 136, probably following Montgomery's Survey, cf. H.A. Jefferies in *Seanchas Ardmhacha* 1996–7, 55, 70; and Sir James Ware, cited in *Bishopric of Derry and the Irish Society of London* I, 406. Conall was the son of Éanna Boghaine, great-grandson of Conall Gulban (*a quo* Cineál Chonaill/Tír Chonaill), from present southwest Donegal. His father Máine was also Caol. His feast day is 22 May. Conall was a very common name in early Ireland.

the *baile biataigh* named in *Rawlinson A 237*: Largimack Inanny,[96] clearly the name McEneny/McAnena even if the Gaelic form is less than clear: Mac Con Aonaigh?/Mac Nainneanaigh (of Cineál Eoghain na hInse)?

Erenagh lands

One ballibetagh, unnamed, according to the Appendix.

Two balliboes, unnamed, according to BD & ISL I, 56, 106; CS III, 403 gives Camos, one half quarter or two balliboes.

BD & ISL indicates glebe land at Beharnagh alias Leagharnagh I, 149 confirmed by CS III, 408 as Beirnagh, one balliboe.

CEAPACH MHIC CHUARTA/CAPPAGH

Name

Ceapach (pronounced Cappagh) is a plot of ground for tillage. On occasion it meant an area of grass in front of a house. In either case the name suggests a settlement of people who needed the sort of food grown in a smallish area. 'Ceapach' was probably similar to the modern terms 'luibhghort', a vegetable garden, and *úllord*, an orchard. What did they grow? Onions, garlic, leeks, celery, cabbage, peas, broad beans, either carrots or the plant now called alexanders (used in salads), chives, various herbs for medicinal purposes. Also grown for dyes were woad/*glaisin* and madder/*madar*. The parish name according to the *Inquisitions* is Cappaghquoart. Mac Cuarta/McCourt is suggested as the second part of a difficult word on the strength of two of its clergy being so named in the records of annates paid to the papal court at Avignon on disputed benefices there in the fifteenth century.

The old parish church is at Dunmullan. *Dún*, 'a fort', usually applied in Old Irish (the language as prior to AD 1000) to the residence of a lord, king or dignitary, consisting of an earthen (sometimes stone) rampart inside which the house or houses were erected. The flat area within the 'dún', where the residence was located was the 'lios' (pronounced 'liss'). In the case of a royal residence there might be three circumvallations around it with a moat in between. 'Dún' is a prestige term, often used in Irish as the equivalent of fortress or city – e.g. Downpatrick, Dungannon, Dunseverick, etc. In the case of Dunmullan we are therefore talking about a place that has been inhabited for over

---

96. *Anal. Hib.* 3 (Dublin: Stationery Office of Saorstát Éireann, 1931), 156.

a thousand years. The rampart was for protection from possible attack, from robbers and enemies, of course, but also from wild animals like wolves. The last wolf in Ulster was killed in the 1750s between Feeney and Draperstown in Co. Derry.

In the parish there took place one of the important battles in Ulster history when an alliance of Ó Dónaill and Ó Néill defeated Mac Lochlainn at Caméirí near the site of the present Church of Ireland church (in Cummery) and determined that Ó Néill would replace Mac Lochlainn as ruler of Ulster east of the Foyle.[97] The army that came south to battle in 1242 by way of Sliabh Truim [Bessy Bell], crossed the Strule, proceeded along the eastern (*Dunmullan*) bank of the river and over the shoulder of Carrigan (an *Carraigín* – meaning 'little rock') (now *Mary Gray*) and clashed with the other along the river. This may mean that there was a substantial road near *Dún Maoláin*, since an army would need width to travel together and in safety. It was Sliocht Airt Óig Ó Néill, of the same lineage as the victors, whose territory, based on the town they built, was to become the barony of Strabane. It included most of Cappagh and Lower Badoney, since (rather unhistorically) joined to the Omagh Council area.

Patron

Like Ard Sratha/Ardstraw and Leamhchoill/Langfield (Drumquin), the medieval patron of Cappagh was St Eoghan (incorrectly translated as Eugene). *Eoghan* means literally 'born of the yew', a tree which was sacred to the pagan Gael; the name *Eugene*, Greek in origin, means 'well-born'. Born in Leinster, educated along with St Cairbre of Coleraine by St Ninian at *Candida* Casa ('white house'), now Whithorn in Galloway, he came north as a missionary and founded his church at Ardstraw, then the capital of the kingdom of Uí Fiachra Ard Sratha. That he became the patron of Cappagh as well shows that Cappagh formed part of that kingdom, subsequently overrun by Cineál Eoghain. If there was any local patron before or after that, there is no trace of his presence extant.

Erenagh

The name of the erenagh does not occur anywhere, but it seems reasonable to suggest Mac Cuarta.

---

97. The second last high king was Muircheartach Mac Lochlainn, less than one hundred years before.

Erenagh lands

The erenagh lands of the parish of Cappagh are stated to have been four ballyboes/*bailte bó* and two sessiaghs: Tawnamore, Golan, Kangarrowe, Sessioghtemple and Doonbrin. Sessiagh is Irish *seisreach* from *sé*, meaning six: as a measurement of land it is uncertain, but it was the area of ground a plough team of six oxen (or horses after the thirteenth century) could plough in a season. In contemporary England the 'acre' was the area that could be ploughed in a day.

- Tawnamor/*Tamhnach Mór* (large arable, grassy place – *tamhnach*: *originally a grassy clearing* in forest).
- Golan/*Gualainn* (shoulder of a hill).
- Kingarrow/*Ceann Garbh* (rough headland).
- Seissiaghantemple/*Seisreach an Teampaill* (ploughland of the church).
- Doonbrin/*Dún Bhriain* (Brian's *dún* or mansion).

There were also two ballyboes of glebe: Reaghan and Erganagh, which were usually for the upkeep of the vicar/curate. Reaghan is mentioned in a thirteenth-century poem about the battle of Caméirí by Giolla Bríde Mac Con Mí, where it is written Ríoghdhonn: *ríogh* means 'royal' and *donn* means 'brown'. The erenagh land of the Franciscan house in Omagh was Shergrim in Cappagh.

Towards the end of the fourteenth century the Bishopric of Derry was vacant due to the resignation of the last bishop in 1394, and Archbishop Colton of Armagh seized the opportunity – as he claimed that he could in law at that time – to make an official visitation of the diocese. He set out on 8 October 1397. He came to the diocese by way of Termonmaguirke (Carrickmore) with the sizable retinue that accompanied him and crossed the mountains 'de Glewgavyn'. The notary, Richard Kenmore, from the diocese of Meath and from the Pale got the name wrong. Glewgavyn is *Gleann Gamhna*/Glengamna ('valley of the calf'). They arrived at the church of 'Keppagh' in the Derry diocese. Colton and his companions stopped to recuperate at Cappagh, but the curate and the erenagh pointed out that he was in the diocese of Derry, whereupon Colton gave them a lecture about the powers of oversight of the Archbishop of Armagh, especially when a suffragan see was vacant and 'deprived of the solicitude of a pastor'. He then instructed his notary to draw up a public document stating his powers and those of his predecessors in such circumstances. Then, since Cappagh did not have the accommodation or the ability to provide adequately for his party, he instructed the vicar/curate and erenagh to send on a supply of beef to Ardstraw, where he intended to spend the night. It was the custom at the time that, when the bishop was on visitation to a parish, the erenagh had to provide for him. On this occasion curate and erenagh accepted the primate's request and decided to send the meat of one fat bullock after the archbishop to supply his needs and those of his company. One interesting thing to remember is that this exchange probably took place in Latin.

CLUAIN LAO/CLONLEIGH

Name

According to DIL, *cluain* means 'meadow, pasture land, glade', often low-lying and near water, and *lao* means 'a young calf'. Together they would suggest an enclosed area where cows were brought to calve. It may have been where the calves were kept apart from the cows from a few weeks after birth except during twice-daily milking (it was believed that cows would give more milk when the calves were there). This separation was to ensure an adequate milk yield for human consumption. Why it should give its name to the parish is unclear, though it is typical of the seemingly haphazard way by which our placenames have come about. The name might however be based on the word *laoch*, which may come from Latin *laicus*, meaning 'a layman' (as distinct from *manach*, a monk) and which came to mean 'a warrior'. We cannot hope to work out what might have been the train of thought in that case since we have no sources.

The present parish of Clonleigh includes another ecclesiastical division of the Middle Ages, that known as Teach na Comairce (now *coimirce*), 'the House of Protection/Refuge/Sanctuary'. It was not a parish, but seems to have had an existence of its own. In the Plantation Papers it is described as 'a church or college', which presumably means that it was a collegiate church. A collegiate church was a church where the daily office of worship was maintained by a college of canons, who were a non-monastic, or secular community of clergy, organised as a self-governing corporate body; it had no diocesan responsibilities. Collegiate churches were often supported by lands held by the Church. The relationship between the canons of Teach na Comairce and the chapter of Derry provided a platform which allowed a claim on the deanery of Derry. Collegiate churches were often set up and endowed by donors who wished Masses to be said for their souls. It is not clear if there were any others in Gaelic Ireland but such churches did exist in Anglo-Norman areas, at St Patrick's Cathedral in Dublin, in Youghal and in Galway. In England out of such foundations developed colleges like New College, Oxford, other university colleges, and Eton College. Whether Teach na Comairce served any educational purpose we do not know, although one would like to know where Peadar Ó Cearbhalláin of Clonleigh learnt the canon law that led Archbishop Sweteman to think so much of him.[98]

The canons of Derry possessed a half quarter of lands 'called Feronohaneny under certain covenants to be performed by them for the celebrating of divine service and doing other duties to the bishop' but they came into the possession of the Bishop of Raphoe 'forty-five years since for not performing those conditions,'[99] i.e. in 1554, a date which coincides with that of the election of Eoghan Ó Dochartaigh as Bishop of Derry in succession to Ruairí Ó Dónaill.

How did Teach na Comairce come about? Again we are at something of a loss because of the destruction of records. There is however one incident that may cast light on the matter. During the strife in what is now east Donegal in the last quarter of the twelfth century between Cineál Moain (Ó Gormlaigh/Ó Luinigh), treachery was never far beneath the surface. In 1177 Niall Ó Gormlaigh was at the monastery in Derry, staying with an unnamed cleric. Donnchadh Ó Cairealláin, Lord of Clann Diarmada, married to an Ó Gormlaigh, was also in the city. He set fire to the house of the cleric where Ó Gormlaigh was staying, and when Ó Gormlaigh rushed out to escape the fire, Ó Cairealláin killed him at the door.

The community of Derry was less than impressed by this piece of barbarism on holy ground and Ó Cairealláin had to make peace with Cineál Moain. In reparation to Colm Cille and *Muintir Dhoire* 'the (monastic) community of Derry', Ó Cairealláin undertook *manchaine* on behalf of himself, his family, his descendants and Clann Diarmada until doomsday. *Manchaine* was the service due to an abbot or monastery from a layman. In Ó Cairealláin's settlement it involved the gift to the community of Derry of the *Mac Riabhach*, 'the dark (in colour) goblet', the best of its kind in Ireland, as a pledge for sixty cows, and a *baile biataigh* of land 'in the neighbourhood of Donaghmore'. He

98. See the article on Simon, Bishop of Derry, pp 252–6.
99. Appendix, *Ulster Inquisitions*, 20.

promised in addition to build a house for the cleric who had lost his in the fire and to make good the property he had lost.

Urnaí was the lordship of Cineál Moain (descended from Moen, grandson of Eoghan) and Donaghmore was that of Clann Diarmada. Clann Diarmada formed part of Clann Chonchúir, prominent in east Donegal and descended from Conchúr, brother of Niall Frasach and of Aodh Allán, both of Cineál Eoghain and both High Kings of Ireland. Clann Chonchúir included, in addition to Clann Diarmada, septs who would settle in north Derry, like Ó Catháin, Ó Maoláin, Ó Loingsigh, etc. who left the east Donegal area. One branch that turns up occasionally amongst them is Clann Fhlaithbheartaigh, giving rise to the name Laverty. Where their home base was is unclear but it may have been the origin of the parish of Clonleigh.

Another group in the area were the *Fir Droma Lighean*, 'the men of Dromleen', led by Ó Donnaile/Donnelly and Ó Doibhlin/Devlin. In 1177 Giolla Mac Liag Ó Donnaile, Lord of the Fir Droma, was amongst those killed at Downpatrick, fighting against the Anglo-Norman forces of John de Courcy. When the names Ó Donnaile and Ó Doibhlin reappear in history, the bearers have moved to east Tyrone. The land controlled by Clann Diarmada may have extended beyond what we know as the parish of Donaghmore. Donnchadh Ó Cairealláin had promised land *near* Donaghmore in his *manchaine* to St Colm Cille; the three modern parishes of Clonleigh, Urney and Donaghmore actually meet and where they meet local tradition suggests the presence of an ancient church or monastery.

Unfortunately, references to the erenagh lands give only one name – Ballybogan – for the quarter of churchlands. Ballybogan is now called Churchtown, and presumably these lands were around this old church site. The churchlands as named in the *Civil Survey* were Bellibogan, Clonlee and Ballilast; Ballybogan and Ballylast are contiguous, so it is reasonable to conclude that they make up Donnchadh Ó Cairealláin's *manchaine*.

Patrons
Cluain Lao: St Lughaidh, son of Eochaidh[100] – feast day 24 March; (*named from pagan god Lugh*) his grandfather Iollann, son of Eoghan, was progenitor of Cineál Iollanna, a branch of *Cineál Eoghain na hInse*

---

100. 'Martyrology of Tallaght', *Leabhar Laighean/Book of Leinster* V, 1608. CGSH, p. 13 (#83); Michael O'Clery, John O'Donovan, James Henthorn Todd, William Reeves, *Martyrology of Donegal* (Dublin: Dublin Archaeological and Celtic Society, 1864), 86/87.

of the *Bréadach*, Inishowen East, to which belonged Ó Cearbhalláin, erenaghs of Clonleigh.

Saint Fionntán, of Cluain Lao.[101] GRSH gives the genealogy of one Fionntán, son of Aodh Fionnléith, which would make him the brother of High Kings Dónall Dábhaill (+915) and Niall Glúndubh (+919) of Cineál Eoghain – feast day 19 Sept or 1 Oct, but that seems to be the only reference to him.[102]

Saint Cairneach of Droim Lighean – feast day 28 March and 16 May, described by Kenney as 'a hazy and ubiquitous personage.'[103] Cairneach, 'the Cornishman', a British missionary, founder of Tuilén (Dulane, Co. Meath), is associated with St Patrick and St Benignus in re-writing the Irish laws, allegedly. Tradition makes him the nephew of Earc, mother of High King Muircheartach Mac Earca. (She may in fact have originally been a pagan goddess. She was also, allegedly, mother of St Columba's father Féilimí, from a union with Fearghus Ceannfhada, son of Conall.) Be that as it may, when she was dying she sent for her nephew the bishop and repented her sins. Her sons had given her a demesne of land at Droim Lighean, taken from the lands of Cineál Éinne, and she left this to Cairneach. The only trace of his presence there in recent times was a holy well, since drained away. It is possible that there were two saints called Cairneach and that one of them may have arrived in Meath with a number of British as refugees, perhaps fleeing from the Anglo-Saxon invasion. There is a genealogy of another (?) Cairneach, descended from Colla dá Chríoch. Father Uaitéar Ó hÉigeartaigh said Cairneach had a successor, Messán.

Patrons

| Teach na Comairce: | Ailfinus, Mochonoc, Mochasoc and Anfegen.[104] Finus Oilithir, Mo-chonóg, Mo-Chasóg and Ainfeigean.[105] Montgomery's Survey gives 'St Aghorogus' as patron.[106] |

---

101. CGSH 145 (#707.389).
102. GRSH 46 (#19).
103. *Sources for the Early History of Ireland* (New York, 1929/Dublin, 1979), 351–2.
104. CGSH 29 (#171) and adds *cum suis omnibus* 'with all theirs'. Perhaps Ss Conna and Cassán.
105. Mac Fhirbhisigh II, 789 (#751.2). *Oilithir/ailithir* means 'pilgrim'.
106. H.A. Jefferies in *Seanchas Ard Mhacha*, 1996/7, 55/71. Ware gives Aghavogus BD & ISL I, 406.

Most of these names would seem to be hypocoristic (pet-names), a common practice whereby terms of affection were added in front of and/or at the end of an abbreviated version of the saint's name. One might guess from the central portion what the names might be. It may show that those who gave the names were not familiar with them, perhaps even that the church was already a long-time ruin.

Erenaghs

Cluain Lao: Ó Cearbhalláin of Cineál Iollanna. (Distinct from Ó Cairealláin.)
Teach na Comairce: Ó Bogáin, Ó Brolaigh/O'Brolly, Ó Tomhrair/O Toner and Ó Braoin/O Breen at Kilfore.[107]

Erenagh lands

Cluain Lao: Unnamed at the plantation; two quarters and two *gorts* of glebe for the vicar.
Civil Survey names Clonlee: two quarters; Carneshanagh: two ballyboes glebe.

Teach na Comairce: Unnamed at the Plantation; one quarter plus one gort and one garden of glebe.
Civil Survey names Bellibogan: one quarter; Ballilast: four sessiaghs.
From these lands, with permission of Ó Dónaill, fishing took place from time to time at night and on the ebb tide, part of the lands of *Teach na Comairce* being the island of Inshcorrill in the river.[108] In depositions taken in the 1680s during contention about ownership of the fishery, Niall Mór Ó Cearbhalláin of Clonleigh, a fisherman aged seventy-seven, names the islands as Gunevarne, Cassyuene, Cassynegeeragh, Dunikilliogh and Cagill. This is confirmed by Matthew Strong. Féilimí Mac Loingsigh/MacLinchy, aged thirty, names Islandmore, Corkan and Cagill and separately, Gunevarne, Cossynegeeragh and Dunikilliogh, plus fishing at Gribbin, Sooly and Soolyburnshott. Dónall Ó Cearrbhalláin, a fisherman aged seventy-two, confirms Niall Mór's list, adds Coostra and names the cot (small boat) fishing places: Garysillagh,

---

107. Mac Fhirbhisigh I, 335 (#142.4) makes them belong to Cineál Binnigh of Tulach Óg, a branch of Cineál Eoghain. Ó Brolaigh is also found among Cineál Eoghain *na hInse* (Cineál Aonghusa) I, 347 (#149.6). Kilfore was a grange of the Cistercian abbey at Ballyshannon.
108. BD & ISL I, 28–30. Later papers claim these islands belonged to Clonleigh.

Cumlug (Conlug), Legnagopill, Legacullin.[109] Niall Mór Ó Cearbhalláin insisted that he knew the fishing rights because he was there when the sheriff of Donegal had given possession to established Church Bishop Bromwell [*sic*: Bramhall?], and that they had stayed to eat a salmon that he had roasted on the lands of Clonleigh.

DOMHNACH CHAOIDE/DONAGHEDY

Name

Domhnach (< Latin, *dominicum*, from *dominus* 'lord') is the earliest word in Irish for a church. The name then goes back to the early days of Christianity in Ireland. It is one of the churches said to have been founded by St Patrick in *Dulo Ocheni*, the valley of the Faughan, as was Both Domhnaigh/Badoney. Caoide is the name of the patron (Caideus or Caidinus in Latin). The *Martyrology of Donegal* names Caoide but gives no detail about him and he is not found in the genealogies of the saints.

The Martyrology gives five insertions about Donaghedy, which is unusual in a work that is sparing in its use of comment, including:

Caoide easpag ó Dhomhnach Chaoide cois Dianaide/Caoide bishop from Donaghedy beside the Dennet.

Caoide ab ó Dhomhnach Chaoide i dTír Eoghain diaec Derensis, 25 October ... Caidinus i Laidin. Tá a chill, a chlog agus a bhachall ar fáil/ Caoide abbot from Donaghedy in Tyrone, diocese of Derry, 25 October ... Caidinus in Latin. His church, his bell and his crozier are extant.

Domhnach Chaoide vulgo S. Cadini paróiste. Teampall Uí Bhuidhe in Oireacht Uí Chatháin sa fhéil ... /Donaghedy commonly called the parish of St Cadinus. Teampall Uí Bhuí in Ó Catháin territory and his feast ... (unfinished entry).

Ó Catháin country is usually considered to be modern north Co. Derry. However Altashane/*Alt Inse Uí Chatháin* suggests that they had some interest in the area, perhaps before they moved into Cianacht in the Roe valley. Where Teampall Uí Bhuí/Ó Buí's church might be is a teaser. *Buidhe/buí* means 'yellow', and Ó Buí is not a recognised surname. The only similar surname in the locality is Ó Blí/Blee; the original in the manuscript may have been misread, *Teampall Uí Bhlidhe*/O Blee's church. The word *teampall* seems to be a medieval word for a church, so we may be dealing with a much later church

---

109. BD & ISL II, 75–9 (*Ceasaí* is a plank [narrow] bridge; *súlach* might be foam, suds or muddy water).

than that of Donaghedy itself. In the course of a millennium or so
there would have been many churches, not necessarily all on the same
site. That leads us to the problem of the name Dunnamanagh/*Dún na
Manach*, which means on the face of it 'the fort of the monks'. *Dún*, 'a
fort, usually applied in Old Irish (the language of over 1,000 years ago)
to the residence of a lord, king or dignitary, consisting of an earthen
(sometimes stone) rampart inside which the house or houses were
erected. The word makes an unlikely combination with monks. When
the first flush of monastic fervour had passed in the early Church, the
word *manach* was applied, not so much to the monk, as to a tenant
on land belonging to a monastery. There is no need then to posit the
existence of a monastery in that particular place to explain the name
Dún na Manach. Of course monasteries were small and accessible in
many cases, at least at first. The discussion must go from the tradition
of a monastic presence there to the name, without reading too much
significance into the name, because the meaning of the name itself is
not clear-cut.

Patron

St Caoide, variously said to be bishop and abbot.
His feast day is given variously as 24 or 25 October, and John Colgan
gives 28 October. Colgan also says his name may be Caidinus, Caidanus
or Caidocus.[110] Although associated with a very early church, founded
allegedly by St Patrick, he is not mentioned amongst the disciples of St
Patrick. In addition there may be some confusion with Caedi/Caoide/
Coeti +711, Bishop of Iona, venerated at the same time.

Erenagh

Ó Blí, perhaps, if Teampall Uí Bhuí is properly Teampall Uí Bhlí.
Ó Duimhin/O Devine, otherwise. The rector in 1610 was Terentius O
Dovin/Tarlach Ó Duimhín. The name is spelt differently: Ó Duimhín/
Duibhín/Daimhín. The older pronunciation in English put the stress
on the first syllable. The sept belongs to the Cineál Binnigh branch of
Cineál Eoghain. Members are found amongst the clergy of Donaghedy
and surrounding parishes, so that, as with many septs within Cineál
Binnigh, they were prominent in Church affairs. Since the Cineál were

---

110. *The Martyrology of Donegal*, 283, 284–5 n; *Acta Sanctorum Hiberniae* (J. Colgan,
OFM, 1645; ed. B. Jennings, OFM, 1948), 162 b n.2., l.50a; A. O'Sullivan (ed.),
Book of Leinster VI (1948), 1644, l. 50366 (Coeti).

associated with the monastery in Derry before 1200, Ó Duimhín may have been erenaghs at *Gráinseach Bhun Dianaide*/Grange of Bundennet belonging to that monastery but within the parish of Donaghedy, with two ballyboes of land (unnamed) and 'two parts of the tithes of fishing in two pools of the River of Loughfoile, adjoining or lying within the said county of Tyrone.'

Erenagh lands
Ardkemie or Ardkeyne, Tiremoylan, Leytrim, Boynowen (BD & ISL, I, 56, 62, 106).
Plus vicar's glebal land, four acres – (later increased by Crewcallanagh, Clontegoran, [*Est. Church*][BD & ISL I, 149]), Clondegarrelan, Crikalloghan and Craghan (CS III, 409). Faany, Ardkane, Letrim, Bonony (CS III, 462).

DOMHNACH MÓR MHAIGHE IOTHA/DONAGHMORE

Name
Domhnach (< Latin *dominus* = lord) is the earliest word in Irish for a church. It was presumably called *mór* (= large, either due to its size or its effect). The title *Domhnach Mór* is quite common throughout Ireland. Maigh Iotha means the 'plain of corn', but has many mythological associations and occurs frequently in the historical record (see p. 78). It is important partly because of its location between Barnesmore and the Foyle and partly its fertility for growing the corn that gave it its name. The erenaghs paid the bishop four score methers of malt and they paid yearly to the lords of Glanfyn/Glenfinn four methers of butter and eight methers of meal.[111] The malt went to make the bishop's beer, a necessary constituent in the limited diet of the time – which underlines the importance of the area.

'Patrick came over Barnas Mór into Maigh Iotha and to Domhnach Mór Maighe Íotha and there he left Dudubhae/Dudubhan, son of Corcan, one of his household.'[112] His name does not appear in the listing of members of *muintir Phádraig*/the household of Patrick. He is also known as Dubhán. There is a somewhat confusing reference in Mac

---

111. Irish *meadar* = mether, was a (square) wooden vessel, cup or bucket, holding up to two gallons or so.
112. W. Stokes, ed., *Tripartite Life of Patrick* (London: H.M. Stationery Office, 1887), I, 150/1. John Colgan, *Trias Thaumaturga* (Louvain 1647: Edmund Burke Publisher, Dublin, 1997), 144b.

Fhirbhisigh to a Dubhán, one of seven brothers associated with *Fiodh Mór*, 'great wood'.[113] Colgan recounts that after leaving Dubhán, Patrick went on to meet Eoghan, son of Niall Naoighiallach, in *Fiodh Mór*. Unfortunately it is a common placename.

The historical record shows Maigh Iotha[114] as a place of conflict: the Norse defeated there by High King Niall Caille in 843; Éigneachán Ó Dónaill raided the area in 1206 and many were drowned and killed; in 1417 Ó Néill attacked Neachtán Ó Dónaill at Carn Glas, capturing horses, arms and armour and 'eleven were killed or taken prisoner';[115] in 1432 Ó Néill was back with a great army, 'many were killed and wounded', towns were burnt. The Anglo-Normans were not to be left out: John de Courcy and Edmund Mortimer made their contribution. The area was of course eagerly sought out at the Plantation. None could outdo the locals, however, who left Donaghmore, Urney and Ardstraw desolate in 1179, or as the Four Masters record 'emptied'. The local lords were Ó Cairealláin, Ó Gormlaigh, Ó Laifeartaigh, Ó Luinigh and of course the rising power of Ó Dónaill. Churches bore the brunt because people lived near them before castles were built from the fourteenth century on, because things of value were kept in churches for safety, and because attacking a lord's church was an assault on his worth. Maigh Iotha had all the disadvantages of being fertile, accessible and thus desirable. One can only marvel at the resilience of the people.

Patrons
St Patrick – feast day 17 March; said to be the founder.
St Dubhán, son of Corcán, disciple of St Patrick; feast day unrecorded.

Erenaghs
Ó Galáin/O Gallen, a sept of Cineál Iollanna branch of Cineál Eoghain na hInse, as were their Ó Cearbhalláin neighbours in Clonleigh. Also possible is Ó Gaillín, found among the surnames of Cineál Chaolbhaidh. Or Ó Doiréidh, a sept of *Cineál Chaolbhaidh Mac Fhearghasa* of Cineál Eoghain, amongst whom are the Ó Maolfhábhaill lords of Carraig Brachaí, northwest Inis Eoghain. These septs are named in Plantation sources as 'Mointergallon' and 'Mointergarredie'. Mointer is *muintir*, 'people', the traditional title with a family name. *Muintir Ghaláin* is

---

113. II, 747: 727.11.
114. Also known historically as 'an Lagán/Logán' = low-lying country.
115. This may have led Neachtan to build the castle at Castlefin.

readily decipherable. Mointergarradie/*Muintir Dhoiréidhe* surprisingly indicates retention of the 'd' when one would expect it to be almost silent in such an ending. Ó Doiréidh/O Derry were also one of the erenaghs on the monastic lands of Derry, although they are easy to confuse there with Ó Daighre/O Deery.[116]
Eochaidh Ó Doiréidh, airchinneach/erenagh, died 1064 (AFM).
Saorbhreathach Ó Doiréidh, airchinneach/erenagh, died 1205.

Erenagh lands
Four quarters of Donaghmore, Maharashanbally, Carrick, Emlah (BD & ISL II, 472).
Four quarters: Croghogerran, Machrishanvaly, Numlagh, Carrick, plus two sessiaghs at Kilcadden (CS III, 49).
Glebe: one sessiagh and one gort (unnamed); perhaps 'Altrangilla, juxta proportion Manistir/prop Killimgardan' (BD & ISL I, 149).
Earlier Plantation sources are coy about naming the churchlands here.

DROIM RÁTHA/DRUMRAGH

Name
Droim 'back' here refers to a wide-backed hill with a *ráth* or hill-fort on top. Hill-forts were dwelling places surrounded by a rampart or embankment usually of earth, sometimes of stone. The purpose was to protect, primarily from wild animals like wolves, but of course to defend against attack from humans as well. Its location on a ridge was to provide a field of vision. The rath in this place must have been important because the church was located near it so as to be easily accessible. There are a number of townlands in the area beginning with 're' or 'ra' (from *ráth*), showing that this kind of habitation was not uncommon. That a church was provided here near the river probably suggests a sizable population at the time. *Droim Rátha* was quite a common placename, which makes its history difficult to discover.

We know that the area was evangelised quite early because of the presence of Donaghanie/*Domhnach an Eich* 'the church of the steed' between Omagh and Beragh. It was a place of pilgrimage, associated with St Patrick. Whether we choose to accept the presence of St Patrick and the accompanying folk story of the horse or not, the word *domhnach* (from Latin, *dominus* = 'lord') brings us back to

---

116. Cf. BD & ISL I, 30.

that time, since it is the earliest word in Irish for a church. On the other side of Omagh, in the direction of Drumquin in the townland of Mullaghmenagh/*Mullach Meánach*, 'middle summit' there was a holy well, said to have a cure for sore eyes, called Tubberdoney/ *Tobar Domhnaigh*, again a common placename often translated as 'Sunday's Well'.[117] (The word *domhnach* changed in meaning to bear the additional sense of Sunday, as it still does).

According to the *Ulster Inquisitions* Appendix, there was a church at Coolaghy in the northwest of the parish along the Fairey Water. The name of this river in Irish is *an Féarach*, no doubt due to the fact that, for this part of Tyrone, its uncharacteristically sluggish waters encouraged the growth of surface vegetation. Its 'English' name is probably due to misunderstanding the sound of its name in Irish.

At any rate, the church here was a chapel of ease by 1600. There is no doubt then that the area had become Christian quite early. Who was the original evangeliser is a more difficult question. Neighbouring Cappagh seems to have belonged to the kingdom of Uí Fiachrach Ard Sratha, with St Eoghan/Eugene as its patron. Drumragh was drawn into the ambit of Cineál Binnigh, the branch of Cineál Eoghain who seem to have gone through what is now Co. Derry in their role of military strike force for Cineál Eoghain and continued through Termonmaguirk to Drumragh. They brought their devotion to St Columba with them but left, unfortunately, few traces of what had been there before their arrival.

The patron of the church at Coolaghy is said by Ware to have been St Masianus, recorded by Mongomery as Lanus.[118] There is one reference to a St Lann, daughter of Becc (+594) of Uí Tuirtre (south Derry/east Tyrone now), and King of Airghialla, and niece therefore of St Lurach of Maghera. The Montgomery version records a name with a masculine ending Lan*us*, which would seem to rule out a woman. Nothing is known of St Lann but one might speculate that it could be she who is meant, if the Drumragh area belonged to the kingdom of Uí Fiachrach Ard Sratha at a time, since Uí Fiachrach and Uí Tuirtre were closely related. A confusion attaching to her name is not improbable, particularly since the contribution of women religious to evangelisation in early Ireland has long been underestimated.

---

117. Mullaghmenagh seems to have disappeared with other townland names into what was renamed Mountjoy Forest West. In the poorer, smoke-filled housing of earlier times eye trouble was a persistent problem.

118. For Ware, see BD & ISL I, 406; for Montgomery, see Jefferies, op. cit., 57/73. For St Lann, see CGSH 50 #307.

Another suggestion is that of the late Uaitéar Ó hÉigeartaigh who mentions a Messan, successor of St Cairneach at Drumleen near Lifford. Unfortunately the reference cannot be checked. It is possible that by 1600 the chapel of ease had gone out of use, because the lands attached to it had been taken over by the secular lord, presumably Sliocht Airt, the branch of the Uí Néill who founded Omagh. This was a frequent source of complaint by churchmen in late medieval times.

One of the more intriguing townland names in the parish is Sedennan. The first part 'sed' suggests the Irish *suidhe* (nowadays spelt *suí*). As it happens *suidhe* is common in placenames: *Suidhe Finn*/Seefinn/Finn's Seat near Maghera; the same thing *Suidhe Fhinn*/Seat of Finn/Seein near Sion Mills (a name of which it is no doubt the origin); *Suidhe Goill*/Seegull/Seat of Goll (*mac Morna*, of the Fianna). In *suidhe* the 'h' indicates that d at the end of the word has become silent. In early Irish this was not so. Sedennan may well begin with *suide* and end with *Éanán*. There are a number of early saints called Éanán, one of whom as it happens is associated with *Droim Raithe*, said to be Dromraney in Co. Westmeath.[119] There is another Éanán, however, of Cineál Moain, a branch of Cineál Eoghain, although said to have become confused with St Earnán of Tory Island. In the *Onomasticon* there is a reference to *Enóc Druim Rathe*, which – the editor suggests – seems to refer to the northern half of Ireland and then adds 'Omagh is in Druim Ratha'. *Enóc* may be a hypocoristic form of *Éanna* and of *Éanán*. Perhaps in the name Sedennan we have a trace of an early apostle of Drumragh.

A Norse army crossed Drumragh in 746 and burnt the *dairtheach*, oak church, with 150 people in it.[120] Again, since the placename is common and no other detail is given we cannot be sure that it happened here. We are on more certain ground when we reach the thirteenth century. The Cineál Binnigh branch of the descendants of Eoghan, son of Niall Naoighiallach, had provided the erenaghs to lands belonging to the monastery at Derry, the *Dubhreglés*. By the end of the tenth century the erenagh family was *Mac Con Choille* (anglified McEnhill), notably in the persons of Conghalach, who died in 1112 at the age of ninety-four, and Bébhinn, described as the daughter of Mac Con Choille and female erenagh of Derry, who died on 23 December 1134, probably the daughter

---

119. CGSH 8, #42; Hogan, ed., *Onomasticon Goedelicum* (Dublin: Hodges, Figgis & Co. Ltd, 1910), 368. The entry referred to by Hogan is in Bollandists, ed., *Codex Saltamanticensis, Lives of the Irish Saints*, 356.

120. AFM ad ann.

of Conghalach. She is the last of the family mentioned in connection with Derry. The next to occur in the annals is St Conchúr Mac Con Choille, Archbishop of Armagh, who died in 1175 at Lemenc in Savoy on his way back from Rome. Before becoming archbishop he was prior of the house of Canons Regular of St Augustine in Armagh.

This raises again the intriguing question of relations between Derry and Armagh, between the tradition of St Patrick and that of St Columba, which were frequently fraught over the centuries. At first, it was a matter of the relative importance between Armagh and Iona. When the relics of St Columba were brought to Ireland and eventually to Derry, raising the status of Derry (demonstrated by its change of name from Doire Chalgaigh to Doire Cholm Cille), some way of normalising relations had to be found. The simplest explanation is that St Giolla Mac Liag Mac Ruairí, Abbot of Derry, went to Armagh as archbishop, succeeding St Maolmhóg Ó Morgair who had resigned, while Flaitheartach Ó Brolcháin, as representative of Clann Síonaigh, the power behind the *comharbacht* in Armagh, replaced him as abbot in Derry.

Flaitheartach was made a mitred abbot of the Columban 'order' and 'arch-abbot' of the churches of Ireland in 1158 at the synod of *Brí mhic Thaidhg* near Trim and had carried out visitations in his capacity of successor of Colm Cille. He died in 1175.[121]

In the same year the death took place of St *Conchúr Mac Con Choille*/Conor McEnhill, described in AFM as 'Abbot of the church of St Peter and Paul at Armagh and successor of Patrick afterwards'. His association was with Armagh and no longer Derry, as had been that of the family. The position he had held in Armagh was that of Prior of the Canons Regular in Armagh, and of course the monks of the monastery of Derry at this stage became Canons Regular, seemingly abolishing the rule of the Columban Order with its 'arch-abbot'. Whether the Mac Con Choille link with Derry had been broken or not at this stage or whether the break was due to Ó Dónaill–Ó Dochartaigh encroachment on the city after the Anglo-Norman threat had ended, we next find them in

---

121. AFM ad ann. A mitred abbot was an abbot given the right to wear a mitre, like a bishop. The first 'mitring' of an abbot by the pope was in the mid-eleventh century. There were some twenty-four monasteries with mitred abbots in medieval England. Legally, it gave the abbot no more authority, just prestige. Since the papal legate was present at the synod, presumably it was he who 'mitred' Flaitheartach at 'the request of the clergy of Ireland with the successor of Patrick' and gave him the *ardabdaine ceall Éireann* 'the archabbacy of all the *cealla*/churches (monastic, presumably) of Ireland'.

Drumragh, where they brought their devotion to Colm Cille as patron and the Black Bell of which they were the custodians.

In the summer of 1440, Canon of Derry and Rector/Parish Priest of Drumragh, Aodh Mac Cathmhaoil/Hugh McCaul considered himself to be under threat. A *laïcus barbatus*, 'a bearded layman' one *Pádraig Mac Aodha*/Patrick McHugh had arrived in his parish. Contrary to divine and human law, he had begun arguing about the faith and sacraments of the Church, preaching about, even deriding the clerical state and, daring temerariously to usurp the laws of the Church, he had begun blaspheming and slandering clergy and ecclesiastical persons. Under the terms of synodal and provincial law of Armagh, Clogher and Derry he had incurred excommunication. In spite of that he had proposed to found a new monastery within the bounds of the parish (although he had been restrained several times) and in prejudice to the views of the parish priest. Because of these insults and blasphemies committed in public *Aodh*/Hugh had excommunicated him, but Bishop *Eoin Ó Gubúin*/John O Gubbins of Derry had absolved him.

Fearing that similar grave matters would now be imputed to him again, Aodh Mac Cathmhaoil had appealed to the Holy See and in the meantime sought protection from the Archbishop of Armagh, John Mey. The archbishop inhibited the Bishop of Derry and others from further action to the prejudice of the appellant and calls on Bishop Rossa Mag Uír/Maguire of Clogher and Lochlann Ó Gallachair/O Gallagher of Raphoe to enforce the inhibition, if necessary calling on the help of the secular arm. In Omagh the secular arm was *Sliocht Airt* (Ó Néill). We do not know how the case finished up. It does however tell us something about the foundation of the convent of the Franciscan Third Order Secular at Omagh. They were a community both lay and clerical who came together to live a deeper spiritual life and to undertake the education of the young. Many of the immediate companions of St Francis would have been 'bearded laymen'. It may also tell us a little about the lifestyle of clergy in the fifteenth century, even if it would be too much to expect the parish priest to go into detail of what *Pádraig Mac Aodha* had criticised. He probably originated in the parish of Urney.[122]

Involving the secular arm of the time is interesting because Brian Óg Ó Néill of Newtown, grandson of *Anraí Aimhréidh*/Harry Avery,

---

122. Quigley and Roberts, eds, *Registrum Joannis Mey* (Belfast: HMSO, 1972), #182, pp. lxxxi/182–3.

neighbour and cousin of Sliocht Airt, had been excommunicated in 1407 for laying violent hands on Bishop Eoin Ó Flannúra/John O Flannery of Derry, taking his clothing, horses and other goods, even the rings off his fingers, and ordering the bishop's servants to be beaten up, even killed.[123] If the convent was founded around 1440 it could only have happened with the support of Sliocht Airt, because it would need to be given land to support itself. The land given is outside the parish of Drumragh and in Cappagh, perhaps even taken from land previously held by Sliocht Anraí Aimhréidh. By 1600 the 'secular arm', presumably Sliocht Airt, had taken over churchland at Coolaghy.

In 1529, Archbishop Cromer commissioned *Cormac Ó Muiríosa/* Morris, *Brian Mac Giolla Sheanáin* (Gilsenan)/Bernard Monsenan and *Donnchadh Mac Cathmhaoil*/Donatus O Cawoyll/Donnchadh McCaul, canons of Derry, to try the appeal of *Muiriach Mac Somhairle*/Mauritius McSoyly/McSorley against the decision made by Bishop Ruairí Ó Dónaill in a lawsuit between Mauritius and Thomas McKawoyll/Mac Cathmhaoil/McCaul. In 1530, Donatus McCamayll/Mac Cathmhaoil, Cormac O Murghan/Ó Muiríosa or Ó Mongáin, canons of Derry cathedral, and Catholicus Magensenan/Cathal Mac Giolla Sheanáin/ Gilsenan (or McElhennon), vicar of Cappagh, are commissioned to assess his suitability for the office of Dean of Clogher since he has been accused of perjury, public concubinage, robbery, etc. In 1535 Mauritius McCawell and Féilim McSomnagh/Mac Somhairle were in dispute about the vicarage of Drumragh and Bishop Ó Dónaill had given sentence against Féilim and pronounced him unfit to hold this or any other vicarage in his diocese. Féilim appealed to the archbishop who referred the case back to a court of Derry priests including the *officialis* of the diocese, Niall Ó Cearbhalláin.[124]

Patrons

Saint Colm Cille, abbot – feast day 9 June.
? Saint Éanán – feast day perhaps 25 March.
? Saint Lann V. or ? St Messan. Nothing more known.

Erenagh

Unnamed. There were probably at least two.

---

123. H.J. Lawlor, ed., *Catalogue of the Register of Abp Fleming* (Dublin: Hodges & Figgis, 1912), 113 #8.
124. A. Gwynn, *The Medieval Province of Armagh* (Dundalk: Dundalgan Press, 1946), pp. 193–4.

Perhaps Mac Cathmhaoil/McCaul, who were important in the diocese of Clogher.
Or Mac Con Choille, custodians of the Black Bell of Drumragh.

Erenagh lands
DRUMRAGH:

Eleven ballyboes: Nahany, Killifoure/Kellysoure, Drombeniue/Dombenine, Clonachro, Nadun Iny, Lavarine, Ballintemple, Lassan/Lessan, Tollaghmore, Cuilin/Cuyllin, Lishariny/Lisarune. (BD & ISL I, 56, 106)
Glebe (unnamed): house, garden and nine acres of land. (BD & ISL I, 62 [expanded 1636]). Tatereogh, Edergoule, Nedooneny. (BD & ISL I, 148)

COOLAGHY:

Four ballyboes/townlands: Molniharnan, Buskill, Kilmore, Molantomocke (BD & ISL II, 122) (Part of Mollantomock called Garvhill and Molandevert).
In a note pertaining to a legal case about ownership of these lands, witnesses mentioned were James Young, Turlough O Gormley, Patrick Grum (*gruama*=glum) O Gormley, Manus O Lynnym (?), Mory McChillcallum (Mac Giolla Chalma or Choilm/McElholm), Donnell McCanny (of Dromore), Hugh McLaughlin (of Dromore), Turlough O Mullogh (O Mullan?) (BD & ISL II, 122–3).
The land of the Franciscan convent of Omagh was Shergrim in Cappagh.

LEAC PHÁDRAIG/LECKPATRICK

Name

Leac means any flat slab of rock or stone. It can describe anything from bedrock to a gravestone or altar stone or monument. It is common in placenames. In the grants of lands by James I to Bishop Montgomery of the established Church at the Plantation it is called Magherineleck/*Machaire na Leice*, 'the plain of the flat rock'. The parish of Leacke occurs in *Inquisitions* twice but Magherineleck is treated by Montgomery as belonging in the parish of Urney, as is Camus, and 'Clonekirry'/*Cluain*

Coirre?, a division that does not seem to appear in later documents.[125] In Rawlinson A 237, of the religious centres named, one is given as 'Lackmackolin'. It does not name Leckpatrick as such.[126]

Patron
Saint Patrick – feast day 17 March.

Erenagh
Unnamed, although the opaque name 'Lackmacolin' is intriguing. The rector according to Montgomery, in 1609–10 was Eneas Maghinnie, perhaps Aonghas Mac Nainneanaigh/Mac Con Aonaigh/MacAneny, of the erenagh sept at Camus, who may have had a similar position here.

Erenagh lands
Two balliboes of which the erenagh has one sessiagh free of rent. (Appendix).
One ballyboe at Magherineleck and one at Clonekirry (BD & ISL I, 56). Half a quarter, two balliboes at Lecke (CS III, 403).
One acre of glebe belonging to the vicar (c.1610: Appendix), expanded to one ballybo Coolermoney, and half the ballybo of Killogrewhy by 1626, 'near Cloghogoall'.

LEAMHCHOILL/LANGFIELD
Name
Leamhchoill is an elm wood. The wych elm, *leamhán* in modern Irish, is the only species of elm native to Ireland. The 'elm wood' would perhaps suggest a *fidh-neimheadh*, a sacred grove like *doire*, initially pagan, but usually in later times attached to a church. In early law the elm was not rated as one of the 'noble trees of the wood': oak, ash, hazel, holly, yew, pine, apple, but one of 'the commoners of the wood'. Nonetheless the fine for cutting a branch off an elm without permission was one sheep or its equivalent, and for felling the tree one milch cow. Removing the tree resulted in a fine of two and a half milch cows. The elm in tradition is associated with protection and fertility. Many of its associations were

---

125. BD & ISL I, 56, 80,106; II, 335. Leckpatrick occurs as a separate entity without 'Clonekirry' in I, 110, 149., *Ulster Inquisitions*, page 11/12 (unnumbered) of the Appendix.
126. *Anal. Hib.* 3 (Dublin, 1931), 158.

with saints and holy wells. Elm timber is resistant to water so it was used for piles under bridges and causeways, for water troughs, for early water pipes and even for coffins.[127]

Leamhchoill occurs in the martyrologies in connection with three saints: Colmán, Fiontán and Colum, the last named being a woman.[128] The editor of the *Martyrology of Oengus* identifies the place as Lowhill in Offaly, but this can be no more than an opinion. However, there is no evidence of any early saint associated with Langfield other than St Eoghan/Eugene. *Droim Caoin* occurs in the annals once: '*Droim Caoin* with its churches was burned by Cineál Eoghain without the consent of Ó Néill.'[129] This is an example of the unfortunate tendency of the annalists to report an event without giving any context for it. Why Cineál Eoghain should choose to burn the churches of Drumquin in their own bailiwick, with or without the good will of their king, makes little sense. Was it vandalism, an attempt of *Clann Chonchúir* to force out remnants of *Uí Fiachrach Ard Sratha* or a further episode in the mayhem that marked the area in the 1170s? Or might it be *Droim Caoin/* Drumkeen in modern east Donegal?

Patron
Saint Eoghan/Eugene, bishop and abbot – feast day 23 August.
That he was the patron shows that the original church of *Leamhchoill* was in the *paruchia* and kingdom of *Uí Fiachrach Ard Sratha*. There is no evidence to substantiate any link between the area and the saints mentioned above.

Tearmannach (Erenagh with termon land)
Ó Baoighill/Ó Baoill/O Boyle, who belonged to *Clann Fhlaithbheartaigh/Laibheartaigh*/Laverty, of the *Clann Chonchúir*, branch of *Cineál Eoghain*. Conchúr was nine generations in descent from Eoghan. Two brothers were high kings and this one died in mid-eighth century, probably. The *Topographical Poems* puts Ó Baoill amongst *Fir Mhaighe Iotha* 'the men of Magh Iotha', a name applied to varying branches of *Clann Chonchúir* at various times and sometimes seems to have involved *Cineál Moain*. As defined by the *Topographical Poems*, the make-up of Fir Mhaighe Iotha was Ó Baoill/O Boyle, Ó Maoil

---

127. Niall Mac Coitir, *Irish Trees: Myths, Legends & Folklore* (Cork: The Collins Press, 2003), pp. 130–3, passim.
128. CGSH #707, 258.400; 708.76; *Mart. Oeng.* 76, 389.
129. AFM, ALC, ad ann. 1212; AU ad ann. 1213.

Bhreasail/perhaps Russel now, Ó Coinn/O Quinn and Ó Cionaoith, probably now McKenna. Of them the *Poems* say that they 'guarded the borders'. Which borders or whose we are not told. Fir Mhaighe Iotha seem to have been a fighting force. In 1193, Eochaidh Ó Baoill was slain by Uí Fiachrach Ard Sratha. By that time the ruling group of Uí Fiachrach had been ousted by Cineál Eoghain from Ardstraw and are found with allies from Fermanagh attacking Cineál Eoghain. Eochaidh may have met them on a border crossing. Caoinchomhrac (*gentle meeting*) Ó Baoill, Bishop of Armagh from Pentecost Sunday 1099 to 1106, may have belonged to this sept. He was the last old-style bishop before the early stages of the Twelfth-Century Reform began under Ceallach, made *uasaleaspag* 'noble bishop' at the request of the men of Ireland in 1106. Usually *Clann Chonchúir* and *Fir Mhaighe Iotha* describe Ó Catháin/O Kane, Ó Cairealláin/Kerlin and Ó Maoláin/ Mullan, etc. as more newsworthy members.

Erenagh lands
Four balliboes: Ballianwoy, Ballycullin, Ballineclogins, Dromchintaramon, plus one half-sessiagh (said to be about sixty acres) of glebe land (unnamed).[130]
Longfield churchland: four ballyboes.
One ballyboe: Magheryryne; and one ballyboe: Lagvuldcarne and Glanrowne (CS III, 367). The last named ballyboes might be glebe lands for the curate.

The fact that this was a *tearmann* is unusual, since the more widely recognised tearmann was quite near, that of Termonamongan-Termonmagrath, associated with Lough Derg. It suggests that *Leamhchoill* may have been connected with the other, and perhaps that that termon land was divided at a time. It was claimed that the separation was due to the military exercise that Bishop Giolla an Choimdhe (Germanus) Ó Cearbhalláin was accused of perpetrating. However, it would surely have been impossible for a bishop to undertake such aggrandisement without at least the consent of neighbouring lords. It would seem more likely that the detachment of Termonamongan from Termonmagrath, and from the diocese of Clogher, was more probably due to the dismemberment of the kingdom of Uí Fiachrach Ard Sratha

---

130. BD & ISL I, 56, 62, 106, 148; II, 335, 341. Dromchintaramon = *Tearmann Droim Chaoin*/Drumquin Termon.

by Cineál Eoghain, in particular by Cineál Moain (Ó Gormlaigh-Ó Luinigh-Mac Conallaigh) who are found in that area in *Ceart Uí Néill*. Clogher claimed to be the diocese of the *Airghialla*, to which grouping Uí Fiachrach belonged. All churches had some sanctuary rights but the concept of *tearmann*/sanctuary, allowed to agreed churches, was found all over Europe in an age of fairly ruthless punishment when someone accused of a crime might expect execution, loss of hands or eyes or castration. Being in sanctuary meant that the criminal might lose his land and property but at least his person was inviolate.[131] He could leave and face the music with some degree of protection.

TEARMANN UÍ MHONGÁIN/TERMONAMONGAN

Name

Tearmann Uí Mhongáin/O Mongan's termon was also known as Kylchyrryll/*Cill Chairill*/'St Caireall's church'. It appears once in the annals, in 1537, as *Tearmann Uí Moain*. Along with *Tearmann Mhic Craith*/Termonmagrath in the diocese of Clogher, originally part of the wider *tearmann*, known as *Tearmann Dáibheoig*/St Dávog's termon, getting its name from the patron, associated with *Loch Dergderc*/Deirg it was attached by force to the diocese of Derry in an operation that allegedly removed modern west Tyrone from Clogher, an operation which was said to have been conducted by Bishop Giolla an Choimdhe ('servant of the Lord' – Latinised 'Germanus') Ó Cearbhalláin, but was probably the result of political and civil trouble which brought about the demise of the kingdom of *Uí Fiachrach Ard Sratha*, the pressure of Cineál Eoghain expansion forcing the ruling body of Uí Fiachrach Ard Sratha to seek their niche with other Airghialla septs in Fermanagh/ Monaghan. Both the Bishops of Clogher who claimed the return of the area to their diocese were Ó Bracáin/O Brogan, a name that occurs in 1179 in Ardstraw in the context of the mayhem resulting in the many deaths and much destruction brought about through the rivalry of Cineál Moain and Clann Diarmada.

There may have been other factors at work that cannot be uncovered due to the paucity of the remaining records, but *Ceart Uí Néill* – the record of Ó Néill claims to levies and taxes on Ulster, dating in its final form from the sixteenth century – indicate that Cineál Moain

---

131. Cf. Robert Bartlett, *England under the Norman and Angevin Kings 1075–1225* (Oxford: Oxford University Press, 2000), pp. 445–6.

were established at Killeter, suggesting a primacy, in Ó Néill's eyes, of *Mac Conallaigh*/McConnolly (now Connolly)/McNally (descended probably from Conallach Ó Luinigh [+1178]) over Ó Gormlaigh. Ó Néill's claim on Cineál Moain was 200 beeves and 150 marks silver, plus entertainment and sustenance when he visited, and 150 men for military service.[132]

What references we have apply in the main to the wider Tearmann Dáibheoig and are in the main a record of plunder, cattle rustling and armies passing through on the way to attack someplace else. One interesting pointer to the role of the *tearmannach* occurred in 1496 when Mac Craith (Ruairí, son of Diarmaid) confronted the forces of Conn Ó Dónaill who were in pursuit of Mag Uír. In his position as *Comharba Dháibheoig* ('successor of St Dávog') Mac Craith warned Conn not to violate his protection and that of the *Tearmann* by attacking Mag Uír. His warning was ineffective. Conn Ó Dónaill took control of the road and Mag Uír's party had to try to cross a bog and quagmire, in the process leaving behind 110 horses, having twelve of his band killed and being taken prisoner himself. On the other hand, in 1471 Colla Mag Uír killed Ruairí Mag Uír at Mac Craith's house in Alt Ruaidhin, but he and his son were killed 'through the vengeance of God and of St Dávog'. An entry in the annals in 1440 tells of a newly appointed *comharba* being ordained.

Patrons
Saint Patrick, bishop – feast day 17 March.
Saint Dáibheog/Dábheóc/Mobeóc/Beog – feast day 1 January.
Dáibheog was one of the chief saints of Ireland, amongst them Colm Cille, Ciarán of Clonmacnoise and Molaise, who came to fast, ineffectually, against Diarmaid mac Cearbhaill after Diarmaid had violated the sanctuary given by St Ruadhán of Lothra to Aodh Guaire, until St Brendan provided fifty blue-eyed horses as a ransom for Aodh Guaire.[133] One genealogy suggests that Mobeoc/Dáibheog was the son of Brachan, King of the Britons, and of Dina, daughter of the King of the Saxons. Another suggests that he belonged to Dál Fiatach in modern east Co. Down.[134] In either case he came as a missionary, either from

---

132. Éamon Ó Doibhlin, Diarmaid Ó Doibhlin, eds, *O'Neill's 'Own Country' and its Families* (Donaghmore: Donaghmore Historical Society, 1998), p. 51.
133. C. Plummer, *Lives of the Irish Saints* (Oxford: Clarendon Press, 1922/1997) II, 85#185.
134. CGSH 178, #722.89; GRSH 82; Mac Fhir Bhisigh II, 737 #723.5.

Britain or from the area first associated with St Patrick. This would suggest that he came with St Patrick. As to what his name was we have more of a problem. As it stands it is hypocoristic (a pet name). *Dá* at the start and *og* at the end are terms of endearment (as in 'He's gone to school *wee* Hughie and him not four'). That leaves us with the *be* in the middle. He is also called Beog, which may mean that someone as puzzled as we are at the problem of the hypocoristic name simply lopped off the *Dá* at the start. Once again we are up against the destruction of records. Montgomery gives his name as 'Beotis', which Sir James Ware construes as 'Boetius', perhaps the result of an association of ideas.

The original Boëthius or Boethius (who died about AD 525) was a Roman *philosopher*. He was venerated under the name Bestius. There are saints whose name begins with Beo- (=live). Colgan quotes Gerald of Wales who called him Beanus and suggests that he was also venerated on 28 October (*recte*, 26 October) and 3 December under the name Beoan, but the martyrology associates the first date with St Beoan of Lough Brickland in Co. Down and the second with Feighcullen in Offaly, although, intriguingly, this one is said to be a son of Nessán and brother of Caireall.[135] Perhaps the most likely candidate is a member of St Patrick's retinue, one of his so-called artisan-smiths, *Bite*. Not every list of the retinue includes his name (pronounced with two syllables), and he is not named in association with any other church, which does lend some credibility to our thesis. It also accords with his seniority.[136] He may have had a sister called Síneach, as had St Colm Cille. Colgan adds that Beog foretold the coming of St Colm Cille.

Saint Caireall, of *Cill Chairill*. There are a number of saints of this name, but perhaps the most likely originated amongst the Ulaidh in east Ulster.[137] One of the sons of Nessán, venerated at Eanga (Termoneeny) was named Caireall, although they were from Leinster. It might even be St Cyril of Alexandria.

Erenagh
Ó Mongáin, as tenants of Mac Craith – as claimed by Clann Chraith. The surname is not found in the genealogies, where examples of

---

135. VT 390b, 449a; MD 157, 285; CGSH 46# 284.
136. For Montgomery, cf. H.A. Jefferies, op. cit., 57; For Ware, BD & ISL I, 406; For Bite, *Mac Fhirbhisigh* II, 698#695, who is unclear about his origins; CGSH 118#471.12 – given as #471.11 in the index; for Síneach, 156, 708#147.
137. GRSH 99. *Mac Fhirbhisigh* II, #727.26; #748. 7.

Mongán as a Christian name are found mostly in east Ulster – *mong* describes a thick growth of long hair, a mane. We are fortunate to have confirmation of their possession by Archbishop Fleming of Armagh, probably in 1412, in a letter confirming 'Patrick Omongan in the lands of Kylchiryll, which from time immemorial he and his ancestors have held by charter from the Church of Derry.'[138] In 1557 Ó Néill (*Seán an Díomais*: Shane the Proud), escaping on foot with only two companions after his heavy defeat at the battle of Balleeghan by the forces of Ó Dónaill, had to swim the Deel, Finn and Derg, all of them in spate. At *Tearmann Uí Mhaoin*, as the annalists tell us, he bought a horse from Ó Maoin, which must have been a sterling animal for in spite of the heavy rain he reached *Aireagal Dá Chiaróg*/Errigalkeerogue by daybreak. The 'Ó Maoin' pronunciation was confirmed in the course of a decision made by Lord Deputy Wentworth in a legal squabble between James Magragh/McGrath and the established Church Bishop of Derry about ownership of the churchlands of the parish. Marcas Rua Mac Craith testified that the McGraths had been in possession of the lands of Termonmagrath and Termonamongan time out of mind, that the prior of Lough Derg had had two quarters of termon as of right of the monastery of Lough Derg since the first abbot's time, and furthermore that Miler McGrath, established Church Archbishop of Cashel (who belonged to the *comharba* family), had bought the lands back from Captain Edmond Lee who was in possession of the land by letters patent. Miler was the son and heir of Donncha Mac Craith (*an Giolla Gruama* – the gloomy fellow) to whom 'the Omongans were tenants and paid rent'. This was confirmed by Calbhach Bán Mag Uír.

The evidence of these deponents was rejected by Wentworth and the Council as contradictory. James Dubh McGrath, a descendant of the *comharba* of St Dáibheog and *tearmannach* of *Tearmann Dáibheoig* had argued that the Council could not rule in favour of the bishop because there was no such place as Termon O Mongane, that the parish at issue was Termon O Moyane. This delayed the decision until the Council in Dublin was informed that, while it was called Termon O Moyane by the Irish, it was known as Termon O Mongane by the English. The following year, 1635, Sheriff William Ancketill took 'quiet and peaceable possession of the lands and ordered that they be delivered to Bishop

---

138. H.J. Lawlor, ed., *Calendar of Register of Abp Fleming* 149 (Dublin: Hodges Figgis, 1912). The see of Derry must have been vacant.

John Bramhall.[139] Bishop Bramhall was in the position of having to recover lands leased liberally by his predecessor, George Downham. Both of them seemed content to act as though erenagh land had belonged to the bishop.

Erenagh lands

Termonamongan was omitted when the *Inquisitions* set out to determine churchlands, just as Termonmagrath seems to have escaped direct consideration: 'by reason of the ignorance and unsettledness of the times sundry parcels were omitted', as the letter on behalf of Charles I put it. Only one of the jurors, Ruairí Ó Gormlaigh, was from west Tyrone and none were from the erenagh families, unlike the jurors for Coleraine and Donegal. They seem to have been a little confused about which of the new counties the area should be considered to belong in. It is surprising that none of the ten English jurors, usually so well tuned in to the potentialities, were aware of Lough Derg. As a result, the name and nature of the lands only begin to emerge in 1630, 'two townlands and a sessiagh'. By 1675 the lands are named as Carraghro and Meenenergus by William O Carrowlan/*Uilliam Ó Cearbhalláin* and Loughlin Backagh McKew/*Lochlann Bacach* (= lame) *Mac Aodha*, and as Seogrenan and Meenevergus by Morris O Mungan/*Muireadhach Ó Mongáin*.[140] In the *Civil Survey* (1654–6) they are given as Croy, Ballimongon and Aghilonring (one balliboe), Magherekill, Gortnagrosse and Kilteeragh (one balliboe) and the half cessue of Carragh hoe.

URNAÍ/URNEY

Name

Basically *Urnaí* means an activity rather than a place. It means 'praying' and secondarily, prayer. From there it came to be applied to a place where prayer was carried on, an oratory (from Latin, *orare* = to pray). The parish takes it name from the convent founded by St Cognat and from the primary activity that was carried on there. The *Life of St Eoghan* (Eugene) of Ardstraw speaks of him visiting, in the company of St Tiarnach of Clones, a convent in *Ros Cay in terra Metheorum* (in the

---

139. BD & ISL I, 195, 200–2. This also shows a connection between the surnames Mongan and Mone.
140. BD & ISL II, 19–20; CS III, 366.

land of the ?Methei?) whose abbess was called *Mosseta*. Since Urnaí was known as Urnaí Mhaighe Iotha in later times, it is not impossible that Urnaí was the place in question – *in terra Maighe Iotha* – with its name garbled by a later scribe unfamiliar with the area. Local knowledge may decide if *Ros Cay* can be identified. The only suggested date for the death of St Eoghan (Eugene) is the year 550. The account of his life is late and not particularly reliable.

Convent

Unfortunately, we have no historical record of anyone with a name like *Mosseta* in the convent of Urnaí. Founded by St Cognat, it was one of two convents in the diocese whose success in evangelisation was such that their achievement was remembered. The other was at Camas na Banna/Camus-juxta-Bann, which had a link with St Comhghall and Bangor. It was unlikely that either survived the ravages of the Norse and GaillGhaeil (of mixed Hiberno-Viking ancestry, with the bad habits of both), but some of the religious in both were remembered.

Parish
URNAÍ:

Urnaí returns to the light of history in the twelfth and thirteenth centuries when, after the Twelfth-Century Reform of the Church, parishes as we know them were being created in place of the 'federal' church of the monastic *paruchia* where local churches were linked to a monastery, sometimes different from another church near them. The development of Urney and Donaghmore shows most clearly one basis for division. Donaghmore was the *tuath* (state/kingship) of Clann Diarmada/Ó Cairealláin (Carlin/Kerlin) whereas Urnaí was the *tuath* of Cineál Moain/Ó Gormlaigh (O Gormley), two ruling septs who were continually at loggerheads, until Ó Gormlaigh on one side and Ó Dónaill on the other, squeezed out Ó Cairealláin who moved closer to their ally and overking, Mac Lochlainn, at Derry. There they gave their sept name, Clann Diarmada, to the parish of Clandermot/Glendermott.

Ó Gormlaigh in alliance with their overking Ó Néill were to prove the stronger. Ó Gormlaigh's territory came to include the present parishes of Urnaí, Mourne, Sion Mills, Camus and maybe Leckpatrick. Cineál Moain's home territory, as it were, was what is now Urney and Mourne. Later Ó Dónaill forced them across the River Mourne, and later still they were displaced towards Gortin by Ó Néill where they left the name of their branch of their sept in Munterloney/*Muintir Luinigh*.

Although Ó Gormlaigh were the most prominent sept there were other surnames emanating from Cineál Moain: Ó Luinigh, Ó Tiarnaigh, Mac Giolla Uír/McAleer, (Ó) Mac Gairbhéidh/McGarvey, Ó Peatáin. Similarly, Clann Chonchúir included Ó Muireadhaigh/Murray, Ó Baoill/Boyle, Ó Laibheartaigh/Laverty, as well as the more prominent Ó Cairealláin and of course Ó Catháin/O'Kane. Some of these must have had a hand in the parishes around Urney, but they are not recorded as belonging to any definite place. Ó Catháin began to make their mark when they moved to the Roe valley. For all we know, they may have been helped on their way – perhaps from Donaghedy or Leckpatrick – by their neighbours.

BALLENELINNIE:

There was a capella/chapel of the parish of Urney at Ballenelinnie, which may indicate the area belonging to Ó Luinigh: *Baile Uí Luinigh*. The chapel was dedicated to St Constantus, which is almost certainly St Constans. Since Constans belonged to *Uí Mic Cairthinn* and had a church dedicated to him at Stradarran (Banagher), the chapel at Ballenelinnie must have been in the kingdom of *Uí Fiachrach Ard Sratha*, close relatives of *Uí Mic Cairthinn*, until Cineál Moain came on the scene and attached the area to Urney. Urney is in the barony of Strabane (Sliocht Airt Óig) while Balleylumy/Ballenelinnie is in the barony of Omagh (Sliocht Airt). It is interesting that three of the townland names of Urney point to septs of Cineál Moain: Ballyfatten/Baile Uí Pheatáin; Killigormley/Coill Uí Ghormlaigh; Ballimcleer/Baile Mhic Ghiolla Uír (CS III, 387–8).

Patrons
URNAÍ:

Feme, now *Féimhe* (pronounce *fay've*) – feast day 21 January.
She was the sister of St Dáigh, of Cineál Dalláin in Cineál Eoghain na hInse (originating in the Moville area of Inishowen). Dáigh was one of the acclaimed artisan-smiths of sacred vessels of early Ireland, said to have been a disciple of Ciarán of Clonmacnoise, founder of Inishkeen (Co. Monaghan) and died in 587.
Cognat – feast day 11 February. There is also a saint called Coinet.[141]
Fainche (pronounce *fan'che: -ch-* as in *loch*) – feast day 1 January. She is perhaps confused here with Féimhe; also known as *Fainche Gharbh*

---

141. GRSH 50–1; CGSH 127, 215, #690.10.

(= the rough), said to refer to the texture of her skin, resulting from a long swim to escape an unwanted marital suitor.

Neas (pronounce *ny'as*) – feast day 4 September.

Sáfann (Sámhthann) – feast day 18 December, later became abbess of Cluain Brónaigh (Clonbroney) near Granard (Co. Longford), well-known spiritual director, +739. The convent is unlikely to have survived the Viking era since it would have been too accessible to the Norse who made their base on the Foyle.

BALLENLINNIE:

Saint Constans, also known as Cuanna – feast day 14 November.

Also said to have been called Connachtach/the 'Connachtman'. He is described as an anchorite or hermit who lived on Eo-inis in Loch Erne and died in the year 777. Eo-inis is in fact an island in Loch Uachtar/ Oughter in Co. Cavan.[142] Eo originally meant 'tree' but later came to mean 'yew' and *inis* is 'an island'. Constans is at the later end of the lists of early saints, and the Latin name 'constant, firm, steady' must mean some sort of religious profession. Why he should be called *Connachtach* is not apparent.

Erenagh
URNEY:

Mac an Bhaird, a branch of a sept named Ó Ceallaigh/O Kelly, a common surname because Ceallach was a common Christian name; it comes from *ceall*, meaning a church or monastic foundation. *Ceallach* has a homonym meaning 'contention'. *Aodh Mac an Bhaird* was erenagh about 1609. A *bard* was a poet with lower qualifications and lesser studies than a *file*. There were sixteen subdivisions amongst the *baird*. It was part of his role to declaim the poetry written by the file:

> ... the action and pronunciation of the poem in the presence of the principal person it related to was performed with a great deal of ceremony in a Consort of Vocal and Instrumental Music. The poet himself said nothing but directed and took care that everybody else did his part right. The bards, having first had the composition from him, got it well by heart, and now pronounced it orderly, keeping even pace with the harp touched upon that

---

142. Mac Fhirbhisigh, op. cit., II. 87 #340.14/15; 721#713.6/7; III, 462#1129.1. GRSH 66. CGSH 9, #51, 74, #583.

occasion, no other musical instrument being allowed for the said purpose but than this alone.

Where this branch of Ó Ceallaigh originated is impossible to tell. There was the sept of the name who were erenaghs at Fahan, from whom descended Mag Rabhartaigh/Magroarty, but perhaps more likely it is a branch of Cineál Eoghain na hInse, descended from Eochaidh, son of Eoghan, and known as Cineál Eachach or *Cineál Eachach an Chodaigh*. *Codach* means a pact, covenant, treaty of friendship. What exactly the *codach* was we do not know. Eochaidh had six sons. One called Dáigh is described as King of all Uí Fiachrach and he was killed by Uí Mic Cairthinn at the battle of *Áth Ghort an Chatha*, 'the ford of the field of the battle', probably Gortica near Drumahoe, and would suggest that *Cineál Eachach an Chodaigh* were making inroads on the territory of *Uí Mic Cairthinn* of the Faughan valley, probably pushing them back farther up the valley, perhaps in the process creating the area around the lower Faughan, called Annagh by the sixteenth century, a recognised discrete portion of the barony of Tirkeeran. The battle is recorded in the genealogy only so we cannot date it, but it may count among the early attempts of Cineál Eoghain to break out of their exiguous homeland; if the genealogies are anything to go by, probably the result of population pressure.

If he was, as described, King of Uí Fiachrach, it shows that they had also overcome the relatives of *Uí Mic Cairthinn, Uí Fiachrach Ard Sratha*. Their grip on the kingship did not last very long anyhow, because they relapse into obscurity. Like Cinneál Binnigh, the length of their genealogy suggests an importance not borne out by the annals. When septs lost political power they moved into other fields of activity. Some became erenaghs, Mac Doinnshléibhe became a medical family under the name Mac an Ultaigh. It was not uncommon for them to move into a poetic or bardic role. Féilim, brother of Dáigh, was the ancestor of Ó Ceallaigh, descended from *Ceallach Leathaigh* (Dubh Dúin Ó Ceallaigh was eleven generations from Eochaidh).

The genealogy includes another family with the surname Ó hEachach and says they are found *ag an Chamabhainn*, 'at the crooked river'. The River Camowen joins the Drumragh at Omagh to form the Strule. That might seem too far away, but it could have been the eastern boundary of the kingdom of *Uí Fiachrach Ard Sratha* since the area that became the parish of Cappagh seems to have been within it. *Mac an Bhaird Uí Cheallaigh* may well then have been of Cineál Eoghain and may have moved or been moved sideways by a resurgent Uí Fiachrach or by more powerful branches of the Cineál Eoghain that came along.[143]

An entry in the annals gives us a view of the status of the erenagh. In 1178 Cineál Moain banished Dónal, son of Dónall Ó Gormlaigh, to Inis Eoghain and Conchúr, son of Conallach Ó Luinigh,[144] took the *taoisíocht* (chieftainship). Three months later Ó Luinigh was deposed and Ó Gormlaigh was reinstated. Supporters of Ó Gormlaigh killed Ó Luinigh in Ó Gormlaigh's house while he was under the protection of the erenagh of Urnaí (unnamed), who was along with him. For this act of treachery Cineál Moain expelled Ó Gormlaigh again.

BALLENELINNIE:
Mac Aodha/McHugh. Mánas Mac Aodha in 1509.
The antecedents of Mac Aodha are not clear. The name Aodh/Hugh was so common that they might originate in any sept but they do not occur in any Ulster genealogy. However, in *Ceart Uí Néill* they are treated for tax purposes as belonging to Cineál Moain,[145] and Islandmachugh, presumably their headquarters, is in one of the Baronscourt lakes, perhaps in that referred to in *Ceart Uí Néill* as *Loch Uí Mhaoldubháin*, although that seems to be where *Mac Con Mí* is found.

Erenagh lands
The *Ulster Inquisition* jurors did not know anything about Urney and left any estimate of area to a new inquisition. Surprisingly, none of the Tyrone jurors were of erenagh families. The few local jurors like Ruairí Ó Gormlaigh may have kept quiet. Be that as it may, Bishop George Montgomery had it worked out when it came to the grant of churchlands to himself in 1610, as follows:

Urney: four ballyboes: Aghenedonagh, Cogan, Nurim, Longford. (BD & ISL 56)

By 1615, in the grant to Bishop John Tanner, four sessiaghs of Ballilast had been discovered, as had, by another Inquisition in 1611: a half of one quarter (two ballyboes) in Ballyunelynny (BD & ISL 80), which were added to Aghnedawnagh, Cogan, Nurnin, Longford (do. p. 106). The

---

143. H.A. Jefferies, op. cit., 56/71; *Mac Fhir Bhisigh* I, 347 #148–9.3.
144. Conchúr, son of Conallach Ó Luinigh, may have been the first Mac Conallaigh/ Connolly/McNally.
145. Op. cit., 51–3. However, Mac Aodha, Ó Ceallaigh, Mac Connallaigh, Ó Gormlaigh, Ó Duibhin, Ó Flaitheartaigh and Mac Con Mí occur in the taxation list, even though some have no genealogical connection.

Civil Survey identifies one sessiagh of churchland called Concrewar (III, 408).

Ballinlinnie: had one sessiagh of glebe, according to the *Inquisitions*, Appendix.

Aghenedonagh looks as if it includes 'domhnach', a very early church. Nurin might be *An Urnaí*, and Longford might indicate a Norse encampment.

The medieval parish of Urney had two churches in Urney and one dedicated to St Maolrubha on the island of Islay off the west coast of Scotland. Saint Maolrubha had founded a monastery at Abar Crosáin/Applecross on the Scottish mainland opposite Skye and was one of the great apostles of Scotland. By ancestry he belonged to the *Cineál Binnigh* branch of *Cineál Eoghain*. His mother Subhthan was by ancestry of Dál nAraí in Antrim and was said to be the sister of St Comhghall of Bangor, although their dates make this unlikely (St Comhghall was dead by 605 and St Maolrubha died on 21 April 721). Maolrubha is said in some sources to have been Abbot of Bangor also. There is no obvious reason why there should be a link between Maolrubha, Islay and Urney.

On 20 September 1535, two priests Magonius Ogarquinclayder/Mánas Ó Gormlaigh and Torreletus McAeder/Tarlach Mac Aodha appealed to Primate Cromer of Armagh, They, along with Nellanus Ocerballan/Niall Ó Cearbhalláin, held between them the rectory and the vicarage of Urney. The rectory of St Maolrubha was held by two Scottish priests: Patrick Roisse/Ross and Macolinus Macmiradhy/*Maolcholm Mac Mhuireadhaigh* (Murdock, now). Odo MacAbarde/*Aodh Mac an Bhaird* had come up with the idea that all these scattered benefices would be better managed if he held them all and had gone to Rome and obtained his provision to the united position. The provision was challenged on legal grounds. The appeal was to go to Rome, but Henry VIII renounced any allegiance to the pope in the meantime. The appeal was probably still born.

The case is interesting because it shows us Mac Aodha of one erenagh family in the parish pitted against Mac an Bhaird from another, and Ó Cearbhalláin of the erenagh family of Clonleigh involved also. The sept of Ó Gormlaigh was to act on two levels, Mánas as one of the appellants, and Eoghan Ó Gormlaigh, 'captain of his nation', along with Ó Dónaill (Aodh Dubh), asked by the primate to provide civil protection until all was settled.[146] The solution, if one was found, was overtaken by the religious crisis then looming.

This concludes our survey of the medieval endowments of the parishes of the diocese of Derry. It is highly ironical that, because of the studied annihilation of medieval Gaelic political and ecclesiastical arrangements, we are dependent for any detailed enumeration of them on the records drawn up for the purpose of their expropriation. Nonetheless, even these documents bear unwitting testimony to a highly organised political and ecclesiastical system, which evidences a very original response on the part of Gaelic society to a problem which exercised peoples all over Europe in the Middle Ages: how to reconcile the financing of a Church system with the necessity to find an appropriate role for the Church within civil and social organisation.

SOME BISHOPS' LIVES

It was regrettable that the Anglo-Norman invasion of Ireland followed so hard on the heels of the process of reform, which had been progressing favourably in the country in the course of the twelfth century. From that time on, racial and political discrimination bedevilled Church administration in regard to appointments, visitations, finance and discipline. It was not always easy for an Anglo-Norman prelate to enforce his authority among the Gaelic-speaking population. On the other hand, the colonial authorities in the country distrusted Gaelic-speaking clergy and discriminated against them in appointments. The end result was a Church organisation divided and disorganised, without the unity of purpose or transparency of discipline, which would have created countrywide the conditions to permit the kind of spiritual and cultural renaissance that developed at this time in more fortunate European countries.

Furthermore, the permanent presence of a foreign political entity upon the island threw the indigenous population back into the wetter north and west, or into areas protected by forest and marsh. The earlier effort towards the emergence of firstly provincial and subsequently national kingship was permanently frustrated or diverted into purely local ambition and contention. The resulting instability of political

---

146. For St Maolrubha, CGSH 6 #17; 175 #50, 86. A. Gwynn, *Medieval Province of Armagh* (Dundalk: Dundalgan Press, 1946), pp. 194–7.

society made an unpromising context for the organisation – let alone the enrichment – of the Christian life. Yet what evidence we have for late medieval Derry reveals a functioning system and even spiritual idealism, like the development of the Franciscan Third Order in west Tyrone.

Undoubtedly, behind the belligerent antics of the aristocracy – which monopolise the headlines as it were – in the annals, normal social conditions continued. Civil organisation under the *clann* system maintained a stable society for centuries. The ecclesiastical system of the *airchinneach* (or erenagh) code persisted similarly and maintained Church life. Hospitality in the widest sense flourished, it too underwritten by the erenagh network. Travelling scholars, scribes and poets were welcome in the houses of the nobility. Pilgrims, strolling musicians or professional storytellers found food and lodging in the *brúnna*, or hostels, that dotted the countryside. The sick poor and lepers (in the medieval sense) were catered for by charitable foundations like, for example, the Franciscan Third Order, who, with their herb-gardens and traditional skills, provided a rudimentary health service. In spite of the strict hierarchy in society, no obstacle seems to have been placed in the way of the advancement of people of ability and character in Church or society.

Nonetheless, abuses abounded: a turbulent and sometimes murderous aristocracy, the decline of clerical celibacy and the alienation of Church property. In spite of it all, the remarkable fact is that when the merciless harassment of Catholicism began in the sixteenth and seventeenth centuries, the native Church, as created by the medieval reformers, found the spiritual resources and energy to put up an effective resistance.

It is difficult for the modern reader to envisage what life was like in a medieval society anywhere in Europe. To begin with, we must divest ourselves of expectations of democracy, egalitarianism, public order, even the measurement of time – all the fruits of the French Revolution and of the Industrial Revolution. Life expectancy and health, diet and hygiene, personal comfort and all the benefits of modern technology must be set aside. In all the countries of Western Europe society was controlled by a military aristocracy, arrogant, aggressive and avaricious, contemptuous of a merchant and financial class still only emerging in the city-states of Italy and oblivious to the underorders who tilled the land and performed menial tasks.

It was in such a context that the Christian message of mutual goodwill and equality before God fought to survive and make its presence felt.

The bishops and leaders of the Church, themselves often drawn from the ranks of that self-same aristocracy, must have struggled to realise in themselves the implications of the Christian message, as well as protecting and advancing the organisation in which it was embodied, its clergy, its finances, to say nothing of its spiritual mission.

The records of medieval societies, and therefore our historical sources, are dominated almost entirely by these two orders – the nobility or aristocracy and the international organisation of the Christian Church. This is no less true of medieval Ireland than of anywhere else, with the added problem of the wholesale destruction of such sources by foreign invasion and its effort to erase all trace of indigenous civilisation.

It is essential to bear these realities in mind when we attempt to throw some light on the leadership of the diocese of Derry in the later Middle Ages. Regrettably, there is barely an existence of sources to help write the stories of the ordinary members of the Church whose commitment is crucial to its mission. The destruction of records in medieval Ireland leaves little more than the phenomenon of their perseverance, given that at times they had to confront the vicissitudes of ordinary living and the turpitude of some of their leaders in an age that ended with the certitude of hostile government. In this context we propose nonetheless to attempt to outline biographical sketches of some ecclesiastical leaders involved in diocesan affairs from the later Middle Ages into early modern times, and perhaps thereby to show something of the travails of the Church in those centuries.

As at any era in Church history, there were bishops who were venerated as saints, like Muireadhach Ó Cofaigh, patron of Killelagh (+1173), and Giolla Mac Liag Mac Ruairí Abbot of Derry and Archbishop of Armagh (+1166). Some, however, were not. There were Franciscans – one of whom was nationally famous as a preacher, Dónall Ó Fallúin (1485–1500) – Cistercians, Dominicans and Canons Regular, those who appear to have been good administrators like Nicholas Weston (1466–84) (or *Sar Nicol Uasdún*, as the *Annals of Ulster* call him) and bishops who may not even have entered the diocese (not always their fault). Most of them are little more than names, unfortunately, sometimes barely that much. It is interesting that, to judge from their surnames, more than half the Bishops of Derry in medieval times were not natives of the diocese.

Giolla Mac Liag (Gelasius) Mac Ruairí

To anyone who interests himself in the history of medieval Ireland, it soon becomes an evident fact that social mobility was quite uncommon.

Family groups devoted their energies to a particular line of activity generation after generation. If one comes across names like Ó hUiginn, Mac Con Mí or Mac an Bhaird, it is *filíocht* (poetry) that comes to mind. Other hereditary occupations included history (Ó Cianáin), medicine (Ó Caiside/Mac an Ultaigh/Ó Siail) and law (Ó Breisléin/Ó Deoráin). Sometimes, however, there are exceptions that surprise. The Twelfth-Century Reform was led by St Malachy Ó Morgair whose surname is not to be found elsewhere with the exception of his brother, Giolla Chríost (*Christianus*) Bishop of Clogher, and who is squeezed into the genealogy of Cineál Chonaill (Ó Dónaill/Ó Dochartaigh, etc.) where he clearly does not fit. Saint Malachy's successor St Giolla Mac Liag belonged to the Mac Ruairí family in what is now south Tyrone, who were amongst the descendants of Aodh Allán, high king (+743), none of whose other descendants would seem to have been churchmen. Whatever about a proximity to Armagh, they certainly had no connection with the Church of Derry where he became abbot from a young age (1121–37), before going on to succeed St Malachy in Armagh. The position of abbot was usually handed down within the descendants of those who made the original grant of land. Maybe he was 'head-hunted' for the position by those who were serious about reform at that time, even perhaps by Dónall mac Ardghair Mac Lochlainn, high king +1121, who had made Derry his capital.

Mícheál Mac Lochlainn OFM, Bishop (1319–49)

Mícheál Mac Lochlainn, also known as Mauritius (perhaps Muircheartach), was theologian of the Franciscan convent in Armagh. He was elected to Armagh in 1303 but not consecrated (probably because it was deemed unacceptable in the English lordship) and became Bishop of Derry in 1319.[147] Few of Clann Lochlainn were churchmen before him. Mac Lochlainn fortunes had reached a low ebb by the fourteenth century. Muircheartach Mac Lochlainn (+1166) had been the second-last High King of Ireland. Shortly after his death the Anglo-Norman invasion came about.

We usually see Norman occupation in Ireland as a matter of occupying the best land in Leinster, north Munster and south Connacht. We forget that the Normans drove right along the coast, leaving settlements behind them in Down and Antrim, and occupying

---

147. See T.W. Moody, F. X. Martin, *New History of Ireland* IX (Oxford: Oxford University Press, 1984), pp. 269, 279.

Derry. Like the Moors in Spain or the Greeks in Sicily, Irish armies could not withstand the ferocious charge of Norman cavalry on their heavy, mailed horses when underfoot conditions were in their favour.

In the process they weakened the power of Mac Lochlainn with the result that an alliance of Ó Dónaill and Ó Dochartaigh were eventually able to seize Inishowen and Derry. Ó Néill in alliance with Ó Dónaill crushed Mac Lochlainn power at the battle of Caméirí near Omagh in 1241, in the process killing ten of their *deirbhfhine* (family members from whom a new leader might be chosen). Ó Néill finished off what the Normans began; Clann Lochlainn retreated to east Inishowen and obscurity.

In Inis Eoghain, the Normans built the castle now known as Greencastle and looked set to maintain themselves there with valuable access to the sea. The Brown Earl of Ulster, William de Burgo, had a prisoner – Walter, son of Walter de Burgo – starved to death 'in the prison of the New Castle of Inishowen' in 1333. The following year the Brown Earl (*an tIarla Donn*), the last de Burgo Earl of Ulster, was murdered in revenge and the power of the Normans in west Ulster waned. In the person of the Red Earl (*an tIarla Rua*) (+1326) they had arrogated to themselves rights to revenue and patronage of the church in the city of Derry during the episcopate of Gofraí/Geoffrey Mac Lochlainn (1297–1315). Now Mícheál seized the opportunity of the Brown Earl's death and the disharmony amongst the Normans to petition Pope Clement VI to have diocesan emoluments returned. We do not know if he succeeded at that time but time was on his side since the Normans were in retreat in any case.

Simon _____ OP, Bishop (1349–c.1380)

Simon's surname is nowhere recorded. He served as prior of the Dominican house at Roscommon and was nominated as Bishop of Clonmacnoise, only to find that that diocese already had a bishop. Accordingly, Simon was translated to the vacant see of Derry. What we know about him comes from the Register of Archbishop Milo Sweteman of Armagh.[148] In spite of all sorts of letters and requests from the primate addressed to 'Brother Simon', we do not have a single word of what Simon's reply might have been. In considering his life we need to bear in mind that the view we have is that of his opponents who had captured the 'media' of the time, the Church records.

---

148. H.J. Lawlor, *Calendar of the Register of Archbishop Sweteman* PRIA. XXIX, C, 8 (Dublin: Hodges & Figgis, 1911), passim.

In August 1365, the primate commissioned the dean and prior of the Armagh chapter to carry out a visitation in his name of 'the clergy and people of Derry', but 'matters pertaining to the person of the bishop are exempted from their jurisdiction'. As far as one can gauge, relations between primate and bishop began to become somewhat strained over the occupancy of the deanery of Derry, which would remain an intermittent bone of contention in the diocese until the diocesan chapter went under at the Plantation of Ulster.

The problem originated in the fact that the deanery had emoluments, usually land, in three different civil polities of the diocese in the fourteenth century: at *Nuachongbháil* (Faughvanvale) in Oireacht Uí Chatháin within the jurisdiction of Ó Catháin, Teach na Comairce at Lifford in that of Ó Gormlaigh and at *Fathain/Teampall Mór* (Fahan/Templemore) in that of Ó Dochartaigh. They had different erenaghs,[149] loath to share their benefits with anyone else. As a result, at any given time, one could have three deans of the chapter: *Mac Bhloscaidh* from Nuachongbháil, *Mac Giolla Bhríde*[150] from Fahan/Derry city and *Ó Cearbhalláin* from Clonleigh/Lifford. In 1367 Petrus (Peter, probably *Giolla Pheadair*) Ó Cearbhalláin/Carolan (always referred to as 'Master' in the Primate's Register: one might suppose a canon lawyer) received a dispensation to succeed his 'natural and legitimate' father Donncha as Dean of Derry from the primate, who sent covering letters to Augustinus Mac Thaidhg, *comharba Chainnigh* (successor of St Cainneach at Tearmann Chainnigh/Termoncanice) and to Canon Eoin Ó Cuaig (Quigg). Both of these were from Ó Catháin country, therefore – one would think – supporters of Toimlín Mac Bhloscaidh, Ó Cearbhalláin's rival. Ó Cearbhalláin was, as they say, 'well got' with the archbishop who had appointed him to carry out in his name a visitation of the diocese of Kilmore. It may have been relevant that Ó Cearbhalláin was also related in fosterage[151] to the wife of Ó Raghallaigh, Lord of east Breifne.[152]

---

149. Erenagh, *aircheannach*, person who farmed the land set aside for upkeep of priests and parish, and paid tithes, etc., to the bishop. Cf. earlier essay on *The Diocese of Derry in an Age of Reform* [=pp 74–86 above].

150. Mac Bhloscaidh/McCloskey is a branch of Ó Catháin, descended from Bloscaidh Ó Catháin. Mac Giolla Bhríde/McBride, Mac Dáibhid/McDevitt, Mac Fheabhail/McCole, Mac Ailín/McCallion, Mac Dhónaill Óig/McConologue are branches of Ó Dochartaigh.

151. Fosterage/*altram*/*aice* was the primary method of educating young people between the ages of seven and seventeen.

152. *Pilib*, or perhaps *Cúchonnacht*, who retired in favour of his brother Pilib and took holy orders in 1367.

Ó Cearbhalláin began the visitation in August 1366. Someone else was appointed to continue it in October but Peadar was reappointed in November. Perhaps Peadar's father had died in the meantime, leaving a vacancy at home to be sorted out. By 1367 he had become also a canon and the Chancellor of Armagh and was appointed to conduct a visitation of Raphoe. The only fly in his ointment was that the deanery was in the possession of Toimlín (Thomas) Mac Bhloscaidh who not merely had no intention of resigning but had the support of Bishop Simon, at least some of the diocesan chapter and Ó Catháin (perhaps Cú Mhaighe na Coille).

The primate excommunicated Ó Catháin, who was absolved by Simon. Simon refused to appear before the archbishop and he was excommunicated and incurred a sentence of greater excommunication for intruding Mac Bhloscaidh into the deanery, thus 'displaying contempt for the jurisdiction of the Church of Armagh'. It would seem to have become quite nasty at that stage as Simon is accused of imposing burdens on chapter, clergy, erenaghs and people of the diocese. In June 1367 a witness, whose name is lost, testifies that it is well known that Simon has been excommunicated for over ten years 'in Derry and elsewhere', that he is the father of the daughter of *Bean Mí* (no surname) and of the son of *Aifric* (again no surname) and that this is 'notoriously true', all corroborated by Muireadhach Ó Casaide (Mauritius Ocacidi), Canon of Armagh, who heard it from 'Master Peadar and others'. Peadar asks the primate to confirm that Simon is suspected of perjury and is a 'notorious fornicator'. He is excommunicate in Rome and in Ireland because he has not paid the taxes due to the apostolic *camera* on his appointment, nor the fines imposed for notorious concubinages and adulteries. Addressed to 'Master Augustinus Mac Thaidhg',[153] *Comharba Chainnigh* and canon, the mandate of appointment of Ó Cearbhalláin was to be served on Mac Bhloscaidh and others at the cathedral in Derry, but he was actually found 'in the chamber of Br Simon Bishop of Derry in his manor of the church of Aghadowey'. Mac Bhloscaidh did not appear on being cited and was declared contumacious and excluded from further opposition to Ó Cearbhalláin.

In February 1368, Simon was told (1) to remove a man who was underage from the rectory 'de Ardo' (Tamlaghtard), usually conferred

---

153. 'Augustinus', Latinised distortion of some Irish name, probably. *Mac Thaidhg* = McKeague/Montague. *Comharba Chainnigh* 'successor of St Cainneach' at *Tearmann Chainnigh*, Termoncanice (Limavady), a very important 'dignity' in the diocese.

on a canon of Derry, and confer it on someone else on the advice of dean and chapter; (2) that he give the episcopal a third of his income of the rectory of Derry to the fabric of the church, 'as law demands'; (3) that he place Ó Catháin's lordship under interdict, since he was excommunicate, until Ó Catháin gives security to the dean and his subjects; (4) that he pay his debts owed to the archbishop by giving the settlement to the dean as the dean advises, i.e. seventeen marks due from the time of Archbishop Fitzralph and fifty-two marks, plus two marks[154] due from the last visitation of the diocese. The archbishop must have really endeared himself to Simon by adding that 'he wonders that the bishop does not follow the counsel of his dean without whose counsel – if we could have the advantage of his presence – we would do nothing of difficulty, as we did not in the past when he was with us'.

By 1380 Simon was accused of simony, squandering the goods of his church, neglecting to correct the sins of his subjects, falsely obtaining a papal bull from Gregory XI with the help of the Abbot of Cella Nigra, Derry, and using it to oppress many people. At some stage he had appeared and confessed his excesses 'in the chapel of the archbishop's manor in the lake near Armagh'. On that occasion he volunteered to pay a fine of ten marks on 1 May and a further ten marks on 24 June but in fact paid neither, with the result that the archbishop threatened to write to the pope to have him deposed.

Business continued throughout, however. In 1368–9 the primate gave a lease of the manor of 'Kyllroe' to Brother Simon from 1 May 1369 for a rent of forty shillings (two pounds), one hundred middle-sized and sixty large eels and 'other customary burdens', the lease being void if Simon 'transfers the land to any layman for cultivation or custody'. By 1 July 1370, Simon is cited to appear in Armagh cathedral on 15 July 'to pay ten marks, due by his oath, for the redemption of his penance and four and a half marks and eels, rent due from the manor of Kyllreo [sic], and to show cause why he should not be proceeded against for perjury'.

Kyllroe is most probably Kilrea. Interestingly, Kilrea turns up in the *Ulster Inquisitions* at the Plantation of Ulster, where the jurors state that Kilrea possessed ten *bailte bó* or townlands of churchland, with a rector and vicar, who had been presented for the previous 170 years by the abbot of Saints Peter & Paul, Armagh, to whom the tithes were paid.

---

154. *Mark*, worth 13/4 (thirteen shillings and fourpence), currency unit used in Church finances (= c.67p/€0.80, but vastly greater in purchasing power).

Clearly there is a connection between Kilrea and Armagh pre-dating that 170 years. The only clue as to why may lie in a claim based on St Caomhán of Kilrea having been a member of *Muintir Phádraig*, the retinue that travelled with St Patrick. Simon appears to have outlived the primate, but there we take our leave of him, aware that diocesan life may well have seemed quite dull without him.

An Archbishop Comes Calling (October 1397)

After Simon, some short-stay bishops claimed Derry, some of whom may in fact never have arrived there. The Benedictine John Dongan, who technically held the see, transferred to Down in 1394 and Seán Ó Mocháin, priest of Achonry, probably from the erenagh family at Cill Athracht in Sligo, died in 1395.

Unlike modern canon law, in which a bishop is answerable directly to the pope, in medieval times the Archbishop of Armagh claimed authority over his suffragan bishops, and, like the *comharba Phádraig* abbots of Armagh over the centuries, he claimed the right to carry out visitation of their dioceses in person or to appoint commissaries to do it in his name.

Although his name may sound as if he were born Ó Comhaltáin in west Tyrone, in fact John de Colton was a Norman cleric, born in Norfolk, educated at Cambridge, becoming a doctor of canon law. He had given proof of loyal service to the English lordship in Dublin (where at a time he led a troop of twenty-six knights with success against Ó Móra and Ó Broin), had served as chancellor and lord justice before going to Armagh. He had a reputation for virtue and learning and was affable and popular, a man of talent, enterprise and action. Thus, in 1397 when the see of Derry was vacant, Archbishop John de Colton decided to carry out a visitation in person. Although accompanied by a retinue, both clerical and lay, Gaelic and English, thirteen of whom are named, much of his discussions with those he met – clergy and erenagh – must have been in Latin.

He would seem to have come into the diocese from Termonmagurk in Armagh by way of Achadh Leathan (Mountfield), Loch an Tairbh, Léana and across the shoulder of Mullagharn through *Glengamna* to Cappagh where he stopped for a rest, rather than what we might consider the more likely way through Gortin Gap. At Cappagh he insisted on his right to visit the diocese so forcefully, having it written down by the notary and re-asserting it again later, that one wonders if it all went as smoothly as the record suggests.

Since the buildings at Cappagh were inadequate to house his company, the curate and erenagh there (both unnamed) complied with his order and sent a *mart* (cow or ox killed and salted) after him to Ardstraw for their next meal. At Ardstraw, where they clearly had no problem in finding accommodation for more than thirteen travellers, for each house in which men and horses of the archbishop were lodged, they were provided with bread, butter, milk, meat for men, halters, corn and bedding for the horses. The locals also established watchmen in different parts of the town and especially around the archbishop's house overnight.

The next day, 9 October 1397, at the urgent request of the curate, Laurencius Obogyll/Lochlann (?) Ó Baoill,[155] of the erenaghs and people of Ardstraw, he reconsecrated the cemetery, which had been polluted by the spilling of blood.[156] Then he was provided with seven or so horses to carry his baggage and provisions and he set out for Urney. At Urney he was received by the rector Dónall Ó Cearbhalláin who saw to it that provisions for men and horses and a night watch were made available free to the company. The next morning, having attended Mass, he was again given seven horses or so to be loaded and he set out for Leckpatrick. The horses at Leckpatrick were scattered in the fields, grazing, and the archbishop could not wait for them to be brought in, so the inhabitants of Leckpatrick found sureties to pay to Urney to allow their horses to be taken on to Derry.

They crossed the Foyle by boat and were welcomed to Derry by the dean of the cathedral, Uilliam Mac Cathmhaoil/McCawell, clerics, friars and laymen. They brought the primate to the monastery, the *Dubhreglés*, where suitable chambers were found and they received provisions in abundance and without charge. On 11 October in the monastery church, after a sung Mass and another without singing, he summoned the canons and inquired of them if there was anything relating to the state of the monastery that they needed to tell him about. Events would show that he had a shrewder idea of life in the monastery than they perhaps realised.

They withdrew to discuss and one of them, on behalf of the rest, returned to say that on the resignation of their last abbot Raghnall Ó hÉigeartaigh, Aodh Mac Giolla Bhríde Ó Dochartaigh had been

---

155. No doubt of the erenagh family at Leamhchoill (Langfield).
156. In medieval times, a cemetery was open public ground where business was transacted, children played and pigs rooted. Clearly an occasional fight was only to be expected.

deputed guardian of the monastery. He had taken away the Great Seal of the monastery, normally kept in the house under triple lock and the canons wished it to be returned. Mac Giolla Bhríde handed over the Seal to the primate who kept it until Sunday 14 October. The spokesman for the canons raised other issues of complaint (unstated). The archbishop tried to persuade Raghnall Ó hÉigeartaigh to remain as abbot but he refused, which was reluctantly accepted. The primate asked every canon in turn if he was willing to accept Aodh Mac Giolla Bhríde (Ó Dochartaigh) as abbot and all agreed unanimously, whereupon the primate publicly proclaimed that anyone who wished to object should do so at his sitting on the next day.

The dean, Dr Uilliam Mac Cathmhaoil, was ordered to convoke 'on imminent peril to their souls' the archdeacon, the chapter and all clergy of Derry to appear before the primate. On 13 October after Solemn High Mass in the cathedral, seated in the choir, the primate wished to inspect the letters of appointment of the archdeacon, members of the chapter, all those appointed to dignities, benefices, orders and dispensations, together with the charters of erenaghs, letters dealing with lands, possessions and any other office. A crier was sent to call for the archdeacon and chapter to come, and when they did not, the primate 'graciously awaited them in the same place'. No reason is given for their non-appearance, but it may have been a reluctance to recognise his authority. Many of the others came and exhibited their letters. The canons of Dubhreglés came to ask him to confirm Mac Giolla Bhríde as abbot, and after consultation he confirmed and instituted him in the abbacy.

After refreshments at the abbey, Colton returned to the cathedral and sent the crier for archdeacon and chapter. When they did not appear they were declared contumacious and cited to appear before him in the town of Diarmaid Ó Catháin the following Monday. This proclamation was declared in a loud voice by the crier (which would suggest that they were not so far away), and the archbishop withdrew from the cathedral. On 14 October the primate went to the church of St Breacán in the land of Clooney ('which lands are known to belong to the Church of Armagh') where the Dean and Rector Dr Mac Cathmhaoil asked him to reconsecrate the church and cemetery, polluted by the shedding of blood, and to celebrate Mass for the thousands of people gathered there.

As the primate was about to say Mass at an altar set up at the western door of the church to accommodate the crowd, archdeacon and chapter appeared (as a result of diplomatic negotiation on the part of Conchúr mac Cormaic Ó Dónaill, Bishop of Raphoe), asking that the sentence of excommunication be lifted so that they could join in the Mass. The primate commissioned the Bishop of Raphoe to absolve them under pain of being excommunicated again if they refused to follow the primate's mandates and ordinances. Then he celebrated the Mass, blessed the new abbot and returned the Great Seal to Canon Dónall Ó hÉigeartaigh to hold in the common chest under triple lock. He then proceeded to the town of Diarmaid Ó Catháin.[157]

On 15 October dean, archdeacon and chapter came into the presence of the primate to ask that they meet him again in Banagher to sort out the matters that they had been summoned to discuss at the cathedral. The primate agreed. Later that day Úna, daughter of Ó Conchúir and lawful wife of Ó Catháin (Mánas), 'captain of his nation' (Oireacht Uí Chatháin) came to complain that Mánas had put her away 'without the judgement of the Church' and taken another in her place, and to seek redress. When he found out that Mánas was nearby he summoned him to appear immediately 'on account of imminent peril of soul' and answer the petition. Ó Catháin was told to show cause why he should not be compelled to take Úna back and do canonical penance. Mánas asked for time to consider. After consulting with his *oireacht*, he returned to say that he had never contracted marriage with Úna. On being asked for witnesses, Úna produced Dónall Ó Catháin and Simon Ó Fianachtaigh/Feeney[158] called *dominus*, presumably rector. The archbishop adjourned the case to Banagher the next day.

Caitríona Ó Dochartaigh next appeared and she asserted that she had contracted marriage with Mánas Mac Giollagáin and that the Archdeacon of Derry and Dr Eoin Mac Thaidhg – judges appointed in the matrimonial tribunal – had adjudged her so. Notwithstanding his promises, Mánas Mac Giollagáin had divorced her without reasonable cause and 'taken other women in her stead'. Mánas appeared and denied the marriage contract and any legal adjudication. Being put on oath, Caitríona called as witnesses the two clerics mentioned, who were examined by the primate, the Dean of Armagh and Dr Thomas Ó Luchráin, and who deposed that they had in fact made the above

---

157. Location unspecified but most probably Enagh.
158. Simon Ofynnachaich, priest of Derry, had been Rector of Camus on the Bann and became Perpetual Vicar of Tamlaghtfinlagan before 1423. Presumably he was ordained priest while in Camus. Cf. M.A. Costello, ed., *De Annatis Hiberniae* I Ulster (Maynooth: St Patrick's College, 1912), 137.

decision. The case was adjourned to Banagher the next day. Once again erenaghs and local people provided horses and provisions for the company free of charge.

On 16 October, the primate proceeded to the house of Canons Regular at Dungiven where he reconsecrated church and cemetery, again polluted by the shedding of blood. After doing so he enjoined the inhabitants of the town to provide for his company and animals and send all to Banagher, where he was to remain overnight. On reaching Banagher he summoned Archdeacon Uilliam Ó Catháin and the chapter of Derry before him as he sat in front of the high altar and expounded to them that he came to Derry to exercise legitimate oversight of the spiritual and temporal state of the diocese during the vacancy as he and his predecessors had exercised that right in the past, there and in other dioceses. Then he decreed:

1) that Aodh the abbot aforesaid must dismiss within three days and never take back Caitríona Ó Dochartaigh 'whom you are said lately to have taken in concubinage' and that you make no such promise to any other woman;

2) that you restore to the said house whatever goods you have alienated so that neither you nor any other canon may expend or promise any goods of the said house for the keeping of any woman;

3) that no woman be introduced by you or any other canon within the precincts of the house, or sleep or rest within it;

4) that you and all the canons eat together in the common refectory, having devout and holy reading during meals and that you sleep in one dormitory;

5) that every Lord's Day and on every solemn feast all the Canonical Hours and one Solemn Mass with singing and another without singing be devoutly celebrated in the choir of the church, and on every other day one Mass at least be devoutly celebrated in the church, and the Canonical Hours recited, provided always that each brother, who is to celebrate, approach the altar sorry for his sins and after confession in true penitence. 'Moreover, we give the dean of the cathedral church power to compel you to observe this'.

Amongst the clergy present in Banagher were Dean Uilliam Mac Cathmhaoil, Archdeacon Uilliam Ó Catháin, Canon Muireadhach Ó Catháin, Lochlann Ó Maolainfe – Rector of Donaghmore, Lochlann Ó Baoill – Perpetual Vicar of Ardstraw, Pilib Ó Cearbhalláin – Rector of

Clonleigh, Dónall Ó Cearbhalláin – Rector of Urney, Eoin Mac Thaidhg, Dónall Mac Lochlainn, Dáibhid Ó Muireasain, Lochlann Mac Giolla Mhuire, Muireadhach Ó Conallaigh, Simon Ó Fianachtaigh, Aodh Mac Thaidhg, Muireadhach Ó Catháin and Eoin Ó Caisile, all described as 'doctor'.

The representative of Mánas Mac Giollagáin came forward to assert that before Caitríona Ó Dochartaigh 'had contracted in any manner whatsoever' with Mánas, he was already lawfully married to Máire Mhac Bhloscaidh. Not being able to resolve the issue, the primate gave it over to the examination of Uilliam Ó Catháin and Eoin Mac Thaidhg and entered his lodging. The erenagh of Banagher and people provided sustenance and the night watch.

On 17 October the primate put his decisions about the Dubhreglés in Derry into writing at the request of the dean and he gave them to the abbot in person. The archbishop gave the dean letters of admonition, suspension, excommunication and interdict against Ó Dónaill, Ó Dochartaigh, Ó Catháin, Ó Gormlaigh, Dónall and Brian Mór, sons of Anraí Ó Néill,[159] for usurpation of the rights of the Church of Derry. Then Colton settled a row between two inhabitants of Banagher about the office of erenagh[160] and collated Diarmaid Ó Maolagáin to the rectory of Dromagarvan/Drumagarner. Taking about five horses for his baggage and retinue the primate set out to return to Armagh, accompanied for two miles or so by dean, archdeacon and chapter, through the 'trackless wastes of Glenelly'[161] to Desertcreat.

Nicol Uasdún/Nicholas Waston/Weston Bishop (1466–84)

In reporting his death 'before Christmas 1584', the *Annals of Ulster* know him as 'Sar Nicol Uasdún', 'sar' being a gaelicised version of English 'sir', a title of honour deriving ultimately from Latin *senior*. The Four Masters report his death twice, in 1474 and 1484. Weston himself must remain something of an enigma. His is the only non-Gaelic name amongst the medieval bishops. There would be a prominent Weston family around Dublin one hundred years later. When appointed by Paul II, Nicholas was a Canon of Armagh and Rector of Ballyclog in that diocese. He was appointed to succeed the late 'Joannes'. Most commentators posit the

---

159. Anraí Aimhréidh (+1392) who built *an Seanchaisleán/the old castle*, the origin of Newtownstewart.
160. The erenagh of Banagher, at least in later times, was Ó hÉanaigh.
161. *Colton's Visitation* indicates the relative importance of places, the quality of accommodation and roads.

appointment of a bishop 'John' after Bartholomaeus Ó Flannagáin. Eoin Ó Gubúin (1433–55) Canon of Derry, was in Rome when appointed bishop which might be expected to indicate validity, whereas the resignation of Ó Flannagáin may have raised a doubt about validity so the reference to Joannes/John perhaps refers back to Eoin (Ó Gubúin). The notice of appointment of Weston's successor, Dónall Ó Fallúin OFM, on 16 May 1485, speaks of 'the Church of Derry, vacant by the death of Nicholas, during whose lifetime it was specially reserved by the present pope'. Since that 'present pope' was Innocent VIII, elected on 29 August 1484, less than a year previously and four months before Weston's death, it is hard to see what this could have meant.

Weston claimed that when he got to Derry he found things in a parlous state. The cathedral was almost roofless. There was only one chalice, in tin, and vestments were badly needed. For all practical purposes there was no cathedral chapter. Mánas Ó Dónaill in his *Beatha Cholaim Chille*[162] claims that the saint built a church at Cluaine 'in the port of Doire Chalgaigh' and foretold that an easpag gallda would knock his church to build another with its stones in the place called Bun Seantoinne and composed a verse after building:

Mo thrua, tiocfaidh Gaill go Cluaine,	Alas, strangers will come to Cluaine,
Agus beirfidh siad mo theampall	and they will bear away my church
go Bun Seantoinne fuaire	to cold Bun Seantoinne.

Bun Seantoinne would seem to have been at the water's edge, not all that far away. Mánas Ó Dónaill duly reports the fulfilment of the prophecy when *tháinig easpag gallda go Doire darb ainm Nicól Bastún* 'a foreign bishop called Nicól Bastún came to Derry', who knocked down that church to build a *cúirt*. *Cúirt* is translated 'palace' in the *Beatha*, but probably meant no more than the 'manor' of Bishop Simon at Kilrea did (see above), an area controlled by a lord. In any case, according to Mánas, the *cúirt* was left unfinished 'by reason of a miracle of Colm Cille'. Colm Cille would not have used the word 'gallda', or indeed 'teampall' of a church – a term that is probably post-Crusades.

---

162. A. O'Kelleher and G. Schoepperle, eds (Illinois: University of Illinois, 1918), #90, p. 85. By the time of Mánas Ó Dónaill, *easpag gallda* would have had the overtone 'English bishop'.

As Primate Colton was aware earlier in the century, while Clooney was where St Cobhrán, a nephew of Colm Cille, was buried, the land at Clooney belonged to the Church of Armagh, so the legal position is unclear. It would look as if Weston met opposition from the Columban community in Derry. He may have had a difficult time there.

Séamas Mac Mathúna/James MacMahon (1503–19)

The Annals of Ulster report that at Epiphany in the year 1486 there was a quarrel between clerics in Clones involving the son of Donncha Mac Mathúna, the *pearsún* (parson, rector, parish priest), Giolla Phádraig Ó Conallaigh, Abbot of Clones, Séamas, son of Pilib, son of the *Comharba* Mac Mathúna and Art, son of Mac Domhnaill of Clann Cheallaigh, and that in the row the last-named, perhaps the only non-cleric amongst them, was slain. Two, if not all three, of the survivors occur in Roman Annate lists in the 1490s, indicating that they had undertaken to pay the tax levied on their appointment to benefices, the right to appoint to which had devolved to Rome for legal reasons. Perhaps their original journey to Rome was in requital of some ecclesiastical sanction imposed after the first incident, but we find Séamas Mac Mathúna, a canon of Clochar, appointed in 1491 Rector of the *plebania* of St Tiarnach's parish church, Clones, and Archdeacon of Armagh in 1492, and Ó Conallaigh in 1493 in receipt of the rectory of the parish church of Kilmore and of Saints Peter and Paul's Augustinian abbey, Clones. The latter died bishop-elect of Clochar in 1504, a position for which Séamas Mac Mathúna would also seem to have pressed his suit.

Séamas Mac Mathúna (James MacMahon), son of Philip, son of James, son of Rúraí, son of Ardghal, was the son of *Comharba Thiarnaigh* and heir to the immense prestige accruing to the position of 'successor of St Tiarnach' at Clones. He belonged also to the royal house of the *Airghialla* (in modern Louth/Monaghan). He was provided to the see of Derry on 5 July 1501 but his bulls of appointment had not been expedited when Alexander VI died, and it was Julius II who supplied the deficiency in November 1503. He was consecrated bishop in 1507, it appears, but it is not likely that he had any effect on the diocese of Derry, and on 6 July 1508 he was made commendatory prior of the abbey of Knock, Louth, which was united to his bishopric because the latter was insufficient for his sustenance 'being much reduced by wars and the oppression of chiefs', as Primate Octavian's Register has it. He was present as co-consecrator at the consecration of the Bishop of Killala by the primate in 1508 and died in 1519. It is not unfitting that his title 'epscop Doire' (Bishop of Derry) is omitted in the English translation of the *Annals of the Four Masters*.

Ruairí Ó Dónaill/Rory O'Donnell (1520–50)

Ruairí (*Rudhraighe*) Ó Dónaill belonged to the ruling house of Cineál Chonaill. He was grandson of Aodh Rua I (lord: 1461–1505), nephew of Aodh Dubh (lord: 1505–37) and first cousin of Mánas, son of Aodh Dubh (lord: 1537–55). Aodh Rua I had seven turbulent sons by three wives.[163] As troublesome as any was Donncha *na nOrdóg* ('of the thumbs'), whose mother was descended from Anraí Aimhréidh Ó Néill, builder of 'Harry Avery's Castle' near modern-day Newtownstewart. Donncha had two full brothers, Dónall and Seán. The latter became a Franciscan, perhaps at the Donegal friary which Aodh Rua founded in 1474 at the persuasion of his mother, Nuala Ó Conchúir, and his second wife, Nuala Ó Briain, who became a Franciscan Tertiary after his death.

Donncha *na nOrdóg* (+1503) spent much of his life in captivity because of his rebelliousness. He had three sons, Ruairí, Dónall and Eoghan. Ruairí profited enough from his father's example to abandon his dynastic prospects and became Rector of Templecrone and Dean of Raphoe. When he was made Bishop of Derry by Leo X on 11 January 1520, he was allowed to retain his deanery. All that is known about his administration is what appears from the registry of Primate Cromer, who, in 1535, heard appeals from priests of Derry about decisions made by the bishop, from Drumragh (Mac Cathmhaoil/McCaul vs Mac Somhairle/Mc Sorley) – and from Urney (which then included the rectory of St Maolrubha in the island of Islay) – Mac an Bhaird (Ward/O Kelly) vs Mac Aodha (McHugh), Ó Gormlaigh (Gormley), Ó Cearbhalláin (Carolan). These cases indicate that he was active and decisive in his diocese.[164]

In 1514 Conn (Cornelius) Ó Catháin had been appointed Bishop of Raphoe by the pope on the recommendation of Henry VIII. This had resulted in a feud between him and the Ó Gallachair septs who felt they had a proprietary interest in many Church benefices in Raphoe. Ó Catháin embraced the schism of Henry VIII to buttress his position. His attempt was unsuccessful because Éamann Ó Gallachair had appointed himself bishop. Because this was doubtfully valid, Art Ó

---

163. Wives, I suggest, because their surnames indicate probable political alliances.
164. Cf. Aubrey Gwynn, *Medieval Province of Armagh* (Dundalk: Dundalgan Press, 1946), pp. 188–96.

Gallachair, Dean of Derry, threw his hat into the ring with the backing of the Raphoe chapter. James V of Scotland was persuaded to write to the pope in favour of Art, asking the pope to appoint Ruairí Ó Dónaill and the *officialis* of Moyle to study the problem. This was done and on 1 July 1538, judgement was given that neither Conn nor Éamann had a right to the see, moving that Art be provided.

Rome was not convinced, because Art was not appointed until 1547.[165] In 1538 Cormac Ó Gallachair had Bishop Ó Dónaill deprived of the rectory of Templecrone (which he had retained on going to Derry) with the help of Aodh Mac an Bhaird (Ó Ceallaigh) of Urney, who had had legal difficulties with the bishop in 1535 as we have seen, both perhaps supported by Éamann Ó Gallachair who also would have had a score to settle.

Meanwhile Mánas Ó Dónaill, Lord of Cineál Chonaill since 1537, had become leader of a union of north and south, the Geraldine League, formed to protect the life and interests of the young Gerald, successor to the Fitzgerald earldom of Kildare, after Silken Thomas' revolt. In July 1538, the bishop, along with James Delahide, Thomas Leverous and Robert Walshe was sent to the King of Scotland by Mánas and young Gerald. At the end of the year Ruairí wrote to Pope Paul III recounting the misdeeds of Henry VIII's deputy and his adherents who burn, spoil, destroy, ravish maidens, kill priests who pray for the pope or compel them to erase his name from the Canon and torture preachers who do not repudiate his authority.

The real point of the letter is at the end when he asserts that, since the four archbishops had withdrawn their obedience to Rome, he should be given authority as a papal legate to remove and appoint bishops and clergy, to absolve and reconcile schismatics, etc. Mánas was preparing for a major revolt against Henry VIII's anti-papal policy and wanted Ruairí, his cousin, in the role of spiritual leader. Unfortunately for him, the ship of the bearer of his letter was blown into South Shields by storms and he was captured. The letter ended on the desk of Thomas Cromwell and its bearer was summarily executed.[166] Ruairí's attempt to become the most important figure in the Church in Ireland came to nothing.

In 1539 he is said to have been sent to Scotland to obtain 6,000 'redshanks' (galloglass mercenaries) and on to Rome. It is hard to

---

165. See John J. Silke, *Disputed Succession to Raphoe and the Henrician Schism,* 1950. passim.
166. *Letters and Papers (Henry VIII),* 14.1.516.

know what to make of these allegations because they result either from 'confessions' or from gossip. Reports about bishops – even quite unlikely figures – going to Rome become increasingly frequent as the century wears on, evidence of the growing paranoia of the colonial government in Dublin.

The Geraldine League seemed militarily formidable, and for it to assume a religious character was undoubtedly ominous for the colonial government. By mid-summer, Galway merchant Thomas Lynch reports to that government that the clergy of the north were preaching holy war, where death was martyrdom and its reward that of Peter and Paul. However, in August 1539, the northern forces of the League, laden with booty, were confronted at Bellahoe in Meath by Lord Deputy Gray's small but modern army and were completely defeated. The reason for the alliance disappeared when in 1541 the young Fitzgerald was sent away to Florence and the northern leaders submitted to the government, accepting Henry VIII as King and Head of the Church. When Mánas submitted, did Ruairí do so also, submitting his papal bulls of appointment to Henry's authority? The answer is unclear. Rome made no attempt to appoint another to Derry during his lifetime and he is mentioned as being 'of good memory' in the provision of his successor.

On 31 August 1541, says Fr Gwynn, Primate Cromer issued a commission to four prelates to carry out a visitation of Raphoe: Cornelius (O Cahan) Bishop of Raphoe, Hugh Scheyll, primate's chaplain, Conocius Scheyll Abbot of Kildare and *Henricus Darensis*. Father Gwynn submits that *Henricus Darensis* should read *Ruricus Derensis*, because the only bishop called Henry at the time was de Burgo of Enaghdun. If this is so, does it mean that Ruairí accepted the schismatic Cromer as his lawful metropolitan? Is it more than just coincidence that this happens just after Mánas submitted to St Leger? Conocius Scheyll must be Cú Chonnacht Ó Siail, Abbot of Eas Dara (Ballisodare) and chaplain to Mánas Ó Dónaill. The names indicate that all had connections with what we would call Donegal, and this may have been an overriding consideration with Cromer, perhaps determined to show that things were proceeding as normal.

Again the evidence does not convince. In 1543, Henry VIII issued a brief naming nine bishops 'in whose fidelity and diligence we confide' and charging four or more of them to invest and consecrate George Dowdall as archbishop. The nine were Thady Reynolds of Kildare and all the bishops of the province of Armagh except Dromore. Reynolds may have been named in place of MacGennis of Dromore (who is not mentioned and had not submitted), or it might be another *Darensis/ Derensis* confusion. The others seem to have submitted to Henry, except for Ruairí Ó Dónaill of whose position nothing can be said with certainty. The bishops named by Henry VIII are the suffragans of Armagh, as one would expect.[167] Real proof would be their attendance, but there is no record of that. Could Ruairí have escaped the demand to submit, given that he was so prominent at the time of the Geraldine League? The answer may not have been as pressing as it may seem to us.

In 1542, St Ignatius Loyola sent two of his first Jesuit disciples, Brouet and Salmeron, to investigate the situation in Ireland, at the request of Papal Primate Robert Wauchop of Armagh. Ó Néill and Ó Dónaill refused to meet them, afraid of being accused of treason, but they spent Lent in Ulster, preaching, hearing confessions, giving dispensations and proclaiming indulgences. They met an unnamed local bishop who welcomed and helped them. They made a very gloomy prognosis to St Ignatius about the future of the Church in Ireland. The bishop was probably Ruairí Ó Dónaill, since they came through Scotland, had met the brother of the bishop of the Isles who lived on Iona, and had come to see Mánas Ó Dónaill.[168]

Ruairí the bishop might have been annoyed, as we are intrigued by an incident in 1542 which is reported by the Four Masters: 'Mac Con Midhe [Brian Dorcha, son of Solamh – *Solomon*], a man skilled in poetry and literature, a rich and affluent man, who kept a house of general hospitality for all, died about the festival of St Colm Cille through the miracles of God and St Colm Cille and the curse of O [*recte* Mac] Robhartaigh, because he had profaned and dishonoured the Great Cross, for he had struck it before that time.' Brian Dorcha (*dark*) held an important public position. He was the head of the poetic *Mac Con Mí*/MacNamee family, highly respected, well read, with ecclesiastical connections, probably erenagh. So why did he strike in public and with deliberation the Great Cross and so 'dishonour St Colm Cille'? Do we have here a hidden reference to the influence of Reformation theology in Ulster, from a time before the government made being Protestant a political choice? Had he, like several members of Scottish poetic families at the time, absorbed Reformed ideas at the University of Glasgow?

---

167. See list in *Arch. Hib.* I, pp. 253–7.
168. See Gwynn, op. cit., pp. 225–49

In 1549, the government appointed Ruairí one of three judges in a lawsuit about trespass and damage between Mánas and Mac Suibhne (MacSweeney) Fánaid. In the winter of 1549–50, Primate Wauchop visited Derry to meet Ó Dónaill and Ó Néill in a fruitless effort to push an anti-English alliance with France. Ruairí may again have been present.

Ruairí Ó Dónaill died on 8 October 1550 (or as some say, 1551). He was buried at his own request in the Franciscan friary of Donegal, founded by his grandfather, in the habit of the order.

Eoghan Ó Dochartaigh/Eugene O'Doherty (1554–68)

When we first meet Eoghan Ó Dochartaigh he is engaged in the process of obtaining an income for himself. In August 1530 he promised to pay Rome the annates on benefices in Derry and Raphoe: the parish churches of Desertegny, Moville, Clonmany and Kilmacrenan, and in February 1531 he promised the annates of the rectory and vicarage of the parish church of Northburgh, *alias* Moville, which are to be erected into a canonry and prebend of the Church of Derry for his lifetime. Finally, when provided to the see of Derry on 25 June 1554, he was already Abbot of the House of Canons Regular of *Cella Nigra* at Derry, a position Pope Paul IV dispensed him to retain. He is described in the provision as being of noble race on both sides and born in lawful wedlock. He must have become Abbot of *Dubhreglés* after 1531 when Cú Chonnacht Ó Fríl was abbot.

In May 1555, one Cornelius Odacartard (Ó Dochartaigh) attempted to oust Art Ó Gallachair, Bishop of Raphoe, from the deanery of Derry because he had no legal entitlement to it. Cornelius had been dispensed some time before as the son of an unmarried man and a spinster of noble birth to receive tonsure and 'even' holy orders, and hold together two benefices with care of souls. Having been dispensed and then ordained he obtained the rectory of Moville, and is made dean.

In Bishop Montgomery's *Survey* of one of his three new dioceses c.1609, he notes that the rectory of Moville and vicarage of Clonmany and the rectory of Culdaff are all held by 'Cornelius O Doghartie', who, according to Montgomery, was the son of Eugene the bishop. It is possible that we are dealing with the same man in both cases. The Dean of Derry at the time of the Survey was Uilliam Mac an tSagairt (Mac Taggart), who later became established Church Rector of Termoneeny. If Cornelius the dean was the son of Eugene the bishop, they would have had a very considerable responsibility for the Church in Derry, and especially in Inishowen, between them – in Templemore,

Faughanvale and Glendermott (Cornelius as dean) and Culdaff, Moville, and Clonmany (Cornelius as rector). Moville-Culdaff was a *plebania* i.e. permanently combined parishes.

Eoghan Ó Dochartaigh is not mentioned by name in any contemporary document. He did not attend the Dublin parliament of 1560. In 1566, Sir Henry Sidney acted on an English plan to take Seán Mór *an Díomais* Ó Néill (so-called 'Shane the Proud') from behind by occupying Lough Foyle. He sent Colonel Edward Randolph by sea from Bristol and, on learning that he had reached Lough Foyle, Sidney set out to join up with him, accompanied by the Earl of Kildare, Bagenal, Calbhach Ó Dónaill and Seán Mag Uír (Maguire). They marched through Ulster by way of Armagh, Benburb, Clogher and Lifford, where they met Randolph. On 12 October they encamped in Ó Catháin country, wrote Sidney later, 'over against Derry where there came to us no one but O Doherty and his brother Cathaoir with the Bishop of Derry, a gentleman of that surname'. Ó Dochartaigh and the bishop entreated him to pass over into Derry and offered him 'the platte of ground where the ancient city of Derry stood, now totally ruined and yet some monuments remaining, in the hope that your Majesty would build, or cause to be built, a city there'. Sidney accepted it in Queen Elizabeth's name, which was probably why he had come in the first place. Perhaps Ó Dochartaigh was putting a brave face on what was unavoidable.

Sidney went on to Raphoe to sign a treaty with Ó Dónaill, witnessed by Ó Dochartaigh 'chief of his name', by which all the principal men of Tirconnell recognise fealty and service to the queen, and amongst other promises agree that the queen shall have 'the donation of all bishops and other ecclesiastical persons in Connalia'. Another witness was Dónall Mac Congail (McGonagle), Bishop of Raphoe, one of three Irish bishops who attended the Council of Trent.

It is most likely that the bishops took the oath of allegiance or fealty since it was not in Sidney's interest at that juncture to risk testing them with the oath of royal supremacy in the Church or uniformity of worship. At any rate the provisions of the treaty were not adhered to, because Calbhach Ó Dónaill died shortly afterwards and his brother and successor Aodh Dubh allowed them to lapse.

Randolph's English garrison found Derry an unpleasant spot. The coldness of the weather, disease and lack of provisions (due to non-delivery of the corn promised by Calbhach Ó Dónaill) decimated his army, and then Seán Ó Néill attacked. The garrison repulsed him with the 'loss of three hundred men', but for the English too the battle was a defeat because Randolph was killed. The end of the Derry garrison was disastrous. On 21 April 1567, a windy day, sparks from the forge set fire to the powder stored in the ruined church of St Columba. A number of men were killed in the resultant explosion and all the wooden buildings were burnt out. The remaining troops took ship the next day for Carrickfergus while the cavalry rode through Ulster to safety. This is traditionally seen as the cause of the end of the Columban monastery.

However, a word of caution. Sidney's description (on previous page) is hardly that of a thriving monastic city. In addition, in a letter written perhaps in 1568 from prison in Dublin, the papal legate, Jesuit Fr David Wolf stigmatised Ó Néill (Seán an Díomais) as a 'cruel, impious, heretical tyrant' who burnt the church of Armagh, the abbey of Killodonnel, the monastery and church of Derry, the monasteries of Moville, Muckamore, Errigal, Fahan and Devenish. Obviously Wolf had little sympathy with the plans of Seán an Díomais, but that in fact was perhaps mutual. Seán's view of it all was quite simple – that the Church should not remain neutral but should offer him support and aid in his war since, in his view, he was fighting for his religion. No doubt he attacked some 'to encourage the others' – particularly if they were in the territory of Ó Dónaill. However, it is not morality that is in question here. If Wolf is right, it was in fact initially Seán who had damaged Derry. This would help explain the eagerness of Seán Mór Ó Dochartaigh and the bishop to suggest to Sidney the occupation of the ancient city.[169]

Amongst the papers of Cardinal Morone for 1568–9, a letter of Archbishop Richard Creagh tells of an undated Church synod in Ulster to which the Bishops of Derry and Raphoe did not go 'because of wars', and recommends one *Daniel* to the bishopric of Derry. A minute added to the letter records that Derry is vacant by the death of Eugene, the last bishop. Thus, we learn of the death of Eoghan Ó Dochartaigh from a note in Rome, curiously fitting for a man whose story must remain elusive. Even the date of his death is uncertain.

Réamann Ó Gallachair/Raymond O'Gallagher (1569–1601)

Réamann Ó Gallachair is often called *Redmond* in English, perhaps in imitation of Edmond > Éamann, but there seems no very good reason

---

169. Cf. Sidney's account in *Ulster Journal of Archaeology* III (1855) and Ciarán Brady, *Shane O'Neill. HAI* (Dundalk: Dundalgan Press, 1996), pp. 60–3

for not using the usual English, Raymond. He signed his name in Latin *Remundus Derensis.*

A late tradition, impossible to authenticate, suggests that he was born at Lifford. He was born in or around 1521, a first cousin of *an Calbhach* (Calvagh) Ó Dónaill, son of Mánas who built the castle of *Port na dTrí Námhad* at Lifford and who was married five times. Lynch says Réamann was the son of *Giolla Dubh* ('the black fellow'), but this does not help much since it is probably a sobriquet or by-name. There is however one *Giolla Dubh* mentioned in the *Annals of Ulster*. In an episode of blood-letting within Cineál Chonaill in 1497, for which the annal – as is not uncommon – gives no reason, Éigneachán Ó Dónaill is slain along with *Féilimí mac an Ghiolla Dhuibh* and *Tarlach mac Chathail mhic an Ghiolla Dhuibh Uí Ghallachair.* It is possible that this uncle and nephew represent the beginning of a sept within *Muintir Ghallachair* descended from this Giolla Dubh, similar to *Sliocht an Easpaig* and to *Sliocht Aodha,* and that Raymond belonged to this distinct grouping. Be that as it may, as any reading of papal letters or reference to other contemporary Church documents will bear out, to belong to any branch of Ó Gallachair was a distinct advantage when seeking Church preferment in west Ulster in the fifteenth and sixteenth centuries.[170]

The suggestion in *Ibernia Ignatiana* that Réamann Ó Gallachair was the '*dilectus filius Raymundus*,' to whom Conn Bacach Ó Néill had entrusted a letter to Pope Paul III and to which the pope had replied in 1541 (which led to the Jesuit mission of 1542 referred to earlier) seems to have no warrant other than his name, particularly bearing in mind that he would have been just twenty years of age.

On 6 November 1545, Réamann Ó Gallachair, described as a cleric of Raphoe, was appointed administrator of the diocese of Killala in spiritual matters in succession to the late bishop, Richard Barrett.

170. Fr Paul Walsh was unable to trace Réamann's ancestry. He quotes Grattan Flood to the effect that he was dispensed *ex defectu natalium* before his consecration. This could mean illegitimacy or marriage within the forbidden degrees (third cousins or closer, a common problem in a closely linked society like Ireland) or the son of a priest. Cf. 'Septs of Muintear Ghallchubhair', *Irish Chiefs and Leaders,* Pól Breathnach (Dublin: Sign of the Three Candles, 1960), pp. 206–15. Calvagh Ó Dónaill's mother was a daughter of O Reilly of Bréifne. Cf. Paul Walsh, ed., *Beatha Aodha Ruaidh Uí Dhomhnaill* (Dublin: Irish Texts Society, 1948/57), II, pp. 194–5. So if Réamann was a cousin of Calvagh's he was more probably related on the father's side, his mother perhaps a sister of Mánas (and cousin of Bishop Ruairí Ó Dónaill).

Because he was only twenty-four he was to wait three years before being consecrated. Some have seen this as proof of his sterling qualities, but it might also be relevant that Mánas Ó Dónaill was making strenuous efforts at the time to extend his sway over north Connacht, and no doubt Muintir Ghallachair were not unwilling to follow behind. It would seem he had a sister married in the area, but unfortunately we do not know her name or her husband's. If we did – after all, her husband may have been a Barret – we might have a further indication of a reason for his promotion.

Details of his administration are sparse and vague. He detached a farm from the lands of the see and gave it to his brother-in-law, preferring to see it in his hands than to lose it completely to the Church. Lynch condones this alienation by saying it must have happened during the reign of Edward VI when it would have ended otherwise in the hands of a foreigner, but that looks like the wisdom of hindsight. Julius III wrote to him in 1553, perhaps in connection with the reforms of the Council of Trent. He was invited to the Parliament of 1560, but there is no evidence that he attended. In 1556, along with Bishops Andrew O Crean of Elphin and Eugene O Hart of Achonry (who had attended Trent) and a large number of clergy, he presided as senior bishop at a provincial synod at Tuam to promulgate the decrees of Trent.[171]

Shortly after this Ó Gallachair ran into trouble with Shane mac Oliver, the Mac William Burke of Lower Connacht. On the plea that he was suspect of undue familiarity with a nobleman's wife, according to Lynch, he was imprisoned, had his possessions confiscated and finally was exiled from his diocese. In his trenchant style papal commissary, David Wolf corroborates much of Lynch's account, without giving a reason for the ejection however:

> Those of the see of [Raymond O Gallagher] are barbarians, untamed, ferocious and of bestial habits. At one time they pursued the said bishop with intent to kill or take him prisoner, and he fled to Portugal and abode some years in Lisbon whence he went to Rome: he is now in Ireland in a different see. The bishops of Ireland are hirelings and dumb dogs and acknowledge Queen Elizabeth as Head of the Church, all except three besides the said Bishop Raimund.

171. See John Lynch, *De Praesulibus Hiberniae*, J.F. O'Doherty, ed. (Dublin: The Stationery Office, 1944), II pp. 325–7.

'Undue familiarity with a nobleman's wife' was not a common reason for an outburst of public morality at the time, nor for attempted murder. Perhaps it had something to do with the brother-in-law and the acquisition of churchland, or with the rows between competing *clanna* in northwest Connacht – Barrets, O Dowds, Burkes – especially with the change of leaders in the O Dónaill dynasty in 1566 on the death of Calvagh.

Archbishop Richard Creagh recommended one *Daniel* (Dónall, no doubt) to succeed Eoghan Ó Dochartaigh as Bishop of Derry. The minute added to his letter adds in Latin about the vacancy: 'Two Irishmen from the said diocese have come to the Curia to obtain it *viz. Cornelius Ocervalan* with some letters from Fr David Wolf and others from the Rector of Louvain. Also Abbot *Magonius* recommended by letters from the Bishops of Raphoe and Kilmore with the approbation of the chapter of Derry.'[172] Information is lacking at the moment to identify any of the three candidates, Dónall, Cornelius (probably Conchúr/Conor) Ó Cearbhalláin (probably from Clonleigh and perhaps a Franciscan) and Mánas (*Magonius*), presumably Abbot of Derry. Two of these candidates are in Rome seeking the bishopric, both highly recommended. At this stage there arrives in Rome from Lisbon an experienced bishop armed with a reputation as a reformer, perhaps also bearing a letter from David Wolf,[173] and aware of the contacts in Rome built up by the Ó Gallachair interest over the years.

As a result, Réamann Ó Gallachair was absolved on 22 June 1569 from the bond of the Church of Killala and translated to Derry with permission to retain the priory of *Eachinis*, a house of Canons Regular of St Augustine, and all things annexed to it in Killala.[174] He is described in 1571 in State Papers as being lately come from Rome, armed with many faculties, no doubt to spearhead the papal programme of reform after Trent.

We know little about his administration in Derry. On 13 April 1573 he received a faculty from Rome to act as primate while Richard Creagh

---

172. *I.E.R.* I, pp. 358–9; P.F. Moran, *Spicilegium Ossoriense* (Dublin: W.B. Kelly, 1874), p. 39.
173. Cf., Myles Ronan, *Reformation in Ireland under Elizabeth* (London: Longmans, 1930), p. 470. Wolf sent clerics to Rome to be confirmed in loyalty and to be made bishops, three of whom went on to Trent. Ó Gallachair did not, as is sometimes claimed. Cf., *New History of Ireland* III (Oxford: Oxford University Press, 1976), p. 592.
174. Probably the priory of Aughris, cf. Gwynn and Hadcock, *Medieval Religious Houses in Ireland* (London: Longmans, 1970), p. 158.

was in prison,[175] presumably because he was in the Armagh province and was senior to Ó hAirt of Achonry who had been recommended for the position. Apart from the year that Edmund Magauran, Creagh's successor, spent in Ireland, Ó Gallachair exercised this vice-primacy until his death in 1601.

On 6 June 1575, he was written to by Pope Gregory XIII who was particularly concerned to implement the decrees of Trent dealing with bishops' visitation of their dioceses and the formation of the clergy. In this case he gives instruction about promoting to Holy Orders and to benefices those born out of lawful wedlock. In January 1579, he is reported to the government as one exercising papal power to grant licenses and indulgences, doubtless using the faculties of 1571, confirmed in 1575. In 1580, he is mentioned on a Vatican list as an Irish bishop who has not taken the oath of allegiance. He is not on the list of those who attended Perrot's parliament in 1585.[176]

On 28 January 1586, Sir John Perrot and the Dublin governing Council wrote to the Privy Council on the state of the realm and included Maguire's confession to the effect that 'the pretended Bishop of Derry is the chief instrument in the invasion of Philip, having travelled into France, Spain and Scotland and being now again gone abroad with great assurances of effecting it.'[177]

As the sixteenth century wears on, the Dublin government becomes increasingly paranoid about the influence of bishops, seminary-trained priests and Jesuits as it becomes clearer that its own policies are being rejected. One would tend to be sceptical about the purpose of these journeys, if they took place at all except in the mind, or sometimes as a consequence of the tortured body of the informant. The government was afraid of the invasion that eventually arrived in the shape of the Spanish Armada, but it is clear that, when it did come, the Spanish did not want to land in Ireland and the Irish leaders had not planned a rising out to greet them.

If Réamann did travel abroad in 1586, he was back in 1587 when he was one of seven bishops and other clergy who met in provincial synod somewhere in the diocese of Clogher to promulgate the decrees of

---

175. Cf., *Spicilegium Ossoriense*, p. 71.
176. James McLaughlin, *Brief Memoirs of the Bishops of Derry* (Dublin: J. Dollard, 1879), p. 28.
177. Perrot Papers, in *Analecta Hibernica* 12 (Dublin: Stationery Office of Saorstát Éireann, 1930), p. 34.

the Council of Trent.[178] It would appear that he presided as senior by consecration and as acting primate.

By 1588, in preparation for the feared and much foretold Armada, the Dublin administration had terrorised the country. Sir John Perrot in 1584 had established garrisons at Dunluce, Ballycastle and Coleraine, although Dunluce had been regained by the Scots. On 2 July 1588, Ó Gallachair wrote in Latin to Conchúr Ó Duibheanaigh (Conor O'Devany), Bishop of Down and Connor, delegating him for one year to dispense 'with salutary penance' in all cases where Ó Gallachair himself could, in virtue of his apostolic brief and primatial dignity because he cannot visit the area 'due to imminent dangers and hazards to life'. The letter is signed *Remundus Derensis Episcopus ac Vice-Primas*, and was written at *Tamlat*, which is almost certainly Tamlaghtard Magilligan, part of the bishop's mensal lands. It looks as if he had intended to cross the Bann and had been persuaded by discretion to write instead, probably because of the garrison at Coleraine. As luck would have it, the letter fell into English hands when Ó Duibheanaigh was captured, escaped, was recaptured and lodged in Dublin Castle for two years where he nearly died of starvation. The letter was in government hands by 26 October 1588 (CSPI).

Faced with a storm from the south west on 12 September 1588, the officers of *La Trinidad Valencera* felt they had no choice but to run with the wind and trust to luck or providence. On 14 September they found a good anchorage in Kinnagoe Bay, Inishowen, but the ship had sprung a leak and was sinking. The locals who soon thronged the shore agreed, at a price, to ferry the ship's company of four hundred ashore. It took them two days to do so before the ship sank with forty crew and some of the Armada's finest guns still on board, the first of the Armada ships to sink off the Irish coast. It took four days for the survivors to make their way to Seán Óg Ó Dochartaigh at Elagh, where they tried to negotiate a safe conduct, advised by a bishop in a neighbouring castle, presumably that owned by the bishop at Fahan. The agreement worked out was that the Spanish should advance and fire their arquebusses at the castle, and the Ó Dochartaigh garrison would yield. In this way the Irish could claim they had been overcome. When the Spanish did advance, some of those in the castle 'discharged a piece of artillery towards the part where the queen's garrison was.'

---

178. L. Renehan, *Collections* I, p. 435.

Don Alonso de Luzon became suspicious, and retreated to another dismantled castle nearby, near a marsh. A mixed English/Irish force answerable to Henry and Robert Hovenden, foster-brothers and clients of Hugh O'Neill, in the Queen's service, approached and after skirmishes and parleys, Don Alonso accepted 'terms of war' from a Major Kelly, including an English promise that each man be allowed to keep his best suit of clothes. The Spanish laid down their arms. They were however attacked and left naked anyone who resisted being killed. After protest, the officers were guarded, while the ordinary soldiers were left naked nearby. At dawn 'the remaining soldiers were made to go into an open field and a line of the enemy's harquebusiers approached them on one side and a body of cavalry on the other, killing over three hundred of them with lance and bullet; one hundred-and-fifty Spaniards managed to escape across a bog, many of them wounded, and sought refuge in the castle of *Duhort* (O'Doherty) where Bishop Cornelius received them and conveyed one hundred or so who were unwounded, to the island of Hibernia'.

The only bishop with the Latinised name *Cornelius* in Ulster at the time was Ó Duibheanaigh of Down and Connor, but he was certainly in prison in Dublin in October 1588 after being arrested twice. It is just possible that it was Conor O'Devany, but that demands a very tight schedule. No charge of giving help to the Spanish was laid against Conor during his imprisonment at this stage or during his trial before execution in 1612. There is a distinct probability that the bishop in question here was Ó Gallachair, particularly since another official residence of the Bishop of Derry was at Fahan, not far from the scene of the action. In that case the name Cornelius might result from confusion, since many of the Spanish were later ferried to Scotland by the MacDonnells of north Antrim in the diocese of Connor. The letter of a certain Patrick Foxe to Walsyngham in September 1588 would seem to connect Ó Gallachair with the incident and calls him 'a most seditious papist, and a man like to procure great aid to the Spaniards if he can' (CSPI).

On 4 October 1589, Captain Francisco de Cuellar wrote a letter that has been described as 'a mixture of fable, satire, parable, epic and cautionary tale' on 'a basic framework which is verifiably true', recounting his adventures after his ship was wrecked on Streedagh Strand in Sligo in September 1588. Over the course of the winter he pursued his hero's course north towards Ó Catháin's country and safety. It is hard to follow the course described by Cuellar, but he seems to have crossed the Foyle near Derry in the direction of the Ó Catháin castle at Limavady and to have been brought to a bishop

> ... who was living in retirement in a castle seven leagues away whither he had fled from the English. This bishop was a truly Christian man; he went about disguised as a savage [Cuellar's view of anyone not fortunate enough to be a hidalgo] ... He had twelve Spaniards staying with him until he could pass them over to Scotland. He was much pleased at my arrival. During the six days I spent with him he treated me with all possible kindness ... This bishop was called Don Reimundo *Termi* and he was Bishop of *Times*, an honourable and just man.

He talked to Cuellar about matters relating to 'the loss of the kingdom, and the help His Majesty had given them'. Don Reimundo is obviously Raymond O'Gallagher[179] with details that Cuellar picked up wrong. *Termi* might be 'Terri'. The directions and distances are vague, but it could be that the bishop had returned to his mensal lands at Tamlaghtard. The place has to be fairly near the Coleraine garrison, from a further escape Cuellar claims to have had when he went to speak to Ó Catháin.

The presence of survivors of the Armada brought informants into operation, and Patrick Eustace wrote to Sir Henry Bagenal in late October 1588:

> I was on Sunday last at Strabane where O Neill is and the Bishop of Derry and a friar from Donegal. These last two told me of 1,500 Spaniards in MacSweeney country [west Donegal] and they are like to perish for lack of food. The bishop goes to Rome presently and I judge he will go to Scotland or elsewhere in that ship [i.e. a ship to be provided for the Spanish].

Ó Gallachair was then sixty-seven years of age. There is no way of authenticating if he went abroad or not. On the face of it, it is as liable to be accurate as is the large total of Spanish in MacSweeney country.

At the end of 1590 Miler MacGrath, Queen Elizabeth's Archbishop of Cashel, former Papal Bishop of Down and Connor, sometime

---

179. See Felipe Fernandez-Armesto, *The Spanish Armada: The Experience of War in 1588* (Oxford: Oxford University Press, 1988), pp. 247–63. Evelyn Hardy, *Survivors of the Armada* (London: Constable, 1966), pp. 29–31; 122–9.

Conventual Franciscan and member of the *tearmannach*/erenagh family of Termonmagrath (Lough Derg) reported on the state of the Church in Ireland (CSPI):

> First in Ulster is one Redmundus O Galligher, Bishop of Derry, *alias* Deren, Legate to the Pope and *Custos Armaghen (custodian of Armagh)*, being one of the three bishops that were in the Council of Trent. This bishop uses all manner of spiritual jurisdiction throughout all Ulster, consecrating churches, ordaining priests, confirming children, and giving all manner of dispensations, riding with pomp and company from place to place as it was accustomed in Queen Mary's days. And for all the rest there, they use all manner of service now, as in that time, and not only that, but they have changed the time according to the pope's new invention. The said Bishop O Galligher has been with divers governors of that land upon protection, and yet is suffered to enjoy the bishopric and all the aforesaid authorities these twenty-six years past and more; whereby it is to be understood that he is not there as a man without authority or secretly kept.

Clearly the political temperature had cooled since the days of the Armada and the bishop could operate freely again as bishop and as vice-primate. Miler allows us a glimpse of Counter-Reformation west Ulster, with a self-confidence that allowed the use of the Tridentine Mass, to introduce the Gregorian calendar and to rebuild churches, as Ó Gallachair did that of Clooney.[180] In June 1590, Bishop Ó Gallachair ordained Patrick MacTaggart of the diocese of Clogher in the cathedral in Derry (which therefore must have been restored since Randolph's destruction in 1568) in the presence of the Dean of Derry, William MacTaggart, and Maurice O Hegarty and other priests, and of laity. He had given Patrick MacTaggart minor orders at Enagh in 1588 and sub-diaconate at Drumachose in 1589, and issued the relevant documents as might be done after such a ceremony anywhere. It is possible that, as vice-primate, he ordained the martyr-to-be Blessed Giolla Phádraig Ó Luchráin (Patrick O Loughran) of Donaghmore (Armagh) about 1600. The protection by Gaelic leaders that Miler speaks about was necessary if Réamann was to avoid the fate reserved for recalcitrant bishops by the government Miler was reporting to.

---

180. The ruins of this church are in St Columb's Park, Waterside, Derry.

There is no evidence that Ó Gallachair ever set out to be a martyr. The long-held suspicion of the Dublin government of the trustworthiness of most things Gaelic was reinforced and simplified when Pius V fatefully excommunicated Elizabeth I in 1570. Now it would be doubly easy for the New English members of the administration to recognise their enemies. The mirror image of this was the acceptance by many of the Gaelic Irish and of the Old English that their religion could best be protected by war, which meant that many of the Counter-Reformation clergy were to be found as scribes and advisers to the political leaders.

Thomas Jones, Royal Bishop of Meath, sent a letter to the lord deputy in 1592 which had come into his hands, written, he said, in 'the hand-writing of that traitorous Rome-runner, the Bishop of Derry'. It read: 'Faculty by Remundus *Derensis episcopus ac Primatis locumtenens* to William Nugent to hold lands, possessions and tithes pertaining to churches and monasteries'. It was written '*in Coenobio de Lios Gabhail*'[181] and dated *19 Aprilis 1592*. Since Nugent belonged to the prominent Catholic family in Westmeath, it may be unkind to wonder if the indignation of Bishop Jones was in proportion to the effect of the grant on his revenue. It may well have been in the nature of a political 'sweetener' to William. One might wonder if Réamann was also conscious in his role as Abbot of Derry of the lost lands of the Columban houses of Meath.

Archbishop James O Hely of Tuam managed to evade the attention of spies and bring safely with him a number of letters from Irish leaders to the pope and the King of Spain, one of them, dated 8 May 1593 and signed by Hugh Maguire of Fermanagh, Theobald, Richard and John Burke, and Brian Óg Ó Ruairc, and by the northern bishops: Edmundus (Magauran) of Armagh, Remundus of Derry,[182] Richardus (Mac Brady) of Kilmore, Cornelius (O'Devany) of Down, Patricius (McCaul) of Dromore and Niallanus (O Boyle) of Raphoe. The letter tells of the increasing fury with which the Queen of England's Deputy is pursuing the princes of the north since they assisted the survivors of the Armada. They ask King Philip for military aid and declare that if an army of ten thousand or at least eight thousand is sent to the northern coast of

---

181. Lios Gabhail is Lisgoole Abbey south of Enniskillen. Originally founded for Canons Regular of St Augustine it had been transferred to the Franciscans 1580–3.
182. Remundus Diren. Epús. (*Dirensis Episcopus – Bishop of Derry*), Conor O'Devany signed, almost anonymously, Fr – i.e. *frater* ('friar') – C.D. ac C. Epús.

Ireland the English will be vanquished. Primate Magauran brought a sense of purpose to the alliance on his return from Spain, but he was killed in June in a battle in Roscommon.[183]

Cardinal Allen wrote to the Senior Bishops of Ulster, 'Remundus of Derry, Richardus (Mac Brádaigh) of Kilmore and Cornelius (Ó Duibheanaigh) of Down, probably in late 1593 (because he does not mention Magauran), giving them our faculty

> ... to absolve penitents from all their sins no matter how enormous and in all cases whatsoever ... even from heresy and schism and any censures that may have been incurred ... and to preach, administer the sacraments of the Church and perform universally even in profane places all functions profitable to the welfare of souls and which are usually exercised by bishops or by those delegated by bishops. In particular, we authorise you to celebrate Mass in fit and convenient places even before daylight on portable altars and to bless vestments, etc., having regard to decency and such propriety as circumstances in those places will admit of.

He further gives them certain privileges concerning marriage. Allen, accepting that war was justified, is here making provision for it and no doubt encouraging the three bishops to take their cue from him. This atmosphere promoted a hysterical attitude on the other side, like that of the Bishop of Cork and Ross who wrote to Burghley in 1595 about Ó Néill: '[The Earl of] Tyrone has the pope's legate with him, one Gallaghore, the Bishop of Derry, who directs him in all his doings', which has to be an exaggeration.

Later that year Bingham accused him of taking the profits of the bishopric of Killala, which may refer to his retention of the abbey of Aughris on leaving for Derry. It is unlikely to be a confusion with his successor in Killala, Donncha Ó Gallachair (who was translated to Down and Connor in 1580 and died in 1582). It is in this year that George Montgomery first shows interest in Derry we are told, although there is no direct evidence of the patent that he applied for, and did not mention, ten years on.

---

183. See Micheline Kerney Walsh, 'Archbishop Magauran and his Return to Ireland', SA XIV (Armagh: Cumann Seanchais Ard Mhacha, 1990), pp. 75–6. The lord's spiritual sign on the left of the page and the lay lord's on the right.

We get a clearer idea of what the relationship between Bishop Ó Gallachair and Aodh Mór Ó Néill might have been in May 1596. Ó Néill was on his honeymoon with his fourth wife, Caitríona Nic Aonghasa (MacGuiness) of Iveagh, fishing at Castle Roe on the Bann, when a Spanish ship arrived at Killybegs with letters for the Irish leaders. Ó Néill rode to Lifford to meet the envoys. Also present at the meeting were Henry Hovenden and the Bishop of Derry. Hovenden was the earl's secretary, and so it is not unlikely that Ó Gallachair served a similar role, as scribe, Latinist, or perhaps the adviser on relations with Spain. He also had the advantage of writing a neat, clear hand. He was present at a number of these meetings dealing with Spanish matters.[184]After all, he had spent those years of exile in Portugal.

In July 1596, he accompanied Aodh Rua Ó Dónaill on an advance into Connacht where we find him using the faculties given him by Cardinal Allen, absolving from heresy those who deserted from the English army and came across to Ó Dónaill. On 8 August 1596, he appointed Bernard Macaghowan, Vicar General of Tuam and John O Dongal, guardian of the diocese of Mayo. In October of that year, it would seem, he was back in the north to meet an envoy from Spain and to entrust a letter to a messenger, Bernard O Donnell, for Pope Clement VIII. There was an assembly of Gaelic lords to discuss a letter from King Philip of Spain and reply to it. They 'desired the Bishop of Derry who was present to reply to the king's letter in their name but it yet pleased them to use the writer's hand', i.e. O Donnell's. O Donnell was captured and found to have a large bag of letters, ten from Aodh Ó Néill alone.

Ó Gallachair tries to give the pope a picture of 'the Satanic fury of English tyranny' and asks the pope to 'cast a kindly glance at your Ireland which now presents such a dismal appearance, so wretched, so mournful, suffering so many disasters inflicted by heretics' and the struggle the lords are putting up 'against malicious oppression' while awaiting aid. He urges the pope to act now 'since opportunity is bald on the back of the head'. He does not actually ask for military aid but

---

184. It is interesting that, although the subject of many accusations in the State Papers about his influence on political leaders, Ó Gallachair is not mentioned by name *even once* in Ó Cléirigh's *Beatha Aodha Ruaidh Uí Dhomhnaill*, Paul Walsh, ed., ITS, xlv 1943/1957. There is one reference to a 'faithful Catholic bishop' through whom news of an assassination plot is passed on to Aodh Rua (Dublin: Irish Texts Society, 1948), p. 290, but that is very vague.

leaves the details to be told by the bearer.[185] Had the bishop but known it he was at least one pope too late. Clement had already concluded that war against Elizabeth was no longer a realistic option. The struggle as envisaged and to be conducted by the Irish leaders was already being seen as an anachronism.

There were pastoral matters to be decided as well. In July 1597, Sir Conyers Clifford had marched north to capture Ballyshannon. With him was Lord Inchiquin, who was an Ó Briain and one of the most powerful loyalists in the west. On the night of 30 July, Inchiquin was sent with Sir Calisthenes Brooke to seize the fort at Áth Cualáin, west of Beleek. The operation was successful, but Inchiquin was shot dead. His body was recovered by Cormac Ó Cléirigh, a monk of the Cistercian Assaroe Abbey, where he was buried. When the Franciscans of Donegal heard of his death they demanded his body because the lords of Inchiquin were always buried in a Franciscan church, but the Cistercians refused to let it go. The dispute came before Ó Dónaill (Aodh Rua) who appointed the Bishops of Derry and Raphoe to help him decide. They judged the Franciscans to be in the right, ironically, and ordered the body to be reinterred.

The battle of the Yellow Ford happened in August 1598. The Dublin government seemed about to capitulate, but Captain George Thornton was sent by sea to Inis Eoghain, where in October he landed and 'burnt some corn'. He had a conference with Sir John (Seán Óg) O Doherty who 'with many gentlemen in his country would be good subjects if they were defended'. Thornton added (on 3 November) that the discussion could only take place 'in the hearing of the Bishop of Derry, whom they call the Lord Primate of Ireland, by direction of O'Donnell, who sent the bishop from his camp in Connacht' (CSPI). In his seventy-seventh year one might have thought he was too old for following an army. Perhaps he was sent as a sort of a 'fatherly restraint' on his impulsive relative, Aodh Rua.

Thornton was clearly sent to reconnoitre Lough Foyle. His knowledge came in useful in 1600 when, as captain of one of the ships, he led Sir Henry Docwra, who was sent 'to put a bridle on Ulster'. Docwra landed at Culmore in May. Within a week he had captured O Doherty's half-

---

185. See J.K. O'Doherty *Derriana: Essays and Occasional Verses* (Dublin: Sealy, Bryers and Walker, 1902), p. 125–6, where a translation of the letter is printed.

demolished fort at Elagh, and on 22 May occupied Derry,[186] using the stones of the ruined cathedral to build his fort. On 1 June, Art Ó Néill of Strabane, son of the previous Ó Néill, Tarlach Luineach of Sliocht Airt Óig, came over to the English side. Also, in early June when Ó Dónaill (Aodh Rua) went south to invade Thomond, Docwra took his chance and seized Dunalong up the Foyle in Ó Catháin country, where he built another fort. Then Ó Dónaill returned and captured two hundred of his horses. In the encounter Docwra himself was injured. Docwra's men began to get sick and many deserted.

With things at their worst for the Foyle garrison, Niall Garbh Ó Dónaill joined the English in early October 1600 and his military talent began to make a big difference, particularly when he began by capturing Lifford fort. In January 1601, Ó Dochartaigh (Seán Óg) defeated the English of Derry who had attacked him, but on his return he became ill and died quite suddenly on 27 January. When Ó Dónaill (Aodh Rua) as overlord appointed Seán's brother, Féilim Óg, to succeed him rather than his son, Cathaoir, Aodh Buí Mac Daibhid, with whom Cathaoir had been fostered, and Aodh's brothers, Féilim Riabhach and Éamann Gruama, signed articles of agreement with Docwra on 14 February 1601, which recognised Cathaoir as the queen's O Doherty.[187] Three of the neighbouring *clanna* had now split apart in their reaction to the English presence, each divided by a perceived opportunity for personal advantage. It would not be long before Mánas Gallda Ó Catháin would try his luck also.

This meant that the eighty-year-old Réamann Ó Gallachair was forced to live in a much altered environment in the spring of 1601. In a description of Inishowen in the State Papers dated 12 April 1601 but perhaps at least a month old by that stage, we read 'over against Inch in O Dogherty's country is a castle and a church called the Fanne [*Fahan*], but broken down since our arrival. *Here dwells the Bishop O'Galthar'* [*sic*]. Docwra had made similar notes in March. Given the known antipathy shown by the English towards bishops and the summary

---

186. Described by Docwra as having the 'ruins of an old abbey, of a bishop's house, of two churches, and at one of the ends of it an old castle, the river called Loughfoyle encompassing it all on one side and a bogge most commonlie wett and not easilie passable except in two or three places'. Henry Docwra, *Narration in Miscellany of the Celtic Society* (Dublin, 1849), p. 238.
187. Mac Dáibhid (McDevitt/ McDaid) were descended from Dáibhid Ó Dochartaigh +1208; one of the five branches of Sliocht Eachmharcaigh: Mac Dáibhid, Mac Dhónaill Óig (McConologue), Mac Fheabhail (McCole), Mac Giolla Bhríde (McBride) and Mac Ailín (McCallion).

justice Docwra meted out to prisoners (as can be read in his own words), and now with his own residence at Fahan no longer habitable, it was no wonder that the old bishop decided to move elsewhere.

Although the MacDevitts were staunch Catholics (as Féilim Riabhach was to prove at the scaffold), Ó Gallachair may have feared that association with Ó Dónaill rendered him vulnerable, particularly now that English forces had access to his area. He must have been in some doubt about the trustworthiness of those around him. Lynch is sure that he felt under threat. Niall Garbh Ó Dónaill has long been the subject of obloquy, and Lynch blames him for abandoning Ó Gallachair to Docwra's soldiers. This may be true in the sense that, with the bishop too old to cope any longer with the travelling and constant movement of Ó Dónaill's army – involved in an increasingly bitter conflict – he might have expected at least some limited protection from Niall Garbh. It seems a regrettable but unavoidable fact that Niall Garbh devoted most of his consideration to Niall Garbh. He also seems to have been much on the move, and anyhow would probably have seen the bishop as one belonging to his rival's camp. Furthermore, the area around the Foyle on both sides was being criss-crossed by raiding, marauding, foraging parties. For all these reasons it seems clear that the bishop was trying to make his way to a quieter location, perhaps back to the other episcopal residence at Tamlaghtard, perhaps to the protection of Ó Catháin (Dónall Ballach) or maybe just into the wilds. Lynch recounts the events as he heard them:

> Abandoned by Niall Garbh O Donnell, Henry Docwra, with the Lough Foyle garrison, got on his track and at last seized him in Cumalia, a remote area about a mile from Derry on the road that leads to Strabane, where there was a parochial church. A short time before the bishop had learned the arrangements the enemy had made for getting hold of him, and had in consequence hid himself in a bog, winter though it was; but the bitter cold and his enfeebled old age compelled him to slip into a house at the dead of night. On the approach of the enemy all in the house took to flight, except himself. Unable to fly, he hid himself among some sheaves of corn. The enemy having got up to the house, and having laid hold on a woman and boy, slaughtered them both, and went away. The people of the place then went into the house, and asked was there anyone there still alive. The bishop from his hiding-place, answered that he was still alive. One of the army

servants of the enemy, who was lurking close by, overhearing the voice, hurries off to his party with his utmost speed, urges them to come back, which they do without delay, fall upon the bishop, thus taken by surprise, mangle him with many a wound, and leave him lifeless. That was in 1602 ... The bishop was buried in the graveyard of the parochial church I mentioned, at the side where the eastern window stood, the interior of the church having been desecrated.[188]

From Lynch we learn that the place of death was Cumalia, clearly a mistake for *Cumaria*, now Cumber (Claudy), confirmed by Bishop George Montgomery's *Survey* of the parishes of the diocese, reaffirmed by Bishop Downham's later *Marginalia*. Lynch's distances and the reference to the Strabane road do not really stand up to examination, but the other details have the ring of truth, reported by someone who was an eye witness.

Sir John Bolles (Bowles) was put in charge of the Dunalong garrison by Docwra, and from there he wrote a long excusatory letter to Sir Robert Cecil in London on 7 March 1601, part of which reads:

The Bishop of the Derry (who is said to be the chief contriver of this general defection and combination with the Spaniards, and hath himself been thrice to Rome and oft in Spain to negotiate), God gave into my hand upon Ash Wednesday at night, but, before I could come to him, the soldiers had slain him. We got there about eighty lean cows, and burned many more in the houses, besides sheep, goats, and corn, and slew betwixt eighty and one hundred persons. This was in O Cahan's country, and his people, being gathered in small numbers together, fought with us for the marching of five miles, but so coldly that in all that time they killed but one of our men, and hurt five. I took a scholar there prisoner, whom because he carried no arms, neither ever may, being within orders, and for that my troop is weak, and horse is that which here doth all the service, I have agreed to ransom for some horses and some oats ...

188. Translated by Bishop J.K. O'Doherty, op. cit., from Lynch, *De Praesulibus Hiberniae* II, p. 327. Perhaps because he was a native of Killea, the good bishop identifies *Cumalia*, where Réamann, his predecessor, was killed, with Killea. He begins by presuming Ó Gallachair was fleeing from the city.

The tone of the letter shows Bolles trying to justify himself to Cecil against accusations of being inactive and not keeping Cecil and the government in London adequately informed of how the war is going in his theatre of operations. For that reason, he dwells on anything his superiors will definitely be satisfied with, like evidence that he is fully carrying out their scorched earth policy. He is so anxious about how they will react to his proposing to hold the theologian for ransom that he goes into great detail about him and why he did not kill him, yet he is quite blasé about the bishop's death and calmly blames his soldiers for bringing about what might be thought the really important news that he has to report and which the government should be delighted to hear, that their great enemy who, they thought, had master-minded the war, was finally dead. It sounds as if Bolles for one did not believe the official propaganda.

Interestingly, he also suggests two ways to end the war: the first, that the priests 'who are more desirous of peace than the people', be guaranteed freedom of conscience and continuance in their livings so that they may draw in the laymen; and the second, by refusing to accept any of those who wish to surrender unless they have proved their loyalty by 'bloody service ... so that the peasants, women and children, forced to live off last year's store and kept from ploughing, must the next year of necessity starve'. It is an interesting moral dilemma.

The two accounts of the bishop's death fit together quite well. There was nothing heroic about it. He died the way so many of his people died, casually, in a callous and cruel conflict, fought with the weapons of starvation and homelessness as much as by lance or arquebus. Bolles gives the day of his death: 'Ash Wednesday at night'. Ash Wednesday 1601 was 25 February by the English calendar of the time, or 7 March by the Gregorian calendar now accepted. Réamann Ó Gallachair, Bishop of Derry and Vice-Primate of Ireland, met a solitary death at Cumber in O Cahan country on the night of Ash Wednesday 7 March 1601, when discovered in hiding by a marauding band of soldiers under the command of Sir John Bolles (Bowles) from the English garrison at Dunalong.

It would appear that Docwra's soldiers had not quite finished with the Bishop of Derry. Lord Deputy Mountjoy wrote to Cecil at the end of March 1601 from Drogheda enclosing an extract from a letter that had just come from Derry with the news that the 'garrisons of Derry hath [sic] slain (at a Mass, as is said) the Prior of Derry and twenty of the principal priests in all Ulster in a church'. The only possible explanation for such an assembly at such a time, surely, is that they had gathered to bury the leading churchman of the country, and that, aware of this,

Bolles or some such had returned to ambush the funeral. The prior may have been the prior of *Dubhreglés*, or of the Dominicans or some dignitary of the diocesan chapter.

What are we to make of the career of Réamann Ó Gallachair? By birth he belonged within the élite of Cineál Chonaill. That he was a Counter-Reformation prelate is certain, serious about reform, in law and in practice. He was clearly proud of his position of leadership as vice-primate in the Church in Ireland, consulted by the leaders of the time. That he was bishop at a time of war complicates the issue. Unlike his contemporary Blessed Conor O Devany of Down and Connor, who was proud to be a simple Franciscan friar, uninterested in political affairs to any great extent (which did not save him from being harried into the Pale by Bishop Montgomery and finally executed in 1612), Ó Gallachair, in the position of primate, could not stand aside, or change policy as readily as a pope. He was presumably influenced by the attitudes of his English contemporary, Cardinal Allen, who held the traditional medieval view that war was justified in the peculiar circumstances created by Queen Elizabeth. It would seem that in the early days of the war he is consulted by Ó Néill and towards the end he is to be found more with Ó Dónaill. The war in Ireland was further complicated by the perception, however confused, of the Gaelic Irish leaders and some of the Old English that their world was in the process of being destroyed, a world which was imbued with a certain conviction about Catholicism. The modern historian can analyse and point out the deficiencies in their integrism, but objective analysis, where it exists, is one of the prerogatives of hindsight.

Medieval Religious Orders in Derry

From the earliest beginnings of the Christian Church, men and women felt strongly impelled to live out their lives in a closer dedication to Christ's example and teaching, leaving normal human society to live as hermits or monks. From the cities of the eastern Empire they sought solitude in the sandy deserts of Egypt, or in Ireland they withdrew into isolated oases in the trackless bogs of the midlands. Inspired by a desire for more faithful discipleship to Christ, for the glory of God and the salvation of the world, their lifelong commitment to the counsels of perfection exemplified in the Gospels led to the development of organised communities and associations which we now refer to as religious orders.

A distinction developed between contemplative orders dedicated to prayer and study, and active ones at the service of their fellow human beings. From the point of view of organisation, we distinguish between a 'federal' system like the early Irish *paruchia* or the Benedictines, Cistercians or Canons Regular of St Augustine, and a later centralised constitution like the Franciscans and Dominicans, where a number of dependent houses are organised into provinces.

The twelfth century, with which these essays are largely concerned, saw a reform movement in the religious life as well as in general Church organisation, a reform which demanded a stricter adherence to the ideal of the orders' founders. In this way, for example, the reform of Benedictine ideals gave rise to the Cistercians. And in the thirteenth century, as a result of social, economic and cultural change, like the emergence of cities and early forms of industry and capitalism, a decisive break produced the so-called mendicant orders, like Franciscans and Dominicans. They were inspired by the ideal of a life without material possessions and marked by penitence, preaching and active dedication to the good estate of one's neighbour.

These new orders were personal associations not tied permanently to one place, living under superiors elected for a specific period. Their material support came from their pastoral work supported by begging. This pastoral care became a prominent feature of their lives and was based for the first time on a methodical and orderly education in special schools or *studia*. They included women in affiliated female branches and a noteworthy aspect, particularly of the Franciscans, was the organisation of Third Orders, living either in the lay world as semi-religious brotherhoods and sisterhoods or in monastic communities (Third Orders Regular).

The renewal of the medieval Irish Church bore testimony to all these new departures, of which the first to make their presence felt were the Canons Regular of St Augustine and the Cistercians.

The Canons Regular of St Augustine
Already in the mid-eleventh century Pope Leo XI, one of the earliest reformers, had encouraged communities of reformed canons in order to restore discipline to religious life. These canons followed the rule of St Augustine of Hippo, the great theologian and Father of the Church in the fifth century. With the onset of reform in Ireland, about the year 1140, St Maolmhóg (Malachy) Ó Morgair, as a result of his experience on the continent, was impressed with the canons at Arrouaise in the

diocese of Arras in northern France. He introduced them to Ireland, where they spread throughout the country,[189] often replacing the traditional native monasteries. In the diocese of Derry there were such canons at Derry itself and at Dungiven.

In Derry, the *Dubhreglés, Cella Nigra* or 'black church' founded by St Colm Cille became a house of Augustinian Canons at the beginning of the thirteenth century, marking the formal end of the Columban Order. The abbey in Derry became filial (or subordinate) to the similar house of Ss Peter and Paul in Armagh. Having caught fire many times and been deliberately set on fire on occasion, it was finally occupied by invading English forces under Colonel Randolph, who turned it into a fort – until the powder magazine blew up and destroyed it. By the mid-sixteenth century, the bishop of the diocese was also abbot of the abbey: successively Eoghan Ó Dochartaigh and Réamann Ó Gallachair. When Derry no longer had a bishop, Blessed Conor Ó Devany, martyr Bishop of Down and Connor, and Eoin Ó Cullinan, Bishop of Raphoe, were abbots *in commendam*.

Dungiven had already been a religious centre for there was an early monastery here founded by St Neachtán Néir in the seventh century. An Augustinian Priory was built by Ó Catháin, after that rising lineage had ousted the Ó Conchúir kings of *Cianacht* from power. What is known of its history is that most of its priors were named Ó *Muireadhaigh* and its emoluments included the rectory of Both Domhnaigh, at least in the fifteenth century. It was graced by a round tower, which survived until as late as 1784, although by 1603 the priory is stated to have been suppressed by English government.[190]

There was a similar connection of the Canons Regular with the Agivey/Kilrea area, about which little is known, except that the canons of Ss Peter and Paul at Armagh had lands there, as indeed they had in Desertmartin also.

The Cistercians

In the early twelfth century, no monastic reform movement had had such success as the Cistercians, a development of the Benedictine rule so named from one of its early foundations, Cîteaux, in eastern France. Its success was due to a new constitution of relatively independent

189. See P. J. Dunning, 'The Arroasian Order in Medieval Ireland', *Irish Historical Studies IV*, 16 (September, 1945), pp. 297–315.
190. Gwynn and Hadcock, *Medieval Religious Houses* (Dublin: Irish Academic Press, 1988), pp. 146–8; 168; 174.

monasteries united under a General Chapter, which spread according to a system of mother and daughter houses, founded in the remotest areas, which would be brought to fertility by the labour of the monks themselves. Perhaps the greatest asset of the new movement was the charismatic Abbot of Clairvaux, St Bernard, one of the outstanding figures of the century. It was as a result of the friendship between him and St Maolmhóg (Malachy) and the latter's admiration for their way of life that the order was introduced into Ireland in 1142.

In the diocese of Derry a Cistercian abbey was established at Má Choscáin (Macosquin), south of Coleraine. Like all Cistercian abbeys it was known by an (often poetic) title, *de Claro Fonte* ('of the Clear Spring'), but apart from the fact that it is believed to have been established by Ó Catháin in 1218, little has survived of its history. It may have been founded on the Cistercian mother and daughter principle from Clairvaux itself by way of Morimond in France, Mellifont and Newry.

Cistercians provided three bishops to the diocese of Derry, two from Macosquin and one from the abbey of *Eas Rua* (Assaroe), near Ballyshannon in Co. Donegal. The same abbey of Assaroe had a grange (or outfarm) at Kilfore in the parish of Clonleigh (whose erenagh seems to have been Ó Braoin/Breen). From that same year, 1218, there was a Cistercian convent in Derry itself, but even less is known about it.[191] The only remaining evidence for religious sisters about medieval Derry is in the placenames *Baile na gCailleach* (now, alas, truncated to Galliagh), and *Ros na gCailleach*. *Cailleach* is the older word in Irish for a 'nun', from *caille*, meaning 'veil', which derives in turn from the Latin word of similar meaning, *pallium*.

The Mendicant Orders in Derry

As we have said, the emergence of the mendicant orders in medieval Europe was conditioned by far-reaching social and economic change largely associated with the development of cities. It is not surprising then that the early Dominican and particularly Franciscan friars came to Ireland in the wake of the Norman invasion and flourished initially in the towns and manors of Norman-occupied areas of the country, where they depended on the alms of the communities they served. Gaelic Ireland in the twelfth century, and therefore the diocese of

---

191. See Flannan Hogan, 'Derry: The Cistercian Connection', *Hallel* 23, 2 (1998), pp. 127–9.

Derry, was essentially rural and for some time appeared unattractive to orders organised for urban living. This state of affairs endured until they developed a form of life suited to the conditions of Gaelic Ireland, notably by the development of the Third Order system, which had such phenomenal success there in the fourteenth and fifteenth centuries.

The Dominicans

Nonetheless, the first Dominican convent, as their houses were called, was established at Coleraine as early as 1244, thereby initiating a connection that would last for five centuries. This was followed by a second at Derry itself in 1274, founded during the episcopate of Giolla an Choimdhe (in Latin Germanus) Ó Cearbhalláin, who was probably not a Dominican himself. The lay founder of the new priory was an Ó Dónaill, probably the Dónall who was killed in 1281 and laid to rest there. The new house was dedicated to St Dominic and was situated in what would later be the area of Abbey Street, William Street and Rossville Street.

The egregious Bishop Simon, whose surname we do not know, but who was a Dominican, made something of a name for himself as errant Bishop of Derry from 1349 to 1380. Subsequently, a common surname among the native friars was O'Lynn, which would underline their connection with north Derry – since O'Lynn (Ó Luain perhaps) were erenaghs in Tamlaghtard – as well as with north Antrim, whither Ó Flainn had had to move after having been Lords of Uí Tuirtre in south Derry. Amongst these O'Lynn friars were Thomas, prior in 1480, and John, prior when executed in 1607, as was his namesake again in 1657.

Being in the territory of Cineál Chonaill, the priory had escaped the first suppressions under Henry VIII, but thirty-two members of the community were butchered at some later date in the reign of Elizabeth I.

In spite of this terrible history, St Oliver Plunkett found six friars still in Derry in 1661, and even by 1734 there were eight, who however possessed no buildings. They were by this stage more probably centred in the county of Derry. Members there included the celebrated *Bráthair Bán* (travelling preacher, sheep dealer and writer, Doimnic Ó Brolcháin) – Bishop Patrick O'Brullaghan who, however, preferred being chaplain to the Sardinian embassy in London, and perhaps too the Seán O Brullaghan who almost became bishop of the diocese.[192]

192. H. Fenning, *Dominicans of Derry* in *Derriana* (1978), pp. 53–6; and in Edward Daly and Kieran Devlin, eds, *Clergy of Derry: An Index* (Dublin: Four Courts Press, 2009), pp. 22–4.

The Franciscans

Since Gaelic Ireland initially appeared unattractive to religious founded in and accustomed to urban and feudal environments, it is hardly surprising that we find no record of what we might call mainstream Franciscans establishing themselves in the diocese of Derry in the early enthusiasm of the thirteenth or fourteenth centuries. However, this situation was to change considerably one hundred years later with the development in Ireland of the Franciscan Third Order, in both its forms, secular and regular.[193]

These groups had originated on the Continent in a pre-existing movement of 'penitents' who voluntarily adopted as a means of reparation the lifestyle imposed by the Church on public sinners: prayer, fasting and distinctive dress, and looking to the Franciscans for their spiritual guidance. The groups first consisted of married laymen and women (Third Order Secular), but eventually individuals came together and began living in communal religious life (Third Order Regular).

Both types spread widely in Ireland after 1400 and early references to them from the dioceses of Raphoe, Clonfert, Limerick and Cork indicate just how widespread they were, and nowhere were they more popular than in late medieval Ulster.[194] In the Derry diocese, there were houses of the Franciscan Third Order Regular in west Tyrone. There they were in the territory of and so would seem to have been introduced by *Sliocht Airt*, the descendants of Art, son of Eoghan Mór Ó Néill (d. 1458), who founded the town of Omagh by building the first castle at that strategic confluence of rivers.

As it would happen, a shaft of light is thrown on the relationship of these movements, lay and religious, with the existing clergy, from whom they demanded high standards and were in no way slow to criticise.

The *Register of Primate Mey* in 1449 records evidence of the intense displeasure of the parish priest (*rector*) of Drumragh, Aodh Mac Cathmhaoil (McCaul) of that prominent ecclesiastical lineage. He lodged a complaint with the Primate saying that he had been confronted by one Pádraig Mac Aodha (McHugh today), a *laïcus barbatus* (a 'bearded layman', therefore one not in major orders). This gentleman had the audacity to challenge him, the parish priest, about his lifestyle.

---

193. See Colman N. Ó Clabaigh, *The Franciscans in Ireland, 1400–1534* (Dublin: Four Courts Press, 2002), pp. 80–105.
194. Cf. Canice Mooney, 'Franciscan Third Order Friary at Dungannon', *Seanchas Ardmhacha* I (1954), pp. 12–24.

On top of that, he had arrived with the support of the Bishop of Derry, Seán Ó Gubúin, who had given him permission to build a monastery in his, Mac Cathmhaoil's parish. And to crown insult with injury, when the parish priest had slapped an excommunication on this mere layman, the bishop had promptly absolved him![195]

The Omagh friary had lands at Shergrim. We are informed by the noted seventeenth-century historian of the Franciscans, Donatus Mooney (Ó Maonaigh), that there were other fifteenth-century Third Order Regular foundations in west Tyrone at Corick (*Comhrac*) near the confluence of the Glenelly and Owenkillew Rivers, Pubble (*Pobal*) close to Newtownstewart and Scarvagherin (*Scairbh an Chaorthainn*) near Castlederg.[196] The same historian wrote also that many of the Tertiaries (as they were called) who lived in congregation were engaged in pastoral work and also organised and taught in boys' schools that were attached to their friaries. We know too from other sources that they wore a habit of Franciscan type but grey in colour.

It was traditionally asserted that the founder of Corick friary was Anraí Aimhréidh Ó Neill, who died in 1392 and who built the so-called 'Harry Avery's Castle' near Newtownstewart. It is claimed that he gave the monastery at Corick both cattle and land free of tithe.[197] It would seem more likely however that it was founded after his day, although he was a great-uncle of Art, progenitor of *Sliocht Airt*, the promoters of the Third Order Regular in west Tyrone. Long after this, in the second half of the seventeenth century, Franciscans came again to minister for a time in Derry and Strabane.

---

195. WGH Quigley and EFD Roberts, eds, *Registrum Iohannis Mey* (Belfast: H.M. Stationery Office, 1972), pp. 182–3.

196. Cf. B. Jennings OFM, ed., Brussels MS 3947: 'Donatus Moneyus, de Provincia Hiberniae S. Francisci', *Analecta Hibernica* 6 (Dublin: Stationery Office of Saorstát Éireann, 1934), p. 103, where they are listed in eccentric spelling: *Scairb an Ciothrainn ag cois Dheirge, an Fhomach* (Omagh), *an Comhrac a Muintir Luinidh, an Popul cois Mhoghuine.*

197. Cf. J.K. O'Doherty, *Derriana: Essays and Occasional Verses* (Dublin: Sealy, Bryers and Walker, 1902), p. 65.

5

Some Medieval Parishes in Political Context

The Deanery of Derry:	The Church in Inis Eoghain.
The Deanery of Binneach:	Támhleacht Fhionnlughan, a Scottish dimension.
The Deanery of Maigh Iotha (Tyrone):	Urnaí (Urney) and Ard Srátha (Ardstraw).
The Deanery of Ráth Luraigh (Co. Derry):	Baile na Scríne (Ballinascreen).

THE GREAT REFORM AND RENEWAL OF CHURCH LIFE IN twelfth-century Ireland had the aim and the effect of creating a country-wide diocesan system in which the faithful were to be brought into more intimate contact with Church organisation under the moral and canonical authority of the local bishop. The logical development of this in the following century was the further subdivision within the diocese into a network of parishes, always with the object of more effective organisation of the pastoral ministry and a closer relationship of the lay Christian with the life of his community.

The Catholic parish is of course the basic geographical subdivision in the descending order of ecclesiastical province, diocese, deanery and parish. It presumes two essential characteristics: a body of Catholics within a fixed boundary and a specified priest with responsibility for ministering to them. Since Catholics may worship in any convenient church, even if they do not live in that parish, it follows that a parish is primarily a community of people rather than a purely geographical unit. Nonetheless, convenience of situation, family tradition, personal memories or devotion all conspire to create strong and enduring bonds with the parish of residence. The development of such sentiments of community in the twelfth and thirteenth centuries can only have been slow, but in spite of the paucity of documentation, we can descry elements of it in the way in which local loyalties seem to reflect the *clann* domains or the petty political lordships of the time. They were probably also promoted by the worship in the parish church of their named patron saint, in many cases none other than the first Christian missionary in the locality, remembered in placename together with his *domhnach* (Domhnach Chaoide/Donagheady) or his *both* (Both Domhnaigh/Badoney) or his *cill* (Cill Eoghain/Killowen) or his *díseart* (Díseart Éignigh/Desertegney), or his *tearmann* (Tearmann Chainnigh/Termoncanice).

Quite apart from the religious renewal involved in this parish network, it should be pointed out that it created a completely new sort of territorial jurisdiction and a new sense of place, a religious relationship that would exist alongside political divisions and ultimately outlive them. Much of the culture thus created would be swept away by the confiscations prior to the Ulster Plantation and subsequently by the abandonment of the native language during the nineteenth century. Even so, parish loyalties were to prove extraordinarily tenacious in spite of the vicissitudes of history. To this day, the core inspiration of GAA club competitions is based on intense feelings of belonging to parishes that in essence were originally delimited seven centuries ago.

That original laying out of parish boundaries could, of course, only take place in the context of the political spheres of influence and the social organisation of the time and no doubt with the cooperation of the local power-brokers, particularly when it came to the provision of financial upkeep. The system that evolved from the dedication of particular townlands for the upkeep of the local church, its buildings, its clergy and its administrators, the erenagh élite, raises interesting questions of tenure and ownership. Centuries after that original arrangement, when the Plantation Bishop Montgomery assembled the erenaghs, no amount of pressure would appear to make them say that their lands belonged to the bishop or the Church, nor did the erenaghs themselves claim anything more than the administration of them.

To study something of the conditions in which such fundamental changes took place, we turn here to some examples of these political contexts, chosen from each deanery of the diocese.

The Deaneries of the Diocese

The Catholic diocese of Derry is today divided into three deaneries, which are commonly referred to by the names of the centres in which clerical conferences take place: Derry, Strabane and Maghera. The deanery system has, however, a long history behind it.

As early as 1397, the Rentale which details the episcopal income paid by each parish at the time of Archbishop Colton's visitation of Derry uses the system of dividing the parishes according to the deanery to which they belonged: Inisowyn (*Inis Eoghain*), Mahya (*Maigh Iotha*) and Bennach (*Binneach*). This division was of civil and not ecclesiastical origin. The *civitas* or city of Derry was in the deanery of Inis Eoghain, and Glendermott/Clann Diarmada is not mentioned, so that it must be treated as within the *civitas*. All the other parishes belonging in the area now called Co. Derry together made up the deanery of Binneach.

Eoghan of Inis Eoghain, son of Niall Naoighiallach, had two sons named Eochaidh, distinguished by epithets. One was Eochaidh Binneach and his descendants are known as Cineál Binnigh. Binneach is probably derived from *binn*, meaning 'sweet-sounding'. So *binneach* should mean 'tuneful' when applied to a person, one would think. When applied to a place, *binneach* may derive from *beann* 'mountain' and mean 'mountainous', 'of high peaks', 'pointed'. It has also a homonym, which means an animal horn, and carries the derivative sense of the horn or wing of an army disposed for battle. This meaning suits Cineál Binnigh in many ways for they were in the military vanguard of the eastward expansion of Cineál Eoghain across what is now Tyrone/Tír Eoghain and Co. Derry.

Bishop Reeves, whose views are almost always apposite, was of the opinion that the deanery of Binneach took its name from Cineál Binnigh. There is no doubting their importance if one is to judge from their elaborate genealogy. Unfortunately they had begun to recede into the political background by the time the various annals were compiled and few of them are known to us other than by name.

We can trace their effect through some of the Derry surnames that originate with them: Ó Gormaile/Gormley; Mac Con Choille/McEnhill; Ó Duimhin/Devine; Ó Giolláin/? McGillion; Ó Lagáin/Lagan; Ó Fearáin/Farren; Ó Tuathaile/Tohill; Mac Oirc/ McGurk. They were active in Church affairs as erenaghs, guardians of relics and so forth, carrying with them their veneration for St Colm Cille. Reference in placenames also shows how widely their influence spread, with names like Ó Lachtnáin/O'Loughlin; Ó Cuaig/Quigg; Ó Branáin/Brennan;

Ó Rancáin/Rankin; Ó Cormaic/Mc Cormick; Mac Giolla Choirr/
McElchorr, Corr, and so on. Also belonging to Cineál Binnigh were
St Maolrubha, the great missionary of Pictish Scotland, St Dáchuailén,
Abbot of Derry, and St Fothadh na Canóine, Abbot of Fahan. They
always remained, however, under the ambit of the Mac Lochlainn/Ó
Neill Kings of Cineál Eoghain, which may imply rather that the deanery
was named for its terrain.

According to records at the time of the Plantation of Ulster, the
diocese was then divided into four deaneries: Binneach being divided
in two, with a separate deanery covering south Derry, that of *Ráth
Luraigh*/Rathlury (now Maghera). This may have been due to the
expansion into south Derry in the fifteenth century of Clann Dónall
Donn na Banna, (Clandonnel), a branch of Ó Neill Buí of Clandeboye,
over part of the bailiewick of Cineál Binnigh.

The Deanery of Derry

The Church in Medieval Inis Eoghain

According to the 'old books', the sons of Niall Naoighiallach (of the Nine
Hostages), High King of Ireland who died in AD 453, established 'sword
land' for themselves in what came to be known as Donegal. Conall
occupied the west and south, which became Tír Chonaill. Another
brother took the east, known as Tír Éinne; and the north fell to a third
brother, Eoghan, who gave his name to Inis Eoghain, and eventually
to Tír Eoghain.

The area claimed by the descendants of Eoghan was divided into
three *tuatha* or 'states': *an Bréadach* on the east around Moville (ruled
by *Ó Duídhíorma* – pronounced 'Deeyeearma', and now often turned
into McDermott), *Carraig Brachaí* in the north centred on the Isle
of Doagh, ruled by *Ó Maolfhábhaill* (Mc Faul, Lavelle), and *Aileach*.
Aileach gave its name to the over-kingdom and to its overall ruler, *rí
Ailigh*. According to one source there was a sub-ruler in south Inis
Eoghain, *Ó hÉanaigh* (Heaney). Many of the surnames still common
in Inis Eoghain and Tír Eoghain arise from the sons of Eoghan: from
Féilimí come *Ó Duídhíorma* and *Ó Sléibhín*; from *Cormac* come *Mac
Maonghaile* (McMonagle); from *Dallán*: *Ó hEarcáin* and *Ó Mearáin*;
from *Iollann*: *Ó Cearbhalláin* (Carolan), *Ó Galáin*, *Ó Mianáin*, *Ó
Brannagáin*, *Ó Duibhne* (Deeny, Peoples); from *Aileall*: *Ó Fallúin*
(Fallon); from *Aonghas*: *Ó Brolaigh* (Brolly); from *Fearghas*: *Ó hAgáin*,

Ó Maolmochéirí (Loughrey), Ó Maolfhábhaill, Ó Dufacháin, Ó Ceallaigh (including Mac Rabhartaigh). From Eochaidh Binneach were descended the kindred of Cineál Binnigh, branches of whom were to achieve distinction as a military force and later prominence in the Church – as also did some of the above.

It was, however, from Eoghan's son Muireadhach that the chief branches of the Cineál were descended, within and beyond Inis Eoghain, including Ó Néill and Mac Lochlainn, Kings of Ulster and Ireland, and others who made their mark on history century after century: Ó Catháin, Ó Gormlaigh, Ó Brolcháin, Mac Ruairí, Mac Cathmhaoil, Mac Colgáin, Ó hUalghairg … The history of medieval Ulster is to a large extent the history of these descendants of Eoghan.

The first prize to be won among the branches of Cineál Eoghain was the overall kingship of the descendants of Niall Naoighiallach, the Uí Néill (not to be confused with the much later surname Ó Néill). The contention was between Cineál Eoghain, Cineál Chonaill and distantly related families in the kingdom of Meath. Cineál Eoghain became dominant in west Ulster, but their rule was later to deteriorate into a spasmodic civil war between two alliances that lasted for centuries. One alliance was headed by Ó Néill, descended from Niall Glúndubh (d. 919); and one by Mac Lochlainn, descended from Niall's brother Dónall Dábhaill (d. 915), although even this is disputed. Eventually, by the eleventh century, the rivalry seems to have produced an Ó Néill state based on east Tyrone/Armagh, and a Mac Lochlainn state centred on Derry but including much of west Tyrone/west Co. Derry/east Donegal, as well as Inis Eoghain. The ruler of this western sub-kingdom was known as Rí Ailigh, sometimes as the designated successor of the ruler of the whole Cineál.

By about the year 1100, when our story of Church reform begins, Cineál Eoghain was led by a remarkable man, Dónall mac Ardghair Mac Lochlainn. He was a prince of his time in his effort to build up his dynasty as contemporary rulers were seeking to do on the continent. When he died in 1121, he was recognised as King of Ireland, but only his grandson was able to achieve the same distinction. This was Muircheartach Mac Lochlainn, the second-last High King of Ireland, before the last one, the ill-fated Ruairí Ó Conchúir. Muircheartach lost his kingdom and his life in 1166 when his own people and allies, civil and religious, turned against him after he showed catastrophic bad judgement and lack of principle. He had chosen to be buried at Armagh, unlike his grandfather, Dónall mac Ardghair, who had centred his kingdom on Derry, had lived and was buried there. As the Anglo-Norman invasion pursued its course along the coast of Ulster as far as the eastern shore of Inis Eoghain, foremost amongst its casualties were the dynastic hopes of Clann Lochlainn, which were never really to recover from their onslaught. As the Anglo-Norman tide receded, a power vacuum resulted into which rushed Ó Gormlaigh in west Tyrone, Ó Catháin in what is now Co. Derry, Ó Dónaill in east Donegal and Ó Dochartaigh in Inis Eoghain – and of course far to the east Ó Néill.

The Political Context from Eoghan to Conall

By 1600, Aodh Carrach Mac Lochlainn, head of his much-diminished sept, was living at Redcastle/*Cathair Mhic Uílín*. The defining moment for his ancestors had come in 1241 at the battle of Caméirí near Omagh, when they suffered a cataclysmic defeat and the final loss of their kingdom, already weakened by the Anglo-Normans. The victors were Aodh Ó Neill and Maoleachlainn Ó Dónaill, who had come to lend his support to this rival claimant to Mac Lochlainn. The Ó Dónaills had themselves taken the place of Ó Maoldoraidh amongst the leaders of Cineál Chonaill, in spite of the fact that they belonged to a junior branch – junior it might even be argued to Ó Dochartaigh, since the original Dochartach was in command in 727 at the battle of Droim Fornocht in the Lagán. Be that as it may, Ó Dónaill became leaders of the Cineál Lughdhach branch of Cineál Chonaill and later of the entire Cineál, going on to capture all of east Donegal.

In Inis Eoghain, Ó Dochartaigh took the place of the defeated Mac Lochlainn and spread out in various groupings over his new domain. There were five main branches: *an Ríshliocht*, the royal line, based near Derry at *Aileach Mór* (Elaghmore), the last lord of whom was Cathair Rua. There were the branches of *Muintir na hInse* (Inch), *Tuath Cranncha* (Buncrana), *Gleann Ó gCanann* (Glenogannon), *an Dumhaigh* (Doagh), *an Caisleán Nua* (Greencastle). There were also the Ó Dochartaigh branches of *Sliocht Eachmharcaigh* (Mac Cafferty); *Mac Daibhid* (McDevitt/McDaid); *Mac Dhónaill Óig* (McConologue); *Mac Fheabhail* (McCole); *Mac Giolla Bhríde* (McBride); and *Mac Ailín* (Mc Callion). So the dynasty had spread widely between 1200 and 1610, at which time Sir Arthur Chichester came into it all.

The Medieval Church in Context

As we can see, the political system under which medieval people lived was very different from ours, but it was a system that still affects the way we see ourselves today. If Inis Eoghain and a large part of east Donegal belongs in the Derry diocese, it is because the diocesan border followed the boundaries of the Mac Lochlainn kingdom of the twelfth century, and remained unaffected even by the area's subsequent conquest by rulers whose origin was in another diocese, Raphoe. The monastery of Derry, long the treasure of Cineál Eoghain, came to be identified with Cineál Chonaill and Ó Dónaill though less so, strangely, with Ó Dochartaigh. Parishes as we know them now have their origin in the lesser political lordships or *clann* divisions within each kingdom in the late twelfth and thirteenth centuries.

We can see this particularly in Inis Eoghain, where many of the parish churches were dedicated to St Colm Cille and his successors, indicating a new pattern of religious practice replacing the cult of earlier saints. The cult of these saints has become vague and sometimes dissociated from the original location, with the result, for example, that there is a doubt about the relationship between St Máine and Cluain Máine. Even a prominent early saint like Mura has made little impression on tradition, oral or written, even though he was important enough to be made a part of Cineál Eoghain (by being given a trumped-up genealogical relationship with the Cineál), and although he was recognised as an author and biographer and had worthy disciples in Fahan – Colmán Iomramha, an explorer like St Brendan, and Fotha na Canóine, expert on Scripture and canon law.

Similarly, only the genealogies of Comhghall of Both Chonais and of Dáigh, artist in metal work to St Ciarán of Clonmacnois, survive. Saint Breacán's genealogy goes on to add that his feast day is 16 July, and that he was 'lord and abbot of Má Bhile or Cluain Chatha in Inis Eoghain'. Saint Comhghall's feast was on 4 September and that of St Dáigh on 18 August. Most of the thirty-two saints, male and female, with genealogies indicating descent from Eoghan remain little more than names. Some like Éigneach of Desertegny and Muirdhealach of Malin do not even have a genealogy. We can deduce from the placename *Díseart Éignigh* that Éigneach might have been a hermit, but we can no longer know whether he was a genuine solitary in what would have been then a comparative wilderness, or whether he belonged to some larger monastic establishment like Fahan. The only thing certain is that he must have been a remarkable man (grammatically, the name is masculine) to have left such a lasting impression. Perhaps unsurprisingly, any of the women saints that we can trace belonged to the convent at Urney.

It makes sense that in the course of a millennium and a half of Christian living, there must have been many churches in succession in any given area. What we need to bear in mind is that parishes as we know them are the creation, and in Inis Eoghain probably indicate the divisions, of the area associated with the branches of Ó Dochartaigh and other prominent *clann* groupings (bearing in mind that not everyone in a *clann* would have shared the same descent nor had the same surname). It is also worth keeping in mind that the Church itself would have undergone some sort of important reshaping every three to four hundred years or so.

Church Renewal in Inis Eoghain

The control by kings and secular lords of Church appointments was the root cause of much of that decline in Church life which provoked the movement of reform and renewal all over western Europe in the eleventh and twelfth centuries. While a similar need for renewal was as evident in the Irish Church of the time, the explanation was somewhat different. While the continental situation was due to the original incorporation of Church offices like bishop or abbot into the political administration, the Irish situation could be ascribed to two things: firstly, the early Irish Church had never successfully organised a way of maintaining its secular clergy, and secondly the system which did grow up fell victim to Irish customs of inheritance in a social system based on kindreds.

In early Ireland, political organisation was a grid of little kingships or states (*tuatha*), which numbered in the whole island about one hundred and fifty. There was a bishop in each *tuath* who was responsible for those things that are the prerogative of a bishop: ordaining priests, preaching and acting as *anamchara* or spiritual director, to the king of the *tuath* and its people. As the Church came gradually to be based on monasteries, following the model developed by St Martin of Tours in Gaul (France), the bishop was often a monk in the major monastery while actual power and jurisdiction in the *tuath* was exercised by the abbot. As these monasteries and their communities grew, there were obvious dangers of secularisation, and indeed the day came when there were actual brawls between monasteries, especially after the disruption caused by the Viking inroads. Monks came to be rather lay tenants on monastic lands and often the abbot himself was a layman, generally a member of the local ruling dynasty in the *tuath*. If monasteries viewed their importance in political rather than religious terms, there was an obvious need for reform. Ireland did not as yet have a diocesan system such as existed on the continent. Neither did it have the large towns on which the continental bishoprics were based.

The continent of course had its own problems: a papacy saved from the control of the Roman mob only to fall under that of the German emperors. Often the emperor's or the king's cronies were appointed to Church benefices and usually not for reasons of suitability. The long struggle for reform associated with Pope Gregory VII (under his original name Hildebrand) was to lead to some measure of freedom of appointment in the Church and to an immense renewal of Christian living throughout Europe. Many Irish monks played their part in this on the continent, including one of the founders of the Benedictine monastery of St James at Regensburg in Germany, Blessed *Muireadhach Mac Rabhartaigh* (Marianus Scotus II), who was almost certainly an Ó Ceallaigh of Fahan in origin, and whose family were to become the custodians of *Cathach Cholm Cille*, the Psalter of Columba, the halidom borne before Ó Dónaill into battle.

Because of what they learned from experience on the continent, from the system developed in England by William the Conqueror and Archbishops Lanfranc and St Anselm, and from the reforms initiated in Scotland by St Margaret and her husband Malcolm III 'Ceann Mór', son of Donncha (Shakespeare's *Duncan*), the Twelfth-Century Reform in Ireland went forward, associated in our minds with the name of St Malachy, but in fact brought to completion by High King Muircheartach Mac Lochlainn and by Archbishop Giolla Mac Liag Mac Ruairí (St Gelasius), former Abbot of Derry. This involved the creation of territorial dioceses, which in turn led to the development of parishes, on the lines already referred to.

The Institution of Airchinneach or 'Erenagh'

In the process of reform in Ireland, perhaps the masterstroke was the organisation of a system to support and sustain the secular clergy that this new parish system would call for, and yet which would reconcile in itself the practical demands of the new situation and the customs of a highly traditional society. The centrepiece of this reorganised system was the office of *airchinneach* or, as anglicised centuries later, the 'erenagh'. While the title was a traditional term, the actual role would be very new. The holders of this office credited the original idea to the High King Dónall Dábhaill.

Wealth at the time was measured in land. The system devised set aside in each of these new parishes a number of *bailte bó* (townlands), usually four in number, sometimes more, specifically to support the church building and clergy. These *bailte bó* – singular, *baile bó* – were usually part of the best land in the parish, which would seem to suggest that the choice had the support of a powerful central figure, probably the king, as well as the local lords.

Since all professional occupations at the time – poetic, legal, medical – were passed on in the name, the same became true of the administrator and farmer of the churchlands of the parish. He was given the title that had been the title of the superior in charge of monastic lands (who was often a layman, since many monasteries had ceased to exist in any real sense of the term 'monastic'), that of *airchinneach*, or, transcribed as we have said, 'erenagh'.

At first the position of *airchinneach* was viewed as a quasi-clerical state and the occupant had to receive tonsure, but this seems to have fallen into abeyance. As well as exploiting the churchlands, it was the charge of the *airchinneach* to pay annual tithes to the bishop, to receive and cater for the bishop on visitation, and together with the rector (or parish priest), to care for the church buildings and residences, and provide hospitality for travellers, pilgrims and so forth.

In those days, long before the Council of Trent set up seminaries in the sixteenth century, priests were formed by apprenticeship, as in any other occupation. As a result, the erenagh must have had a significant role in the training and education of the clergy, since in the nature of things over the years, he and his family would build up considerable experience of matters ecclesiastical. Later, records would show that the erenagh was often a man of some education himself and that erenagh families tended to produce many of the vocations to the parochial clergy from their own ranks.

He was appointed and could be removed by the bishop – thus ensuring Church control over Church property. On the death or removal of the holder, appointment would probably have been from another collateral branch of the family, possibly as in political office from within the *deirbhfhine*, and might have been more necessary than would appear at first sight if we consider how rare it is for any business today to pass on intact to a third or fourth generation in the direct line. The drawback with the system is obvious. The temptation was strong to retain as much of the income from parish lands as possible in the hands of the family, which meant that the clergy of any given parish might be qualified by relationship to the erenagh rather than by learning or worthiness of life.

Who were the Local Erenaghs?
The following are the erenagh families of Inis Eoghain as accurately as we can reconstitute them:

- *Cluain Chatha*/Cloncha: Ó hEarcáin (Harkin); Ó Maolmhochéirí (Loughrey); Mac Lochlainn at Greallach, known as *Clann Lochlainn Ghreallaigh*; Ó Dubhgáin at the grange in Cullourt belonging to the Cistercian monastery of Má Coscáin (Macosquin, near Coleraine);
- *Cluain Máine*/Clonmany: Ó Muireasáin/Morrison (Bryson), who was also the custodian there of the *míosach Cholm Cille*, and wore special vestments when he bore the sacred emblem into battle before Ó Dochartaigh. Clonmany had extensive churchlands, more than most parishes, including Dunally, which was free to Donncha Ó Muireasáin, described as *comharba an aba*, 'successor of the abbot'. The abbot was probably St Máine, since *comharba Cholm Cille* lived in Derry;
- *Cúl Dabhcha*/Culdaff: Ó Dufaigh (Duffy), also the custodians of St Buadán's Bell;
- *Díseart Éignigh*/Desertegny: Mac Rodaigh (Magroddy, Roddy);
- *Domhnach Mór Glinne Tóchair*/Donagh: Mac Colgáin (McColgan);
- *Fathain Mhura*/Fahan: Ó Dónaill – sliocht Mhic Néill at Litir, sliocht Mhuircheartaigh at Lisbannagh (Lisfannon?); Muintir Shiail ('mounterheiles' according to the planters, Shields) at Sleave and Millquarter. The Abbot of Derry was Rector of Fahan;
- *Má Bhile*/Moville: Ó Dochartaigh – Sliocht Uilliam Duibh and Mánas Mac Maoleachlainn at Cooley; and Mac Lochlainn at Teevenagallan. In later medieval times, the rector (parish priest) of Moville was also parish priest of Culdaff and the parishes were permanently united. (*In the above*, sliocht *means descendants, sept or sub-branch of a family*)

The extensive parish of Teampall Mór (Templemore) included lands around Derry and into Inis Eoghain, the granges of Inch and 'Drumheard' (probably Burt), and Iskaheen. This was to support not merely the bishop (who had mensal lands, Castlequarter and Machaire Beag, and an official residence, no doubt a tower house, at Fahan), but also the dean of the diocese who was Rector of Templemore. The bishop also had mensal lands at Magilligan.

Many of the surnames on the previous page do not occur in the official genealogies, indicating that they were very anciently established in their area. Ó Muireasáin was clearly so well rooted in Clonmany that the new rulers Ó Dónaill and Ó Dochartaigh had to accommodate him by assuring his charge of the *Míosach*. Many of the other surnames pre-date the arrival of Ó Dochartaigh as we have already seen. Ó Brolcháin (now Bradley) is often mentioned in connection with Both Chonais. They did indeed belong to Cineál Eoghain, being descended from King Suibhne Meann, but the medieval historical record shows them in association with Armagh, where they seem to have been related to Clann Síonaigh, the opponents of Church reform in the twelfth century. Maol Íosa Ó Brolcháin (d. 1086), poet, hymnodist, theologian, was recognised as a saint with feast day on 16 January.

The fact that St Colm Cille is patron of Cloncha, Clonmany and Moville (as well as two of his successors at Iona, St Buadán in Culdaff and St Adhamhnán or Eunan at Greallach), indicates a later stratum of religious practice, dating probably from the rise in importance of Derry in the Church. Saint Mura of Fahan was acceptable in this new dispensation because he was the biographer of Colm Cille, and of course St Patrick was beyond challenge. Éigneach too remains prominent although given a connection with Colm Cille, but Ultán, Órán, Muirdhealach, Aonghas, Diúcholl and others were kept alive only in popular memory or in a placename.

'Rome-Runners'

One of the unforeseen and less desirable consequences of the great Twelfth-Century Reform and the new status of the papacy was the increasing centralisation of the Church with the emergence of a Roman secretariat and civil service, which as ever had to be paid for. One of the ways of doing this developed by Pope Clement IV was to decree a tax on those appointed to ecclesiastical benefices. This amounted initially to the first year's revenue and thus called the 'annates'. Dispensations to hold benefices became necessary for those carrying some legal impediment to promotion to a benefice. Many of these dispensations could only be granted by the papal court, which by this time had moved from Rome to Avignon in southern France on its seventy-year exile there (1309–76). Avignon was more accessible than Rome, which started the habit of presenting oneself in person to argue one's case or to claim a benefice. The man on the spot had all the advantages, particularly if there was a dispute. There was also the advantage that the papal secretary did not know, or maybe care, about the details of a problem from a distant country amongst people whose names he could scarcely write down accurately. Distance was not as great a problem for them as we might think at first, and there were places of hospitality and countrymen at each stage of their journey, not least in Rome itself.

The clergy of Inis Eoghain seem to have been more prone or maybe more adept at using the canon law to put their case. Why this should be so is unclear, but it may have something to do with supporters and allies of the new Ó Dochartaigh lords moving in on a structure of office-holders already in existence, as also happened in the Limavady area where Ó Catháin set about ousting the Mac Thaidhg erenaghs from their position. The happy result of this passion for litigation, from our point of view, is that we have in records of papal taxation, papal letters and rescripts, a much fuller list of the clergy of Inis Eoghain, both rectors (parish priests) and vicars (curates), than are available for most of the rest of the diocese.

Because of the facility and promptness with which these benefice-hunters took off for Rome to seek their fortune, they have earned the nickname of 'Rome-runners'. As good an example as any is Seán Mac Giolla Bhríde, no doubt of Ó Dochartaigh ancestry as we saw above, who contested the deanery of Derry in the fifteenth century with Diarmaid Mac Bhloscaidh (Mc Closkey) of the erenagh family of Faughanvale and with Dónall Ó Cearbhalláin (Carolan) of the erenagh family of Clonleigh (Lifford), and who visited Rome no less than five times that we know of to put his case forward. Were it not for the eagerness of these men for advancement, we would not merely not know of their existence, but with the destruction that occurred in the course of the seventeenth century, particularly to Church records as a result of war and plantation, an interesting insight would be closed off to us into a system of Church organisation which stood firmly for four hundred years, to some satisfaction as far as one can tell, and only fell as a result of pressures from without.

The Deanery of Binneach (North Derry)

Tamlaght Finlagan, a Scottish Dimension

The name of the parish of Tamlaght Finlagan has retained so much of its Gaelic origins that a word of explanation may not go amiss. Most of our townland names and traditional parish names are of course hundreds of years old and with the erosion of time the elements which constitute the name of the parish have been changed both in form and meaning. In the case of Tamlaghtfinlagan, these elements are three in number: *támh* and *leacht* and *Fionnlugh*. *Támh* originally meant 'a plague' and soon came quite understandably to signify 'death'; *leacht* meant 'a funeral mound' and together they indicated 'a graveyard'. Fionnlugh is the local patron saint, so that *támhleacht Fhionnlughan* means 'St Fionnlugh's graveyard'.

The first interesting thing to be noted is the antiquity of the word *támhleacht*. Along with two other elements found in many placenames, *cealdrach* and *cloigeann* ('skull'; found in the name Cleggan), it indicates the presence of a very early graveyard, possibly even pre-Christian. Associated with a church, it suggests that the church was built at or near a very early cemetery or sacred site. The original meaning would even suggest a place of mass burial, since such would have been the result of a pestilence, and a reason for a burial mound. The word *támhleacht* then clearly had a sacred connotation and became quite common in parish names. In Co. Derry alone, we find Tamhlaghtard (*ard*, high) at Magilligan, and Tamlaghtocrilly (*Támhleacht Uí Chroiligh/* O'Crilly's cemetery) at Clady/Greenlough. It probably came to mean a graveyard simply. There is also Moydamlaght (*Maigh dTámhleachta*) at Moneyneana near Draperstown, (the 'clearing or plain of the cemetery'). These sites were often marked by a *lia*, or standing-stone, at or on the mound, and it is to be noted that one of the *bailte bó* or townlands making up the churchlands of the parish was Cloghfyn/*Cloch Fhionn*, which means 'white or bright stone'. We will have more to say presently on the subject of churchlands.

Many of these early churches now stand in remote places, making us wonder why on earth they were built there. It is salutary to remind ourselves that our modern roads connect us with important places and towns that did not exist at that time. Early churches are often an indication of where people actually lived then. Many of our towns date only from the fifteenth century, like Castlederg, Newtown (stewart) and Omagh; Strabane and Lifford date from very early in the sixteenth, to say nothing of modern post-Plantation towns like Moneymore, Cookstown or Draperstown. Others are early, like Maghera, Dungiven or Derry, Limavady or Coleraine, but the centre of the modern towns has moved somewhat from the early foundation.

The Patron Saint and his Name

Once again the saint's name is composed of two elements, Fionn and Lugh. *Fionn* has come to mean 'fair' as in 'fair-haired' or 'fair-complexioned'. It was also the name of the archetypal wise man of Gaelic legend *Fionn File*, whose preternatural powers were passed on to another *Fionn*, the mythological warrior-cum-seer, *Fionn mac Cumhaill*. He alas has come down in the world from having been the leader of a redoubtable army, the *Fianna*, to being seen merely as the thrower of lumps of rock across *Sruth na Maoile* (the north Channel) from Co. Antrim to Staffa, a giant called Finn McCool!

Lugh or *Lú* as he would be pronounced in Irish today was a Celtic pagan god whose name is found in the names of places all over western Europe: Lyon, Leiden, Laudun, Laon, Lauzun and so on. He was known as *Lámhfhada* 'of the long arm' because of the range of his weapons, javelin and sling. He was also called *sámhildánach*, 'possessing all the arts'. He was associated with a fertility cult that centred on the harvest (a time of life or death for those dependent on subsistence agriculture), whose celebratory feast at the start of August gives us the Irish word for August, *Lughnasa* (now *Lúnasa*), and is probably the origin of the Auld Lammas Fair.

In early Ireland, a great annual fair, a sort of Gaelic Olympics was held in his honour, *Aonach Tailteann* (Teltown, Co. Meath), where communal activities and games like horse-racing, ball-games and *ficheall*, an Irish form of chess, took place. The marvellous mythical role of Lugh and his evil grandfather *Balar* ('the one-eyed') has a local connection in that the famous cow, the *Glas Gaibhleann*, belonging to *Gaibhleann*, blacksmith to the gods, used to be milked at *Dún Bó* ('fort of the cow') and was housed at *Leaba na Glaise* ('the bed of the *Glas*', Labby near Draperstown)! The point of all this is to show how early, how near paganism, we must place our saint.

Nowadays, *Támhleacht Fhionnlughan* would be pronounced 'towlachtinluan' in modern Irish. The fact that the *gh* is found in the spelling of the name in Irish and that its effect has carried over into English pronunciation (Finlagin) means that the placename dates back to a time when the *gh* was pronounced, at least a thousand years. The pronunciation of 'St Finlough' in English comes from the confusion with the word *loch*/lough, with which it has of course no connection whatever.

To consider Fionnlugh as a person, we must replace him in the context of the society in which he lived. It was, above all, an aristocratic world in which 'blue blood' was all-important. Right down until the collapse of that world with the defeat of the Irish in the Nine Years War and the Plantation of Ulster, it was customary to preserve quite elaborate genealogical pedigrees. The genealogy of St Fionnlugh reads as follows: 'Fionnlugh and Fiontán, both sons of Díomán, son of Finghin, son of Deamán, son of Caireall (who believed in Christ), son of Muireadhach Muindearg ("red-back").'

The latter was King of the Ulaidh, towards the close of the fifth century. By the time of Muireadhach (pronounced 'murreeach'), modern Muiriach, the Ulaidh controlled only modern Antrim and Down of the province named after them. Muireadhach is said to have been confirmed 'in the kingship of Ireland' by St Patrick, which is useful in that it gives us a rough date; but note the attention given to his son Caireall, which might indicate that Muireadhach 'did not believe in Christ'. Muireadhach belonged to the Dál Fiatach people based in what is now Co. Down. One of the many saints, said to be descended, from Muireadhach is St Mura, Abbot and founder of Fahan. Fiontán, Fionnlugh's brother, was venerated as a saint at Dún Bleisce in Co. Limerick.

The martyrologies give St Fionnlugh's feast day as 3 January, although that of Tallaght places him at Dún Bleisce in Limerick, confusing him with his brother Fiontán. The *Martyrology of Oengus* gives Dún Bleisce also but corrects the location in its notes to 'Támhleacht Fhionnlughan in Cianacht Glinne Geimhin'. In the body of the calendar it describes him as *dearbh*, meaning 'steady', but this might only be in the interests of internal assonance in the poetic line. In the notes it explains his name as 'Lughaidh Fionn'. Lughaidh has come to be seen as the equivalent of the name Louis/Ludovicus/Aloysius, but in origin the names are quite different, Lughaidh also being derived from the god Lugh. Yet another Lughaidh is patron saint of Clonleigh (Lifford).

It is accepted that Fionnlugh is the monk 'Finluganus' in Adamnán's *Life of Colm Cille* who saved the life of the saint when he was attacked by the spear-wielding member of the warband of Conall, son of Dónall, whose family Colm Cille had excommunicated for 'persecuting churches'. Finluganus, we are told, stepped between Colm Cille and his attacker. He happened to be wearing Colm Cille's cowl, which the spear failed to pierce. This is said to have happened on the island of Hinba, where Colm Cille had established a monastery dependent on Iona. It cannot now be identified with certainty. Some think it is Eileachneave/ *Eileach an Naoimh*, where Colm Cille's mother is reputed to be buried; others prefer Jura or Colonsay.

Fionnlugh and Scotland

Adamnán's story connects Fionnlugh firmly with Scotland, and Fionnlugh is venerated in Scotland, in the Western Isles, especially on the island of Islay. This was the Scottish base of *Cineál Aonghasa*, one of the branches of the Dál Riada people who colonised western Scotland from north Antrim, gave their name (the Irish were the original *Scoti*) and their language to the north of the British island then called Alba. Many Scots placenames and surnames are Gaelic as a result, and Gaelic was the language of the Scots court until the thirteenth century (hence Shakespeare's *Macbeth* and Malcolm would have been Gaelic-speakers).

Cineál Aonghasa were not the ruling family of Dál Riada. This would suggest that Fionnlugh went to a people to whom he was related and who spoke his language, perhaps as a missionary, perhaps not. It is hard to be certain what the religious status of Cineál Aonghasa would have been at that stage. Scotland would appear almost to have been the fashionable place for an eager young would-be missionary to go to at the time, as proved by St Colm Cille, St Donnán, the martyr of Eigg, St Maolrubha of Applecross (*Abar Crosáin*) across from Skye, and St Cainneach (whose name is preserved in Termoncanice – he was a native of the Roe valley – and also in Kilkenny, and is remembered by the Scots as Kenneth). Some women went there too, like St Caointiarna/ Kentigerna from Leinster who was widowed, went to Scotland and became a hermit on an island in Loch Lomond.

Fionnlugh and Islay

The Islay, or *Íle* in Gaelic, to which St Fionnlugh went, became centuries later the capital of the Lord of the Isles, Mac Dónaill (MacDonald/ McConnell) at Finlaggan Castle on the banks of Loch Finlaggan, where both loch and castle take their name from the saint. The Mac Donalds were Vikings who settled, governed western Scotland, became Gaelic-speaking, devoted to St Colm Cille, claimed descent from the *Airghialla* of south Ulster and repaid the compliment to their Dál Riada origins by being involved as mercenaries in Irish wars and taking over north Antrim. The Earls of Antrim belong to *Clann Dónaill*.

On an island in Loch Finlagan lie the ruins of St Fionnlugh's church, built by *Eoin Íle*, or John of Islay, Mac Dhónaill Lord of the Isles, who died in 1386. The church of the nearby parish of Kilgarrow was dedicated to St Maolrubha, the missionary mentioned already, and had a rector (or parish priest) and a vicar (curate). By the late-Middle Ages the rectory of a church in the diocese of Sodor (*Isle of Man*) and the Islands, according to a bull of Pope Paul III, was attached to the parish of Urney, diocese of Derry; the diocese presumably receiving its income and appointing the parson in question (*parson* in English, from Latin *persona*, is anther name for 'rector', the ecclesiastic who held the benefice).

Bishop Reeves suggests, and there seems little doubt about it, that this was the church of Kilgarrow. There were also on Islay dry-stone chapels dedicated to early Irish saints: Sléibhine of Iona, Ciarán, Cainneach, Lasair and Comán. These were probably founded in medieval times by the Christianised Norse inhabitants of the island. It seems reasonable to maintain that the presence of St Fionnlugh goes back much earlier than this since Loch Finlaggan retains his name in an island where most placenames were replaced by Viking names in Old Norse. In those days, before the creation of seminaries, aspirant priests were educated by apprenticeship, and sometimes a rectory like this may have been used to provide financial support for such. It is still more than a little mysterious, not least because Urney started out as a convent, founded by St Cognat (modern Irish Cónait).

Fionnlugh by the Roe
It is not clear whether Fionnlugh came back to Ireland or whether he lived and died in Scotland. This raises the question as to whether the church here was founded by St Fionnlugh in person, or whether it was simply dedicated to him after his death. As his genealogy shows, he had no necessary connection with this area. Perhaps he returned to Ireland, as did St Cainneach, and founded a church close to Cainneach's people in *Cianacht Glinne Geimhin*. Perhaps the close relationship between Colm Cille and Cainneach had some bearing on the matter, even if the only association Colm Cille has with this part of the country is his presence at the Convention of Droim Ceat. However that may be, there is no compelling reason for saying that Fionnlugh visited the area. Perhaps even his name and reputation were used by others to christianise the pagan 'támhleacht'.

The History of the Parish

At this distance in time we know little about the early history of Támhleacht Fhionnlughan. When light begins to break again we find the parish mentioned in records of papal taxation. From about the year 1400, partly to finance the policy of centralisation implemented during the exile of the popes at Avignon in France, partly to exercise some control of local misdemeanours, the papacy began to take to itself the right to provide to local benefices in the Church in certain circumstances. (A benefice is a Church office or position to which one is promoted by authority, for example that of parish priest.) Some positions in local churches were left vacant for years so that someone else might benefit from any emoluments attached to it. If a benefice-holder died in Rome, Rome reserved the right to replace him. One result of this practice was that there developed a type of cleric called the 'Rome-runner', someone who made it his business to get to Rome first, or to get to Rome with a request that someone else should be removed from a benefice and presenting evidence of that present holder's unworthiness. *Ecclesia semper reformanda*, as we are reminded: the Church always needs reforming! While one might wish to deplore such abuse, it has had the inestimable benefit that the Roman Curia kept records. While they were unfamiliar with the sort of Christian names that the Irish or Polish or other distant peoples bore and frequently made a mess of spelling them, the clerks in the Curia give us a tiny glimpse of what was happening in Támhleacht Fhionnlughan.

Now, the most influential Church benefice in this part of north Derry was at the time a *corbania* called *Tearmann Chainnigh*. To clarify this, it must be explained that a *corbania* was an exceptional group of parishes permanently joined into a union (Today we might say a 'cluster'). The head of this group had the title of *comharba* (or coarb), said to be the lineal descendant of those who gave the site in the first place. The *comharba* was therefore the successor of the saintly founder of the Church. In the case of the Limavady area, this was the prominent St Cainneach (or Canice), whose name was therefore given to the union: *Tearmann Chainnigh* (or Termoncanice).

This office of *comharba* was of considerable distinction in the medieval Irish Church, shown by its holder having the privilege, usually reserved to the aristocracy, of being addressed by his surname alone. He summed up, as it were, the whole sept or family in his person and only the head of such a sept had that right. Since the union or *tearmann* (from Latin *terminus*) had privileges such as the right of sanctuary, the *Comharba Chainnigh* was known as a *tearmannach* or termoner. It is not always clear whether he was a priest but he was often the rector of this union of parishes, which included Aghanloo (Áth Fhionnlugha), and Balteagh (Both Dhá Fhiach), but not Támhleacht Fhionnlughan. We note that they do not record any rector/parish priest of Tamlaghtfinlagan; the parish existed as a parish independent of the *corbania*, yet the rectors' names have not been recorded.

Political and Economic Background

In the later Middle Ages, the lords of what is now north Derry were, of course, Ó Catháin (O'Cahan, O'Kane). They had come originally from modern east Donegal, whence they were ousted by Clann Diarmada (Ó Caireallain/Kerlin) and by Cineál Moain (Ó Gormlaigh). They made their way from there to the Roe valley, overcame its rulers, the Ó Conchúir (O'Connor) Kings of Cianacht (the barony of Keenaught), and established their own power in their stead. In such circumstances it was of course only the ruling class that changed at first, although in the nature of things once installed they began to expand. Eventually they had castles at Limavady, Enagh near Derry and Dungiven, a residence near Coleraine, and had spread their authority into north Antrim and the Glenelly valley of Tyrone. Before their arrival and up to about 1400, the *corbania/comharbacht* of Cainneach was in the custody of Mac Thaidhg (now McKeague/Montague) who belonged genealogically, as did St Cainneach, to the Cianacht people, until they were squeezed out by Ó Catháin.

Thus, by the time that the parish of Tamlaght Finlagan begins to figure in the records, the *comharba* of Termoncanice is an Ó Catháin. Ó Catháin is also described as erenagh of Tamlaght Finlagan. This term, as we have explained elsewhere, indicates the system by which parishes were financed at the time. Nowadays this is done by the voluntary contributions of the parishioners. In Germany, on the other hand, priests and ministers are paid by the state. In France local government is responsible for the upkeep of church buildings, an expense often resented. There are then very different ways of doing this. In medieval Ireland, it was achieved by setting aside land in each parish that was farmed to provide fodder for horses, corn for bread, meat and milk and vegetables for the table. The person charged with the administration of this land was called the *aircheannach* in Irish, a word that would become 'erenagh' in English. He was appointed by the bishop of the diocese and could not be removed. The system had been established by civil authority – it is said by Dónall Dábhaill, ancestor of Mac Lochlainn and King of Aileach (near Derry) in the twelfth century. The system must have continued to be guaranteed by civil power because the land concerned was always good land, sometimes the best in any parish. An Ó Catháin then was, not unexpectedly, erenagh of Tamlaght Finlagan.

In most parishes there were four townlands involved but in Tamlaght Finlagan there were six:

1. Mulkeeragh (*Maol Caorach*/Sheep Hill)
2. Shanreagh (*Seanriabhach*, formerly cultivated old lea)
3. Drumnacarney (originally *Tír Mhic Cheatharnaigh*/McCarney's land)
4. Tullyhilly (*Tulach Choille*/Hill of the Wood)
5. Moneyrannel (*Muine Raghnaill*/Ronald's Hill)
6. Cloghfin (*Cloch Fhionn*/Bright Stone).

Parishioners were also to pay tithes to erenagh and clergy (as instructed in the Old Testament), which in an agricultural economy were paid in kind. It shows that this was a rich parish, a fact demonstrated by the outgoings paid to the bishop and others, which were larger than those paid by neighbouring parishes. The fact that the churchlands were so extensive would also suggest that the parish had some ecclesiastical responsibilities beyond its own church and clergy.

John Colton, the Anglo-Norman Archbishop of Armagh made an official inspection of the diocese of Derry in 1397 during an episcopal vacancy. He made note of the amount of the statutory episcopal income from each parish in the diocese. The income of the see of Derry was made up of the bishop's income as Rector of Derry itself, the *Tertia Episcopalis* (the episcopal third of each parish's income) and rents due from the erenagh of each parish. The bishop also had the right to exact 'refections', in the form of hospitality, which are not included in the parish totals and which were arbitrary.

It is of interest to compare the totals of parishes' liability. Thus *Civitas Derensis* (Derry city) was liable for twenty shillings, plus four marks from the rectory and the episcopal third paid by the *civitas*. Tamlaght Finlagan was liable for two marks *in temporalibus*, the same as Faughanvale. Aghanloo was at 13s 4d, but it and Tamlaght Finlagan are missing from the list of 'episcopal thirds'. Drumachose does not appear in either list, while Magilligan is divided in three: Duncrun 20/- *in temporalibus*, Tamlaghtard 13s.4d, and Ballinascreen *de Ardo*

6s.8d. This Ballinascreen *de Ardo* is not the Ballinascreen we recognise today, of course, although both shrines had associations with St Colm Cille. This field of parish taxation needs further examination. There must be a reason for absence of liability in the case of certain parishes, which may well have something to do with the position of the rectory.

Just as there are lacunae in regard to the financial liabilities of the parish, so too it is remarkable that we do not have the names of any of the parish priests. Whether this was because the income went towards the education of trainee priests, perhaps in another location altogether, or whether the *comharba* Ó Catháin had more personal plans for it, or whether it was impropriate (that is, annexed), to some other church, we no longer have any way of saying. In this context, it is worth noting the presence among the vicars that have survived of names that would seem to suggest a continuing connection with Scotland. We know of a few medieval vicars (or curates) in the parish from the *Annates* or papal records:

1397 Laurentius Micalmen or Mac Calmer, who met Primate Colton of Armagh. He was dead by 1413. His surname was probably *Mac Giolla Mhuire* (Gilmore), 'son of the servant of Mary'. The name occurs in medieval south-east Ulster and in Moymacilmurry, a townland in the parish of Desertmartin. A priest of the diocese, Henry MacElmurray, executed near Omagh during the 1641 war, had been parish priest in Desertmartin, before being changed to Drumragh. The name is of course also found in Gaelic Scotland.

1413 Nemeas Mackenan: *Aonghas Mac Fhionghuin*. He received dispensation *super defectu natalium*, which means either that he was the son of parents married within the forbidden degrees (third cousins) or that his father was in major orders. Though described as 'a priest of Derry' in the *Annate*, from his name he would seem to be a Scot; the Clann Mac Fhionghuin from Tiree was closely involved with Iona. The name is now McKinnon.

1414 Simon Ofynnachaich: probably Ó *Fianachta* or Ó *Fianaigh*/ Feeney.

1424 Johannes Ofyletan: a Fullen from Co. Derry? or a Scot: Mac Gille Chatain?

1425 Patritius Mackamay: *Mac Thomaidh* (Scots McCombie)? or maybe a truncated version of *Mac Cathmhaoil*/McCaul/ Campbell from nearby Dunboe.

1497 Donaldus Machqunnair: *Mac Conchúir*/MacConnacher/ Mac Naugher? The only mention of the name MacConnacher occurs on Islay in 1541. It is not the same name as Ó Conchúir, formerly Kings of Keenaught.

1498 Goffredus okahan: Gothraí Ó Catháin. Gothraí/Geoffrey was a common name among the Ó Catháin.

1631 Vicar Olynne: no Christian name given; probably *Ó Luain*/ O'Lone, a name associated with the parish of Tamlaghtard Magilligan in medieval times.

These names would seem to show some ongoing connection over centuries between Tamlaght Finlagan in Ireland and the church of St Fionnlugh on Islay, which survived the Viking conquest of western Scotland and was re-established after their conversion and Gaelicisation, and after the formation of the Mac Dhónaill Lordship of the Isles, the strongpoint of which was at Finlaggan Castle, named, like Loch Finlaggan, from the saint. History has still the capacity to surprise.

After the last entry and the Plantation of Ulster, the parish of Tamlaght Finlagan disappears from sight in Catholic Church organisation, and becomes part of the larger entity now called Limavady, which included Magilligan up to quite recently.

Churches of the Roe

The ruins of the narrow medieval churches of the Roe valley at Banagher, Balteagh, Bovevagh, Tamlaghtfinlagan, Drumachose, Aghanloo and Magilligan give the impression that they were designed about the same time. That they are narrow is no doubt due to the span of roof that could be supported. The priory at Dungiven is of course different, probably because its origins and aim were different.

It stands to reason that these represent a later generation of churches in an area long Christian and borne out by the names of their patrons. There are those associated only with the parishes along the Roe, and others whose repute was also widespread in western Scotland. This is most obviously true of Cainneach, known in Scotland now as Kenneth, who was amongst the great missionary and monastic figures both in Ireland and in Scotland, in company that included Colm Cille, Maolrubha, Aodhán/Aidan, Donnán, Brendan and Adhamhnán/Adamnán/Eunan.

It is said that Cainneach grew up among the Cianachta of Gleann Geimhin, but his genealogy shows him to have been of Ulaidh origin, son of Luiteach in Dál Dalláin of Síol Ír east of the Bann. Although not stated anywhere, it may be that he was fostered among the Cianachta. Cainneach is associated with Aghaboe (Co. Laois) and with *Cill Chainnigh*/Kilkenny, which bears his name, as does *Tearmann Chainnigh*/Termoncanice on the Roe. Traditionally, the head of the Church there was called *Comharba Chainnigh*/'successor of St Cainneach'. Apart from that, his connection with the area seems to rest on his link with the Cianachta without evidence of him visiting there in adulthood other than in tradition – not to be rejected out of hand, of course. There is however another factor involved in the story.

Alan Macniven has drawn attention to one of the unrecorded results of the Norse invasion of the mainland and isles of western Scotland. He points out that, according to the Norse sagas, none of the inhabitants of the island of Islay had any trouble communicating with Norse speakers from Iceland or Norway, and that none of them are said to speak Gaelic. Combined with the number of Norse placenames there he suggests that in an abrupt change, Norse language and culture penetrated every level of society on the island. He concludes: 'Unpleasant as it may seem, the most likely explanation for this development is one of ethnic cleansing.' When subdued, the natives would have to be killed or at the very least enslaved and sent abroad in large numbers, either 'to fight as *Gall-Ghaeil* (Viking Gaels) on the battlefields of Ireland, or, the less durable specimens, for sale on the slave-markets of Viking Dublin and Bristol'. The cleansing was substantial, although not necessarily total, but Islay disappears from the records for a couple of hundred years, to return as Gaelic-speaking, of course including the descendants of those early Norse settlers, who had become Christian in the meantime.

If a sizable number of the inhabitants fled or were expelled, one must ask where they may have gone. Alan Macniven points out that by the mid-840s the Gaelic kingdom of Dál Riada was ruled by a Pictish dynasty based in northeast Scotland. They in turn were under pressure from the aggressive Anglo-Saxon kingdom of Wessex to the south. Anyone fleeing western Scotland would scarcely have been welcome among the Picts to the east, the Anglo-Saxons to the south or among the Norse coming from the north. Travel by sea being safer than on land at the time, the most accessible escape route was to the west where there were people with whom they had close links, built up over years in language, social system and, in some cases, close blood relationship. In addition, the area was reasonably secure from the Norse, insofar as anywhere was, because of the strength of the Kings of *Cineál Eoghain*. It makes sense that they should come to the valley of the Roe.

It would appear that, when they came, they brought with them their religious practice and their saints. While Mary was the patron of the medieval priory at Dungiven, each of these parishes has a patron venerated in Scotland. Neachtan Néir of Dungiven had a church dedicated in his memory at Kilnaughton in Islay. The monastery of Iona had considerable land holdings in western Scotland and saints associated with Colm Cille and Iona are found frequently as titular saints: Sléibhín, abbot at Kilslevan; Eithne, Colm's mother, at Kilmeny; Aodhán/Aidan at Kileayan, all on Islay. Islay also holds Loch Finlaggan, capital of the Lordship of the Isles, and Killegan, which recall Fionnlugh, the monk who saved Colm Cille's life from murderous attack. Like Cainneach, Fionnlugh was of north Antrim descent. History is silent as to whether he ever visited the Roe valley in person. Saints associated with Iona are:

Adhamhnán/Adamnán/Eunan, abbot and writer, Aodhán/Aidan, abbot-founder of Lindisfarne and missionary to northern England, and Dubhdúin, abbot. Venerated in Scotland also were St Comán and St Maolrubha, and of course St Ninian of Candida Casa/Whithorn (Galloway), teacher of so many of the saints, including St Eoghan/Eugene, St Tiarnach and St Cairbre of Coleraine.

When we transpose all these names with Scots connections onto a map of the Roa valley and environs we find Neachtán at Dungiven, Adhamhnán at Errigal and Bovevagh. Ringán, said by tradition to be another patron of Bovevagh, turns out to be Ninian, for, just as in the north Gaelic *cnoc* is pronounced *croc*, so 'Sanct Ninian' is pronounced 'Sanc' rinian'. Interestingly, amongst the patrons of churches on Islay is St Comán of Kilchoman (*Tearmann Chomáin* was a medieval name for Termonmaguirk/Carrickmore, which has strong Columban associations too), as well as St Fionnán at Kilfennan, which calls to mind Kilfennan in Glendermott at Derry, and St Fionnán at Moville.

319

Perhaps then Aidan of Magilligan is not simply a confused version of Cadán, disciple of St Patrick, but is in origin a tribute to the life and works of Aodhán/Aidan of Lindisfarne, monk of Iona, and of Killeyan, Islay. Similarly, that Dubhdúin, at a time Abbot of Iona, may be the Dubhdúin of *Ath Lunga*, Aghanloo. Saint Finlaggan/Fionnlugh, the monk whose presence is so markedly remembered on Islay, is of course patron of Tamlaghtfinlaggan (Ballykelly).

In addition to these saints with a Scottish reputation these parishes have their local saints. Muireadhach Ó hÉanaigh at Banagher is medieval and is known only from oral tradition. The patron of Aghanloo is said to be Lugh, but both parts of the name Aghanloo, whether pronounced Aghanloo or Annaloo, are open to surmise. Other saints invoked were Colmán at Balteagh, Aodhán of Cianachta descent at Bovevagh, Eolach also of the Cianachta at Drumachose, Cadán and Beo-Aodh at Magilligan. Cainneach was also patron of medieval Faughanvale that replaced the earlier church of *Magh Dula* (Moigh near Eglinton), where Béascna, said to be a member of St Patrick's retinue, was the patron. Strangely, one person to whom we might expect to find some reference in the valley does not occur at all, St Cianán of Damhliag/Duleek (Co. Meath), also a native son.

If this influx of settlers from Scotland made such an impact we can only wonder how the local Cianachta received it. They had been rewarded with land in the Roe valley for help as mercenary soldiers in the defeat of the Ulaidh at the battle of Crinna. The Ulaidh, having given their name to Ulster (Cúige Uladh)), retreated to what is now Co. Down to become *Dál Fiatach* or as *Dál Riada* to north Antrim and western Scotland. In something the same way, the northern Uí Néill (descendants of Niall Naoighiallach) assisted as mercenaries in civil war amongst the Cruithnigh at the battle of *Móin Mór Doire Lothair* in 557 and were rewarded with land at *Magh Lí* (north of the Moyola) and at *Carn Eolairg* (in Magilligan). By accepting these two areas it would look as if there was between them the land of people who were not to be disturbed, allies of the Uí Néill and already subservient, the Cianachta. Given the disturbances resulting from the strife, population density might have suffered considerably, leaving room for settlers. The Cruithnigh were to become in turn the *Dál nAraidhe* in Antrim.

At any rate, the reign of the Cianachta over their area came to an end, it would seem, with great slaughter ('deargár') at the battle of Belat in 1076 at the hands of Aodh Ó Maol Seachlainn and the Fir Maighe Iotha. Aodh (? + 1083) was probably descended from Dónall Dábhaill, brother of Niall Glúndubh, who is the progenitor of those with the surname Ó Néill. Both Dónall and Niall were High Kings of Ireland. At this time, Aodh was leading the rise of Cineál Eoghain power in central Ulster.

The name Fir Maighe Iotha (Maigh Iotha being the Finn valley) covered a grouping whose membership varied from time to time, but here almost certainly are Ó Catháin, on the move away from the internal rivalries of Clann Chonchúir in east Donegal/west Tyrone, making their way to the Roe, to the creation of a lordship that English shiring would eventually rename Co. Coleraine and later Londonderry. One of the results of their arrival at the Roe among incomers from Scotland was that they were to become interested and involved in Scots affairs and culture. In the course of time they were to join in the effort to defeat Norse incursions there and eventually to intermarry with the descendants of these same Norse invaders, Mac Dónaill/MacDonald, whose Lordship of the Isles had its capital on Eileán Mór in Loch Finlaggan on the island of Islay.

Guests at the wedding of Aongas Óg Mac Dónaill of Islay to Áine Ní Chatháin, daughter probably of Cú Mhaighe na nGall, included the Mac Bheatha medical family, later Beaton, said to descend from a member of Áine's retinue. Other Ulster guests were to be ancestors of prominent Scottish families. The River Roe is believed to provide the ending of the name Monroe. The surname Mac Causland may originate with Aisealán Buí Ó Catháin, said to have gone to Scotland to fight the Norse over a hundred years before that. This may be evidence of genealogical pride in Gaelic ancestry (traceable, allegedly, all the way back to Adam and God!) rather than historical accuracy, but it is a credible challenger to the other suggestion, that the name is a derivative of Absalon, son of Mac Bheatha, the name of a cleric in the early 1200s.

Mention of surnames raises the question as to whether Gaelic names beginning with Mac Giolla, 'son of the servant', came into use first in Scotland, with *giolla* – originally meaning 'bald' or 'shaven' (a monk, therefore) – replacing *maol*, which has the same denotation in Irish Gaelic names: Ó Maoldomhnaigh v Mac Giolla Domhnaigh, for example: (Downey/Muldowney v McEldowney).

THE DEANERY OF RÁTH LURAIGH (SOUTH DERRY)

Baile na Scríne (Ballinascreen)

Since the emergence of the 'Armagh-Clogher school of History', led by the late Cardinal Tomás Ó Fiaich, Fr Éamon Devlin, Bishop Patrick Mulligan, Fr Pádraig Ó Gallachair, Bishop Seosamh Ó Dufaigh and others, it has become accepted that history in Ireland cannot be written without local history and local history without the contribution of local knowledge. This means studying the placenames, the surnames and the *béaloideas* or traditional lore of the people on the spot and even the lie of the land, any one of which can throw a shaft of light on a topic otherwise shrouded in semi or complete darkness.

Of few parishes can this advice be more relevant than of Baile na Scríne/Ballinascreen. To the unsympathetic eye it is an unremarkable small town backed into the glens of the north Sperrins, though it still retains – certainly in the minds of its inhabitants – a sense of ancient and even sacred distinction. Not very long ago, historians were ill at ease with its legends – Cadhan Ó hInnéirí and his gluttonous *cú* or hound, the saga of the bouncing bell of Mac Oirc (Mc Gurk), or were puzzled by the former importance of the old church at the Six Towns, built, as they thought, 'in an inaccessible end of the parish.'

This is an example of the danger of looking at the land with a purely modern eye, because it immediately raises the question: 'inaccessible from where?' After all, Archbishop Colton in his historic visitation of the Derry diocese in 1397 went back to Armagh by way of the Glenelly valley, and might even have paused for a collation at Badoney or the Six Towns. The destinations and the routes that we think important are accessible because of the roads we have built, though they follow tracks that may go back for centuries. We think of them as permanent, but many of our towns in mid-Ulster originated as castles built for defence in the fifteenth century. In our journeys, we often divert through places we have no particular urge to visit: the *bealach mór* is not always the shortest. Even today, the old Six Towns church is at a crossroads, with access to important religious or political destinations of medieval times: through Greencastle towards Ardstraw or Clogher, down the Glenelly valley towards Urney and Raphoe, across Lough Feagh to Dungannon and Armagh. We can join what became later the old coach road across the Brown Knowes towards Banagher and Derry, even before we consider taking the main road towards the other Cross, to Kilcronaghan and to *Feartas Tuama* at Toome, there to join the ancient *Slí Mhíluachra*, one of the great roads of early Ireland. The church at Moneyconey was open to the world long before modern roads led young men from Ballinascreen to Argentina and on to sheep herding in the Falkland Islands.

Our difficulty in visualising the medieval parish lies in trying to work out anew the geography of the area so as to uncover a time when the system of government was very different. The very early Irish Church was organised on the basis of a local church with resident clergy, similar to our own. Obviously, the early churches were built near where the people lived. The more important the *tuath* (state or minor kingdom, of which there were about one hundred and fifty in the entire country) in which they lived, the more important their church. One problem is that, while we can say that Maghera, for example, has been an important centre since at least the sixth century, this cannot be said of any one place in Ballinascreen.

Footprints

We should not find that surprising. The sheer length of time involved means that it is highly probable that a few important centres of population and a few churches could have come and gone in that time. We know that, for example, the Black Hill (*Cnoc na Daireoige Duibhe*: 'the hill of the black oak') was an important point of assembly and debate in medieval times. Being on the parish boundary it is perhaps unlikely to have been a focal place; but it does indicate that we must look to our points of reference. On the other hand it could mean that the 'capital' of Glenconkeyne was at one time in the vicinity of Kilcronaghan. Since the parish system followed on in the thirteenth century from the reform of the Irish Church a hundred years before and was presumably based on some existing civil division of land, we cannot be sure of even earlier local territorial boundaries.

Each townland probably represents one level of *clann* ownership and influence. One uses the word hesitantly in this context because not everybody in a *clann* would have had the same surname. Only when we look past the question of their meaning can we work out what townland names have to teach us about the way our ancestors organised themselves, what they grew and ate, how they used land and so on. Sometimes one can be given the impression that what we now call south Derry was completely afforested. This was not the case. We know that as well as its vast areas of managed woodland there were large areas of cultivation and grazing. Placenames show where the woods were (*Doire an Fhóid*/Derrynoid and *Maol na bhFiodh*/Mulnavoo), where they had been cleared for grazing (*Cluain*/Cloane, *Maigh Ard*/Moyard and *Maigh Chaoráin*/Moykeeran), sometimes where cultivation took place (*Gort an Choirce*/Gortahork in the parish of Kilcronaghan) and we can say that places like *Dún*/Doon, *Dún Mhuirí*/Dunmurray, *Dún Lógáin*/Dunlogan and *Maigh dTámhleacht*/ Moydamlet point to habitation (and burial) in quite early times.

We know that thousands of the small pigs our forefathers kept were reared in the forests of Glenconkeyne and south Derry. A great part of what they ate was the mast (nuts, acorns and so on) from the trees, like those that produce *serrano* ham in modern Spain. Cattle were very important. After all it is estimated that Ó Néill, Earl of Tyrone (Aodh Mór) had over one million head of cattle at about 1600. When a cattle plague happened, starvation often followed. As a result a great deal of space in the Irish law tracts is taken up with animal diseases. Bread, doubtless of rougher quality than our homemade bread, was made from barley, oats, rye and from wheat (less often since the local climate is not really suitable). The making of hay was a later invention. There were varieties of hard and soft cheeses. Beer brewed from barley and at times from wheat may have been important to diet since vegetables and milk in a subsistence economy could run short in winter and early spring. There is no evidence of distilling in Ireland before the thirteenth century.

Much is made by hostile observers of the custom of 'ploughing by the tail', which we would see as cruel to the horse. From the standpoint of the ploughman of the time it was more complicated than that. The really valuable thing was the plough, originally made of wood – the earliest iron ploughs in Ireland date from the seventh century. The furrow would not be as deep as that made by a modern plough, but the owner could ill afford to have his plough broken. It was thus connected to the horse's tail, and when the plough hit an obstacle in the ground, the horse stopped short. It would only have had any point in bad land, and was used all over northern Europe, especially in Poland and Russia, wherever wooded land was being cleared and broken in. Actually in early times much of the ploughing seems to have been done with teams of oxen, four or six (*seisreach*) in harness together.

Patrick versus Columba

Where the earliest church was in this area is unknown. The late James Coulter in his account of Ballinascreen is rightly sceptical about the claim that *Mag Dula*, one of the seven churches allegedly founded by St Patrick near the Faghan, is to be equated with Moyola. Séamus Ó Ceallaigh and Fr Éamon Devlin between them would seem to have proved that the word Moyola describes the land through which the river flows on the lowest part of its course and means *Má Dhá Loch*, 'the plain of the two lakes'. Brian Lacey equates *Mag Dula* with Muff near Eglinton. The *Civil Survey* of 1654–6 refers to the river on two occasions as 'the River of Monola', which is supported by local pronunciation. There may be a different name hidden there, distinct from the English 'Moyola', so that the actual origin of the river name may yet remain to be discovered.

But where did the traditional connection of St Colm Cille with this area come from? We are told that, as he fled north from the plague, then devastating the monastery at Glasnevin, he is said to have crossed the river, then called the *Bior* (but *Bior* is only an early word for 'water'). Since he did not stop, we can say that founding a church there was not on his mind. If Badoney (with its church founded by St Patrick and/ or his disciple St Cormac) was in existence by then, it is probable that there may well have been a church in the area of Ballinascreen also. Where it was or who founded it has been so overlaid by the strength of the later tradition about St Colm Cille that the names are lost, although the dedication of Lough Patrick points to very early christianisation.

The traditional account also asserts that, when St Patrick crossed the Bann into the kingdom of Uí Tuirtre, the local king was unwelcoming and Patrick was forced to go south into what is now east Tyrone. Nonetheless, the existence of Lough Patrick and its pilgrimage would seem to indicate a quite early foundation. The pilgrimage itself is surprisingly enjoyable on a good day. When one realises that one will not go down as in quicksand, the sensation of sinking barefoot into soft bog as one circles the lough is quite a liberating experience. Perhaps more to the point, if, from the top of Slieve Gallan, at about six o'clock on an evening in early autumn, one has had the experience of seeing Lough Patrick suddenly glint in the rays of the westering sun from its dark surroundings of heath and bog, it is perhaps easy to believe that the pilgrimage at the lough may have been created to replace a pagan rite of some sort. It stands to common sense that some early missionary or other must have made his way up along the river and left his mark. It may not have been the national apostle, but it would be surprising if the name of the church were not amongst those early churches claimed by Armagh as it sought to establish its suzerainty over the older foundations. To suggest otherwise would be to reduce the area to being at a level of unimportance that it has not had since.

From Secular to Monastic Control
Modern research into his mission would suggest that beyond the name

of the Lough there is no evidence to show that St Patrick came this way. Many of our local churches date from the late fifth to the early sixth centuries. However, it soon became apparent that the Church system of organisation would have great difficulty providing for the material support of its clergy. The chief reason was that in the society of the time, income was dependant on the role the person carried out in society and on his standing. In a traditionally hierarchical society, rigidly organised, a new occupation would immediately run into problems about status until its relationship to other occupations was sorted out. The society into which St Patrick came did not use money. Wealth was measured in land. Until Christianity had made major progress, its ministers would have been considered outsiders, devoid of the status that would allow them access as clients to the well-to-do who controlled the land and therefore the economy.

Early notables like St Colm Cille, who was of royal blood, were baptised into a Church with bishops and priests like, for example, his own tutor St Cruithneachán (Cronaghan). In a society without towns, as early Ireland was, it was difficult to get sustained access to the scattered population living in rural areas where the mission could be carried on. The same problem had already been encountered in Gaul (France), but had been solved by St Martin of Tours, who instituted a series of small monasteries, spread throughout the countryside, to serve as centres of evangelisation. The very Latin word for 'a country-dweller' was *paganus*, so it speedily came to have its modern meaning of 'pagan'.

The introduction of a similar system into Ireland proved an immense success and small rural monasteries sprang up in place of a local secular clergy, giving rise to many of our placenames beginning with a *Kil*, from *cill*, originally a monastic cell. The system had the effect of fundamentally altering the position of the bishop, who henceforth was now usually a monk of the monastery subject to the authority of the abbot, while performing the essential duties of a bishop, ordaining, confirming, acting as a spiritual guide (or *anamchara*, as the term was) to rulers and those in quest of perfection.

The spread of this monastic system and the time span within which it took place is a matter of argument. Clearly it had emerged well before the system had to be reformed again in the eighth century, but many such minor monasteries could have risen and disappeared again in those hundreds of years for which our information is sparse. Since monastic buildings were more solid than most and protected by rights of sanctuary, it was to them that people would turn for safety or to deposit their valuables. Consequently, they became a target for attack by roving bands of Vikings (no respecters of Christian treasures or rights of sanctuary), or by *Gallghaeil* (war bands of mixed Viking and Gaelic ancestry, combining the worst qualities of both races), such as that defeated by Aodh Finnliath, King of Ireland, in 856 in Glenelly. Ballinascreen would hardly have felt very secure in their proximity.

The Advent of Cineál Binnigh

Aodh Finnliath, whom we have just mentioned, as well as being *ardrí* or high king, was ruler of Cineál Eoghain, that is, head of the dynasty who were the descendants of Eoghan, son of Niall Naoighiallach (d. AD 453) and who constituted, as it were,the royal family of the time. From their original base of Inis Eoghain (also named from Eoghan), they spread south-eastwards until by the fifteenth century, led by the O'Neill descendants of Niall Glúndubh (+ 919), they ruled Ulster from the Foyle to the gates of Dundalk. One of the spearheads of this advance was that branch of the kindred descended from a son of Eoghan, Cineál Binnigh. They would appear to have been the vanguard, even the stormtroopers of Cineál Eoghain power in south Co. Derry (the name the English would give the area when they shired Ulster in the early seventeenth century).

I would maintain that not merely did Cineál Binnigh act in a military capacity but that, in settling in their new home, they brought with them devotion to the patron of all the descendants of Niall Naoighiallach. O Dónaill propaganda had subsequently claimed that Colm Cille was their particular patron, but that is the case only after 1200 or so when they achieved their ambition of controlling the city of Derry. Before that time the group most closely associated with the Columban monastery in Derry was Cineál Binnigh. As they moved southwards, they brought the cult of their patron with them and in the process caused that loss of tradition about earlier local churches and patrons in Ballinascreen, as happened also in Drumragh (Omagh) and in Termonmaguirke. This commitment to Colm Cille, I would suggest, is what lies behind the seemingly fanciful account of Colm Cille's bell bouncing from the cloak of McGillion to that of Mc Gurk. It seems to be a subtle, symbolic way of alluding to a transfer of ecclesiastical legitimacy when Mac Oirc supplanted the earlier Mac Uílín. Mac Oirc is one of the prominent surnames in Cineál Binnigh, but it is not as yet possible to uncover the ancestry of McGillion.

Probably the churches of Kilcronaghan and Desertmartin were promptly brought within the ambit of monastic Ballinascreen, since

Cruithneachán the priest was Colm Cille's foster-father and first teacher, and St Martin was looked on as the patron of their monastic form of life. Martin of Tours became a sort of honorary Irishman to such an extent that he was claimed to be an uncle of St Patrick and it was said that many of his family came to Ireland too, although in fact he was a Roman soldier born in modern Hungary. *Díseart* is a monastic term, pointing back to the life of the original Egyptian monks in the desert, and meaning 'hermitage' in Irish. The word is found also in placenames like Dysart and Brackaghdysart (*Breacmhá an Dísirt*) – breacmhá seems to indicate rough, mountain pasture.

It may well be that the role of Mac Oirc was a great deal more than an honorary one as devotee of Colm Cille. Part of the second stage of the Twelfth-Century Reform of the Church in Ireland, after the creation of dioceses as we have them still, was the setting aside of land in each of the new parishes for the maintenance of church buildings and the sustenance of the clergy. The amount of land varied from parish to parish, but usually about four townlands were set aside for Church purposes. This can only have been organised with the support of the dominant civil power because churchland is usually amongst the best land in any parish. The parish of Tamlaghtard (Magilligan), which had also a *Scrín Cholm Cille*, or 'Shrine of St Columba', was completely given to the Church, for it had to support the bishop and his establishment. Ballinascreen must have been important because here six townlands were given to the Church, the famous 'Six Towns'.

This churchland in each parish was in the care of the *aircheannach* or erenagh. Originally, his was the title of the lay manager of monastic properties. Now with the new diocesan system it is transferred to a semi-clerical role of looking after the Church building, the upkeep of the clergy, and the payment of various dues to the bishop, who also had the right to appoint him in the first place. He also had the obligation of providing hospitality for travellers. He probably also had a role in the education of the clergy in those days before seminaries were thought of and when student priests were educated by being apprenticed to experienced pastors.

Erenaghs were to later claim that they were the lineal descendants of those who had given the land to the patron saint for a church in the first instance, but many of them in fact came into possession of the land centuries later. Like most occupations in medieval Ireland, the position of erenagh passed from father to son, unless a line ran out, in which case the bishop had to intervene to appoint a successor. Thus we can trace Ó Caoilte (Kielt), in Termoneeny, Ó Scolláin in Ballyscullion, Ó Diamáin (Diamond) in Kilrea, Mac Riada (Reid) in Aghadowey, Ó Dúill (Doyle) in Desertmartin, Ó Tuathaile (Tohill) in Desertoghill, Ó hÉanaigh (Heaney) in Banagher, and so forth. The Ballinascreen erenagh leaves no trace. Perhaps Mac Oirc was in turn forced to move out or maybe he was able to bring about a combination of Ballinascreen with Termonmaguirke (Carrickmore), all the time holding on to the Bell of Colm Cille, the source of his distinction. It is to be noted that among the clergy of Ballinascreen in the fifteenth century, are to be found the names of Mac Ailín (McCallion), Ó Caoilte of Termoneeny and an Ó Dúill of Desertmartin. The name Ó hÉigeartaigh (Hegarty) occurs here as it does all over the diocese in places where St Colm Cille was patron. The name Mac Oirc does not appear among the clergy of Ballinascreen at that time.

Civil Boundaries

Also among the medieval clergy is to be found Anraí Ó hínnéirí,[1] one of the same name as that Cadhan Ó hInnéirí who features so prominently in the folklore of this part of the country: the young Cadhan Ó hInnéirí who would not go to Mass, and his monstrous hound, or *péist*, that gave its name to the valley of the Moyola as far as Seefin near Maghera (*Suí Finn*, 'seat of Fionn mac Cumhaill') and Slieve Gallan, the valley of Gleann Con Cadhain. In fact, it can be descried that the mythical story reveals a genuine historical clash.

This was a medieval civil boundary and not just a geographic one. The Ó hInnéirí sept had vied with Ó Conchúir (O'Connor) for the kingship of Cianacht (the Roe valley) up to the eleventh century, until the forces of the Cianachta were defeated, as the Cineál Binnigh had been, by another incoming branch of Cineál Eoghain, Ó Catháin (O'Kane). No doubt Ó hInnéirí made their way over Glenshane in search of a new home and may well have settled around Ballinascreen. Folk tradition almost certainly got it wrong about the name, because the distinctive name among the Ó hInneirí was not *Cadhan* but *Cian*. There has never been a suggestion that the name of the valley is Gleann Con Chéin ('of Cian'), and anyhow the name Glenconkeyne seems to predate the arrival of Ó hInnéirí. These names are examples of those totem animal names which go back to pre-Christian times; *cadhan* means 'a brent

---

1. The name Ó hInnéirí has been anglicised as Henry. Note that this is a different name from Mac Anraí (McHenry) who are a branch of Ó Catháin.

goose' and *cú* 'a hound'. Or it may be part of *faolchú*, 'a wolf'; the last one of which, it is worth remembering, was reputed to have been shot between Moneyneena and Banagher in the 1750s.

However that may be, the conflict between Brian Carrach Ó Néill and the incoming Cian Ó hInneirí was about territory and certainly not about hounds. The sobriquet *carrach* ('rough-skinned') was typical of the O'Neills of Clann Aodha Buí, and the lords of the territory from the Bann as far as *Suí Finn* near Maghera were a branch of just that kindred, known as *Clann Dónaill Doinn na Banna*, the descendants of Dónall Donn ('the brown-haired') O'Neill of the Bann, also known as Dónall Caol ('the slender'). Dónall Donn's father, Brian, died in 1488, and Brian Carrach, Dónall's great-grandson, had a son Seán Buí who died in 1577. If he was the same person, Brian would have lived much too late to have been impressed by any mythic medieval *péist* ('monster'). Since there was a political boundary, then separating Glenconkeyne from Clandonnel, the lands of Dónall Donn, it became for young and thrusting members of the upper class a source of friction and an opportunity to assert themselves.

As the traditional story itself suggests, the conflict between Clann Dónaill and Ó hInnéirí was of short duration and not to Ó hInnéirí advantage. There may have been another factor in the story; the imperialist ambition of the sons of the Ó Néill of the time, Eoghan Mór.

In Glenconkeyne, the scion of the royal house of Ó Néill of Dungannon was *Féilimí Balbh* ('the inarticulate'; d. 1461), son of Eoghan Mór (d. 1456), son of Niall Óg (d. 1402). Lord of *An Arachta* (Orritor, Cookstown), Féilimí asserted control over Glenconkeyne as well. Ó Néill of Dungannon and Ó Néill Clandeboye were inveterate rivals for supreme power within Cineál Eoghain and over most of Ulster. With the arrival of a branch of the *ríora*, or Dungannon *clann*, in Ballinascreen to share a frontier with Clann Aodha Bhuí, the boundary must have become even tenser. Féilimí was however one of a minority of Cineál Eoghain leaders who devoted themselves to matters cultural. He built up a collection of books and manuscripts, and perhaps started that local tradition of Gaelic learning in the area to which the great John O'Donovan drew attention in the nineteenth century. Féilimí's great-grandson Seán may even be the source of the surname McShane, still to be found in the area (although McShane/Johnson also indicates descent from *Seán an Díomais*, 'Shane the Proud'), an 'uncle' of Aodh Mór.

The Long Descent from Kinsale

It was to Glenconkeyne that Aodh Mór Ó Néill, Earl of Tyrone, retreated at the end of the Nine Years War and the 'close-run-thing' that was the Battle of Kinsale (1601) before his eventual submission. His last visit may have come about five years later. In 1607, an event occurred that has had a lasting effect on Ulster and which has never been fully explained. Ó Néill, Earl of Tyrone, decided to leave the country together with Ó Dónaill (Ruairí) and a close group of followers to seek reinforcements abroad. This move, however, had the calamitous effect of leaving central and western Ulster wide open for the Plantation.

Ó Néill travelled fast once his mind was made up, from Dublin, through Dundalk, through the Gap of the North and on to *An Chraobh* (soon to be renamed Stewartstown) to gather his family. His journey continued west and he spent the night of Wednesday 12 September *'i Muintir Luinigh, ar chóngar Loch Beagfhine'*, 'in Muintir Luinigh in the vicinity of Loch Beagfhine'. Muintir Luinigh has been anglicised as Munterloney, and usually refers to the parish of Lower Badoney, the valleys of the Owenkillew and Owenreagh Rivers, but no Loch Beagfhine is to be found there. Loch Beagfhine may be connected with Glenviggan on the borders of the parishes of Ballinascreen and Badoney. (The original parish of Badoney included the Glenelly valley as well.) If that was the case the party must have stayed in the Six Towns, as the only place in the area suitable to offer accommodation to a large party of travellers.

Perhaps it was there that the dramatic scene occurred (if we can believe the hostile gossip of Sir John Davies, one of those responsible for driving Ó Néill out): 'On Wednesday night, they say, he travelled all night with his impediments, that is his women and children; and it is likewise reported that the Countess, his wife [*Caitríona Nic Aonasa*/ Mac Guinness, of the lords of Iveagh, Co. Down], being exceedingly weary, slipped down from her horse and weeping said she could go no farther; whereupon the earl drew his sword and swore a great oath that he would kill her in the place, if she would not pass on with him, and put on a more cheerful countenance withal'. *Pour encourager les autres*, perhaps! She accompanied him on to Rome and into years of exile together, where both were to die.

Glenconkeyne was perhaps the last place in Ireland to fall under English control. As a result it may have been spared the horrendous suffering engendered by Sir Arthur Chichester's scorched earth policy during the Nine Years War, which reduced people to eating grass and brought death from starvation to large numbers of the population.

One consequence of this experience and the loss of land in the Plantation was what has come to be called the '1641 Rebellion', although the Irish in fact rose out in support of what they accepted was the lawful government of King Charles I of England. Some of the planning for war and its outbreak was done in the vicinity of the parish. On 27 April 1643, a parliamentary army led by the renegade *Ruairí Ó hAráin* (O'Harran), known as an *Creachadóir* ('the plunderer'), and Sir Thomas Phillips' son from Limavady (and Bellaghy), including forces from Derry, went through Ballinascreen on their way to Lissan to wreck the iron mine on Slieve Gallan. In Ballinascreen they met Niall Ó Néill, the priest of Cappagh. The account does not go on to say what actually happened to him but the same army killed Eoghan Modartha ('the gloomy') Ó Croiligh, priest of Maghera, the next month.

There has survived a statement from a local 'planter', Robert Waring of Magherafelt, which he claimed to have lost in 1642, including the names of those from Ballinascreen who despoiled him of his property, not names one would have associated with Ballinascreen fifty years earlier, a sign perhaps of the displacement of populations. The 'Henry O'Haggan' mentioned is perhaps *Anraí Ó hAgáin* (son of *Ruairí Buí*) of Moneymore (and perhaps of Loughinsholin also), who had been despoiled by Robert Monroe's forces in 1642. Even at that early stage of the war, people were reduced to eating horse, cat, dog and worse.

The Era of the Penal Laws

The physical survival of the people through the brutality and inhumanity of the long seventeenth century in Ireland is testimony to their unsung resilience and strength of mind. The century had begun with high hopes of control over their own affairs but successively these hopes were raised only to be dashed by one outbreak of total war after another – Chichester, Cromwell, William III – until they ended in the Penal Laws.

The so-called penal system was probably the most meticulously devised and iniquitous legal system ever put together in a country (by the way, *against* the wishes of William of Orange) so that a small minority could control a majority population. However, a couple of comments on the system are called for. Its aim was political and economic rather than religious. The penal system lasted about seventy-five years. Had it had a real religious purpose it would have been accompanied by a concerted effort to convert Catholics to the established Church.

No such effort was forthcoming, because to convert the mass of Irish Catholics would have meant they would have to receive their share in the riches of the country. Those with influence were determined not to allow this. Only at times of political turmoil were the penal laws enforced at all strictly, in order to make sure that events developing abroad (such as the projected invasion of James III, the 'Old Pretender') got no support in Ireland. To enforce them all the time would surely have made the country ungovernable and would have meant that local lords could not benefit from the labours of a quiescent peasantry. It was in their interest that things should remain as calm as possible. The penal laws also restricted dissenters but they were allowed just sufficient rights (in land tenure and so forth) to mark them off from the downtrodden Catholics. Finally, one must add that most Protestants had little sympathy with those who would have liked to enforce the laws as strictly as possible. Accounts exist of Protestants assisting in the prevention of the arrest of priests by priest-hunters.

Nonetheless, the purpose of the system was achieved in the grinding and abject poverty of the Catholics in much of the country. In religious terms, while Mass continued to be said in threshing barns and cottages, though only at times of active persecution at Mass rocks, it was often scarcely possible to provide decent chalices and books. Education of the clergy was a problem not always solved, as a contemporary satire in Irish, *Comhairle Mhic Chlamha*, exploits to great comic effect. Dedicated priests educated abroad came home, often from ecclesiastical positions of note in France, to live an uncertain life. The people ensured that, at least compared to those amongst whom they lived, they were probably reasonably well off as far as the essentials of life were concerned, if not in strictly financial terms.

The trace of penal times still influences the attitudes of Ulster Catholics today. The penal laws brought law itself and officers of the law into disrepute. The idea that laws exist to protect people can fall on stony ground. The hostility of the legal system had the result that, in strict religious terms, practice and cohesion became much more important than any attempt at theological debate with possible disagreement. 'Knowing the catechism' was the important thing. Finding themselves under such sustained albeit impersonal attack, people had to determine what was really important to them. They thus identified themselves as Gaelic Irish and Catholics.

Although in Ballinascreen the people held on to both characteristics longer than in most places in Ulster (except west Donegal and the parish of Badoney), they yielded on the first and clung more to the second for support in a life of misery. The direction taken by this loss of morale was assisted of course by the Great Famine. It was unfortunate that the choice came to be made, critically, in the nineteenth century because the consequence, with the change of language, was that Gaelic religious expression, now being retranslated into fashionable 'Celtic Spirituality', was replaced by forms of prayer based on Italian and French styles (what is now commonly called 'traditional Irish Catholicism'!). Similarly, traditional morality often yielded to a combination of Victorian English primness and bourgeois French stuffiness, clearly what was thought progressive at the time. We are both richer and poorer for the dilemmas our ancestors faced and the choices they made.

The Deanery of Maigh Iotha (Tyrone/Donegal)

The Parishes of Urnaí (Urney) and Ard Sratha (Ardstraw)

The very name of the parish of Urney brings us back to the early years of the Christian faith in Ireland. The original word in Irish, *urnaí*, indicates an activity rather than the name of a place. It means 'praying' or 'prayer', and reminds us that the parish takes its origins from the convent founded there by St *Cognat* or *Cónait* and from the primary raison d'être of that foundation. There are at least two other examples of the placename in Ireland; one in Co. Carlow where the site of an early monastery or convent is still marked by a granite cross, the other in Kildare where the religious site appears to have been overlaid by a Norman castle. As far as can be ascertained, Urnaí and Camas at the Bann near Coleraine are the only two very early convents in the diocese of Derry, although it is clear from St Patrick's *Confession* that he attached great importance for his mission to communities of women dedicated to Christian perfection.

The *Life of Saint Eoghan* (Eugene) of Ardstraw speaks of him visiting, along with St Tiarnach of Clones, a convent called *Ros Cay in terra Metheorum* (in the land of the Methei?) whose abbess was called *Mosseta*. Since the ancient name of the Lagan (east Donegal) was *Maigh Iotha* and in later times the parish was known as *Urnaí Mhaigh Iotha*, it is not impossible that Urnaí was the place in question – *in terra Maighe Iotha* –with its name garbled by a later scribe unfamiliar with the area.

Local knowledge may decide if *Ros Cay* can be identified. The only suggested date of the death of St Eoghan is the year 550. The account of his life, however, is late and not particularly reliable.

The Convent

Unfortunately, we have no historical record of anyone with a name like *Mosseta* in the convent of Urnaí. Apart from St Cónait ('Cognat' in Old Irish) who was its founder, we know the names of some others, all venerated as saints in medieval times, who made the name of Urnaí famous: *Féimhe* (pronounced fay've; in Old Irish *Feme*), whose feast day is 21 January; *Fainche* (pronounced fan'che; ch as in loch) whose feast day is 1 January; *Neas* (pronounced nas) whose feast day is 9 September; and *Sáfann* (in Old Irish *Sámthann*) whose feast day is 18 December. Sáfann later became abbess of Cluain Brónaigh (Clonbroney) near Granard, now in Co. Longford, was well known as a spiritual director and died in 739. The convent is unlikely to have survived the Viking era.

The Parish

Urnaí returns to the light of history in the twelfth and thirteenth centuries when parishes as we know them were being created. The development of Urnaí (Urney) and Donaghmore shows most clearly one basis for division. Donaghmore was the *tuath* (state or kingdom) of Clann Diarmada/Ó Cairealláin (Carlin, Kerlin), whereas Urnaí was the *tuath* of Cineal Moain/Ó Gormlaigh (O Gormley), whose ruling septs were continually at loggerheads, until Ó Gormlaigh got the upper hand and forced Ó Cairealláin to move closer to their ally and overking, Mac Lochlainn, at Derry where they gave their sept name, Clann Diarmada, to the parish of Clandermot/Glendermott. Ó Gormlaigh were allied to their own overking, Ó Néill, who was to run out the stronger in the dynastic contest with Mac Lochlainn. Ó Gormlaigh's territory included the present parishes of Urnaí, Mourne, Sion Mills and Camus. Later, Ó Dónaill forced them across the River Mourne, and later still they were displaced by Ó Néill towards Gortin, where they left the name of their branch of the sept in *Muintir Luinigh/* Munterloney. The centrality of Urnaí is underlined by the fact that the deanery that includes the parishes in east Donegal and west Tyrone in the diocese of Derry was known in medieval times as the deanery of Maigh Iotha.

The Erenagh

Since the conquest of Ireland in the sixteenth century, the Catholic parish church and clergy are maintained by the direct offerings of the people of the parish. This was not always the case. From the thirteenth century, after the Twelfth-Century Reform, to the end of the sixteenth century, land was set aside in each parish for this purpose. The land was farmed and administered by an official called the *aircheannach* or erenagh. He was appointed by the bishop and his office continued in his family. He had also an obligation to provide for travellers and was involved in the education of the clergy in those days before seminaries, when to prepare for the priesthood meant being apprenticed to a serving priest in a parish.

In Urnaí the erenagh family was *Ó Ceallaigh*/Kelly, of the branch known as *Mac an Bhaird* (Ó Ceallaigh). Obviously, as the name shows, they were a literary family. The *bard* was a grade of poet lower than the *file*, whose avocation it was to declaim the poetry composed by the *file*. Being closely involved in parish life, the erenagh families produced most of the priests of the Derry diocese in the Middle Ages. Significantly, in that terrible time of confiscation and oppression in the seventeenth century, the Catholic religion was maintained by one Tarlach Ó Ceallaigh/Terence O'Kelly, who, from 1630 to 1666, was Vicar Apostolic of Derry for some thirty years of that period of one hundred and nineteen years when the diocese of Derry had no bishop.

What the dues paid to the bishop were we get some idea of from the *Inquisitions*, the enquiries which reported to the authorities on the finances of the Church in preparation for the confiscation and the Plantation of Ulster. Unfortunately they give no return for Urnaí. The 'good and lawful men' on the jury claimed that they did not know what the rents and tithes were. Admittedly, most of its members, except for Ruairí Ó Gormlaigh, were from east Tyrone. Since coinage was scarce and hardly used at all at the time, many rents were paid in kind. Thus we know that, at Donaghmore, Ó Galáin, the erenagh, had to pay the bishop, amongst other things, 'four score methers of malt' and Ó Cearbhallain at Lifford paid 'twenty methers of malt' per year. A mether (*meadar* in Irish) was a wooden vessel containing two gallons. The malt was for the beer of the bishop's household, beer being essential to the diet of the time. It is a testimony too to the fertility of Maigh Iotha.

Churchlands

In the erenagh system townlands in each parish were set aside for the upkeep of the parish, usually four, sometimes more. In the English grant of confiscated lands in 1610 to Bishop George Montgomery of the established Church, the erenagh lands are specified as: Aghenedonagh, Cogan, Nurim and Longford. In 1615 his successor as Bishop John Tanner was in receipt of: Aghnedawnagh, Cogan, Nurim and Longford. In addition there were two ballyboes (*bailte bó*) or townlands at Ballinlinny, a chapel of ease of Urnaí, from which the erenagh paid the bishop a yearly rent of two shillings and sixpence. As listed in 1634, the churchlands at Urnaí are still: Aghenedowagh, Cogan, Nurim and Longford; along with half a quarter (= two ballyboes) at Ballynalinney and two sessiaghs of Ballylast near Lifford in the barony of Raphoe.

The spelling of these names was of course at the mercy of scribes, unfamiliar with the area and not remotely concerned with rendering the original Irish names with accuracy. It can make for confusion and difficulty in sorting out what the names might mean. The name 'Longford', for example, might point to a settlement of Vikings in the area at one time, since *longphort* in Irish denoted a 'ship-fort' or early Viking naval base. The *Civil Survey* (1654) adds Cooledroman, glebe land, and gathers all the rest under the name 'Urney', leased to Matthew Babington, described as 'English Protestant', although the rest of the parish had been granted to James Lord Hamilton, Baron Strabane, described as 'Scottish Papist'. 'Ballilast' was leased to the heirs of James Spottiswood. The district was planted from Scotland. During his long tenure as vicar apostolic, appointed by the pope to run the diocese since there was no bishop, Terence O'Kelly probably lived under the protection of the Hamiltons at Urney.

Clergy in Medieval Records

- *Uilliam Mac Cathmhaoil*/William MacCawell(McCaul/ Campbell), Rector (parish priest) of Urney and Dean of Derry in 1397, died before 1407.
- Donatus Okerbulan/*Donncha Ó Cearbhallain*/O'Carolan, Rector of Urney 1397.
- Johannes Ochasalaid/*Eoin Ó Casaile* (Cushley), Canon of Derry, vicar, resigned before 1413.
- Donaldus Macauhemail Ocheallayd/*Dónall Mac an Bhaird Ó Ceallaigh*, vicar, provided 1413, dead by 1430. A Dónall Mac an Bhaird was deprived in 1432 for concubinage, perjury and dilapidation of parish property.

- Donaldus Obryn/*Dónall Ó Braoin* (Breen), vicar, deprived of office of curate for letting a parishioner die without the sacraments after being widely sought, 1482. If proved, *Aodh Ó Cearbhalláin* is to succeed.
- Cormacus Micromnige/*Cormac Mac Con Mí* (Mc Namee), Canon of Derry, Rector of Urney, 1489.
- Florentius Mac Varde/*Fógartach Mac an Bhaird*, Vicar (curate) of Urney, 1607.
- Connougher Omungan/*Conchúr Ó Mongáin*/Conor O'Mongan of Urney and Termon O'Mungan was 'amongst the Catholic clergy who were kind to non-Catholics in the area occupied by the forces besieging' Derry in 1689. This army of James II was commanded at the time by General Richard Hamilton, grandson of Sir George Hamilton, brother of the Earl of Abercorn.

The Parish of Ard Sratha/Ardstraw

The 'fifth', or province, of the *Ulaidh* or Ulster people (*Cúige Uladh*) in ancient times, we are told, included everything north of a line between the Rivers Boyne and Drowes. About the time of St Patrick this kingdom came under attack, was defeated and reduced eventually to the area east of the Bann. The centre of Ulster was taken over by peoples known collectively as the *Airghialla*, claiming a common ancestry and gathered into a sort of loose federation of *tuatha* or states.

One of these peoples, the *Uí Tuirtre*, were based in south Derry and a branch of the dynasty, descended from one Fiachra and therefore calling themselves the *Uí Fiachrach*, crossed the mountains into what we now call Tyrone and established a kingdom for themselves in the good land at the foot of *Sliabh Troim* (now baptised 'Bessy Bell') where the valley of the Derg meets that of the Strule. Perhaps they used as their centre the *crannóg*, or lake fortification, in storied *Loch Laoire* (now Lake Catherine in Baronscourt) or perhaps the nearby *lios* and *ráth*. Loch Laoire gets its name from Laoire Buach, the hero-warrior mentioned in the *Ulster Cycle* of mythological tales.

Established there, this people became known as the *Uí Fiachrach Ard Sratha* and their territory may have included the modern parishes of Cappagh and Langfield as well as the lower Derg and perhaps down river to what is now Strabane – but almost certainly not Badoney, at least initially. *Ard Sratha* (Ardstraw) owed its importance to good land and to the fact that it lies at an important crossroads, the Derg giving access to Fermanagh and south Donegal, to Lough Erne and the sea, while the other river valleys open into central Ulster or towards Lough Foyle.

A Monastic Church

The founder of the Christian Church in Ardstraw was St Eoghan (now wrongly translated as Eugene), who unlike many early patrons is always described as 'the Bishop Eoghan', *an tEaspag Eoghan*. The relationship of bishop to abbot in what became a markedly monastic Irish Church is still argued about by historians. It was often the case that the bishop lived in the monastery and under the authority of the abbot. According to law, there was to be a bishop in each *tuath*, but he had often less jurisdiction over that territory than the abbot, who was seen as the successor of the saintly founder. The bishop performed the sacramental and pastoral duties of a bishop: preaching, ordaining, acting as *anamchara* (spiritual director) to rulers and so on. As we have seen, it was only with the reform of the twelfth century that Ireland came to have dioceses as we know them.

We should bear in mind as well that our conception of what is meant by 'monastery' and 'monk' has been greatly influenced by the later Benedictine style of monasticism. Monasticism in Ireland was more ascetic than that of the Benedictines, but in earlier times at least, it did not involve strict enclosure. The buildings were less fort-like, on a more human scale and more accessible, and the dress less 'monkish'. It is reasonable to assume that the early monasteries were established near where the local rulers lived most of the time even if they seem to us often to be in out-of-the-way places. Nor should we forget that the important places to which people would wish to go then need not be those that we consider important nowadays.

Ardstraw after Eoghan

With the destruction of documents over centuries during which the area was subject to warfare and conquest, it is not surprising that a succession list of Bishops of Ardstraw cannot be established. Two later bishops are named in the annals: Maolfothartaigh who died in 678 and Coifiánach who died in 705. The latter is venerated as a saint with his own feast day, 26 November. By the next century, ecclesiastical power at Ardstraw had fallen into the hands of the ruling family of Uí Fiachrach because we learn that Aonghas, son of Maelcalada, *comharba easpaig Eoghain Ard Sratha*, 'successor of Bishop Eoghan of Ardstraw' died in 878, described in the *Annals of Ulster* as *princeps*, 'superior'. It does not follow that he was in fact a bishop but he was certainly in charge of the land and property of Ardstraw. Furthermore, two of his brothers were kings within the Airghialla federation. It became common to find churchland in the control of local rulers and their relatives, ostensibly because they had given the original grant of land to the founding saint. It was precisely this state of affairs that would provoke the great movement of reform in the twelfth century.

There is no information about whether the Vikings visited Ardstraw on their depredations, although we do know that the *Gallghaeil* (an interbred group of Vikings and Gaels based in the Hebrides, and who combined the worst qualities of both races) were defeated in a battle by Cineál Eoghain in Glenelly in 856. The Airghialla federation had come to grief in 827 at the battle of Leathcham near Armagh when they were defeated by Cineál Eoghain. Before that the kingdom of Uí Fiachrach had fallen to another branch of Cineál Eoghain, and notable as one of the origins of the surname Ó Ceallaigh/Kelly. The latter in turn were to lose out to Ó Gormlaigh. The last King of Uí Fiachrach was Murchadh Ó Críogáin who died in 1202 and whose family name may be preserved in the townland of Magheracreegan. By the tenth century, the church of Ardstraw had become part of the *paruchia* or monastic system practised in the monasteries who looked to and venerated St Colm Cille as founder, like Derry, Drumcliff and Drumhome.

Ardstraw in the Twelfth-Century Reform

After the end of the Viking period, effectively brought to a close at the Battle of Clontarf in 1014, it became increasingly obvious that the Church was in serious need of reform. The movement began on the continent, initially in a mixed group of laity and clergy, in an attempt to eradicate cronyism and control by local lords and kings in appointments to Church offices. Ireland had special problems because of the lack of towns in the European sense and of its system of Church organisation based on monasteries. It became clear that any reform would have to include the creation of territorial dioceses.

As in other countries, the dioceses came to be based on the political divisions of the country. The present diocese of Derry was originally divided between two such divisions. What is now the County of Donegal (including Inis Eoghain) was to be a diocese to be called either Derry or Raphoe. East of it was to be the diocese of Ardstraw, which was to stretch from *Sliabh Larga* ('The Pigeon Top' near Omagh) to *Carn Glas* ('The Tops' at Castlefin), and from *Loch Craoi* (perhaps

Lough Lee at Drumquin) to *Binn Fhoibhne* (Benevenagh). The historian Fr Aubrey Gwynn has suggested that two bishops named Ó Brolcháin (the name is now made 'Bradley') named as Bishops of Armagh in the annals were in fact (due to a misprint) bishops of this new diocese of Ardstraw, but this seems unlikely since they were related by marriage to those who headed the unreformed party and were hostile to St Malachy in the Church of Armagh.

Ardstraw was chosen as seat of the diocese in the new system because of the prestige of St Eoghan as bishop, because it had a suitable Church building in its *daimhliag* or stone church (one of the few in Ulster; early church buildings were generally of wood, such as one can see in modern Scandinavia), and because the authorities in Armagh seem to have been afraid of the power that would accrue to Derry if it had the prestige of being both head of the Order of Colm Cille and the seat of the bishop. Ardstraw's difficulty seems to have been that it found itself in a disputed area since Ó Gormlaigh (Gormley), based on what became the parish of Urney, and Ó Caireilláin (Kerlin/Carlin), from the parish of Donaghmore, both laid claim to the territory.

The former won and ousted the latter who departed the scene and gave their name to the parish of Glendermott near Derry. The Bishop of Ardstraw also departed and took up residence at Maghera or *Ráth Luraigh* in south Derry, becoming known as the Bishop of Cineál Eoghain. It was only in 1254 that Derry became the episcopal seat while Giolla an Choimdhe Ó Cearúlláin (Germanus O Carolan) was bishop. In the meantime, the Order of Colm Cille had declined and become part of the Canons Regular of St Augustine. The *Registry of Clogher* claims that he was the bishop who detached the lands of the kingdom of Ardstraw from Clogher by force of arms, but the boundaries set at the Synod of Rath Breasail (1111) discussed earlier would seem to disprove this, except perhaps for Termonamongan.

Henceforth, Ardstraw would be reduced to a constituent parish of the deanery of Maigh Iotha of the diocese of Derry. Its brief episcopal prestige did not protect it from destruction by John de Courcy and the Anglo-Normans in 1198 anymore than its monastic character had protected it a century before from neighbouring Ó Catháin lords or Ó Briain kings from Munster. Attacking churches was a way of undermining the status of the local ruler who would be expected to be able to afford them protection. Furthermore, they tended to be the safe places where valuables were deposited in times of turmoil and so an inviting target for the elastic conscience. Traditionally too, the bridge at Ardstraw was a frequent meeting place for those on either side (Ó Gormlaigh v Ó Cairealláin; Ó Néill v Ó Dónaill) who wished to negotiate terms of peace, with terms accepted and sworn to on the relics preserved in the church there.

Financing the Reform

Although the Twelfth-Century Reform of the Church was primarily concerned with the establishment of dioceses and the raising of spiritual standards amongst the people (liturgical reform; appointment to Church benefices; keeping Sunday holy; marrying according to the norms of canon law, and so on), it raised a further problem. How was this new diocese, and the parishes which followed as a consequence from it to be financed? In Ireland, occupations were passed on in the *clann* (which was more like a limited company than what we mean by 'family'. Not everybody in the *clann* would have had the same patronymic or descent, nor an equal stake in the *clann* possessions). A bold decision was taken to confide the financial management of the parish to the laity and to appoint in each parish an *aircheannach*, or 'erenagh' (as it is anglicised).

In those days the only source of wealth was the land, and so a number of townlands in each parish was set aside for the maintenance of the church buildings and the support of the clergy. These lands were administered by the erenagh or head of the *clann* to whom had been entrusted the hereditary position and its duties. The bishop of the diocese had the right to appoint the erenagh if the family succession broke down, and the erenagh in turn had to pay dues to the bishop and receive him on visitation, to provide hospitality for travellers, and at a time when priests were trained by apprenticeship to a serving priest, he probably had a role in the education of the clergy.

It is a measure of the importance of Ardstraw that four *bailte biataigh* and eight *bailte bó* were set aside for the Church. That constitutes no less than twenty-four *bailte bó*. (The *baile bó*, or 'cow-land' is the origin of the modern 'townland'.) Four centuries later when it came to confiscating these lands for the established Church, each *baile bó* or townland was reckoned to contain sixty Plantation acres. By 1610, the erenagh paid twenty shillings, the pastor and his vicar or curate two shillings apiece annually to the bishop.

The erenagh family of Ardstraw was Ó Farannáin, a branch of Cineál Eoghain. The earliest of the name are Maolbhríde ('servant of St Bríd') Ó Farannáin who died in 1127 and Giolla Domhnaigh ('servant of the

Lord') who died in 1179. Donncha was a canon of the Derry chapter in 1530 and the last certainly of the name to occur is Tarlach, Vicar or Curate of Ardstraw in Bishop Montgomery's *Survey* at the Plantation of Ulster. He was a contemporary and perhaps a relative of 'Denis O Farran', probably another Donncha Ó Farannáin, pastor of Donaghedy and erenagh at Ardstraw. The surname is different from Ó Fearáin/Farren, but since the name Farnan has disappeared in west Tyrone, it is probable that the surname changed and has come down to us in another form derived from a byname. One possibility is *Mac Con Mí* (McNamee), still common in the area, who occur amongst the clergy in late medieval west Tyrone, although they are better known as *filí*, a poetic family – court poets to Ó Néill, Ó Dónaill, Ó Gormlaigh and others. It was not uncommon for poetic families to become involved in Church affairs as well.

A Snapshot of Medieval Ardstraw

In the year 1397 the Archbishop of Armagh, John Colton, decided to conduct a visitation of the vacant diocese of Derry. From his name one might have thought that he was a native of the parish of Droim Rátha, an Ó Comhaltáin, but in actual fact he was 'de Colton', Anglo-Norman French, born in Norfolk, educated at Cambridge, a doctor of canon law, appointed lord treasurer of the English colony in Ireland, made Dean of St Patrick's in Dublin, lord justice in 1381, chancellor and in 1392 Pope Urban VI made him Archbishop of Armagh, which at that time could only be held by an Englishman. He died in 1404 and is buried in Drogheda. He resided at Dromiskin in the Pale, and came to Armagh *inter Hibernicos* (the Gaelic-speaking north of the archdiocese) only on occasion. The bishopric of Derry was vacant due to the resignation of the last bishop in 1394, so Archbishop Colton seized the opportunity to assert his authority and, as he claimed that he could in canon law at the time, make an official visitation. He set out on 8 October 1397.

In the record of the visitation we find the erenagh of Ardstraw fulfilling his function. The archbishop entered the diocese from the direction of Termonmaguirke (Carrickmore), and with the retinue that accompanied him crossed the mountain 'de Glewgavyn'. The notary, Richard Kenmore, from the diocese of Meath and native of the Pale, misspelt the name but it is clearly Gleann Gamhna/Glengamna. They arrived at the church of 'Keppagh' in the Derry diocese, and stopped there to recuperate. It was *Ceapach* or Cappagh of course and the curate and the erenagh there pointed out that he was no longer in his own diocese, whereupon Colton gave them a lecture about the powers of oversight of the Archbishop of Armagh especially when a suffragan see was vacant and 'deprived of the solicitude of a pastor'. He then instructed his notary to draw up a public document stating his powers and those of his predecessors in such circumstances.

Then finding that the parish of Cappagh at Dunmullan did not have adequate accommodation for his large entourage he moved on to *Ardsraha* to spend the night, having ordered the Vicar (curate) and Erenagh of Cappagh to send such supplies to Ardstraw as they would for their own bishop. One interesting thing to remember is that this exchange probably took place in Latin.

It was the custom of the time that, when the bishop was on visitation to a parish, the erenagh had to provide for him. They decided to send the meat of one fat bullock on after the archbishop to supply his needs and those of his company.

When he arrived at Ardstraw he sent for priest and erenagh and ordered them to provide security for his retinue and their belongings. Having attended to this, they provided bread, butter, milk and meats and heat – it was October – for humans (fourteen of whom are named) and straw and fodder for their horses. The establishment at Ardstraw must have been substantial. The notary provided us with the name of the curate, *Lochlann Ó Baoill* ('Laurencius Obogyll'). He belonged no doubt to the erenagh family of the parish of *Leamhchoill* ('elm wood'/ now Langfield).

The next day, at the request of the priest, the primate reconciled the cemetery, which had been polluted by the shedding of blood. He entered the church, said the litanies, blessed salt, ashes, water and wine and sprinkled the cemetery as laid down in the *Pontifical*. This reminds us that customs in medieval Europe were very different from nowadays. The graveyard was regarded as public property or a sort of village green where all sorts of things happened, fairs, public meetings, people rambling about, pigs rooting in the vicinity, and clearly at Ardstraw, an occasional fight.

For the journey to Urney, which was to be his next port of call, the erenagh provided free of charge '*ad numerum vii caballorum vel circiter*' ('horses to the number of about seven') to draw the primate's carriage and to carry his food and gear. From there he went on by way of Leckpatrick to Derry, to Banagher and back to Armagh by way of Glenelly, again reminding us that the roads then travelled were different from now, just as the destinations were different.

The Franciscans in West Tyrone

Probably somewhat after the year 1400, west Tyrone remarkably produced four houses of Franciscans of the Third Order Regular, at Scarvagherin (*Scairbheach an Chaorthainn*, 'stoney place of the rowan tree'), Pubble (*Pobal*, 'people, community, congregation'), Corick (*Comhrac*, 'confluence, meeting of waters') and Omagh, the latter founded in the 1440s, it would seem by one Patrick McHugh 'a bearded layman', which may have been their last. Not a great deal is known about them, but they were in the main lay people who came together to live in community. They seem to have devoted themselves to education, and to have had some very definite opinions about the standards they wished to find amongst the secular clergy. They seem to have been encouraged by Bishop Sean Ó Gubúin (1433–c.1455) and perhaps by Anraí Aimhréidh Ó Néill (d.1392) and his descendants.

The Ó Néill Borderlands

In the fifteenth and sixteenth centuries, political power in west Tyrone was no longer in the hands of Ó Gormlaigh but came within the purlieu of their Ó Néill overlords. Ó Gormlaigh and his *clann*, Muintir Luinigh, were pushed up the Glenelly/Owenkillew valleys by the pressure from Ó Dónaill from the Donegal direction. We learn that Dónall Caol Ó Néill died at Loch Laoire in 1325. His grandson was established at *Sliabh Troim* (now 'Bessy Bell') and built the castle that still bears a bowdlerised version of his name. 'Harry Avery', or Anraí Aimhréidh Ó Néill to give him his correct name – 'Henry the Awkward' – built the castle to protect the increasingly threatened border with the Ó Dónaill lordship in what is now Co. Donegal. Anraí is given a dubious character in folk tradition (not always the best guide), while the contemporary annals praise him highly. He is credited with coming to the aid of the Franciscan house at Corick when they were destitute, but their foundation may date from later than his time. His became known as the 'Old Castle', before the *Baile Nua* was built which provided its name to Newtown, to which the name of the incoming planter, Stewart, was added after the Plantation of Ulster. There were, however, other strongpoints in this strategic area: *an Caisleán Maol, an Carraigín*. Long before the Plantation, the descendants of Anraí Aimhréidh had rebelled against the chief Ó Néill dynasty or *ríora* and had lost their political importance.

A power later than their time in this district was that of *Sliocht Airt*, descendants of Art Ó Néill who built in the mid-fifteenth century the castle around which the town of Omagh grew. A century later still, *Sliocht Airt Óig*, another junior branch, was responsible for the fortification of Strabane to confront the castle of *Port na dTrí Námhad* at Lifford, erected by Mánas Ó Dónaill. The second last Ó Néill (only the chief of the name had the right to be addressed by it alone) was Tarlach Luineach, so-called from his domain of *Muintir Luinigh*. His sons, Cormac and Art, rebelled against Aodh Mór, Earl of Tyrone, the last to bear the name Ó Néill in Ireland, who left the country after defeat in the Nine Years War and died in Rome in 1616. In spite of their siding with the Crown, Tarlach's sons still lost their lands in west Tyrone and had to move to the other end of the county. Their lands were given, amongst others, to the Abercorn/Hamilton family, relatives of the Kings of Scotland and of the last Catholic archbishop of St Andrew's. Some of them had remained Catholic, as indeed were some of their immigrant tenants, who had no doubt found themselves uncomfortable in the Scotland of 1610.

Tarlach Luineach Ó Neill was buried in 1595 in the royal mausoleum of Ardstraw. Nowadays as the traffic thunders through the middle of that cemetery, few recollect the antiquity of the tradition to which it bears mute witness.

6

Defenders of the Faith

Tarlach Ó Ceallaigh (Terence O'Kelly), Between Two Worlds (1629–71)

UST AS IT HAD TAKEN MANY YEARS FOR THE REFORMS OF THE twelfth century to bed down throughout the Church, so it would be after the even more radical Council of Trent in the sixteenth. In Ireland, the renewal of Catholic life contemplated by the Council was to be immensely complicated by the English conquest and the violent introduction of the Reformation. The tranquil system planned by Trent of a parish unit centred on its parish church and cemetery and manned by a parish priest trained theologically in a special seminary and charged with the catechesis of his people by preaching and teaching, all this would be a pipe-dream amid the destruction and removal of populations in late sixteenth-century Ireland. The best an often-hunted clergy could do was to discharge their duty as best they could, when they could, in the absence of church buildings or public tolerance. It is hardly to be wondered at that the renewal proposed by Trent should be at best patchy or that older practices should continue through lack of formation or the demands of simple survival. The wonder was that anything of the ancestral faith maintained itself at all.

At this point, caught in that battle for survival, in transition between two worlds, the medieval and the modern, we come upon the enigmatic but nonetheless remarkable figure of Tarlach Ó Ceallaigh.

After the death of Bishop Ó Gallachair in 1601 there was to be no Bishop of Derry for at least 119 years. In that hiatus the diocese was run by vicars apostolic, the most celebrated of whom is the third appointed Terence O'Kelly – Tarlach Ó Ceallaigh as he would have been known to his own.

Since much basic research remains to be done on his life it is necessary to proceed to an extent by hypothesis. Tarlach, or Terence, was one the first students to attend the Irish College in Rome after its foundation in 1628, and the first of its students to be ordained priest for the diocese of Derry, in what circumstances we do not know because it would appear that he was expelled from the college. While there, however, it is reasonable to accept that he was in contact with members of the families or entourage of the Earls of Tyrone and Tirconnell. It is probable that it was due to his contacts in Rome that he was promoted to be Vicar Apostolic of Derry. We know that his predecessor, Eugene MacSweeney, sought such support in Rome to advance his case to be made Bishop of Derry. That he was subsequently made Bishop of Kilmore shows that it was not his character that was the obstacle. It is quite possible that Terence had enough influence in Rome to keep him out of Derry.

At the end of the medieval period the vast majority of the diocesan clergy came from the erenagh families, and what evidence we have shows that this continued to be the case well into the seventeenth century. It seems reasonable to suggest then that Terence O'Kelly belonged to the family that figures so largely in the clerical roll of medieval Urney, sometimes as *Mac an Bhaird*, and sometimes as *Mac an Bhaird Uí Cheallaigh*. Like Mac Con Mí in Ardstraw they were a poetic family. Mac Con Mí enjoyed the status of *file*, belonging to a highly organised corporation demanding twelve years of study for the seven grades of *filí*, and was thus superior to the *bard* in qualifications and prestige. Mac an Bhaird (sometimes Macbard/Macabarde/Ward) were also the erenagh family at Urney before the Plantation of Ulster. Unusually the *Ulster Inquisitions* cannot name the erenagh lands of Urney, but the first established Church Bishop George Montgomery was given a grant on 3 August 1610 of the 'possessions of the see of Derry' in each parish which included for Urney: *Aghenedonagh, Cogan, Nurim* and *Longford* [sic].[1]

The Vatican *Per Obitum* lists contain the names of certain benefices reserved to Rome, which were vacant because of the death (hence the name of the list) of the holder outside the Roman Curia, giving his name and that of his successor. In 1626, a Terentius Killy is

---

1. Cf. Moody and Simms, *Bishopric of Derry and the Irish Society of London I 1602–1705* (Dublin: Stationery Office for the Irish Manuscripts Commission, 1968), p. 56.

provided to the deanery of Maigh Iotha (Strabane/Tyrone deanery) and to the perpetual vicarage of Donaghmore, with permission to hold both together. This clearly suggests that Terence was a native of that deanery. The appointment of what would now be called a vicar forane (VF) or rural dean would not normally be a papal appointment, so it may indicate that the candidate was already in Rome and aware that there was no bishop back at home. Then seven years later, in 1633, we learn that Terentius Kelly, Dean of Derry, has died outside the Curia and that Eugenius Colganus (Eoghan Mac Colgáin) is provided in his stead (probably he of that name, fellow-student of Terence O'Kelly in Rome). On 10 January 1629, Terentius Kelly was appointed Vicar Apostolic of Derry.[2] There are obviously two people named Terence Kelly involved here and, if we are to judge from the vicar apostolic's subsequent career, perhaps father and son. The older man, the dean, died in 1633 when Terence Óg had graduated from being vicar forane to being vicar apostolic. That, of course, can be no more than surmise.

Sir Thomas Phillips had been granted lands near Bellaghy and at Limavady in the Plantation of Ulster. As a result he was in a good position to observe how the London Companies performed in carrying out the duties laid on them by the English government. He was soon engaged on a campaign against them for their lack of thoroughness in achieving these aims, not least for their tolerance of popery, especially since the financial gains accruing to popery were clearly greater than those to the government. Fortunately for us he gathered evidence in 1631 to support his case and submitted it to the authorities. His letter gives three different lists of priests that overlap. The first is a list of the clergy of the parishes in Co. Derry living on the lands of the London Companies who have been appointed, Phillips adds, by the 'vicar general', Turlogh O'Kelly. There are twenty-one from the diocese of Derry and four from Armagh. The second list names seven mendicant friars. The third list is that of an ecclesiastical court made up of twenty members, fourteen of whom are named, convened by Turlogh O'Kelly, the vicar general, as he calls him.

---

2. Vicar apostolic was a priest not in bishop's orders nominated by the pope to run a diocese as a way of getting round the government's antipathy to Counter-Reformation bishops, many of them associated at first with Ó Néill and later in the century with the Stuarts. The system arose when Clement VIII decided that military action against Elizabeth would fail. Cf. P.J. Corish, *The Irish Catholic Experience* (Dublin: Gill and Macmillan, 1985), p. 92.

Phillips accuses the local magistrates, and especially county sheriff Richard Kirby of allowing Donncha Ó Catháin, priest of Cumber, to take four actions in the Sheriff's Court against people who did not pay the priest's dues. The witness Cormac O Mullan (Ó Maoláin) had been excommunicated for two-and-a-half years by this priest (presumably for being one of the four). Shane MacTegart (Seán Mac an tSagairt) corroborated.

There was worse, however. Owen O Quigg (Eoghan Ó Cuaig) was owed a debt by Thomas O Lunnan (Tomás Ó Luanáin) and had taken out a decree against him at the King's Bench. O Lunnan had escaped, but the vicar general had intervened and excommunicated O Quigg. O Quigg appealed against the sentence and the vicar general had assembled a court of twenty priests, which included at least two friars – O Lunnan is probably the friar Thomas O Human in the second list – to consider the matter. The court agreed that Ó Cuaig be absolved but that he should first be whipped. This was done, and he was told to beware how he meddled with priests again. In mitigation it must not be forgotten that the experience of many contemporary priests before the King's Bench had been far from comfortable.[3] Sir Thomas Phillips goes on to analyse the income of the parochial clergy:

- for every married couple: 2 shillings;
- for every single person: 6d;
- of every plough: 20 sheaves;
- of every churning one churning which they call 'mescan frive' (*meascán an phríomh-mhaistridh*: pat of butter from the main churning);
- of every marriage: 1 shilling;
- for Extreme Unction which they call *Cuyrollo* ('cur ola' – literally 'putting on of oil') or in lieu thereof 1s;
- a Mortuary (which is a cow or mare or some such large beast) of such as be possessed of goods; and of the poor sort, some part of what they die possessed of, as also their upper garment as their mantle or brackin (*breacán*, 'plaid'); offerings at Christmas and Easter of some 2d, some 3d; some 4d, some 6d, some 1s; none comes empty; at burials, daily beggings, of

---

3. See *Diocese of Derry in 1631* in *Archiv. Hib.* v (1916), pp. 1–6, and an examination of the priests' names in *Derriana* (1980), pp. 9–13. Two of the priests on the lists, Eoghan Modartha Ó Croiligh of Balteagh and Drumachose and Muiris Mac Rodáin, a friar, were killed during the 1641 war. Cf. *Analecta. Hibernica* 3, pp. 8, 15.

corn, sheep and other necessaries for their Mass and for help of poor scholars, amounts to a good sum each year.

It is certain that the priests receive in duties with the jurisdiction from the pope as much as amounts to 1000li (£1000) per annum. There are also mendicant friars who come abroad twice a year and receive, besides the beggings, which is of no small value, 8d a couple per annum, twenty sheaves of corn of every plough [*land*] and a churning of butter [*from*] every churn. These 'vagrant priests are not beneficed and yet live upon the people's labour'.

Phillips noted that there were eight Mass houses on the 'London Plantation'. Even if Phillips was concerned to make the case against the companies as black as he could, it is still clear that a system had been put in place that enabled the Church to carry on fairly well, despite having lost all the churchlands that supported it before the Plantation. It is clear that this was done openly, supported to an extent by some agents of the state. We can distinguish in this the beginnings of the system of funeral offerings, stipends and harvest dues, which maintained the clergy down to our own times. While we cannot be sure that O'Kelly was responsible for initiating the scheme, he was certainly not going to allow it to be ignored.[4]

Terence O'Kelly was Vicar Apostolic of Derry from 1629 to 1670, during the 1641 war with its terror and starvation, its massacres, armed bands toing-and-froing across the diocese which was never under the control of the Catholic Confederacy, armies which were intensely hostile to priests, further dispossession of Gaelic landholders – very many of whom with no obvious means of support took to living on their wits and on what they had learnt during the war, as the *ropaire* or *tórai*.[5]

---

4. Saint Oliver Plunkett offers some corroboration of the system, when he says that he has tried to stop priests accepting offerings of one shilling for a baptism, two for a marriage or anointing, etc., but his clergy replied that without these they would not have adequate support, and that 'it is the custom of the country since the beginning of the Reformation'. Cf. John Hanly, ed., *The Letters of St Oliver Plunkett 1625–1681: Archbishop of Armagh and Primate of All Ireland* (Dublin: The Dolmen Press, 1979), p. 78.

5. The established Church Rector of Urney was 'frighted away by the Tories' in 1668. Cf. Moody and Simms, eds, *Bishopric of Derry and the Irish Society of London, 1602–1705* (Dublin: Stationery Office for the Irish Manuscripts Commission, 1968), I p. 423.

If the surmise is correct that Tarlach lived in the Urney area, the probability is that he had powerful protection, and that this, not improbably, came from the Hamiltons, a family who had both Catholic and Protestant members and who survived the 1641 war with no obvious ill effects.[6] In 1671, Oliver Plunkett wrote of O'Kelly: 'He had such power with the Protestants that he made my two primate predecessors tremble (Hugh O'Reilly and Edmund O'Reilly) and had more than one of the visitors imprisoned'. It is clear that, even though St Oliver had the strong backing of the Earl of Charlemont, president of the province of Ulster, he was himself more anxious about Terence's influence than he was prepared to admit.

On 20 July 1665, the Vicar Apostolic of Derry signed statutes to be observed in the diocese of Derry. Priests are to avoid public houses and inns under pain of fine and suspension. They are to preach the teaching of the provincial synod, to live in a definite place so that their parishioners can find them and to find such a place within a month – which indicates that what he calls 'vagabond ecclesiastical persons' were quite a problem, and when care of souls permits, they are to study practical theology and Christian doctrine. Priests are, always and without intermission at the end of Mass on Sundays and holydays, to say three *paters* and *aves* for Charles II and for a happy and peaceful reign. Priests are ordered strictly on pain of suspension to inform him within two days of any machination or treasonable action they become aware of and he will report it to the civil authorities. Priests are not to go to fairs and markets. They are to explain these statutes on Sundays to the people in Irish and in English and exhort the people to be peaceable, and to write out a copy of the statutes that they are to keep carefully and not lose. Finally, the last statute reads: 'Having completed what is written above, I ask and beseech again and again my most dear brothers (*confratres*) whom I have attended to in this diocese for the last thirty-seven years to say one Mass (*unum sacrum de passione Domini Nostri*

---

6. The Hamilton family tree included James, second Earl of Arran, heir presumptive to the Scottish throne in 1543; his cousins James, Bishop of Argyll, and John, Abbot of Paisley and Catholic Archbishop of St Andrews who was executed, both of whom had illegitimate children; Sir George, 'brother to my lord Abercorn, came out of Ireland, comforted [Gilbert Kennedy, a priest] and gave him an hundred marks' in 1614. Cf. David McRoberts, ed., *Essays on the Scottish Reformation 1513–1625* (Glasgow: Burns, 1962), pp. 49, 231. The *Civil Survey* (1664–6) notes Sir George Hamilton of Dunalong, deceased, and his son James: another James Lord Hamilton, son of Claude, baron of Strabane (with lands in Urney), all 'Scots papists'.

Jesu Christi) within the next twenty days for my happy death which cannot be long away'.[7]

The prompt fulfilment of this prophecy would have made life easier for St Oliver Plunkett. The clash between Terence O'Kelly and Oliver Plunkett is in many ways that of reform versus tradition, that of the late arrival versus one who had been long in the field and borne 'the labours of the day and the heats', between one who was aware of international attitudes and developments and one whose horizons had been limited by adversity and who had furthermore grown used to doing things according to his own agenda, between one whose 'model of the Church' (as it is put nowadays) was lived in the vestiges of medieval practice and one who saw the necessity of adhering to modern canon law and accepted moral standards. It was probably fuelled by the memory of bitter, self-defeating argument between Old English and Gaelic Irish during the Confederacy, which had shown that ancestral rancours were far from healed. The status of the dispossessed was probably a factor also. It is perhaps a pity that the only source for their disagreement is an occasional reference to the matter in St Oliver's letters. Tarlach's attitudes and state of mind are beyond our reach.

Terence O'Kelly presented Oliver Plunkett on his appointment in 1669, with what he came to see in the early years of his primacy as the most difficult and pressing problem confronting him. Saint Oliver claims that Terence had been 'a solemn simoniac'[8] for some years. O'Kelly had also been living in public concubinage, for twenty years, the primate says in one place, or thirty years, as he says in another, with a number of children. Incidentally, if we take St Oliver's dating as accurate, the length of concubinage would suggest a case of 'mid-life crisis'. As it was a source of scorn to Protestants, and of embarrassment to Catholics the result was that the diocese of Derry was turned upside down. Plunkett had O'Kelly's jurisdiction suspended at the Synod of Clones in 1670. He then went in person to the diocese of Derry, called the clergy together, suspended the vicar apostolic's jurisdiction and appointed Eugene Conwell in his place. The only one to object in Derry was Eugene Colgan, the Archdeacon of Derry. With O'Kelly he

---

7. See *Bishopric of Derry and the Irish Society of London* I. pp. 390–9. What there is published can only be an extract from the statutes of those canons applicable to clerics.

8. Hanly, op. cit., p. 135/7: the number of years is lost in the damaged original letter. Saint Oliver cites no evidence for the charge, unfortunately. No cleric in Derry seems to have disagreed with it.

had been one of the first students of the Irish College, Rome and is described by the primate as 'a rather elderly man who is learned and of good life'. His objections were, it would seem, procedural: that, since the vicar apostolic had been appointed by the pope, only the pope could remove him, and secondly, that he (Colgan) as the last surviving member of the diocesan chapter should have the authority rather than Conwell, an outsider. The primate got a brief from Rome to back up the appointment of Conwell and that ended the matter. Colgan is probably the same as the 'Eugenius Colganus' provided to the deanery of Derry in 1633 in succession to Terentius Kelly (see page 335).

O'Kelly made accusations against the primate before the civil tribunal in Dublin following his dismissal, but both the Viceroy and the Governor of Ulster, the Earl of Charlemont, rejected his plea. The primate himself triumphantly gives the reaction of Terence to his failure: 'He cried out at the top of his voice: "The Italian primate, the Roman primate has unhorsed me!"' In the Italian original of his letter to Archbishop Baldeschi, St Oliver has underlined Terence's words, thereby underlining at the same time his own sense of relief. On 16 September 1671, St Oliver wrote, somewhat priggishly, to Airoldi, the internuncio in Brussels: 'The unhappy wretch (Terence O'Kelly) died in the course of this summer amid the embraces, as they tell me, of his mistress and his bastards. God help us, as he lived so he died, as the popular saying goes'. Perhaps he had not read Terence's final plea to his clergy in his statutes of six years before.

The *Bráthair Bán*

Although the subject of this article leads us beyond the medieval period in the strict sense, it presents such a vital individual in the history of the faith in the Diocese of Derry that we may claim indulgence for including him in this list of exceptional figures in our story.

The wars of the seventeenth century ushered in the century-long period of anti-Catholic legislation and intermittent persecution that we call the Penal Age. In the worst of that time a remarkable man played an essential role in preserving the Catholic faith and Gaelic culture among the native-born people of the north of Ireland and even of Gaelic Scotland. This man was Doimnic Ó Brolcháin, whose memory lived on among his people down to our own times, and deserves not to be forgotten.

Doimnic Ó Brolcháin was born around the year 1666 in the townland of Beitheach (Beagh) near Swatragh in what is now Co. Derry. As a result of the eviction and exile of Ó Neill of Tír Eoghain in 1607, the failure of the revolt of 1641 and the Williamite War, Catholics no longer owned any land in the north. His father was a farmer and would therefore have been a tenant-at-will on the lands of the London Companies, to which most of the land of Co. Derry had been handed over. Doimnic was one of a family of four. His eldest brother Proinsias was also a priest. His sister was the mother of Micheál Mac Donncha, Bishop of the Diocese of Kilmore (Cavan–Leitrim) from 1728–46. His brother Seán was the father of Pádraig Ó Brolcháin, a Dominican friar like his uncle Doimnic and later Bishop of Derry in 1751.

It is difficult for us to imagine the desolation of northern Catholics in the time of Doimnic Ó Brolcháin. Reduced practically to the status of serf-labour on the lands confiscated from their nobility or displaced to the mountains and marshes, they owned nothing. Their churches had been ruined by the wars, and the buildings and lands and cemeteries handed over to the established Church. With their traditional leaders living in exile on the Continent or surviving as guerilla bands in the hills and forests, the only organised group who could stand by them were the Catholic clergy.

Their precarious position meant that for a long time priests lived on the run, until eventually in 1704, the English government admitted failure in stamping them out and allowed one priest to reside in each parish, provided he registered with the authorities, who could then keep an eye on him. Priests, however, were so scarce that only twenty-seven registered for the whole Diocese of Derry. This of course applied only to diocesan priests; Dominican and Franciscan friars were totally banned from the country, although a number of such men remained on unregistered, disguised as laymen and moving around as pedlars, day-labourers, sheep-dealers (as tradition asserts of Doimnic), or wandering musicians, in the manner of the celebrated 'bard of Armagh', who was the bishop in disguise.

It is from this official list of 1704 that we learn that Doimnic's older brother, Proinsias, was a parish priest, living probably with his own people around Swatragh, and officially parish priest of Maghera. An English spy sent in a report to Dublin in 1695 denigrating him:

> Proinsias Ó Brolcháin, thirty years of age or so, tall, fair-haired, unlettered and arrogant. He was captain of a company (in the

army of King James) in the late war. He lives near Swatragh. He is a diocesan priest.

He had, in fact, been secretly ordained in 1693 in Creagán (Creggan) between Omagh and Cookstown by Bishop Tadhg Mac Eochagáin of Cluain Fearta (Clonfert, Co. Galway).

We know rather more about Doimnic than about his brother. He too was fair-haired, hence his name among the people, 'an Bráthair Bán', the fair-haired friar. Unlike his brother, he had become a member of the Dominican Order, who had a long and intimate connection with the Diocese of Derry as we have seen already. The order had been in Oireacht Uí Chatháin (O'Cahan's Country, subsequently Co. Derry) for hundreds of years. They had had convents (as their houses were called) in Derry and Coleraine, both of which were destroyed by the soldiery of Queen Elizabeth I. Thirty-two friars were martyred in Derry and twenty-one in Coleraine, and the stones of their buildings in Derry used to partly build the city walls. When the newly appointed Archbishop of Armagh, St Oliver Plunkett, secretly inspected the Diocese of Derry in 1671, he reported to Rome that there were still six friars ministering secretly around Derry and ten in Coleraine. They must have been living outside these places, because in the plantation towns Catholics had to live in shanty towns (called 'Irishtowns', as one can still see in Omagh or Limavady or the Waterside), outside the boundaries. At sundown a curfew bell was rung in Coleraine and all Catholics had to leave town. This bell continued to be rung down almost to this day, once a month, to remind everyone of the past.

Being clearly a gifted young man, Doimnic Ó Brolcháin was smuggled out of the country to study for the priesthood. He headed first for Salamanca in Spain, where there was already an Irish College. He was eventually ordained priest in the Irish Dominican College in Louvain in Spanish Flanders (modern Belgium), and in the great university there was awarded the highest degree, that of STM, Master of Sacred Theology. Although he could no doubt have looked forward to a successful career on the Continent, he had himself smuggled back to Ireland, where he was to spend fifty years ministering clandestinely to Catholics in Ulster and in Scotland. He became prior of the Dominican house outside Coleraine in 1722, where he had a community of eleven, one of whom would be his nephew Pádraig, known as an Bráthair Óg or an Bráthair Dubh, to distinguish him from his uncle.

The learning of Doimnic Ó Brolcháin is shown by the fact that he wrote a book as guide for clandestine missionaries in a persecuted country. It was called *Opusculum de Missione* ('A Booklet on Mission'). It was printed in Louvain in 1736, and was so successful as to have been reprinted there in 1747. It is the earliest example of a subject that has since gained great importance – missiology or Mission Studies. A single copy survives in the Library of Maynooth College.

Much of the advice given by him to prospective missionaries reflects his own experience in the difficult conditions of eighteenth-century Ireland. For example:

'In the summer season, from Easter to harvest-time, go round from parish to parish, from village to village, and, if necessary, from house to house, teaching all that is necessary for the salvation of souls.' Or again: 'Rise early, read your office and hear confessions. Around nine o'clock or so, having prepared the altar, teach the catechism until midday. Begin saying Mass then, and after reading the epistle, continue with the catechism until those poor people arrive who have had a long way to travel, in case they should be disappointed by finding themselves late. Read the Gospel then, and go on with the Mass ...' Or: 'In winter, from Hallow Eve to Christmas, gather the young people around you in whatever house you are staying at the time, and teach them their prayers, the catechism and how to prepare for Confession until half past nine. Then say the Litany and the other prayers in Irish ...'

Doimnic Ó Brolcháin wrote other works as well, including an account of the Pilgrimage to Loch Derg, which was published in 1725.

Two relics of this saintly friar were preserved down to our own time. The first was a yellow metal pyx, probably brass, which he used to carry the Host to the sick. And the second was a pewter inkstand, circular in shape and decorated, in relief work, with the symbols of the four Evangelists, a man for St Matthew, a lion for St Mark, a bull for St Luke, and an eagle for St John, a fine example of Continental metal work. Their whereabouts today, if they still survive, seem to be uncertain.

Doimnic Ó Brolcháin was popularly regarded as a saint and many stories about him circulated as long as Irish was spoken in south Derry. When he died poems were written lamenting his loss. It is not inappropriate that these glimpses into the history of the faith in the Diocese of Derry should conclude with our brief account of a heroic figure who did much to ensure the survival of the Catholic community and its faith during their time of trial.

Appendix 1:
How Did People Live?[1]

Weather

An expert on gardening has said that, in spite of our perceptions, in the Irish climate wind gives rise to more problems than rain because few days are completely calm. For the centuries 850–1300, during what is called the Medieval Warm Period, land that had been too wet or too boggy was brought into use, as happened in Fermanagh/West Tyrone. Since much of the country was sparsely inhabited, especially in mountainous areas, the cattle could be brought seasonally to ungrazed land – the origin of *buailteachas* or transhumance. While the livestock was elsewhere, the cultivation of land at home near the clachán or cluster of houses in which people lived was more straightforward. The mildness of the climate meant that people saw little need to make hay, particularly during the Warm Period. There followed a colder period, or Little Ice Age, from 1300 onwards for five hundred years or so. However, in either period, given the prevalence of wind and rain for much of the year, the difference in the sort of crops that could be grown was effectively limited.

The historical records of course, like the newspapers, tend to record chiefly bad news. The early 1670s were a time of famine throughout Europe. Nearly a thousand years earlier in 773 there was little bread due to drought. Animals suffered in the hot summer and drought of 1129. Sheep were kept near the homestead where they could be better protected from wolves for example, and pigs roamed the forests, dining on mast (acorns, hazelnuts, etc.) On occasion, as in 748, deep snow meant that the cattle could not graze, as happened again in 764, when excessive

---

1. Fergus Kelly, *Early Irish Farming* (Dublin: Dublin Institute for Advanced Studies, 1997); K. W. Nicholls, *Gaelic and Gaelicized Ireland in the Middle Ages* (Dublin: Lilliput Press, 2003); A. T. Lucas, *Cattle in Ancient Ireland*, (Kilkenny: Boethius Press Ltd, 1989).

snowfall followed by drought led to dysentery and famine. In 825 there was a great famine and pestilence that caused the deaths of the old, the infirm and the very young. In 1104 heavy snow brought about a great loss of cattle, sheep and pigs. In 818, 856, 917, 941, 945 and 1234, we are told, rivers were frozen and passable dryshod. In winter 1156 'most of the birds of Ireland died as a result of the deep snow and severe frost'. A storm in 1178 felled one hundred and twenty oak trees in *Doire Cholm Cille* alone, but in what season we are not told. Heavy rain in 1012 destroyed the corn, as did gales in 1077. Lightning storms had the same effect in 1328, whereas in 1471 the damage to crops was caused by two-inch hailstones. In 1224, prolonged rain brought an outbreak of disease in cattle from the grass they ate and then in humans from their milk, a startlingly modern experience. According to a ninth-century writer, an ideal year should have 'a fine frosty winter, a dry windy spring, a dry showery summer, and a heavy-dewed fruitful autumn'. A people dependent on what they grow themselves are always at the mercy of the weather.

Land
The *baile bó*, or *baile fearainn*, the origin of our townland, would have had permanent fencing, either by hedge or earthwork. There is part of such a ditch on the boundary of the diocese of Derry with Armagh below Slieve Gallan that may be there since the division came about in the late twelfth century. In general fencing into fields was temporary. The cycle of cropping was a biannual one, which fitted in with the life of a wattle fence. Much of the cultivation in Gaelic Ulster would have followed the hill slopes down from the grazing or calving areas to make manuring easier. The plough used was much cruder than the modern implement, or even than the 'Scots plough', introduced much later. The coulter and mould-board were relatively late inventions in medieval Europe and iron was scarce, often limited to the soc or ploughshare at the front of the plough. The work required the efforts of three men, one to lead the horses (or originally oxen), one to hold the plough and one to hold down the ploughshare. The plough was often attached to the horse's tail. It is unclear whether this preceded the invention of the horse-collar or was done, as in other forested areas of northern Europe, to protect the valuable plough, since the horse would obviously stop if the plough hit a rock or a tree stump. If the latter were true it would be particularly useful in bad, thin soil or recently cleared ground. It is clear that cultivation was productive and widespread. Foreigners like Sir Henry Docwra described the 'champaign' or open country of the

Ó Catháin lands in the early 1600s, and officers of English army raiding parties were wont to boast of the amount of crops and the numbers of animals destroyed in the scorched earth policy with which the Nine Years War was waged.

The primary source of wealth was livestock. The Irish sheep, of a breed now extinct, had a fleece that was more hairy than woollen in appearance and this was plucked rather than clipped. Horses were kept in great herds and were a valuable export. Expert horsemanship was common although men rode without saddle or stirrups. *Eachaí*, the man who rode an *each* or steed, is the origin of a Christian name and a surname (Haughey, Mc Gaughey), while the more general term *capall* was a draught-horse, and *gearrán*, perhaps originally meaning a gelding, may have been the workhorse. Horse rearing, which was part of the obligation of Ó Gormlaigh to Ó Néill, is reflected in placenames like Liscapple (near Gortin) – *Lias Capall* – a horse corral.

Cattle were very suited to the climate and were kept in huge numbers. It is claimed in the State Papers that Ó Néill (Aodh Mór) possessed one million head, however that total could have been counted. In summer in central Ulster at least these herds moved from place to place accompanied by herdsmen and guards, living in temporary shelters, in a unit called a *caoraíocht*. Since it was not the practice to make hay, the system allowed the less populated areas to be grazed and pasture nearer home to be rested. The system was referred to as *buailteachas*, translated as transhumance, although it may have been more a permanent feature than just summer grazing. Terms relating to cattle raising are common in placenames, like *inis*, an area for milking, in Iniscarn (near Desertmartin); *leamhnacht*, new milk, in Killunacht (Feeney), or three names at the foot of Mullagharn on the Badoney-Cappagh borders, *Loch an Tairbh* ('Bull Lake', now Mountfield Lough), *Srath Damhán* ('bullocks' holm') Stradawan; and Gleann Samhaiscí ('heifers' glen') Glensawisk. Near them is *Ros na Muc*, which would suggest an afforested area for rearing pigs. The *caoraíocht* had the additional advantage that livestock was readily moved in times of conflict or of the sort of cattle rustling that passed for tax gathering as well as proof of political virility by a newly declared lord and leader.

Social Custom

There were no inns or lodging-places except at the ports. However, the traveller was welcomed into any house. He had no trouble getting something to drink but he might not receive a meal until the main meal of the day, which was taken in the evening. Since money was rare and lack of generosity deemed inexcusable, there was no question of payment, and most commerce, even rents, was by exchange of goods. In Gaelic Ulster the welcoming of travellers was part of the function of the erenagh in each parish.

Some evidence from archeological examination of human bones found in medieval cemeteries would suggest an extension of the shinbone at the joints in some remains resulting from routine squatting to do low-level tasks like tending the fire. This was mostly found, it would seem, in female skeletons. Disease of the joints from an early age due to occupational stress, dietary deficiency of iron in particular, and poor dental health, perhaps due to a lack of variety in diet, made life burdensome, particularly for the less well-off.[2]

When they met, both men and women greeted each other with a kiss, noted a Spanish visitor who was in southwest Ireland around 1580 in the company of James Fitzmaurice Fitzgerald as he planned rebellion. That he recorded this fact means at least that he was surprised. He went on to add:

> Although lacking in *educatio urbana*, 'refined education', [the Irish] behave so peaceably and affectionately towards one another that in those six full months I never saw soldiers have recourse to arms, a peace to which even horses and dogs seem subject, so that I think it is to be ascribed to the quality of the region and its air. They are content to sit on hay, grass, straw and avoid benches and rocks. If there is nowhere to sit except a stool or a box they spread rushes, hay or straw under them.

The Spaniard was fortunate in his choice of time and place. He notes their trust and foolhardiness. 'They do not break faith with their lords at whose will they accept peace or war. In war it is more courageous for each to leave the ranks and even to attack alone, paying little attention to what his comrades are doing.' As for fleetness of foot, they could run as fast as or faster than a horse, later corroborated by Lord Mountjoy in 1602 and by the Ambassador of Venice in 1611: 'The Irish, cradled in hardship, are most agile and dexterous, and swifter on foot than any

---

2. Denis Shine and Ciara Travers, 'Unmarked medieval and post-medieval burial grounds: Athboy, Co. Meath', *Ríocht na Midhe* XXIII (Meath: Meath Archaeological and Historical Society, 2012), 37.

other nation ... They catch their horse by the left ear to mount and do not have stirrups. Neither do they wear leggings.' It was agreed that they were superb horsemen. 'They are great walkers and inured to toil,' confirmed Spanish Captain Cuellar in 1568. At meals the person of honour was seated in the middle, with the second in importance at his right, the third at his left, the fourth on the right and so on in a circle around the walls, 'but all have their face to the door, never their back, lest an enemy should come around and catch them unprepared.'

The system of land tenure within the *fine* or kin group restricted the rights of women who 'married in.' A woman could administer land obtained during the marriage, but if her husband died or divorced her all she had to fall back on was what she had brought into the marriage as her dowry, which might of course be substantial. Wives also suffered as a result of the frequency of divorce and rejection by their husbands without ceremony, particularly among the nobility. They could of course invoke the sanction of Church tribunals, as happened when Archbishop Colton visited Derry in 1397. Clandestine marriages involving only the consent of the two parties were valid until the Council of Trent (1563) made it obligatory that marriage be a public ceremony before a priest and witnesses. Amongst the results of the older state of affairs had been confusion, bigamy and the misleading of the guileless.

In the closely-knit kin structure of Irish society, marital alliances were not infrequently between those who were third cousins or closer, which rendered the 'marriage' invalid at the time. Trial marriage and concubinage were not uncommon. One special power given to a woman was in the 'naming' of children. A woman who had a child as the result of a casual liaison could make a sworn declaration as to who the father was. The child was then recognised by the father and shared with his other children in his estate. Thus Matthew was affiliated and recognised by Ó Néill (Conn, first Earl of Tyrone), after his mother, the wife of a blacksmith in Dundalk, claimed that Matthew was a product of their brief affair. Matthew was a teenager at the time the claim was made. Seán an Díomais Ó Néill (Shane the Proud, legitimate son of Conn's marriage), like others among the Uí Néill, was less than impressed by this. Seán went on to become Ó Néill and lead a revolt. Matthew, also known as Feardorcha, was father to Aodh Mór, second earl. Counter-Reformation preaching and perhaps a touch of persecution would help bring acceptance of Church marriage laws. All in all, it had the symptoms of a society in disarray, as was to be the case throughout Europe at the advent of the Reformation.

Religious Practice

We might recall first of all that the rite used at Mass for much of the Middle Ages followed the so-called 'Celtic Rite', which seems to have been in use only in Ireland and Gaelic Scotland. Saint Margaret, queen of Malcolm III, *Maolcholm Ceann Mór*, King of Scotland (1058–93) led a reform of the Church in Scotland, seeking advice from the archbishops of Canterbury. Given the close relationship between Ireland and Scotland at the time it is not surprising that the Church in Ireland was to follow a similar course during the twelfth century.

One of the changes was the gradual replacement of the 'Celtic Rite' by the so-called 'Roman Rite', which had been developed in fact from practices in different countries within the Latin Church. The change was gradually put into effect by the Synod of Kells (1152) and the Synod of Cashel (1172). The Mass was in Latin because it was believed that the only proper languages for liturgy were those written on the Cross: Hebrew, Greek and Latin. It is not clear at what stage Mass came to be offered every day. In the early monasteries it seems to have happened on Sundays and feasts of saints. In the early Church in Ireland, a priest could say Mass twice on such a day but no more. If there were priests together they concelebrated, while a bishop said Mass on his own.

At first there seems to have been two colours of vestments, white and purple, but a few centuries later, yellow, black, red and green had been added, although the yellow was probably golden. The chasuble was a full circle of material with embroidery, reaching to the ground, which had to be hitched up when the priest had to perform any action. It was expected that there would be a choir, supported by a harp. Mass took place very early in the morning, presumably because the participants had been fasting since the evening before. Mass began with a short penitential rite, followed by the *Kyrie Eleison* (Lord, have mercy) which was continued by a short litany directed at the apostles asking their prayers. There seems to have been three readings in Ireland and what we would call the Prayer of the Faithful came before the gospel. The dead to be prayed for were named after the Offertory.

The core of the Mass was the Roman Canon, now known as the First Eucharistic Prayer, which has been in use in Ireland from at least the eighth century and included another longer litany of the saints, men and women, both native and non-native, as part of a long prayer for various groups of people. The Blessing may have come after the Our Father. People received both host and chalice – women had to be veiled – and both were reserved for communion of the sick. The custom in the Eastern Church of confirming and giving communion to infants after baptism seems to have obtained at a time. Burial in consecrated ground was a requirement from the eighth century.

Whether confirmation took place regularly or not is not clear, perhaps because there were problems obtaining the oil at times. We know, for example, that chrism was unobtainable in 1074. Though the Irish Church invented the idea of the *anamchara*, or spiritual director, and private confession, St Bernard insists that in twelfth-century Ireland the practice was no longer followed, presumably because he was told so by St Malachy and his entourage. Saint Bernard was laying stress on the sanctity of his great friend (they were buried in the same grave) who had to withstand so much at home and his account may show the trace of prejudice.

It is worth remembering that St Bernard, the 'conscience of Europe', was a man of his time and place when it was thought that anyone who did not live in Christendom (between Normandy and Central Italy) could not be properly regarded as a Christian. Hence there were wars in Spain, Sicily, Lithuania and Prussia to bring 'true faith' to the peoples there. The English had just made it because they had had the good fortune to be invaded by the Normans. The first Norman Abbot of St Albans said of his Anglo-Saxon predecessors, as he destroyed the shrines of their saints, that they were 'uncouth and illiterate'. When St Bernard said of the Irish that they were 'Christians only in name, pagans in fact', he was reflecting the way that the Roman model had come to shape the thinking of men like St Malachy to the extent that they had come to believe that the Irish could only be Christian when they accepted Roman norms.

Since Canterbury had made claims to jurisdiction in Ireland it was a short step to the papal bull *Laudabiliter* of 1156 and the commission to Henry II of England to reform the Irish Church. Before waxing indignant at this intrusion, we have to remind ourselves that in the twelfth century the idea of the nation-state lay far in the future. Adrian IV merely saw the need to reform religion and wanted Norman support. He may well have trusted Henry II to bring about reform without bias. Henry's 'adventurous, acquisitive and pious' Anglo-Norman barons, who invaded on the invitation of Diarmaid Mac Murchadha, would prove to be not quite so disinterested.

In 1580 as James Fitzmaurice Fitzgerald, himself of Anglo-Norman descent, was planning rebellion, a Spanish agent in the country records that the people he stayed with were in the habit of getting up at midnight to pray and meditate, some for an hour, some for half an hour. He added that at Mass they stood for the Lord's Prayer. Where he stayed was an area deeply marked by Counter-Reformation spirituality, but it is impossible to say how general such attitudes may have been. There were two days of abstinence in the week, *an Chéadaoin* ('first fast'), Wednesday, when they abstained from meat; and *an Aoine* ('the fast'), Friday, when they abstained from milk products. It could hardly have been further from the epithets hurled in the *Book of Fenagh* at the prelates and princes of around 1300, when, in the author's view, morals were so bad that it was like the end of the world.

While the Franciscans did sterling work in evangelisation, not least from their four Third Order Secular houses in west Tyrone, and while Nicholas Weston and Observantine Franciscan Dónall Ó Fallúin, 'who diligently taught and preached throughout Ireland for thirty years,'[3] seem to have been serious bishops, little evidence survives about parish life. We learn of an allegation in 1497 that the archdeacon of Derry, Aodh Mac Bhloscaidh (Mc Closkey), had neglected the parish church in Dunboe to the extent that the people were living, cooking and keeping their tools and utensils in it. Since, however, the complainant was a Mac Cathmhaoil (Mc Caul/Campbell), belonging to the erenach family of Dunboe, and Mac Bhloscaidh belonged to the rival erenagh family of Faughanvale, one might well wonder what was the full story.[4]

The mayhem that broke out from time to time among medieval nobility must have made regular religious practice difficult in certain areas, particularly since it often involved the destruction of churches. The Church building was where valuables were often taken for protection in times of danger and so sometimes became a target. The lack of stable government and effective central authority, since Anglo-Norman rule in distant Dublin made them no more than just one other of the competing powers, resulted in the breakdown of the efforts which were being made to achieve unitary rule in the century and a half from the death of Brian Bóramha. This in turn lent an extra measure of opportunity to the fissiparous and self-aggrandising lesser lords, typical of medieval nobility throughout Europe. Having others to do the manual work and provide food, they could devote themselves

---

3. AFM ad ann. 1500.
4. Cf. *Derriana* (1976), H.A. Jefferies, 'Clerics of Derry', 39; cf. Annates of Ireland (Ulster).

to derring-do and proving their manhood in bloody squabbles. In the deanery of Maigh Iotha particularly, the need simply to survive must have dominated the lives of most ordinary people in the thirteenth and fourteenth centuries. It is remarkable, it must be said, that such a large crowd, 'thousands' we are told, turned up with only a couple of days' notice for Archbishop Colton's Mass held in the open air at the church of St Breacán, Clooney, on Sunday 14 October 1397, perhaps because it was such a break in the tenor of their days.

When the papacy at Avignon began reserving benefices to papal appointment, even if the main purpose was to raise revenue, the system laid itself open to those who might use it for personal gain, since Avignon could not know the situation at first hand. After the papacy returned to Rome, Eoin Mac Ghiolla Bhríde Ó Dochartaigh (McBride O Doherty), for example, went there five times in the 1460s to pursue his claim to the deanery against other claimants.[5] Another abuse was for son to succeed father in Church office by having the latter disqualified on various grounds. Sometimes the son may have been born before ordination, sometimes not. It was particularly common among the nobility in higher Church benefices, but then of course the various annals only reported the activities of the prominent. There were cases of clerical concubinage, how prevalent is not clear. One can guess at the deleterious effect all this may have had on belief and practice.

Drink

Like ourselves people drank water, which was easy to come by. In an agricultural community milk was a common drink, except that it might be in short supply in winter. The unavoidable deficiencies in diet, especially the case in winter, meant that beer was a common drink. The brewer was a *scóaire* or a *cerbsire*. Even St Patrick was credited with having his own *cerbsire*, the priest Mescán, who is perhaps associated with the parish of Cumber. (The name he bore may be connected with *mesc*, meaning 'intoxicated' or 'confused'.) What the brewer produced was *scó* or *coirm* (beer), *leann* or *laith* (ale). *Beoir*, a more usual word for beer nowadays, came into Irish from the Norse. Most beer was made from malted oats or barley and it was there that Maigh Iotha

---

5. Mac Ghiolla Bhríde is the name of one branch of Ó Dochartaigh, as are Mac Daibhéid/McDevitt/Mc Daid; Mac Dhónaill Óig/McConologue; Mac Fheabhail/McCole, etc.

and the parishes along the Finn came into their own. They were obliged to provide the malt needed by the Bishop of Derry and by Ó Dónaill himself. A little beer was malted from wheat. There was also *brocóit*, made from malt and honey. As far as can be seen, the only additive to beer was honey until late medieval times when hops came into use to add flavour. Another drink was *midh*, now *meá*, mead, made from fermenting honey with water. There is no mention of *uisce beatha* (whiskey) being distilled in Ireland until the thirteenth century, although it was claimed that St Patrick introduced it! Commentators on late medieval Ireland draw attention to how fond of it the Irish had become in the meantime. The first casualty recorded was one Risteard Mag Raghnaill (Mc Reynolds) who died of drink in 1405. The annalist makes the wry comment that is was for him *uisce marfa* ('water of death'), not *uisce beatha* ('water of life').

Wine, of course, was also consumed, principally by the nobility. The Venerable Bede claimed in the eighth century that the Irish 'had no lack of vines', but the climate was scarcely suitable for vines on that scale. Wine was necessary for the Eucharist, of course, but from quite early times Gaulish and Frankish traders visited the country, especially from Bordeaux. Tradition insists that all dioceses touch the sea or the Shannon, allegedly to ensure wine for religious purposes. However, since the dioceses were based on civil boundaries there must have been more to it than that, for wine was also seen as a festive drink. In later times, when Ó Dónaill was described as *Rí na nIasc* ('King of Fish') because of the value of the Tír Chonaill fish trade, there was obviously a thriving coastal commerce. This would have included Basque as well as French and English vessels.

Our Spanish visitor to the country about 1580 records seven sorts of drink: beer, milk (*serum lactis*), wine, broth (*iusculum*), mead (*mulsum*), *uisce beatha* (*aqua vitae*) and water (*aqua pura*). The beer, he adds, was brewed from water and barley.[6] Since whey on its own has a sour taste (it was often drunk as a penitential diet in early times), it may have been *treamhanta*, made by boiling milk and adding buttermilk. When the curds were strained off, it made a somewhat acid drink. There was, of course, also *bláthach* (buttermilk). There were several words for types of whey drunk, presumably with different additives to make it palatable. The broth mentioned above may have been gruel.

---

6. Reginald Walsh, ed., 'Irish Manners and Customs in the 16th Century' (1916), *Archiv. Hib.* V–VI, 17.

Food

The staple diet was, as one would expect in this country, bread and milk. It was common belief that a man would eat a loaf in a day and another at night. Our anonymous Spaniard tells us that 'they eat plenty when there is plenty, but can fast patiently for two or three days'. He adds that at meals, before grace after meals is said, if a bishop or priest is present, he gives a sermon, which is listened to 'with great attention'. Since wheat was hard to ripen, most bread was of barley or oatmeal, sometimes fire-dried. Bread came in the form of a *bairín* (loaf) or *sruán* (oatcake), garnished (*tarsann*) with butter, suet, cabbage, fruit, edible seaweed, honey, etc., depending on the season. The food in summer was mostly dairy produce, curds (*gruth*), soft cheeses (*grus, cáis, milseán, maothal*), while in winter there was salt meat, nuts, apples, onions and hard cheese (*tanag, mulachán*). *Tanag* was so hard that it could be hurled as a missile from a sling, and is said to have brought about the death of Queen Méabha in ancient times. One cheese was so hard that it had to be chipped with an axe. Grain crops were the material for *cáfraith* (sowens) from soaking bran in water, *leite* (porridge), *meanadhach* (gruel) and *brachán*. Food might be served on a wooden dish or *mias*. Before the arrival of the fork in northern Europe in the early seventeenth century, solid food was eaten with knife and fingers.

Veal from bull calves and meat from bullocks would have been common since most cattle kept for over-wintering would have been female. The meat would have been dried for winter consumption, but supplies would scarcely have been adequate by the time spring came.

Hens were less well-fed than now and their eggs were smaller, but they played a significant part in diet, as did those of wild birds. Geese were eaten and their eggs prized, especially as food for nobles, ducks perhaps less so. Deer, wild boar, hare, trout and *pollán* (by hook and line), salmon and eel (at weirs), wild duck, wild goose, whooper swan, snipe, woodcock, red grouse and capercaillie (*capall coille*) were hunted, by sling, spear and hunting dog (*míolchú*), although the *gadhar* may have been the dog that scented out the game. These two differed from the *árchú* (guard dog), *conbhuachaill* (herd dog) and *measán* (lapdog or pet). The word cat is borrowed into Irish from Latin, which suggests that the species may have been introduced, though much earlier than the rabbit, donkey, mute swan, pheasant, pike and perch, all introduced by the Normans.

The *Annals of Inisfallen* have to resort to Latin to describe the size of an unusual arrival in 1105, a camel, presented to King Muircheartach

Ó Briain, by King Edgar of Scotland.[7] The *corr réisc* (heron) and the vegetarian *corr mhóna* (crane) sometimes became pets, but were not eaten. Cranes no longer visit Ireland. Sea fishing seems to have been less practised than one might expect – one of the anomalies of an Ireland surrounded by sea – although shellfish were on the coastal diet. It is to be presumed that the wine traders who visited the country from Britanny and Bordeaux kept the country supplied with salt from western France, or it could have come from north-western England. Salt may also be obtained by burning seaweed and boiling the salt out of the resulting ash – a wearisome task. Pepper (*sciobar*) was introduced into Ireland in the early Christian period.

Since some of the monks of early Ireland were vegetarian, the result was that monasteries had gardens. Saint Columba was said to have lived on a diet of nettle soup. The houses of the well-to-do followed the monastic example and had a *luibhghort*. Gardens of some sort are essential to the provision of a balanced diet, in quality and quantity. According to medical opinion of the time, diet had to be thought of in terms of the four 'humours' that shaped the individual's make-up. The word *hortus*, Latin for garden, is cognate with Irish *gort*, which denotes cultivated ground. Amongst the common vegetables were garden peas and beans (round and small), celery, leek (*borrlus*), onion (*caineann*), wild garlic (*creamh*), cabbage (*praiseach*), chives (*foltchib*), watercress (*biolar*) and sorrel (*samhadh*). Vetch (*peasair*) and acorns (*dearcáin*) were eaten by humans only in hardship. Turnips and carrots may have come from Roman Britain, having originated in Asia, while parsnips are European. All of these are known in Irish as *meacan* (root vegetable) with a qualification, usually of colour. Fruit consumed included *úll* (apple), *airne cumhra* (plum), *cnó* (hazelnut), and fruits probably introduced by Norse or Anglo-Norman whose names are borrowed into Irish, *péire* (pear) and *sirín* (cherry). Common wild fruit were consumed too: *fraochóg* (bilberry), *sméar* (blackberry) and so on.

Clothing

Raymond de Perelhos came from southern France in 1397 to visit St Patrick's Purgatory on Loch Derg, spending Christmas with Ó Néill on his way back. He wrote in his account of his journey that he thought the Irish the handsomest men and the most beautiful women he had met anywhere, but that they lived in poverty. His contemporary Archbishop

---

7. Eóin Mc Néill, *Annals of Inisfallen* (Dublin: Hodges, Figgis & Co., 1933), ad ann.

Colton gives a different impression. However, winter visiting would not catch the country at its best, both in weather and meagerness of supplies. According to the latter's experience the men went barefoot, and the dress of both men and women did not meet his standards of modesty. What that might mean by the standards of our day is unclear. Sources agree that the men wore heavy cloaks (often day and night), sometimes with short loose coats and tight calf-length trousers, not unexpectedly without underwear. Wool and linen were widely available. The cloaks of the nobles were embellished with strips of leather of different colours. The women wore linen turbans made up of yards of material. Flax was one of the common crops grown, particularly in Inis Eoghain. The men carried small knives, larger than a dagger, according to the Spanish visitor. Whether for carving, defence or to demonstrate virility is not clear.

Early Education
Education in early Ireland was by fosterage. At a time of little social mobility, children between seven and seventeen were prepared for the state in life that would be theirs. In the nature of things, its length probably varied, as in primary schools later. There was fosterage done in affection, *altram seirce*, and *altram ar iarradh*, fosterage for a fee. The fee depended on the rank of the child and was greater for a girl than a boy. The son of a king had to be supplied with a horse, suitable clothing and taught the board games *fícheall* and *brannaíocht*, swimming, horsemanship and marksmanship. The king's daughter was to learn sewing, cloth-cutting and embroidery. A farmer's son was to learn how to care for lambs, calves, kids and piglets, while his daughter had to learn how to use the hand-mill, kneading-trough and sieve. There was specialised training for the member of a medical or legal family, for the *airchinneach* (erenagh) in Latin, reading and writing, for the artisan (*saor*), the *maccléireach* (clerical student) and the *maccailleach* (novice nun).

The son of the *file* (poet) would have been a more exceptional case, given the position of respect, almost of awe, accorded to the poetic order or *aos dána*. They spent years in training, learning complicated metres and traditional lore, composing their works after fasting and prayer, and often sent on diplomatic missions by the lord to whom they were accredited. Such was their importance within the Gaelic system that they drew down on themselves the unrelenting hostility of English government. Lower in status than the *file*, were the *bard* and *reacaire* (reciters of what the *file* composed). According to law, even the food foster-children were to receive was to accord with their rank, but obviously that would also be reflected in the relationship. Children could be also fostered by those who wished the protection of the child's parents but did not actually have responsibility for rearing the child.

It is interesting that the pet names children have for their parents in modern Irish are borrowed from English, as a result of the original pet names in Irish, *aite* and *muimme*, being used for foster parents, words which nowadays have come to mean a teacher (*oide*) and a nurse (*buime*) (like the alternative word for a foster mother, *banaltra*, now also meaning a nurse). The pet names show how close the relationship between child and foster parent was, sometimes closer than that with their parents. The degree of support given to leaders by their foster family is noticeable, for example, in the case of *Seán an Díomais Ó Néill* (Shane the Proud), also known as *Seán Donnaileach*, who received throughout his turbulent life the unquestioned backing of *Muintir Dhonnaile* (the O Donnellys), holders of the position of hereditary *marascal* (marshal) to Ó Néill. The development of education with the Franciscan Third Order Regular in fifteenth-century Tyrone suggests that a demand for change was making itself felt.

Early law was even clear on the colours of clothing that foster parents could provide for the children: *lachna* (grey-brown), *buí* (yellow), *dubh* (black) and *fionn* (white), for commoners. Children of lords might wear *dearg* (red), *glas* (grey-green) or *donn* (brown). Sons of kings might wear *corcra* (purple) or *gorm* (blue). If this was possible to enforce it would have given the appearance of a uniform for each different class. Perhaps it also reflected the availability and cost of the various dyes in use at the time. The purple may have come from shellfish, but most of the dyes came from plants. *Raithneach* (bracken) produced a yellow-green; *aiteall* (juniper) gave brown; *crotal* (a lichen) gave crottle, a reddish-brown; *cróch* (crocus) gave an orange yellow, as did the onion. *Glaisín* (woad), which was widely grown, gave blue and, after the extraction of all the blue, dyed cloth pink. The word *roide* describes a reddish-coloured mud (as in *uisce roide*, 'spa' water) and may come from *roid*, which is madder, the roots of which provided a red dye, useful also as a cosmetic.

Law

The system of law, called *féineachas* (or 'brehon law' in English, from *breitheamh*, 'a judge') operated in Gaelic areas. With the arrival of the

Anglo-Normans, who brought a version of the Common Law with them, there were areas of Ireland where *féineachas* applied, areas of Common Law and areas where legal systems were variable combinations of both. It is obviously impossible to set down the legal system here, but we may draw attention to the importance of the *fine* (pronounced 'finna') or kin-group, descendants of the same great-grandfather. The head of kin or *ceann fine* was elected to speak for them in public and to ensure that their rights and obligations were honoured. This group owned the land, although the individual member worked his share, and each member was considered to some degree responsible for all the land. The kin group was responsible for the behaviour of each member, including his wrongdoing. The system accepted that payment could atone for crime. Such payments seem to have been made, even though there was no central government to enforce them. Killing was punishable by a fixed penalty, which could be very expensive for the killing of a person of high rank. If the killing was done by one of its members, the *fine* was expected to contribute to the payment. Similarly, the person responsible for injury to another was obliged to provide sick maintenance if the injured one did not recover within nine days. After that the culprit must pay for medical treatment, provide food and accommodation, and provide a substitute to do the man's work. If the victim was married an additional payment was required. All this is not to say that execution or mutilation (blinding and castration) for crime did not happen. It was for this reason that *tearmann* (termon, 'sanctuary') was provided in certain places to allow the culprit a chance to obtain due process.

Appendix II:
Surnames of the Northwest

The word *sloinneadh* seems to have begun its life, according to the *Dictionary of the Irish Language*, as meaning 'to declare', 'to tell who you are' or 'to name' before giving rise to *sloinne*, 'a surname'. In Ireland surnames date from about the year 1000. Since a surname is only necessary among people who have moved to where the individual is not well known, it would suggest that they became necessary when over kingdoms began to expand and leaders like Dónall Ard Macha (+ 980) felt the need to stress that his grandfather Niall Glúndubh (+919) had been high king, thereby setting a headline for himself. Henceforward he was known as Dónall Ó Néill; a later relative of the same lineage was content with the importance of his own father and called himself Mac Lochlainn.

There can be considerable difficulty in finding an authentic original version of some surnames. There follows here a selection of the more common names which originate before AD 1200 within the diocese of Derry, according to the genealogies; the forms are given firstly in classical medieval form, secondly in Modern Irish usage if different, and lastly in 'anglicised' form:

CINEÁL EOGHAIN (Branches of)

Cineál Eoghain **na hInse**/Inis Eoghain/Inishowen
Ó Duídhíorma/Mc Dermott; Ó Treabhláin/Trolan; Ó Sléibhín/
Slevin; Ó hAirmheadhaigh/Ó hAirmhigh/Harvey; Ó hOitéin/
Hutton, Houghton; Ó hAircheallaigh/Ó hAireallaigh/Harley;
Ó Mianáin/Meenan; Ó Cearbhalláin/Carolan; Mac Céile/Mc Gale;
Mac Conghail/McGonagle; Ó Grúgáin/Groogan; Mac Maonghaile/
Mac Maonaile/(Mc) Monagle; Ó Galáin/Gallen; Ó Duibhne/Deeny/

Peoples; Ó hEachach/Haughey (from *an Camabhainn*, Camowen River, tributary of the Strule); Mac Naineannaigh/?Mc Anena. (*Naineannach* seems to mean 'warlike'. All the various Gaelic versions suggested for the surname McAnena/McAneney are problematic; surprisingly it does not occur in Gaelic records).

Cineál Eoghain/**Cineál Moain** (Urney)
Ó Gormlaigh/Gormley/Grimes; Ó Luinigh/Lunney; Ó Peatáin/Patton; Mac Gairbheith/McGarvey; Ó Criagáin/Creegan; Ó Duineachaigh/ Donaghy; Mac Giolla Uír/Mc Aleer. (This last seems to have been Mac Giolla Adhuair from *adhuar* meaning 'very cold', but was changed to *odhar* meaning 'dun' or 'grey–brown' – therefore now 'son of the brown fellow', giving rise to a change of accent from the 'u' to the 'i' in modernised spelling. This might also explain the variant McClure.)

Cineál Eoghain/**Clann Chonchúir** (mostly moved from Donaghmore in Donegal to north Derry).
Ó Catháin/Ó Kane; Mac Bhloscaidh/Mac Loscaidh/Mc Cluskey (branch of Ó Catháin); Ó Corráin/Curran; Ó Muireadhaigh/Ó Muirí/ Murray; Ó Láithre/Lowry; Ó Dubhagáin/Ó Dúgáin/Duggan; Ó Maol Bhreasail/Ó Breasail/?Russell; Ó Godáin/?Goodwin; Ó Maoláin/ Mullan; Ó Loingsigh/Lynch; Ó Baoill/Boyle (based at Drumquin, distinct from Ó Baoighill/Ó Baoill/Boyle of south Donegal); Ó Coinn/ Quinn, distinct from Ó Coinne of Baile Uí Choinne/Newmills in east Tyrone; Ó Dubhda/Ó Dúda/Duddy; Ó Cairealláin/Kerlin/Carlin. (This last belonged to the Clann Diarmada branch of Clann Chonchúir who gave their name to the parish of Clondermot/Glendermot when ousted from Donaghmore, and distinct from Ó Cearbhalláin on previous page.)

Cineál Eoghain/**Cineál Fearaigh** (south Tyrone; west Tyrone; Dunboe).
Mac Cathmhaoil/McCawell/McCaul/Campbell; Mac an Ghirr/McGirr; Ó Maol Gheimhridh/Winters; Ó Brolcháin/Bradley.

Cineál Eoghain/**Cineál Fearghasa** (northwest Inishowen; some moved to east Tyrone).
Ó hAgáin/O'Hagan/Hagan; Ó Coinne/Quinn; Ó Maolfhábhaill/ McFaul/Lavelle; Ó Ceallaigh/O'Kelly (one branch of whom became Mac Rabhartaigh/Magroarty); Ó Branagáin/Brannigan; Ó Bracáin/ Brogan.

Cineál Eoghain/**Cineál Tiarnaigh**
Ó Muirgheasa/Ó Muiríosa/Morris; Ó Mealláin/Mellon,Mallon; Ó hEodhasa/Ó hEosa/Hussey; O Coinneagáin/Cunningham.

Cineál Eoghain/**Cineál Binnigh** (widely scattered in West Tyrone-East Donegal, Derry).
Ó Tomhrair/Toner; Ó Brolaigh/Brolly; Ó Bogáin/Bogan; Ó Giolláin/ Gillan/?Mc Gillion; Ó Duimhin/Ó Duibhin/Devine; Mac Con Choille/ Mc Enhill; Ó Fearáin/Farren; Ó Cuaig/Quigg; Ó Lachtnáin/O'Loughlin; Ó Tuathaile/Tohill; O Rancáin/Rankin; Ó Dónaill (Lord of Cineál Binnigh Locha Droichid in south Derry and distinct from Ó Dónaill of Tír Chonaill); Ó Lagáin/Lagan; Ó Gormaile/Gormley/Grimley (distinct from Ó Gormlaigh on previous page); Mac Oirc/McGurk; Ó Maol Mhartain/Martin; Mac Fhorbhallaigh/Mc Corley.

Cineál Eoghain/**An Ríora** (the royal line i.e. Ó Néill, Mac Lochlainn, and branches).
Ó Farannáin/Farnan (has been generally subsumed by Farren in this area); Ó Maol Tuile/Flood; Ó Duibheanaigh/Devaney; Mac Cú Uladh/ MacCuladh/Mc Cullagh; Mac Ualghairg/McGoldrick; Ó Braoin/ Breen; Mac Ghiolla Mhartain/Gilmartin; Ó Fearghail/Farrell; Mac Murchaidh/(Mc) Murphy; Mac Ruairí/McCrory; Ó Flaithbheartaigh/Ó Laifeartaigh/Laverty; Ó Cairre/Kerr in east Tyrone (from Carrbaethán, sobriquet of Aonghas, son of Niall Caille +846. Mac Giolla Cheara/ Carr/Kerr of Donegal has a different origin).

Cineál Eoghain/**Fir Droma Lighean** (Drumleen, Lifford, moved to east Tyrone).
Ó Donnghaile/Ó Donnaile/Donnelly; Ó Doibhlin/Devlin; Ó Banbháin/?Bannon; Ó hEochaidhéin/Haughian.

Cianacht (of the **Roe** valley).
Ó Conchúbhair/Ó Conchúir/O'Connor (distinct from Ó Conchúir of Connacht, high kings); Ó Céin/?subsumed by O'Kane (both these families were the royal house before conquest by Ó Catháin); Ó hInnéirí/Henry.

AIRGHIALLA (Branches of)

Uí Tuirtre (**South Derry**)
Ó Flainn (moved across into Antrim); Ó Tomaltaigh/Tumelty; Ó hUrthuile; Ó Maolruanaigh.

Uí Fiachrach **Ard Sratha** (branch of Uí Tuirtre at Ardstraw in west Tyrone). Mac Fothaidh/Fahy; Ó Críocháin/Creegan/Creehan; Ó hAodha/O'Hea, probably 'translated' to McHugh.

Uí Mic Cairthinn (branch of Uí Tuirtre in **Faughan** valley).
Ó Colgan/Colgan (distinct from Mac Colgan); Ó Conaill/O'Connell (distinct from Ó Conaill in Munster); Ó Cormaic/Cormick/mostly Mc Cormick now.

CINEÁL CHONAILL in Gleann Fhinne
Mac Loinseacháin/Mc Glinchey.

CINEÁL CHONAILL Ó Dónaill
Mac Meanmain/Mc Menamin.

CINEÁL CHONAILL Ó Dochartaigh (Inis Eoghain after c. 1200) (branches).
Mac Daibhid/McDevitt/McDaid; Mac Ghiolla Bhríde/Mc Bride; Mac Fheabhail/McCole/Mc Cool; Mac Dhónaill Óig/Mc Conologue; Mac Aindilis/? McCandless. (Since *Eachmharcach* [='horseman'] was a common first name among Muintir Dhochartaigh, it is probable that Mac Eachmharcaigh/Cafferky/Mc Cafferty is a branch of Ó Dochartaigh.)

Of Uncertain Origin
Ó hÉigeartaigh/Hegarty does not appear in the genealogies and the name occurs only once in the annals (1050) and then at Lorrha, now in Tipperary. A family of that name had an important role in connection with the Church in Derry and occurs often in Church records there. The lords of *Clann Sneidhghile* or *Cluain Eidhile*/Clanelly, a district to the west of Letterkenny, were Ó *Taircheirt*, a surname that has disappeared. They are last mentioned in the annals (AU) at 1213 and 1232, entries unrecorded by the Four Masters, which presumably means that AFM considered them of no significance. In 1098, the death in battle at *Fearsaid Súilí* (a narrow, tidal part of the Swilly) of Éigeartach

Ó Taircheirt is recorded. His descendants, having lost political power, may have changed their surname to Ó hÉigeartaigh and found a new role as Church erenaghs – not an uncommon move. Something similar was accomplished by *Ó Maol Doraidh*, Kings of Cineál Chonaill. When ousted by Ó Dónaill they moved to west Fermanagh and became *Mac Giolla Fhinnéin* (anglicised Leonard). Such changes were of moment only to the ruling group within the *clann*.

Mac Fhearghail/McGarrigle were Lords of *Tír Bhreasail* according to *Ceart Uí Néill*, although Seán Mór Ó Dubhagáin in his *Topographical Poems* suggests as lords there Ó Donnagain and Mac Gairbheith, who may stem from Cineál Moain like Ó Gormlaigh in Urney. Where exactly the boundaries of Tír Bhreasail were is unclear.

Propaganda

Not everything in local records can be taken at face value. *Ceart Uí Néill* describes the rents and services that Ó Néill claimed as lord's entitlement from lesser lords with his lordship. Some of it at least seems fanciful. With regard to Inis Eoghain it names three lords among whom the home territory of Inis Eoghain was divided by Ó Néill, it would claim, when he moved east towards Dungannon. The three named are Ó Duídhíorma in *an Bréadach* (Moville area) in the east, Ó Maolfhábhaill at *Carraig Brachaí* (Ballyliffen) in the northwest, and Ó hÉanna. The first two occur in all records. Boundaries are given which have been identified by Seoirse Ó Dochartaigh.[1] There is, however, no evidence of the existence of the name Ó hÉanna amongst the descendants of Eoghan in the genealogy of Cineál Eoghain. It seems not unlikely that the name was created to sow confusion. Adjacent to and south of Inis Eoghain lay the territory of Cineál Éinne (with leaders *Mac Dhubháin* and *Ó Lapáin*), whose name the author of *Ceart Uí Néill* used to create a surname and *clann*. His purpose was to write Mac Lochlainn, traditional rivals of Ó Néill, out of history. They were certainly the overlords in all of Inis Eoghain until about 1200. The eclipse of Mac Lochlainn at the hands of the Anglo-Normans, who built Greencastle, resulted eventually in the rise of Ó Néill and Ó Dónaill and the arrival of Ó Dochartaigh in Inis Eoghain. With their rise the power of Ó Duídhíorma and Ó Maolfhábhaill in Inis Eoghain and of Ó Maol Doraidh and Ó Canannáin/Canning in Tír Chonaill went into decline.

---

1. Seoirse Ó Dochartaigh, *Inis Eoghain – The Island of Eoghan: The Placenames of Inisowen* (Seoirse Ó Dochartaigh, 2011), p. 25.

Some Important Dates

AD 431	Palladius sent by Pope Celestine 'to the Irish believing in Christ'.
432	Saint Patrick comes to Ireland to preach the Gospel.
453	Death of Niall Naoighiallach (of the Nine Hostages).
546	Colm Cille makes a foundation at Derry.
557	Battle of Móin Mór Doire Lóthair; Cineál Eoghain come to north Derry.
563	Colm Cille founds his monastery at Iona.
795	The first Viking raids on Ireland.
1002	Brian Bóramha becomes undisputed High King of Ireland.
1014	Defeat of the Danes at Cluain Tarbh (Clontarf).
1083	Dónall mac Ardghair Mac Lochlainn becomes King of Tír Eoghain.
1088	Death in Regensburg of Muireadhach Mac Rabhartaigh (Marianus Scottus).
1106	Ceallach consecrated as Reforming Bishop of Armagh.
1111	Synod of Ráth Breasail; reform of the Church launched; dioceses created.
1132	Saint Malachy (Maolmhóg) becomes Archbishop of Armagh.
1152	Synod of Ceanannas (Kells); Armagh recognised as primatial see.
1157	Consecration of Mellifont, first Cistercian monastery in Ireland.
1169	Arrival of first Norman invaders.
1176	High King Ruairí Ó Conchúir divides Tír Eoghain between Mac Lochlainn and Ó Néill.
1224	Arrival of Dominicans, first mendicant order in Ireland.
1231	Arrival of Franciscans.

1241	Battle of Caméirí; Mac Lochlainn coalition defeated by Ó Néill.
1254	Seat of diocese transferred from Machaire Rátha Luraigh to Derry.
1305	The Norman 'Red Earl' builds Northburgh (Greencastle) in Inis Eoghain.
1397	Visitation of Archbishop Colton.
1425	Pope Martin V authorises Third Order of St Francis in Ireland.
1460	Defeat of Brian Rua Ó Néill at battle of Dún (Downpatrick).
1541	Henry VIII of England declared 'King of Ireland'.
1600	English under Docwra destroy monastic city at Derry.
1601	Martyrdom of Bishop Réamann Ó Gallachair. Defeat of Ulster lords at Kinsale.
1607	Bishop George Montgomery assembles the erenaghs.
1608	Ulster Plantation begins.
1629	Tarlach Ó Ceallaigh appointed Vicar Apostolic of Derry.

Index A:
Names of Persons

Index B:
Names of Places
and Population Groups

Names of parishes in Derry diocese are printed in bold. Two place-names – Ireland/Éire and Derry, which occur passim – are omitted, but two Irish forms of the latter, Doire Chalgaigh and Doire Cholm Cille, are included. Abbreviations: bar. = barony; dioc. = diocese; par. = parish; tld = townland.

Index C:
General

Index D:
Authors, Sources
and Abbreviations